Muslim Fula Business Elites and Politics in Sierra Leone

Rochester Studies in
African History and the Diaspora

Toyin Falola, Series Editor

The Jacob and Frances Sanger Mossiker Chair in the
Humanities and University Distinguished Teaching Professor

University of Texas at Austin

Recent Titles

Population, Tradition, and Environmental Control in Colonial Kenya
Martin S. Shanguhyia

Humor, Silence, and Civil Society in Nigeria
Ebenezer Obadare

Nation as Grand Narrative: The Nigerian Press and the Politics of Meaning
Wale Adebanwi

The Rise and Demise of Slavery and the Slave Trade in the Atlantic World
Edited by Philip Misevich and Kristin Mann

The Power of the Oath: Mau Mau Nationalism in Kenya, 1952–1960
Mickie Mwanzia Koster

Cotton and Race across the Atlantic: Britain, Africa, and America, 1900–1920
Jonathan E. Robins

*Islam, Power, and Dependency in the Gambia River Basin:
The Politics of Land Control, 1790–1940*
Assan Sarr

Living Salvation in the East African Revival in Uganda
Jason Bruner

On Durban's Docks: Zulu Workers, Rural Households, Global Labor
Ralph Callebert

*Mediators, Contract Men, and Colonial Capital:
Mechanized Gold Mining in the Gold Coast Colony, 1879–1909*
Cassandra Mark-Thiesen

A complete list of titles in the Rochester Studies in African History and the
Diaspora series may be found on our website, www.urpress.com.

Muslim Fula Business Elites and Politics in Sierra Leone

Alusine Jalloh

UNIVERSITY OF ROCHESTER PRESS

First published 2018

University of Rochester Press
668 Mt. Hope Avenue, Rochester, NY 14620, USA
www.urpress.com
and Boydell & Brewer Limited
PO Box 9, Woodbridge, Suffolk IP12 3DF, UK
www.boydellandbrewer.com

ISBN-13: 978-1-58046-917-3
ISSN: 1092-5228

Library of Congress Cataloging-in-Publication Data

<<CIP DATA>>

This publication is printed on acid-free paper.

Printed in the United States of America.

For my late older brother, Dr. Chernor M. Jalloh, Esq.,
and my son, Benjamin J. Jalloh

Contents

Photographs follow p. 102.

Acknowledgments

This book would not have been possible without the research support of the Africa Program at the University of Texas at Arlington, which I founded in 1994. Its generous funding allowed me to make multiple research trips to Sierra Leone. In addition, a Fulbright grant in 2012–13 at Fourah Bay College (FBC), undergraduate alma mater, University of Sierra Leone, in Freetown—the capital city—enabled me to gather more information for this project. I would like to thank the J. William Fulbright Foreign Scholarship Board for this prestigious opportunity. And my gratitude also extends to the Department of History and African Studies at FBC for hosting me, particularly the Department's chair, Joe A. D. Alie.

To my twin brother, Alhassan Jalloh, and to Abdul A. Mansaray, I extend special gratitude for their research assistance. Furthermore, in the course of my research, I profited from discussions with many Fula, particularly Alhaji[1] Mohamed Malal Jalloh Jamboria[2]—father of the author; Alhaji Abu Bakarr Tejan-Jalloh, Almamy[3] (Alimamy) Agibu Jalloh, Alhaji Chernor Maju (Sowe), Alhaji Almamy Muhamadu Alieu Seray-Wurie, Alhaji Almamy Baba Allie, Alhaji Sanu Barrie, Alhaji Mohamed Lamin Sidique, Alhaji Mohamed "Texaco" Bah, Alhaji Almamy Dr. Honorable (Hon.) Chief Justice Abdullai B. Timbo, Hon. Alpha B. Barrie, Alhaji Ambassador Sulaiman Tejan-Jalloh (son of Alhaji Tejan-Jalloh), Professor M. Alpha Bah, Alhaji Chernor Sie, Alhaji Ambassador Amadu M. B. Jalloh, Chief Justice Umu Hawa Tejan-Jalloh (daughter of Alhaji Tejan-Jalloh), Alhaji Abu Bakarr Jalloh, Alhaji Ibrahim I. Tejan-Jalloh (son of Alhaji Tejan-Jalloh), Dr. Allieu Shaw, Chernor Jalloh, Mrs. Fatmata Momoh (née Shaw), Lamin Bah, Mrs. Fatmata Binta Stevens (née Jalloh), Alhaji Umaru Monorma Bah, Almamy R. Seray-Wurie (son of Alhaji Seray-Wurie), Hon. Bai Sheka Wurie, and Almamy Jaia Modibo Kaikai (son of Alhaji Almamy Dr. Jaia Kaikai). My research visits to Sierra Leone were assisted by Kadiatu Ngele; many thanks for your hospitality. My longtime colleague Allen M. Howard generously shared research materials on the Fula. Additionally, I owe a deep debt of gratitude to my former student, treasured friend, and colleague Harold Harris for his strong support over the life of this project.

I also wish to thank the staff members of the Sierra Leone Library Board (SLLB), the FBC Library, and the Sierra Leone Public Archives (SLPA) for their assistance and professionalism. In particular, I would like to thank Salieu Turay, chief librarian of SLLB; Albert Moore, senior Sierra Leone government archivist of the SLPA; Rev. Frederick Lavai, deputy librarian, FBC Library; and Alfred K. Fornah, assistant Sierra Leone government archivist of the SLPA. These individuals were most helpful and provided the necessary documents with speed and professionalism. Moreover, my gratitude also extends to the anonymous reviewers for their constructive feedback, which helped to improve the manuscript.

I have presented portions of the book at two international conferences: "Sierra Leone Past and Present 2012" at the FBC in April 2012 and the International Academy of African Business and Development Conference at the University of Florida in Gainesville in May 2008. I thank the audiences at these gatherings for their helpful observations and suggestions, some of which have influenced the final product. I wish to thank the Africa Program, the Department of History, the Office of Graduate Studies, the College of Liberal Arts, and the Charles T. McDowell Center for Critical Languages and Area Studies at the University of Texas at Arlington for providing a travel grant to the first conference in Sierra Leone. The Africa Program and the Department of History funded the second conference in Florida.

Finally, I have dedicated this book in part to my late elder brother, Dr. Chernor M. Jalloh, Esq. Among other things, Chernor inspired me to pursue and earn at age twenty-nine a PhD in history on a graduate assistantship from his beloved undergraduate alma mater—Howard University, where he was a professor emeritus of philosophy. After receiving his PhD in philosophy from Pennsylvania State University, Chernor combined his academic career with a private law practice in Washington, DC, after receiving his doctor of law (JD) degree from the Georgetown University Law Center. My most enduring debt is to my son, Benjamin, to whom I have co-dedicated this book. He missed out on bonding with his dad during my long research absences. Thank you for your understanding and support!

Abbreviations

ACRM	Anti-Corruption Revolutionary Movement
AME	African Methodist Episcopal
APC	All People's Congress
AIM	Ansarul Islamic Mission
CAST	Consolidated African Selection Trust
CBE	Commander of the Most Excellent Order of the British Empire
CID	Criminal Investigations Department
CP	Commissioner of Police
DELCO	Sierra Leone Development Company
DICORWAF	Diamond Corporation of West Africa
DIMINCO	National Diamond Mining Company
ECOWAS	Economic Community of West African States
EIU	Economic Intelligence Unit
ERP	Economic Recovery Program
EUB	Evangelical United Brethren
FBC	Fourah Bay College
FCC	Freetown City Council
FPU	Fula Progressive Union
FSLMO	Federation of Sierra Leone Muslim Organizations
FYO	Fula Youth Organization
FWA	Fula Women's Association
GDO	Government Diamond Office
GGDO	Government Gold and Diamond Office

HMO	Hanafiyatu Muslim Organization
IMF	International Monetary Fund
JP	Justice of the Peace
MBE	Member of the British Empire
MI/Q	Ministry of Interior Index Number
MOR	Member of the Order of Rokel
MP	Member of Parliament
MP	Minute Paper
MRU	Mano River Union
MWL	Muslim World League
NAIB	National Association of Indigenous Businessmen
NDB	National Development Bank
NDP	National Democratic Party
NIC	National Interim Council
NPLF	National Patriotic Front of Liberia
NPRC	National Provisional Ruling Council
NRC	National Reformation Council
OAU	Organization of African Unity
OBE	Officer of the Most Excellent Order of the British Empire
OBBA	Old Bo Boys Association
OIC	Organization of Islamic Conference
PDG	Parti Démocratique de Guiné
PEER	Public Economic Emergency Regulations
PEPU	Protectorate Educational Progressive Union
PNP	People's National Party
PP	People's Party
PZ	Paterson, Zochonis and Company

RSLMF	Republic of Sierra Leone Military Forces
RUF	Revolutionary United Front
RWAFF	Royal West African Frontier Force
SAP	Structural Adjustment Program
SLAFA	Sierra Leone Amateur Football Association
SLBA	Sierra Leone Butchers Association
SLBS	Sierra Leone Broadcasting Services
SLDC	Sierra Leone Diamond Corporation
SLEF	Sierra Leone Employers Federation
SLFA	Sierra Leone Football Association
SLICTU	Sierra Leone Indigenous Commercial Traders Union
SLIS	Sierra Leone Islamic Society
SLIL	Sierra Leone Islamic League
SLIPTA	Sierra Leone Indigenous Petty Traders Association
SLLB	Sierra Leone Library Board
SLLC	Sierra Leone Labor Congress
SLMDU	Sierra Leone Motor Drivers Union
SLMB	Sierra Leone Muslim Brotherhood
SLMC	Sierra Leone Muslim Congress
SLML	Sierra Leone Muslim League
SLMPM	Sierra Leone Muslim Pilgrims Movement
SLMMWA	Sierra Leone Muslim Men and Women's Association (Kankalay)
SLMWA	Sierra Leone Muslim Women's Association
SLMRS	Sierra Leone Muslim Reformation Society
SLMU	Sierra Leone Muslim Union
SLMWBO	Sierra Leone Muslim Women Benevolent Organization
SLPA	Sierra Leone Public Archives

SLPIM	Sierra Leone Progressive Independence Movement
SLPM	Sierra Leone Pilgrims Movement
SLPMB	Sierra Leone Produce Marketing Board
SLPTA	Sierra Leone Petty Traders Association
SLPP	Sierra Leone People's Party
SLPWA	Sierra Leone Pilgrims Welfare Association
SLWMP	Sierra Leone Women Muslim Pilgrims
SLSIC	Sierra Leone Supreme Islamic Council
SLST	Sierra Leone Selection Trust
SOS	Sierra Leone Organization Society
UAR	United Arab Republic
UDP	United Democratic Party
UICPTA	United Indigenous Commercial and Petty Traders Association
UMJ	United Muslim Jama`at
UPP	United Progressive Party
WAFA	Western Area Football Association
YMMA	Young Men's Muslim Association

Map 1. Sierra Leone–Guinea Region

Introduction

This book investigates why and how Muslim Fula[1] business elites participated in the postindependence politics of Sierra Leone. The Fula are one of the country's main entrepreneurial groups. Arguably, they are the most successful African business minority in this West African country, which has a long history of entrepreneurship, considerable agricultural potential, and vast resource endowment including diamonds, gold, and bauxite.[2] The study focuses on elite Fula who engaged in import and export business enterprises, as well as large-scale retail trade, and were the highest-ranking members of the socioeconomic hierarchy of the Fula people. The Fula business class, comprising both immigrants and native-born individuals, was a component of a larger multi-ethnic business community. Others included Temne, Mende, Krio, and Mandingo,[3] as well as non-African groups like Indians and Lebanese.[4] As Muslims, the Fula played a major role in the spread of Islam through their proselytizing efforts and establishment of educational institutions. They are part of a larger Islamic presence in West Africa, extending from Senegal to Cameroon.[5]

The book examines Fula political relationships with the Sierra Leone People's Party (SLPP) during the prime ministership of the brothers Dr. Milton A. S. Margai and Albert M. Margai, as well as with the All People's Congress (APC) under the leadership of Siaka P. Stevens and Joseph S. Momoh. The history recounted here begins in 1961, the year of Sierra Leone's independence,[6] with the Milton Margai administration. But in 1964, Sir Albert became prime minister after the death of Sir Milton. Then, in 1967, military coups ensued after the electoral defeat of the Albert-led SLPP by the opposition APC. However, in 1968 the APC was reinstated in power with Stevens as prime minister, who became president in 1971 when the country adopted a republican constitution. In 1985 President Stevens retired and was succeeded by Major-General Joseph Momoh. This made history, as Sierra Leone became the first African country to hand over a civilian-constituted government to the military chief. The period under study concludes in 1992, when the Momoh presidency was ousted in a military coup d'état led by Captain Valentine E. M. Strasser. As a result, the National

Provisional Ruling Council (NPRC) was established to govern the nation. This work examines previously overlooked actors and events in constructing a fresh narrative about the political and business history of twentieth-century Sierra Leone.

The book argues that although the reasons for Fula business elites' involvement in national politics were varied, they centered on immigration and business. They were interconnected, with immigrants forming a large segment of the Fula business community, as well as being central to Fula cross-border trade networks and commercial organization in the country. Fula immigration is examined from two perspectives: domestic politics and Sierra Leone–Guinea relations. Neighboring Guinea was the single largest source of legal and illegal Fula immigrants. Immigration was a unifying and radicalizing force and the primary factor in giving birth to a Fula organization—the Fula Progressive Union (FPU)—which drew together foreign-born and Sierra Leonean–born Fula into political activism beginning in the 1960s. By the 1990s, the Fula were organized into an effective interest group that deployed its resources for political action. Such resources included money, membership, information, and business expertise. The FPU's political activities centered on lobbying, monitoring legislative debates, and participation in national elections. Immigration brought citizenship concerns to the fore and influenced political and economic debates. Furthermore, it pushed the Fula to the center of the political scene for a period of several decades, with the Fula population focusing its attention on advocacy and conducting voter turnout drives in nationwide elections.

The Fula political agenda was also shaped by business. The involvement of Fula business elites in electoral politics was motivated by their strong interests in such key enterprises as livestock, merchandise, diamonds, and motor transport. Since the colonial period, the Fula had dominated the livestock trade that connected the capital city of Freetown with the Provinces and neighboring Guinea. A central component of this trade was the butchering business, characterized by cross-ethnic competition and intra-ethnic Fula business rivalry. Besides the livestock trade, the vast majority of the Fula business class was involved in retail trade as urban shopkeepers in the merchandise sector, which included provisions, textiles, and produce. This trade was hierarchical, trans-ethnic, and highly competitive. By the 1960s, the diamond trade based in the Kono District began to emerge as a primary source of capital accumulation among the Fula. By the 1980s, it had become the single largest source of Fula capital.

Profits from the diamond trade were then invested in such sectors as real estate, livestock, and motor transport, the latter being one of the fastest-growing sectors of the Sierra Leone economy. The Fula were importers, owners, and drivers of various models of commercial vehicles from countries such as Japan, France, Italy, Germany, South Korea, the United Kingdom, and the United States. Fula-owned commercial vehicles transported goods and passengers both within Sierra Leone and into Guinea. In the politics of business examined in this study, new light is shed on the Fula as lobbyists and on their interactions with political leaders and politicians of each party, as well as with government officials in ministries dealing with Fula businesses.[7]

To achieve their goals in the country's political landscape, Fula business leaders pursued diverse strategies that focused on fostering intra-group cooperation and building bipartisan alliances with multi-ethnic local political actors and organizations, which reflected their political pragmatism. Fula intra-group collaboration involved traditional, political, and business leaders, as well as Western-educated, native-born professionals and civil servants. Women, many of whom were wives of Fula businessmen, were also a part of this broad-based partnership to advance the Fula political plan of action. Mobilizing the large Fula business group was a linchpin of the political approach of the Fula business elites. Moreover, as Muslims they worked within trans-ethnic local Muslim organizations such as the Sierra Leone Muslim Congress (SLMC) in strategic leadership positions, resulting in close personal ties with government officials and politicians that helped to influence government policies affecting the Fula people.

The Significance of the Project

The nexus between business and politics is one of the most important areas of study in business history.[8] As it pertains to Africa, however, the literature on this subject from both country-based and comparative perspectives is relatively small. Many of the scholarly writings have been by political scientists, economists, and anthropologists whose primary focus has been such topics as corruption, underdevelopment, foreign investment, state enterprises, and nationalization of businesses. When specific firms have been studied, the focus has generally been on non-African enterprises. Significantly, a large gap exists in the historical literature on the interconnections among African minority business groups, governments, and political parties in postcolonial Africa.[9]

The present volume, therefore, seeks to help fill this void in our historical knowledge of the intersection of business and politics in postindependence Africa. It is the only book-length examination of business elites in the political history of Sierra Leone. Moreover, it is the first comprehensive work on twentieth-century Muslim Fula business-government relations. The book combines business and political history, drawing on private business records, oral sources, government documents, newspapers, and periodicals in order to show the dynamic interplay between business and politics. This book expands on my own previously published work as well as multidisciplinary works by scholars such as M. Alpha Bah, Arthur Abraham, John R. Cartwright, Gershon Collier, Earl Conteh Morgan, S. T. Cox, Sheikh Batu Daramy, G. K. Deveneaux, Mac Dixon-Fyle, C. Magbaily Fyle, Fred M. Hayward, Allen M. Howard, Kelfala Kallon, Jimmy D. Kandeh, Martin Kilson, William Reno, David E. Skinner, and A. Zack-Williams that have examined history, politics, business, immigration, Islam, and ethnicity in historical and contemporary Sierra Leone.[10]

In illuminating the case study of Sierra Leone, this book makes a significant contribution to our understanding of both historical and contemporary Africa. Moreover, it enriches our insights into broad comparative themes such as immigration, the political relationship between immigrant communities and host societies, minority business elites, the interactions between immigrants and their homelands, political parties, interest groups, intergenerational relations within minority communities, political leadership, political fundraising, elections, and the intersection of ethnicity and national politics. If we are to understand contemporary Africa, with its boundaries inherited from the colonial period, we must understand the dynamics of immigration and ethnicity. African history specialists, students, and the general public interested in the history of Africa, as well as scholars in political science, sociology, anthropology, business, Islamic, and African diaspora studies will find this book most useful.

The Organization of the Book

The book is divided into two parts of two chapters each. Part 1 deals with the prime ministerships of the Margai brothers, Milton and Albert, from 1961 to 1967. This was a short but critical period in the history of Sierra Leone, as it witnessed the first postindependence government, the first administration to be defeated in a national election in postcolonial Africa, and the first military intervention in the country's politics. The second part examines APC rule during that of Stevens and his handpicked successor, Momoh, over a twenty-four-year period. Collectively, the APC era was a political watershed, marked by milestones such as the introduction of a republic and a transition from multiparty democracy to a one-party state.

Chapter 1 examines the political relationship between Fula business elites and the SLPP under the leadership of the first indigenous prime minister, Dr. Margai, between 1961 and 1964. Immigration, which was shaped by both domestic politics and the country's relations with neighboring Guinea, is explored. The related issue of citizenship, one of the most controversial political topics since independence, is also treated. Next, Fula business leaders' efforts to promote their interests through various strategies, including working with politicians, government officials, and lawmakers, are discussed. The chapter concludes with a discussion of the Fula and the 1962 general election, detailing their varied contributions as business leaders, politicians, and Muslims.

Chapter 2, covering the years from 1964 to 1967, explores how Fula business leaders related to the SLPP and the government during the prime ministership of Sir Albert. As a serious perennial problem, immigration is examined from both a domestic perspective and Sierra Leone–Guinea relations. The immigration issue would help frame the country's politics for the next several decades. Explored next is how Fula business elites attempted to advance their interests in the business environment through multiple approaches, including working with politicians, lawmakers, and government officials. The chapter concludes with the crucial 1967 election, examining Fula roles as businessmen, politicians, activists, and Muslims, as well as the challenges they faced, particularly political targeting and violence.

The involvement of Fula business elites in the nation's politics during APC rule under Stevens from 1968 to 1985 is the subject of chapter 3. As one of the persistent and urgent national challenges, immigration is explored from the perspectives both of domestic politics and Sierra Leone–Guinea relations. Next, the political activities of Fula business leaders in pursuit of their broad and diverse economic interests are discussed. The study of the Stevens era concludes with a detailed examination of the contributions of the Fula as business leaders, lobbyists, politicians, activists, and Muslims in the country's three general elections.

Focusing on the years from 1985 to 1992, chapter 4 examines the political relationship between Fula business leaders and the APC under the leadership of President Momoh. Despite competing pressing economic and social issues vying for political attention, immigration was never far from the center of the country's politics. As in previous chapters, immigration is examined here in view of both domestic politics and Sierra Leone–Guinea relations. The activities of Fula business elites in immigration issue advocacy, the use of lobbyists, and involvement in electoral politics are further explored. As an interest group, the Fula were well-organized and well-financed during the Momoh presidency. The potency of Fula political activism drew its strength largely from the Fula's business success, which is examined, as well as the Fula's close personal ties to President Momoh. The chapter concludes with the military overthrow of the Momoh government in April 1992.

Part 1

The Sierra Leone People's Party (SLPP) Rule

1

The Prime Ministership of Milton A. S. Margai, 1961–64

The first postcolonial Sierra Leone government was headed by Dr. Milton Augustus Strieby Margai from April 27, 1961, until his death on April 28, 1964. Dr. Margai was the chief architect of Sierra Leone's independence from Britain. He was born on December 7, 1895, in Moyamba District and received his early education at the Evangelical United Brethren (EUB) church school in Bonthe District and at the Albert Academy in Freetown. Dr. Margai was the first person from the Protectorate (the area outside of the colony later renamed the Provinces) to graduate from FBC in 1921, where he earned a bachelor of arts degree, and was also the first from the Protectorate to qualify as a medical doctor. He studied medicine at King's College, Durham University and graduated in 1926. Before he entered active politics, Dr. Margai set up private practice in the Protectorate after twenty-two years as a medical officer in the British colonial service. Until his retirement as a senior medical officer in 1950, Dr. Margai served in the colony (this area became Freetown and with its environs is referred to as the Western Area) and the Protectorate, where he taught midwifery to indigenous women, contributed to improving health care and hygiene, and boosted adult literacy.[1]

Dr. Margai first entered politics at the local level in the 1930s because he opposed the political marginalization of the Protectorate peoples. He first represented Bonthe as a nonchief member in the Protectorate assembly. By 1950 he was working toward a fair representation of the Provinces in the legislative assembly and had become the head of the politically oriented Sierra Leone Organization Society (SOS) to promote agricultural cooperation. His colleagues in the SOS included Dr. John A. M. Karefa-Smart, whose maternal pedigree was Fula;[2] Sir Albert, Kandeh Bureh, Stevens, and Dr. William H. Fitzjohn.

In 1951 Dr. Margai, alongside others like Alhaji Dr. Muhammad Sanusi (M. S.) Mustapha, helped found the SLPP, which was a merger of the Protectorate Educational Progressive Union (PEPU), the SOS, and the People's Party (PP) founded by the Reverend E. N. Jones (Lamina Sankoh). Dr. Margai provided strong leadership for PEPU in the 1940s after its founding by mainly Protectorate chiefs and others to promote education as a priority in the Protectorate. By 1954 Dr. Margai was chief minister, and in 1958, under a new preindependence constitution, he was named premier. In 1960 he was knighted by Queen Elizabeth II, thus receiving the title "Sir." The SLPP represented an alliance of the traditional and Western-educated Protectorate elites and the Western-educated Krio leaders from the colony. The SLPP was committed to moderate nationalism, political unity, and independence. This emphasis on unity was evidenced in the SLPP's motto: "one country, one people." At independence in 1961, Dr. Margai was both leader of the SLPP and prime minister.[3]

Immigration

A primary reason for Fula business elites' participation in national politics during the prime ministership of Dr. Margai was immigration, which was shaped by both domestic politics and Sierra Leone's relations with neighboring Guinea. Like the British colonial administration, the Margai government was confronted with the problem of illegal immigration. Guinea was the single largest source of both legal and illegal Fula immigrants, accounting for over 80 percent of the Fula immigrant population in Sierra Leone. And the Fula were at the heart of the country's highly divisive discussions about illegal immigration. For many Sierra Leoneans, the Fula were perceived as Guinean-born foreigners. Fula immigration was part of a broader national political debate about immigration, ethnic relations, citizenship, and African unity.[4]

Immigration divided the citizenry in the ethnically diverse nation. A high political priority of Sir Milton was to forge trans-ethnic unity in the Sierra Leone political landscape, which was marked by ethnic politics. This was based on patron-client relationships and a share of the spoils of office. It incorporated large numbers of people into electoral politics and linked the mass of the population to regional and national leaders. Ethnic politics was highly personalized and centered on the prestige of the leader and his ability to reward followers with favors in cash or kind. Some of the patrons were politicians-businessmen. In cases where patrons were not contestants for national political office, they may call on their clients to support political alliances involving relatives or friends. Such action may serve to protect the patron's political, economic, or social privileges in his community.[5]

Immigration, which was one of the most controversial political issues since independence, also affected citizenship. The criteria for Sierra Leonean citizenship were vigorously debated in Parliament and among the general public. Fula politicians of the SLPP such as Alhaji Dr. Amadu Wurie and Hon. Abdulai Bum Mikailu (A. B. M.) Jah[6] contributed to the citizenship debates in Parliament, arguing for inclusion of minority groups like the Fula.[7] One noted political commentator on the public debates on citizenship was Dr. Raymond Sarif Easmon, who advocated broader Sierra Leonean citizenship to include minority groups such as the Lebanese, Afro-Lebanese, and Fula. According to the independence constitution, a Sierra Leonean citizen was defined in section one as

Every person who having been born in the former Colony and Protectorate of Sierra Leone was on the twenty-sixth day of April 1961 a citizen of the United Kingdom and Colonies or a British protected person shall become a citizen of Sierra Leone on the 27th day of April 1961. Provided that a person shall not become a citizen of Sierra Leone by virtue of this sub-section if neither of his parents nor any of his grandparents was born in the former Colony and Protectorate of Sierra Leone.[8]

After two proposed bills and lengthy public debates, Parliament passed an amended Citizenship Act in January 1962. According to the Act,

Any person either of whose parents is a negro of African descent and would, but for the provisions of the above paragraph, have been a Sierra Leonean citizen, may on making application in such manner as may be described be registered as a citizen of Sierra Leone. Such person shall not be qualified to become a Member of the House of Representatives (Parliament) or of any District Council or other local authority unless such person shall have resided continuously in Sierra Leone for 25 years after such registration or shall have served in the Civil or Military Services of Sierra Leone for a period of 25 years.

It was Hon. Jah who made a further amendment to the Citizenship Act which stated that the period after registration be twenty-five years instead of ten years.[9] The Citizenship Act further stated that "every person of negro African descent born in Sierra Leone after April 27 last year shall be a citizen of Sierra Leone at the date of his birth if at that date his father is a citizen of Sierra Leone."[10] Stevens, the leader of the opposition APC, criticized the legislation as "sectional" and said that it deprived some people of the right to contest for Parliament or local government councils. However, J. Barthes-Wilson, deputy leader of the United Progressive Party (UPP), which was formed in 1954, described the Act as fair and added that "any Citizenship Act in any country must be discriminatory, for instance it must distinguish aliens from indigenous people."[11]

Kono District

Kono District in eastern Sierra Leone—the country's diamond mining nexus—arguably best illuminates immigration as a major political subject in postindependence Sierra Leone. The Fula were only one of several African groups like Malians, Nigerians, Gambians, and Liberians, as well as non-African groups like the Lebanese, who migrated to Kono in search of diamond wealth. These new arrivals or "strangers" were mainly illegal immigrants, although some had legal residency. The diamond rush of the 1950s brought an unprecedented number of immigrants, including Fula, to Kono, where they were involved in illicit diamond mining, as well as being licensed diggers and dealers. Competition for diamonds among locals and foreigners resulted in violence that lasted throughout the postindependence period under review. According to one report, "Violence occurred wherever illicit miners worked; chiefs took part in the business by charging for tools, gangs of thugs were formed; sanitary conditions were appalling; Mandingoes arrived in their thousands; and wherever diamonds were found the main beneficiaries were the international traders whose large profits were spent abroad."[12] Alluvial and kimberlite gem and industrial diamonds were first discovered in Kono in the early 1930s. The Consolidated African Selection Trust (CAST) was the first company to prospect and to discover large amounts of diamonds in the area. Its subsidiary, the Sierra Leone Selection trust (SLST), was then formed to mine diamonds. In 1934 the British colonial administration gave the SLST exclusive rights to mine diamonds for ninety-nine years in return for certain payments to the colonial administration. The SLST provided the bulk of the government revenue from diamonds.[13]

Because of widespread smuggling by native-born residents and foreign nationals like the Fula, Mandingo, and Lebanese involved in illicit diamond mining, the colonial administration decided in 1956 to restrict the mining activities of the SLST and grant licenses to individuals to mine diamonds in Kono. This program, the Alluvial Diamond Mining Scheme, brought about a diamond boom that attracted both Sierra Leoneans and foreigners. To curb illegal diamond mining, the British carried out several "stranger drives," which led to hundreds of arrests and deportations.[14] By 1961 illicit diamond mining activities had increased substantially. As a result, the Margai administration adopted a policy to issue residential permits to non-Kono residents. All immigrants or strangers without residential permits were ordered to leave the mining area. Moreover, the Margai government continued the policy of stranger drives against illicit miners, resulting in thousands of arrests and expulsions to their countries of origin, which affected the Fula.

To deal with the influx of immigrants, in 1961 the SLPP government set up an Immigration Quota Committee to grant immigration quotas to foreign nationals, including Lebanese and Indians. In 1962, according to government immigration records, there were fifty-five Asian traders in Kono.[15] In the same year, Prime Minister Margai informed Parliament that, "according to the immigration records 16,810 foreigners have entered Sierra Leone legally since the beginning of 1957. The number of persons who have entered illegally is not known." The prime minister acknowledged that because much of the country's land boundary, particularly the Sierra Leone–Guinea border, was made up of bush without roads, it was impossible to ensure that no one enters the country illegally. He further stated that immigration posts now existed at five border crossing places to enable immigrants, including Fula, to comply with the law. Dr. Margai made it clear that his government was aware of the problem of illegal immigration and had therefore recently formed a new immigration department that was directly responsible to him to ensure compliance with the nation's laws.[16]

In an effort to curb illegal immigration in Kono, the Margai government carried out stranger roundups that led to the arrests and deportations of illegal immigrants. In 1962 some Fula and Mandingo residents were detained but were released when it was discovered that they were members of the tribal authorities (chiefs). This was disclosed in Parliament by Sir Milton in reply to D. S. Bockari (Member of Parliament—MP—for Kono East), who had asked the prime minister to "state how many Tribal Authorities in Kono District have been arrested and committed into prison for residential permits, and if at all these people were non-Konos but issued with exemption certificates and what would the Government do to safeguard the property of such persons who are deported after their various terms of imprisonment." According to Dr. Margai, "no case is known of such persons having been committed to prison for failure to have residential permits. No member of a Tribal Authority in any chiefdom in Kono requires a residential permit or exemption certificate. The second part of your question does not therefore arise."[17]

Parliament became the battleground over illegal immigration in Kono as the SLPP government and the opposition parties disagreed on solutions. In 1962 George W. Mani, MP of the Sierra Leone Progressive Independence Movement (SLPIM), moved "that this House deplores the system of issuing permits to Sierra Leoneans before they can enter certain parts of Sierra Leone with particular reference to Kono. We are all in one country and we should be free to move about. I know the Government members will vote against the motion but it will surely affect our brothers and sisters. People do not all go to Kono for diamonds. How can you drive a Sierra Leonean from a part of Sierra Leone?" The motion was defeated by the majority MPs of the SLPP.[18]

In Parliament both Sir Milton and his ministers defended the SLPP government's immigration policy in Kono. In 1964 Finance Minister Albert Margai, on behalf of the prime minister, stated that "government does not consider that Kono District is thickly populated by foreigners or that the law deprives Sierra Leoneans of any of their rights in this respect." He added that "it is not in the country's best interest to preclude non–Sierra Leoneans from residence in the Diamond Protected Area. Anybody who is not a true native of Kono District is required to have a permit to enter or reside in the Diamond Area and this is strictly controlled." Albert Margai further noted that recently a number of immigrants had their residential permits revoked for unlawful practices, which demonstrated the government's resolve to deal with the issue. He argued for a certain number of non–Sierra Leoneans to be permitted to enter or reside in Kono to engage in the diamond business. He pointed out that it was not always possible for Sierra Leoneans to find the considerable capital necessary to finance the diamond trade in Kono and the country as a whole.[19]

Beyond that, the SLPP minister of lands, mines, and labor, A. J. Demby, informed Parliament that one Sierra Leonean, ten Lebanese, and nineteen privileged Africans had been served with Expulsion Orders from the Diamond Protection Areas in Kono since January 1962 and that two such Expulsion Orders had been revoked to date. This was in response to the APC politician S. A. T. Koroma's (MP for Port Loko South) question regarding how many Sierra Leoneans, Lebanese, and

African foreigners have been served with Expulsion Orders from the Diamond Protection Areas since January 1962 and how many of these Expulsion Orders have been revoked to date.[20] Previously, in 1963 the SLPP government appointed an advisory committee headed by Justice C. O. E. Cole to consider and make recommendations on objections raised on expulsion orders. One of the petitions examined by the advisory committee was that of Henneh Shamel, a Lebanese diamond dealer from Magburaka in northern Sierra Leone.[21]

Also in 1963, Prime Minister Margai, who was also minister of internal affairs, introduced a bill to amend the Aliens (Expulsion) Act, which was passed by the SLPP-dominated Parliament. The purpose of the legislation was to remove the distinction between commonwealth citizens and aliens regarding expulsion. According to the Act, "'Non-citizen' means any person who is not a citizen of Sierra Leone or a person, not being the national of any other country, who would but for any amendment of the constitution have been a citizen of Sierra Leone." In effect, commonwealth citizens could now be deported from Sierra Leone. The legislation was opposed by the APC opposition leader Stevens.[22]

Dr. Margai, in response to questions on immigration in Kono by George W. Mani (MP for Kono South), stated that the residential permits of eighty-seven Lebanese traders and diamond dealers in Kono were revoked in January 1964 but twenty-seven were allowed reentry and their permits renewed following appeals to the provincial secretary. In all, there were 186 Lebanese traders and diamond dealers in Kono. The prime minister also informed Parliament that his administration was considering the introduction of legislation to provide adequate safeguards for indigenous businesses against competition by Syrian, Lebanese, and Indian private enterprises.[23]

Outside of Parliament, the presence of immigrants, including large numbers of Fula, in Kono was a prickly political issue. At a meeting of the APC in the campaign for the Bo Town Council in 1962, a leading APC politician and parliamentarian, Mohamed Bash-Taqi told a crowd of over one thousand that

> The ruling SLPP has done nothing to safeguard the interest of the Africans but strangers are putting up mansions all over the country. There are great difficulties in getting permits for Africans to enter Kono but strangers get permits easily. This is the time that you should begin to show the Government that you do not like the way things are going by voting solidly for our candidates in this election and future elections.[24]

Fula business elites lobbied the Margai government on a number of issues related to the diamond trade, including the issuance of more diamond dealer licenses, residential permits, and diggers licenses to the Fula. Some of the Fula business leaders like Alhaji Momodu Alpha Bah in Kono, used their personal connections with Sir Milton and members of his cabinet to influence key matters: expansion of Fula participation in the diamond business, particularly in Kono; ending of police harassment of Fula in the diamond areas; and integration of Fula immigrants into host mining communities. The granting of diamond dealer and digger licenses was a highly political and divisive issue. Since the 1930s, when diamond mining started in Kono, the Fula had been one of the largest African groups in the diamond trade. Besides the Fula, Lebanese, and Indians, African nationals like the Mandingo from such countries as The Gambia, Guinea, Liberia, and Mali also competed for diamond licenses in Sierra Leone Moreover, given the illicit nature of a large number of Fula diamond-mining activities, the Fula, like many other illicit miners from African and non-African countries, were frequently targeted by the police and government officials in their efforts to curb lawlessness, violence, corruption, and illegal immigration. Here again, Fula business elites provided leadership in working with law enforcement and public officials in ensuring that Fula rights were protected in accordance with the laws of Sierra Leone.[25]

Fula Business Elites and Immigration

The political program of Fula business elites in dealing with immigration matters focused on responding to the surging Fula immigrant population and the Margai government crackdown on illegal Fula immigrants. Fula business leaders formed the core of the Fula interest group that crafted political responses to the Fula immigration question. Though informal, it included politicians from different parties including the SLPP and APC, traditional rulers, businessmen-politicians, professionals, civil servants, and youth activists. Collectively, they worked closely with the SLPP government on immigration legislation and enforcement, as well as explaining immigration policies to the Fula people nationwide.

Prominent Fula business leaders in the interest group included businessmen-traditional rulers like the Freetown-based Guinean-born Alhaji Almamy Momodu Bah, who arrived in Freetown in the early 1900s; Alhaji Momodu Alpha Bah and Alhaji Ibrahima Sowe (previously Taal), both of Kono; Alhaji Almamy Abdul R. Jalloh of Kabala, Koinadugu District in the Northern Province; Alhaji Almamy Wuroh Jalloh Timbo of Rokulan, Bombali District in the Northern Province; and Alhaji Almamy Kulio Yalloh (Jalloh) of Tonkolili District, Northern Province. Other key Fula businessmen included the Sierra Leonean–born sons of the Senegalese-born Fula business titan, Alhaji Almamy Momodu Allie in the colonial era, namely Alhaji Ibrahim M. Allie, Alhaji Baba Allie, and Alhaji Abass Allie; and diamond dealers such as Guinean-born Karim Barrie and Alhaji Mohamed W. Jalloh; and Sierra Leonean–born Almamy Agibu Jalloh, who was involved in the cattle, transport, and produce trade. Businessmen-politicians were also a part of the Fula interest group. They included Freetown City Council (FCC) Councilor Alhaji Tejan-Jalloh, Member of the British Empire (MBE) and Justice of Peace (JP) who was in the produce and merchandise trade; and Alhaji Ali Dausy (A. D.) Wurie, FCC councilor, alderman, and assistant resident director in the Sierra Leone Development Company (DELCO). In 1963 Alhaji Wurie was awarded the MBE in recognition of long and distinguished service in Freetown and the Northern Province.[26]

Native-born Fula politicians included Alhaji Dr. Amadu Wurie, who served as minister of education, after a long distinguished career as an educator, during the Margai administration and held the MBE award.[27] Others included Alhaji Almamy Dr. Jaia Kaikai (Sidiyankei Barrie) of Pujehun District, who held the MBE and was a JP;[28] Sir Hon. Justice Banja Tejan-Sie, who was awarded the Most Distinguished Order of St. Michael and St. George—the second-highest rank in the order— for distinguished public service as speaker of Parliament;[29] as well as Hon. Jah (MP for Pujehun West). These politicians collaborated with top Fula civil servants like Alhaji Muhamadu Alieu Seray-Wurie, who held several key government positions before retiring as director of audit;[30] acting Superintendent of Police Mohamed Pateh Bah, who was in charge of the A District in Freetown;[31] and Alhaji Mohamed Lamin Sidique, who was the second Sierra Leonean to be appointed provincial secretary, the first being A. K. Hyde, a Krio, who was later promoted secretary to the cabinet.[32]

Many members of the broad-based Fula lobby cultivated close relationships with Sir Milton through personal and political ties. Although a predominantly northern group, the Fula did not join others from the same area such as the Temne and Limba in providing mass support for the APC. Instead, most Fula remained loyal to the SLPP under Dr. Margai. Fula chieftaincy traditions, which date back centuries, also help to explain their political support. As prime minister, Dr. Margai promised to protect the institution of chieftaincy. The SLPP leadership showed great respect for traditional rulers, including paramount chiefs, who were an integral part of the SLPP since its inception and whose support was central to the party's electoral success in the country. In fact, Sir Milton had blood ties and a long association with chiefs. And he worked with them and district councils to gain support of the multiethnic people in the Provinces.[33]

In spite of the strong relationship between Dr. Margai and the Fula people, his SLPP government was tough on prosecuting and deporting illegal Fula immigrants through the courts. Prominent Fula business leaders such as Alhaji Bah, Alhaji Tejan-Jalloh, Almamy Agibu Jalloh, and Alhaji Ibrahim Allie contributed cash and in-kind donations to help take care of the dependents of Fula immigrants who were deported to their homelands. Beyond that, they were instrumental in securing legal representation for them in Freetown-based Magistrate courts. They hired Krio lawyers such as Cyril Rogers Wright, Aaron Cole, J. E. Mackay, Johnny Smythe, Livesey Luke, R. B. Marke, George Gelega-King, and Solomon A. J. Pratt to represent Fula defendants in court. The Krio dominated the legal profession in Sierra Leone at this time because of their Western education. The Fula had a long history of working for, and doing business with, the Krio community in Freetown. As immigrants, Fula worked for Krio civil servants, professionals, and businesspeople in menial positions as domestic servants, drivers, and night watchmen. They also rented shops and houses from Krio landlords.[34]

One major consequence of illegal immigration was the deportation of non–Sierra Leoneans to their homelands. Court records show that Fula, particularly those from Guinea, were among the highest number of deportees because of illegal entry into the country. The evidence, however, does not suggest that Fula immigrants were deported to their countries of origin because of political reasons during the Margai administration. The following court cases illustrate the deportation of illegal Fula immigrants. In 1962, ten Guinean-born Fula were each fined £20 or two months imprisonment when they appeared before the senior police magistrate, C. A. Harding, at Magistrate Court No. 1 in Freetown on charges of entering Sierra Leone without valid passports or traveling certificates. They pleaded guilty to the charges and were ordered to be deported to their Guinean homeland. The eleventh Fula accused pleaded not guilty and was granted bail of £50 and one surety in the same amount. He told the court that he was born in Freetown and that he was sent to Conakry, the capital city of Guinea, by his father a few months ago.[35] In addition, three Guinean-born Fula were sentenced to six months imprisonment with hard labor by Magistrate Agnes Macauley. Each pleaded guilty to a charge of entering Sierra Leone without valid passports and traveling certificates and were ordered to be deported to Guinea after serving their terms of imprisonment.[36]

Moreover, in 1963 a Krio lawyer, Livesey Luke, defended a Guinean-born Fula Mohamed Jalloh on charges of possessing gunpowder without a permit and entering Sierra Leone without a passport in Freetown's No. 1 Magistrate Court presided by Acting Senior Police Magistrate J. B. Short. Jalloh, pleading guilty to both charges, was convicted on his plea and fined £25 or three months on the first charge. But before passing sentence on Jalloh on the second charge, Magistrate Short asked the police whether they were applying for his deportation after sentence. After the police application for deportation, lawyer Luke said to the magistrate, "Deportation does not help African unity in view of Addis Ababa" (a reference to the African Unity Charter signed by thirty African heads of state, including Prime Minister Margai, at the Addis Ababa conference in May 1963). But Magistrate Short told him that he was only an administrator of the law and had nothing to say to that. Consequently, he sentenced Jalloh to a month's imprisonment, after which he ordered him to be deported to his birthplace in Guinea.[37]

Additionally, in 1934 Magistrate Short ordered the deportation of a Fula trader, Amadu Bah of Westermoreland Street (later renamed Siaka Stevens Street) after pleading guilty to the charge of entering Sierra Leone without a passport. In his defense, Bah said he had been in Sierra Leone for two years and that during that time his passport and the sum of £10 were stolen. He said he came from Futa Jallon in Guinea and begged the court to have mercy on him. He was sentenced to a month's imprisonment and subsequent deportation to Guinea.[38] In April of the same year, a Guinean-born Fula, Osman Jalloh of Old Railway Line, Brookfields, in Freetown, who claimed to have resided in Freetown for over ten years, was sentenced to a month's imprisonment for entering Sierra Leone without a passport. He produced certain documents in Magistrate Court No. 1 which showed that he belonged to a certain Fula organization in Freetown, but the police prosecution argued that they were not the equivalent of a passport or a traveling certificate. Magistrate Short ordered Jalloh to be sent to Guinea after serving his sentence.[39]

Besides the Fula, the Margai government deported non-Fula Guinean citizens, as well as Nigerian, Liberian Lebanese, and British nationals for offences ranging from political interference to the smuggling of diamonds. In 1962, for example, J. T. Reffel, who was the former Bassa tribal headman or chief, outgoing councilor for Freetown West, and the APC candidate for the November 1962 FCC election, was deported to Liberia. Reffel's deportation was challenged by his lawyer, Berthan Macaulay. The SLPP government had earlier revoked the recognition of Reffel as tribal headman of the Bassa ethnic group in Freetown.[40] The Margai administration also deported John Hatch, the British-born director of Extra-Mural Studies at FBC for publishing an article on Sierra Leone in the left-wing British newspaper *New Statesman*. The Senate of FBC sent a resolution to Dr. Margai stating "that the Senate of Fourah Bay College, the University College of Sierra Leone, views the deportation of Mr. John Hatch with concern. The Senate trusts that no individual would be made to suffer for any opinions honestly and truthfully held. The Senate reiterates its loyalty to the College and Government of Sierra Leone but feels that the fundamental right to freedom of expression ought once again to be affirmed." Prime Minister Margai responded, "We however reserve the right, as any sovereign Government would, to decide what measures to take when there is a clear case of political interference and excessively derogatory comment on the affairs of our county as was the case with the author and the article in question."[41] Beyond that, the Margai administration deported two Lebanese diamond traders resident in Bo District: Naif Mohamed Fackie and Mohamed Alie Jaward. Fackie came to Sierra Leone in 1947 and Jaward in 1954. Before leaving for Lebanon, Fackie stated "I regard my deportation as being unfair, because I was given no reason for the deportation. Since my arrival in this country in 1947, I have never been convicted by any court as I have always obeyed and respected the laws of the land. I have never been involved in the political affairs of the country." Fackie further stated that the SLPP government had granted him a diamond dealer's license and had given him permits to enter Kono for the purpose of buying diamonds. Since 1959 he had done not less than £1 million business with the Sierra Leone Diamond Corporation (SLDC) and the Government Diamond Office (GDO) and had paid about £75,000 in taxes to the government. Fackie also said that he was responsible for at least 15 percent of the total diamonds purchased locally by the SLDC, an indication that he was not smuggling diamonds out of this country.[42]

After meeting with Prime Minister Margai, the Lebanese charge d'affaires, Jean Hazou, said in commenting on the deportation orders that he did not "consider the deportation of the two Lebanese from

Sierra Leone a prejudice against the Lebanese community. The issue was nonpolitical and has no connection with the general good policy of the Sierra Leone government toward foreigners. The government through Sir Milton has always praised the activity of the Lebanese community in this country." Hazou emphasized that although the Lebanese had always cooperated in the economic and social fields, "This does not mean that the authorities might not be dissatisfied with the behavior of a restricted number of individuals, whether Lebanese, Europeans, or Africans."[43]

Sierra Leone–Guinea Relations

Relations between Sierra Leone and Guinea influenced Fula immigration, business, and politics during the prime ministership of Dr. Margai. One of the factors that impacted Fula immigration was the personal relationship between President Ahmed Sékou Touré of Guinea, where most of the Fula immigrants originated, and Prime Minister Margai, who did not share the former's radical political ideology. Margai was a conservative politician who leaned toward the West. The political systems of Sierra Leone and Guinea were in marked contrast. Whereas Sierra Leone had one of the best African multiparty democracies where the opposition could replace the government by free elections, Guinea, by contrast, had one of the most oppressive one-party systems on the continent.[44]

Unlike President Touré, Sir Milton did not perceive the Fula as political enemies. The evidence does not suggest that Guinean-born Fula resident in Sierra Leone participated in political opposition to the Guinean leader. Actually, Prime Minister Margai had a good relationship with the Fula, which reflected his political trademarks of unity and tolerance. His familiar phrase was "one country, one people." One of the closest personal friends of Dr. Margai was the Fula politician Alhaji Amadu Wurie, whom he appointed as minister of education.[45] In a major policy speech appointing Sierra Leone's first ambassador to Guinea, Abdul Karim, a Susu, in 1961, Prime Minister Margai stated that minority groups like the Susu and Fula should not be apprehensive for their well-being since his SLPP government was tolerant and committed to the unity of Sierra Leone. He further pointed out that problems facing minority ethnic groups did not exist in Sierra Leone, unlike elsewhere in Africa. Speaking of Sierra Leone's relations with neighboring states, particularly Guinea, Prime Minister Margai said that he would be friendly with his neighbors depending on their foreign policies. He emphasized that the SLPP government's goal of unity in Sierra Leone would be pursued not only in West Africa but the whole of Africa.[46]

Sir Milton's warm relationship with the Fula was strongly influenced by their shared conservative values in revering traditions and chieftaincy. As a matter of fact, the prime minister, like many of the Fula business elites, came from chieftaincy backgrounds. Fula political culture, which date back centuries, celebrated chieftaincy and recognized incumbency.[47] This was a primary reason for Fula support of Dr. Margai as well as the SLPP government and party. Since the inception of the SLPP in 1951, Sir Milton worked closely with paramount chiefs, who were an integral part of the SLPP. Their support in the Protectorate was central to the SLPP's electoral success. Prime Minister Margai's strong bias in favor of chiefs facilitated their access to government privileges such as mining licenses and building loans. One scholar has argued that this pro-chief attitude alienated many Sierra Leoneans in the Northern Province, and even among some of the youthful supporters of the SLPP in the party's heartland in the Southern Province.[48] By contrast, President Touré abolished chieftaincy as a feudal institution and introduced an administrative reorganization in Guinea to bring about the autonomy of the state.[49]

Although Prime Minister Margai had great respect for traditional rulers and customs, he disciplined paramount chiefs who did not enjoy the support of their people or violated the rule of law. He was a firm believer in putting the interest of the people first. In 1964, for example, Dr. Margai ordered the deposing and banishment of the Temne Paramount Chief (PC) Bai Koblo Pathbana of the Marampa-Masimera chiefdom despite the fact that he was a long-standing personal friend and a strong SLPP supporter. The wife of the deposed PC, Madam Ella Koblo Gulama, was also a staunch SLPP supporter and in 1957 became the first woman elected to Parliament.[50]

While the relationship between Prime Minister Margai and President Touré was cordial, it was not as friendly as the former's connections to fellow conservative African heads of state, President William V. S. Tubman of neighboring Liberia and Nigeria's prime minister, Alhaji Sir Abubakar Tafawa Balewa. This is evidenced by Dr. Margai's absence at Touré's inauguration as president of Guinea in 1958. Instead, it was Albert Margai and Stevens, both of whom by then had resigned from the SLPP and formed the People's National Party (PNP) in September

1958, who visited President Touré to congratulate him, while making it clear that they did not represent the Sierra Leone government.[51] Notwithstanding the absence of Sir Milton at President Touré's inauguration, in order to promote bilateral relations between the two countries, Touré accepted an invitation by the SLPP government through the head of state, Queen Elizabeth II, to visit Sierra Leone in December 1960. Speaking at the state banquet in Freetown, Dr. Margai told Touré, "Our countries have much in common. We have ties of kinship and custom, of history and tradition, and many of our problems, and interests both social and economic are the same. We can gain by mutual cooperation and friendship and it is right that we should do so. It is my earnest hope that we shall find ways and means of helping each other in the years to come."[52] As part of the schedule of events, Sir Milton accompanied President Touré and his Guinean delegation to Tongo Field, which was where diamonds were mined in Kenema District. The Guinean delegation included the Guinean representative in Sierra Leone, Consul-General Camara Gadiri Mangue. Prime Minister Margai's group included MPs, PCs, government officials, and members of SLST, which dominated diamond mining in Sierra Leone.[53]

In spite of the long and widespread Fula presence, as well as growing foreign-born population in the country, especially those from Guinea, there were very few Fula business, political, or traditional elites in Dr. Margai's delegation that hosted President Touré. The sensitivity of Fula immigration to Sierra Leone, as well as the suspicious and adversarial political relationship between the Fula and President Touré, may help explain the low-level presence of Fula, particularly Guinean-born, in the SLPP's delegations that hosted the Guinean leader in Sierra Leone. Members of the Guinean-born Fula business elites such as Alhaji Bah, like many of his ordinary homeland compatriots in Sierra Leone, were highly distrustful of President Touré.

Even after President Touré was reelected for a new seven-year term by the Guinean people in January 1961, Prime Minister Margai did not attend the inauguration ceremonies. Instead, he sent his minister of external affairs, Dr. Karefa-Smart, to lead the SLPP government delegation. Again, there were no Fula political, business, or traditional leaders in the group, despite the large and growing Fula immigrant community.[54] Upon Sierra Leone's independence day on April 27, 1961, President Touré was conspicuously absent at the colorful ceremonies hosted by Sir Milton. Instead, the independence celebration was attended by Dr. Margai's personal friends and fellow conservative leaders, Tubman of Liberia and Balewa of Nigeria. To reciprocate the Liberian president's visit, Prime Minister Margai in January 1964 led a large delegation that joined representatives from sixty-four countries to witness the elaborate activities of the fifth inauguration of Tubman, who had been president of Liberia since 1944.[55]

It was not until January 1962 that Sir Milton made a brief visit to Guinea on the invitation of President Touré. Members of the prime minister's delegation included the minister of natural resources, Albert Margai; the minister of development, R. G. O. King; the minister of information and broadcasting, John Nelson-Williams; the minister of the Eastern Province, Taplima Ngobeh; the minister of the Northern Province, Mahmoud Ahmed; PC Bai Sherbro Yumkella II of Kambia District; PC Alikali Modu III of Port Loko District; and Dr. Sarif Easmon. Conspicuously absent in the delegation were Fula political, business, and traditional elites.[56] While in Guinea, Prime Minister Margai visited Labé, where he was a given a ceremonial parade. Most of the residents of Labé were Fula. The prime minister's three-day visit to Guinea was cut short when he suddenly became ill while in Labé.[57]

After that, in March 1962, Sir Milton embarked on another short visit to Guinea with the same delegation as in January. As in the previous visit, the prime minister did not include Fula political, business, or traditional leaders in his delegation.[58] The focus of the March trip was to discuss two major problems facing the two neighbors: illegal immigration and smuggling. Both Prime Minister Margai and President Touré also discussed broader African issues such as relations between the Casablanca and Monrovia groups in the context of African unity. On arrival in Guinea, Dr. Margai was greeted at the airport by President Touré and members of the Guinean government.[59] In the joint communiqué issued at the end of the visit, both Sierra Leone and Guinea agreed to strengthen the natural bonds of friendship and fraternity between them by (1) taking necessary measures to safeguard and foster the interests of the two brotherly states; (2) cooperating in economic, financial, social, and cultural matters; (3) encouraging frequent contacts between the various organizations of women, youth, arts, and culture; (4) encouraging cooperation at village level and exchanging at the national level practical experience gained in various fields. The two heads of state also agreed to deal firmly with any subversive action directed against their respective governments and peoples from whatever source. They also stated that total independence and African unity constituted the immediate objectives on which depended the peace and prosperity of the world.[60]

Regardless of the ideological differences between Prime Minister Margai and President Touré, both leaders pursued strong relations. For instance, in 1962 both Sierra Leone and Guinea signed an international air services agreement at Lungi Airport in Sierra Leone. The seven-man Guinean delegation included the minister of public works and transport, Toure Ismael, and the director of cabinet in the Ministry of Foreign Affairs, Diallo Abdouleye. Sierra Leone was represented by the minister of external affairs, Dr. Karefa-Smart, the minister of communications, Kandeh Bureh, and the director of civil aviation, R. R. Wright. The minister of communications welcomed the delegation to Sierra Leone on its inaugural flight and expressed the hope that the agreement would be long lasting. According to the Guinean minister of public works and transport, "This morning we bring to you greetings from Sékou Touré, President of Guinea and the people of Guinea. We wish to thank you for this spontaneous welcome. We do hope that the cordial spirit of friendship existing between our countries will continue. The inauguration of this flight will help to develop human relations between our countries." At the end of his speech, the minister said, "Long live the friendship and brotherhood between Guinea and Sierra Leone."[61] But more than that, in 1964 President Touré's government made a major concession to Sierra Leoneans traveling to Guinea by abolishing visas. Jean H. Soumare, acting charge d'affaires of Guinea in Sierra Leone, stated in Freetown that Sierra Leoneans traveling to Guinea did not need visas effective the week of January 17, 1964. He also said that his government was making it possible for all Africans to go to Guinea without visas. This, he added, "is meant to promote and iron out the determination of the African peoples to unite." The Guinean diplomat also stated, "I shall do everything that will make for the strengthening of social, economic, cultural, and fraternal relations between the two sister states of Sierra Leone and Guinea. After all, we are one and the same people. There are a lot of people in the two countries who speak a common language. We were only separated by the colonial masters to perpetuate the economic exploitation of our people for their selfish ends." The Guinean envoy further noted that with the abolition of visas between the two countries, cultural and social ties would be strengthened. He was confident that this kind gesture by the Guinean government would be a major step in promoting the long-standing friendship and mutual cooperation between the two countries.[62] According to Sierra Leone immigration regulations, Guinean citizens were not required to have a visa but only a passport or valid travel certificate to enter the country.[63]

From the perspective of African unity, Sir Milton, in spite of ideological differences, worked with President Touré to promote continental unity. Both were firm believers in African unity and were key players in the formation of the Organization of African Unity (OAU) in May 1963 in Addis Ababa, the capital city of Ethiopia. Besides President Touré, Dr. Margai also collaborated with radical leaders such as Presidents Kwame Nkrumah of Ghana, Gamal Abdel Nasser of the United Arab Republic (UAR, or Egypt), and Modibo Keita of Mali, as well as moderate African leaders such as Tubman and Balewa.[64] According to the monthly *West African Review*, Sierra Leone, despite its small size and population, could play an important role in African affairs given its long history in training leaders from across Africa in such areas as politics and education.[65]

Consistent with the ideals of the OAU in promoting African unity, Prime Minister Margai viewed Fula immigrants in Sierra Leone as African brothers and sisters and sought to promote multi-ethnic unity among the Sierra Leonean population. He was a firm believer in national unity and spent his lifetime trying to bridge multicultural differences in Sierra Leone. Unlike radical Pan-Africanists such as President Touré, Dr. Margai was a gradualist who had a realistic concept of African unity. Because of Sir Milton's political gradualism and pro-West ideology, he was criticized by his domestic political enemies as a "weak traitor, imbecile, and stooge."[66] The birth of the OAU was the result of a political compromise between two major camps: the radical group of African countries known as the Casablanca faction and the moderates who were characterized as the Monrovia group. In January 1961, President Touré, alongside Presidents Nkrumah, Nasser, and Keita, attended the African Summit Conference in Casablanca that was hosted by King Mohammed V of Morocco. These African leaders drew up the Casablanca Charter with emphasis on African unity. They wanted a United States of Africa to replace the newly independent African countries.[67]

In contrast, in May 1961, nineteen African heads of state met in Monrovia, the capital city of Liberia, at the All-Africa Summit to discuss African unity. They included the host Tubman, as well as Margai and Balewa.[68] In addition to Liberia, Sierra Leone, and Nigeria, the other countries represented were Cameroon, Central African Republic, Chad, Dahomey, Congo (Leopoldville), Congo (Brazzaville), Ethiopia, Gabon, Côte d'Ivoire, Madagascar, Mauritania, Niger, Senegal, Somalia, Togo, and Upper Volta. These African leaders decided that "any conception of unity which entailed the surrender of the sovereignty of any African state to another was totally unrealistic."[69] The theme of the conference was, "African solutions to African problems." Speaking at the opening session of the conference, Prime Minister Margai urged attendees to "accept and support" the ideas proposed by President Tubman. He further stated, "We pledge cooperation in defense of the territorial integrity and sovereignty of freedom-loving states in Africa, particularly with a view to curbing internal subversion against lawfully constituted governments of any friendly state. We are prepared to do everything in our power to safeguard the territorial integrity of any African state which might be threatened from within or outside the African continent."[70]

Fula Business Elites and the Politics of Business

Fula business elites participated in Sierra Leone politics in large measure to advance their private enterprise interests in key economic sectors such as the diamond trade, livestock, transport, and the retail trade. For the SLPP government under the leadership of Sir Milton, the Fula were an integral part of the national economy. Nevertheless, the evidence suggests that the prime minister did not have private business dealings or partnerships with Fula business leaders within or outside the country—particularly in the highly profitable diamond trade—nor did he engage in private business or have business surrogates while in office, unlike his political successor and brother, Albert Margai, as discussed in the chapter that follows. To Dr. Margai, politics and business should not intersect in the personal sphere.

A significant political debate during the prime ministership of Dr. Margai revolved around foreign investment in the country. Fula business leaders were particularly interested in this subject because many were foreign born, especially Guineans, and had investments in the nation's economy. In March 1961, Sir Milton told Parliament that his administration's attitude to foreign investment "is an open door policy." He said that the government had no wish of discriminating between one source of investment and another: "All who are willing to invest money in the country are welcome provided that they are prepared to abide by the laws of the country, make genuine attempts to employ local personnel in their business to the greatest, and can satisfy government that they have the technical competence and financial resources to make a success of their investment. It is the policy of Government to allow the repatriation of capital, profit and interest without restriction."[71]

The opposition APC criticized the SLPP government's open door policy. According to an APC statement, "It is a matter of the utmost concern to the APC that our people are being pushed out more and more from smaller trades and industries of the country as a result of the declared open-door policy of the Government."[72] Meanwhile, groups such as the Sierra Leone Business and Professional Women's Club also opposed the involvement of foreigners in certain sectors of the economy like hairdressing, retail trading, mining, and transport. Despite political and commercial opposition, the Margai government did not pass comprehensive legislation to restrict foreign business involvement in the country's economy.

Retail Trade

Retail trade was a core sector of the economy. Since most of the Fula business class was involved in retail trade, Fula business leaders were concerned about the Margai government's trade policies. However, their main challenge was how to protect the growing Fula immigrant retailers against exploitation and harassment by government officials. Fula retail trading activities centered on merchandise. Many were shopkeepers who bought imported consumer goods wholesale from expatriate firms and retailed them to neighborhood customers. By 1963 the cost of living was high and rising, with expatriate enterprises constantly increasing their prices. In order to control consumer prices, the Ministry of Trade and Industry relied heavily on price control officers, who were in short supply. Many Fula retailers faced victimization from these officers. Therefore, they organized themselves—including petty traders, shopkeepers, and wholesalers—under the leadership of Fula business elites like Alimamy Agibu Jalloh in lobbying the ministry to end such unfair actions by price control officers. Their efforts were only partially successful but resulted in improved communication between the Fula business community and the ministry. The parliamentary secretary in the Ministry of Trade and Industry, Hon. Jah, played an important role in helping Fula businesspeople deal with trade questions.[73]

Retail trade was front and center in the political controversy about the participation of foreigners in the economy. As noted earlier, there was growing advocacy by Sierra Leoneans to limit the participation of foreigners including Fula, Lebanese, and Indians in certain sectors of the national economy, particularly retail trade. For instance, in 1962 an MP of the SLPP introduced in Parliament a motion that would bar non–Sierra Leoneans from participating in the rice trade, a measure that the opposition APC supported and which was enacted. After that, in 1963 the acting minister for the Northern Province, W. A. Jackson, stated that by enacting a law to exclude foreigners from the rice trade, the SLPP government had challenged every Sierra Leonean to participate in the trade and become successful. But the APC argued that the Margai government had not put in place the necessary measures such as storage and finance to implement the terms of the law so as to enable Sierra Leoneans to take over the trade.[74]

Livestock

Fula dominated the livestock trade and its related butchering business in the economy. The livestock trade was vertically integrated, with the Fula responsible for raising, purchasing, transporting, distributing, and slaughtering livestock. The success of the Fula in the livestock business can be attributed to five factors. First, they controlled most of the supply networks originating in Guinea and the Northern Province, especially in Koinadugu and Bombali. Second, they controlled most of the retail distribution networks through extensive kinship ties in the country. Third, through employment of kinsmen their operations were cost-effective. Fourth, they had the ability to transport large numbers of livestock legally or by smuggling across the Guinea–Sierra Leone border to the major markets in Sierra Leone. Fifth and finally, the favorable economic environment in Freetown offered many employment and business opportunities and attracted a large beef-consuming population, which expanded the market for meat. This high public demand for meat was complemented by large government contracts for meat.[75]

A major organizational feature of the livestock trade was the supply of cattle, which was essential to the business success of the wholesale butchers throughout Sierra Leone. But access to cattle was uneven among butchers. The dominance of such large butchers as Alhaji Momodu Bah may be explained in large measure by his privileged access to vast cattle supplies from Futa Jallon in neighboring Guinea through his status as chief and his wealth and extensive kinship ties. Over 60 percent of the cattle traded in Sierra Leone came from Futa Jallon, which was the linchpin of the Fula cattle trade with Sierra Leone from a supply perspective, and the Fula played a pivotal role as *julas* (cattle traders). Many of the Fula cattle traders smuggled their cattle from Guinea into Sierra Leone, motivated by higher prices and the desire to avoid payment of taxes to Guinean and Sierra Leonean authorities. The Guinean government's failure to stop the Fula from smuggling cattle into Sierra Leone resulted in the loss of considerable tax revenue.[76]

Of great concern to Prime Minister Margai and Fula business elites were the age-old feuds between Fula cattle herders and own- ers—many of whom were Guinean immigrants—and local farmers, especially in northern Sierra Leone, over grazing lands. In September 1963, there was such a clash in Bombali that resulted in the loss of cattle and crops and deepened the hostility between the Fula cattle owners and the mainly Temne farmers. Fula business leaders, who were also traditional rulers, partnered with the Margai government in resolving these disputes; these leaders included Alhaji Abdul Jalloh and Alhaji Wuroh Timbo.[77]

The butchering business, which involved the purchase of cattle to slaughter for sale of beef in markets in Sierra Leone, reflected the eth- nic diversity of the country. Of the ethnic groups represented, which included Mandingo, Temne, Lebanese, and Susu, the Fula formed the majority. The Fula butchers, who were mostly Futa Jallon immigrants, came from different socioeconomic backgrounds and had varied sources of capital. Organizationally, the butchering business included meat sellers on the streets, sellers of offal and hides, and small-scale retail butchers, who were clients of the wholesale butchers. Usually the wholesale butchers recruited clients from their own ethnic groups, or mostly Fula. Entry into wholesale butchering was limited to butch- ers with long-standing reputation for providing and managing credit, wealth to purchase large numbers of cattle, and established business contacts to market meat on a large scale. Because only a small num- ber of individuals, like Alhaji Bah, possessed the means, the butchering business was dominated by a few.

Among the wholesale butchers there was intense intra-ethnic and cross-ethnic competition to secure the government meat contracts and to sell meat to the public, but ethnic solidarity also existed. The Muslim Fula butchers, for example, exploited their ethnic and religious affin- ity with Muslim Fula julas to prevail over butchers from other ethnic groups. In addition, there was some degree of business cooperation among large-scale butchers of different ethnic groups who were Mus- lims. Competition for the meat market in Freetown—the largest in the country—during the Margai administration was mainly among four wholesale butchers: Alhaji Bah, Alhaji Mohamed Boie Kamara, Alhaji Ibrahim Allie, and Alhaji Kuda Mansaray. Despite the competition,

Alhaji Bah, a close personal friend of Sir Milton, was the single largest government meat contractor. The government contract for meat represented about 40 percent of the meat market in Freetown. Besides meeting the written requirements of the contract, winning the bid involved cultivating the members of the groups awarding the contract, including the permanent secretary and politicians such as the minister of trade and industry. The politics of contracting that involved cultivating human relationships and offering gifts to decision makers in the meat business was similar to that in other sectors of the economy.[78]

The 1962 Election

The May 1962 election was the first since Sierra Leone gained independence from Britain. It marked the first election in a sub-Saharan African country in which political parties contested openly and freely for power. The major parties were the SLPP and the APC. Fula political membership existed in all the major parties, but was concentrated in the SLPP. The SLPP election manifesto covered several areas, including support of the institution of chieftaincy; free primary education and equal educational opportunities for boys and girls; expansion of technical and vocational education throughout the country; expansion of agriculture in areas such as new crops, farm mechanization, and expansion of agricultural credit; effective control of the mining sector for the benefit of the people without nationalization; emphasis on the expansion of preventive health measures and the supply of safe drinking water and other measures for preventing diseases. Furthermore, the program pledged more assistance to FBC to help in the training of additional doctors, dentists, nurses, midwives, and other health workers; expansion of communications, including roads, ports, railway, and air service; support for industrialization in the forms of both public-private partnership and private enterprises; more opportunities for indigenous businesses; provision of decent and adequate housing; and expansion and strengthening diplomatic representation abroad.[79]

The SLPP platform also stated that the party was committed to "fostering good relations with the rest of the world and in particular with our West African neighbors, including Guinea, and with other African countries. The SLPP believes in the eventual unity of all African countries and will do its utmost to promote this goal without interference in the domestic affairs of other countries or by other countries in our affairs."[80] The SLPP policy statement also listed the party's achievements over the past five years, including the areas of adult literacy, communications, education, health centers, agriculture, industrialization, tourism, and Africanization of the public sector.[81]

The APC opposition party's leader, Stevens, criticized the SLPP government on several fronts on the eve of the 1962 election. His criticisms centered on SLPP management of the economy, taxation, the size of the government, immunity for MPs, introduction of trial by judge alone, and the rights of accused persons in native courts in the Provinces. Stevens stated, "It seems to me therefore that if for no other reason that of financial mismanagement alone, the SLPP has failed in its duty to the people and to the country."[82] The APC election manifesto promised better management of the country's economy with fiscal discipline; expansion of scholarships to the underprivileged and recruitment of qualified teachers from overseas; reduction in school fees; building more hospitals and health centers; giving maximum assistance to mission schools; production of more rice for local consumption; and respect for traditional laws and customs on the condition that they be balanced with human rights. Moreover, the APC platform opposed the "open-door policy" of the Margai administration because it displaced Sierra Leoneans in the national economy. Instead, it favored promotion of small-scale industries to be run by native-born citizens and revision of diamond-mining laws to better serve indigenous residents in diamond-mining areas. Like the SLPP manifesto, that of the APC advocated the strengthening of ties with neighboring countries such as Guinea.[83]

Fula business elites participated in the 1962 election as political candidates, voters, and private donors to political campaigns. Their political agenda was shaped largely by immigration and business interests. For the majority Fula business leaders, political priorities for the 1962 election focused on having Fula politicians like Alhaji Amadu Wurie, Hon. Jah, and Alhaji Tejan-Jalloh reelected to Parliament, as well as ensuring that the SLPP was returned to power. The election brought Sir Milton and the SLPP much closer politically to the Fula community. The primary reasons for Fula support of Prime Minister Margai and his SLPP government centered on their political record on Fula immigration, ethnic relations involving tolerance of the Fula as a minority Muslim group, recognition of Fula traditional culture, and an open business environment that gave Fula an opportunity to rise above their humble circumstances. Dr. Margai worked closely with both Sierra Leonean–born and foreign-born Fula political, business, and traditional elites. They included Alhaji Amadu Wurie, Alhaji Kaikai, Hon. Jah, Almamy Agibu Jalloh, Alhaji A. D. Wurie, Alhaji Bah, Alhaji Abdul

Jalloh, and Alhaji Wuroh Timbo. These elite Fula played an important role in mobilizing the Fula business community to provide cash and in-kind donations of livestock and rice for the 1962 election.[84]

In Sir Milton's quest for national unity and to win crucial Muslim support in the 1962 election, although a Christian, he cultivated a good relationship with the multi-ethnic Muslim community, which reflected his trademark political tolerance. As a matter of fact, many of his ministers and close personal friends were Muslims, including Alhaji Amadu Wurie, Sir Banja Tejan-Sie, Alhaji Mustapha, and Kandeh Bureh. In 1961 Dr. Margai attended a Muslim event at the Mandingo mosque, close to the Fula mosque, on Magazine Cut in the east end of Freetown that was attended by prominent Muslim politicians, including Alhaji Mustapha, deputy prime minister and minister of finance; Alhaji Tejan-Jalloh; and the mayor of Freetown, Alderman A. F. Rahman.[85]

Prior to the 1962 election, Sierra Leoneans participated in wide-ranging public political debates about the election and the future of the country. One group advocated continuity with the SLPP under Prime Minister Margai. Yet another wanted change under the APC or UPP. Writing in a local newspaper, one prominent Sierra Leonean encouraged the electorate to vote for the SLPP under Dr. Margai because of its positive political record.[86] Another citizen cautioned the public not to view the different political parties as enemies but as opponents, and to refrain from destructive politics.[87] Political relations between the SLPP and APC had gradually improved since the violence by some APC members after the birth of their party in 1960. However, deep distrust remained between the two leading parties on the eve of the country's first general election.

In a nationwide broadcast marking the first independence anniversary of Sierra Leone, Prime Minister Margai, commenting on the forthcoming 1962 election, told his fellow citizens that they should "vote for the men you honestly believe are best fitted to lead our country further along the right road. In doing so you must look for honesty and sincerity of purpose. The future of our country is in your hands. Do not forget that you must look for men of truth and stability."[88] Earlier in 1961 Sir Milton, during a visit to Koinadugu, advised women not to be frightened when approached to be registered for the election. He was explaining to the women the franchise, which had now been extended to them. A Fula female SLPP supporter, Fatmata Jalloh, who spoke on behalf of the women in Koinadugu, thanked Dr. Margai and his government for extending the franchise to women and expressed the confidence of the women in the SLPP government. Other speakers included the ministerial secretary to the Ministry of Internal Affairs and Defense, A. H. Kande, as well as S. B. Mara and PC Balansama Mara II of Kabala. In addition, Dr. Margai visited many areas in the Southern Province to solicit support from traditional rulers and the grassroots for SLPP candidates.[89]

The political base of the opposition parties like the APC was not as broad and diverse as that of the ruling SLPP. The APC's leaders advertised it as a mass party and that it was opposed to the hegemony of chiefs. This was especially expressed against the backdrop of strong complaints of abuse and exploitation against traditional rulers by northerners, who formed the majority of APC members. While the SLPP candidates came mainly from elite backgrounds revolving around Western education and chieftaincy, the bulk of the APC contestants did not. Instead, they had humble beginnings and modest occupations such as petty trading. Their political supporters largely had such a profile as well. And it was a recurring source of criticism by SLPP leaders and their followers against the APC that the latter's candidates were not sufficiently qualified to govern Sierra Leone.[90]

For the UPP, the 1962 election platform of the "Krio Party"—whose membership included the Fula politician D. M. Jalloh, Barthes-Wilson, J. Hadson Taylor, and C. V. Buxton Thomas—prioritized unity as "the golden key to the ultimate peace and prosperity of Sierra Leone." The party viewed both tribalism and sectionalism as enemies to the realization of Sierra Leonean unity. Its manifesto also advocated decentralization of political authority that would strengthen all local government institutions; modifications to the institution of chieftaincy which would provide that paramount chiefs were elected by their peers through a college of chiefs; and better management of the economy, especially foreign loans. Additionally, the agenda recommended expansion of education throughout the country, full support for higher education at FBC, and acceleration of a broader teacher training program. It also called for the promotion of sports, support for mining activities but with emphasis on seeking the most benefits for the general population, improvement of the railway system, support for Africanization, and full employment for Sierra Leoneans. And the program further supported a rapid transition to a republican form of government. Before the 1962 election, some of the key figures of the UPP, including its leader, C. B. Rogers-Wright, S. H. Robbin-Coker, and Mahmoud Ahmed had joined the SLPP, while others like Alhaji Mucktarru Kallay became members of the APC.[91]

The bulk of the leadership of the PNP and Mende members were absorbed by the SLPP in the preelection period. However, many of the northern backers of the PNP left to join Stevens in the APC. In April 1961, the PNP agreed at its national convention to merge with the SLPP, which announced the dissolution of the PNP at its convention in January 1962. As leader of the PNP, Albert Margai was prevailed upon by several groups to join the SLPP. These included the Mende community and its former tribal headman in Freetown, A. B. Paila. A section of the UPP, including Cyril Rogers-Wright, also joined the SLPP. The SLPP-UPP alliance, which was endorsed at the SLPP convention, was opposed by some supporters of the UPP, leading to the explusion of Rogers-Wright and his followers and the election of a new executive with Neale Caulker as leader and Barthes-Wilson as deputy leader.[92]

Political Fundraising

Political fundraising was an important aspect of the political culture prior to the 1962 election. Since the government did not provide funding for political campaigns and national party conventions, political campaigns were financed primarily by party, private, and business contributions. Nevertheless, in the world of Sierra Leone politics there was no clear boundary between private money and government funds in the financing of political campaigns. The Fula were among the interest groups that provided monetary and in-kind donations to the SLPP and individual candidates for the 1962 election. Fula business elites were essential to Fula political campaign financing, which was organized at the level of chieftaincy, individual businesses, constituency, and kinship. To take but a few examples, the Freetown-based Fula chief Alhaji Bah used his elite position to mobilize the Fula community, especially in Freetown, to contribute cash and in-kind gifts to the election campaign. For Alhaji Tejan-Jalloh, besides self-financing his campaign, he also donated to the SLPP and other candidates such as Alhaji Mustapha. As for Alhaji Amadu Wurie and his brother Alhaji A. D. Wurie, they also gave to the SLPP election fund. Moreover, Alhaji Bah, Almamy Agibu Jalloh, Alhaji Wuroh Timbo, and Alhaji Tejan-Jalloh also organized themselves in certain constituencies such as in Freetown and Bombali to support individual candidates. Kinship was also a basis of Fula organization to raise cash and in-kind support such as livestock and rice for SLPP Fula candidates in the election.[93]

In addition to Fula business elites, the SLPP government exploited its incumbency to obtain financial support from various businesses such as the Diamond Corporation of West Africa (DICORWAF) and the SLST, which gave £25,000 and £20,000 respectively to the party. But it was questionable whether the SLPP secretariat used the financial contributions to support the official SLPP candidates in the election. In fact, some candidates even had to pay their own election deposits and all their out-of-pocket costs, which were a heavy financial burden.[94] Foreign businesses such as Paterson Zochonis (PZ), Kingsway Stores, T. Choitram and Sons, and Freetown Cold Storage Company also provided credit in the form of goods to the SLPP for the election. European banks such as Barclays Bank and Bank of West Africa gave loans with favorable terms to the SLPP for the election. To take but one example, the party received a loan of £12,000. Lebanese merchants such as J. Milhem and Sons, Assad Yazbeck, and E. A. Bamin and Sons also contributed cash and in-kind gifts to both individual SLPP candidates and the party as whole. One writer argues that the SLPP did not expend public funds explicitly for party purposes, in contrast to African political parties like the Convention People's Party in Ghana as well as the Action Group and National Convention of Nigerian Citizens in Nigeria.[95]

Like most political parties in Africa, the SLPP did not have a well-developed fundraising program to fully support its work. The party required a small membership fee and monthly subscription, but these were largely inadequate. Instead, the SLPP relied mainly on its leaders such as Sir Milton and Alhaji Mustapha as financial contributors to its activities, including the election campaigns of the 1962 election. In fact, it was Dr. Margai who financed the SLPP's first newspaper, the *Sierra Leone Observer,* which he founded in Bo District in 1950. The leaders of some of the other main political parties also funded their parties's newspapers. For example, Dr. H. C. Bankole-Bright was founder and owner of the National Congress of Sierra Leone's *Evening Dispatch;* Cyril Rogers-Wright financed UPP's newspaper, *Shekpendeh;* and Albert Margai was a major financial contributor to the PNP's newspaper, *Liberty.* To raise funds, the SLPP also required each of its MPs to contribute to the party's fund through a deduction of an agreed amount from their monthly salaries by the auditor-general. Ministers, deputy ministers, the deputy speaker, and the chief whip made larger financial contributions to the campaign fund.[96]

Election

The 1962 election brought into the open the political infighting inside the SLPP. As a result, SLPP incumbents were challenged by fellow members who were denied the party symbol and chose to run as independents rather than support the party's candidates. According to one Freetown newspaper, many political observers were convinced that the SLPP would not win a single seat in Freetown during the election unless strong party discipline was enforced, which was lacking. This viewpoint was also shared by many SLPP members throughout the country, as well as opposition parties, particularly the APC under the leadership of Stevens.[97]

A well-publicized political contest that showed both the inability of the SLPP central executive to control local party groups and also the extent of intra-party competition took place in Freetown East I constituency, where the FCC councilor Alhaji Tejan-Jalloh, as an independent candidate, challenged the incumbent Temne minister of communications, Kandeh Bureh. He was born as Saidu Bai Kamara at Mange Bure in Port Loko, where he received his primary education at the African Methodist Episcopal (AME) school. He combined Western schooling with Islamic education, learning Arabic under the Islamic scholar Santigie Rembu. In the 1920s, Kandeh Bureh migrated to Freetown, where he attended the Methodist Boys' High School and later worked as a school teacher in the capital city. He helped to found several ethnic-based organizations such as the Temne Progressive Union, the Murkaramin, and the Ambas Geda, which he used to help launch his political career. Furthermore, he contributed to the spread of Islam by supporting the building of mosques across the country, and specifically assisting the Ahmadiyya Muslims to secure lands in several areas of the Provinces, including Rokupr, Boajibu, and Bo. Collectively, these activities were major reasons for his election as Temne tribal headman in Freetown in 1944. As Temne community leader, Kandeh Bureh initiated many social and economic programs. In an effort to promote education among the Temne and work with cross-ethnic Protectorate leaders such as Sir Milton, Dr. Karefa-Smart, and Albert Margai, Kandeh Bureh joined the SOS. When the SOS was dissolved and the SLPP was established in 1951, he became a founding member of the party and contributed greatly to its electoral success from his powerful political base in Freetown as Temne chief. In 1957 Kande Bureh was appointed minister of works and housing. Like Dr. Margai, he was a firm believer in national unity in spite of the ethnic diversity of the country.[98]

Before the 1962 election, Alhaji Tejan-Jalloh had established a strong political record in the nation. His political career was greatly helped by his wife, Haja[99] Isatu Tejan-Jalloh, who was president of the Fula Women's Association (FWA).[100] Haja Tejan-Jalloh was not only able to mobilize Fula women, but also cross-ethnic women, particularly Temne with whom she shared kinship ties. Alhaji Tejan-Jalloh was a high-profile leader involved in bridge building between the SLPP and the Fula community. Further evidence of this can be seen in his collaborative work with Sir Milton and the SLPP government during the state visit of President Touré to Sierra Leone in 1960. Moreover, he played a key role in mobilizing the Fula community to provide a peaceful and orderly welcome, as well as in providing entertainers for President Touré.[101] Alhaji Tejan-Jalloh also supported Fula candidates in both local and national elections. For example, he was a leading campaigner for his fellow Fula politician, Alhaji A. D. Wurie, in the FCC election for the East Ward in 1962. Both Fula and Muslim support was crucial to Alhaji Wurie's electoral success, which resulted in his transition from a councilor to an elected alderman later, in 1964.[102]

As councilor, Alhaji Tejan-Jalloh was one of the few members of the Fula business elite to promote Western education among the Fula and Muslims, especially the education of Muslim girls at a time when the education of girls was not a priority to many Sierra Leoneans. To take but two examples: in 1963 one of Alhaji Tejan-Jalloh's daughters, Khadija, was among three native-born citizens who received scholarships from the UAR government to pursue further studies in Cairo, Egypt. Another daughter, Umu Hawa, attended St. Edward's Secondary School, pursued undergraduate studies at Columbia University in the United States, and would become the first female chief justice in Sierra Leone.[103] A third daughter, Umu Kultumie, earned an undergraduate degree in America as well at Howard University and had a long career in both the public service and private sector of the country.[104] Since 1960 the FCC was responsible for primary education in the city. Previously, the FC had four municipal schools under its management. At the beginning of the 1963 school year in September, this number had reached twenty-one. In the same year, Prime Minister Margai opened the Fatta Rahman Municipal School at Fergusson Street. In his opening remarks, Sir Milton underscored the FCC's challenge of providing primary school education in Freetown. The school was a public-private partnership among the European companies of Elder Dempster Agencies and the British Petroleum Company, as well as the Ministry of Education and the FCC.[105]

The political rivalry between Alhaji Tejan-Jalloh and Kandeh Bureh was also mirrored in Freetown East II, where the independent, Alhaji Sheikh Gibril Sesay, contested the seat held by the minister of finance and deputy prime minister, Alhaji Mustapha, who was a businessman-politician. Alhaji Mustapha held several key cabinet positions during the Margai administration. In 1953 Sir Milton appointed him minister of works; in 1957, he was made minister of natural resources; in 1958 he became the first Sierra Leonean minister of finance; in 1960 he was appointed deputy prime minister; in 1962 he assumed the duties of minister of trade and industry; and between 1963 and 1964, he served as minister of social welfare. Moreover, Alhaji Mustapha, together with Dr. Easmon, organized the Save FBC Committee in the face of British colonial administration's efforts to downgrade the status of FBC to that of a technical college. Alhaji Mustapha, who served as joint secretary, toured many areas of the Protectorate to raise funds and lobby for support of FBC. His commitment to education was also demonstrated by his service on the board of his high school alma mater, the Prince of Wales at Kingtom in Freetown.[106]

The opponent, Alhaji Sesay, was a prominent Temne Muslim leader and a longtime member of the SLPP. In the 1920s Alhaji Sesay studied the Qur'an at Madrasa Islamia and with notable Islamic scholars in Freetown before departing for Barthurst (Banjul) and Dakar, where he studied for sevral years and became a member of the *tijaniyya* (a religious brotherhood founded by Ahmad al-Tijani). During the 1940s Alhaji Sesay studied Islamic law and theology as well as Arabic at al-Azhar University in Cairo on a scholarship from the SLMC. Upon his return to Freetown in the 1950s, he was appointed to the position of deputy and chief imam of the temne central mosque, Jamil ul-Jalil, on Olfield Street in Freetown.[107] He held several positions, including president of the Sierra Leone Muslim Reformation Society (SLMRS)[108] and secretary of the SLMC, which was founded in 1932.[109] In 1961 Alhaji Sesay headed the first group of Sierra Leonean Muslim pilgrims to perform the *hajj*, one of the five pillars of Islam. It was through his efforts that the country's pilgrims were recognized as a national group in 1957. Prior to this time, they had to join either the Nigerian or Senegalese Muslim groups to perform the hajj. Besides working with the broad Muslim community,[110] Alhaji Sesay had a long history of working with Muslim Fula in the Provinces, including his home town, Port Loko, and Freetown. His Fula political and religious colleagues included Alhaji Amadu Wurie and Alhaji A. D. Wurie, who were also from Port Loko, as well as the Senegalese-born chief imam of the Fula mosque in Freetown, Alhaji Ahmadu Sie.[111]

On the eve of the 1962 election, both Kandeh Bureh, a Temne, and Alhaji Mustapha, an Aku, were presented by the SLPP as the official candidates to the electorates in the East I and East II constituencies.

In a meeting of the Temne that was held in East I, a local newspaper alleged that Kandeh Bureh, one of the speakers, said that the Temne should vote solidly for the Temne, including himself, who would be contesting the 1962 election. Kandeh Bureh appealed to the Temne who were APC members to join forces with him. He also urged those in East II to vote for Alhaji Sesay, who also addressed the Temne meeting.[112] Kandeh Bureh later contested the newspaper account and repeated what he said at the meeting as, "I wish leaders of the various tribes would be vigilant in seeking the interest of their people in the interest of the country."[113]

In a political meeting at Cline Town in East I, Alhaji Tejan-Jalloh told his audience that "we should think in terms of Sierra Leone and not as Creoles, Mendes, Temnes, or Lokos." He was referring to an earlier statement made by Kandeh Bureh urging Temne to vote for Temne candidates only. Although he had kinship ties with the Temne, Alhaji Tejan-Jalloh told his supporters that he would not promote ethnic propaganda. He further said that he would advise the people to vote for the person they were convinced would best serve the country.[114] Alhaji Tejan-Jalloh had applied for the SLPP party symbol to the SLPP executive for East I but was denied the symbol in favor of Kandeh Bureh. It was alleged by supporters of Alhaji Tejan-Jalloh that Kandeh Bureh had handpicked the executive to favor him. Prior to the election, Alhaji Tejan-Jalloh and Alhaji Sesay, who were very close personal friends, had reached an understanding to not only contest the election in East I and East II as SLPP candidates, but if denied the party symbol, would contest as independent candidates and support each other other's candidacy. But the decision by Alhaji Sesay to renege on this mutual agreement by supporting Kandeh Bureh led Alhaji Tejan-Jalloh to switch his support to Alhaji Mustapha, a close personal friend.[115]

The election campaigns were not always peaceful. In one instance, the police urged party supporters and those of individual candidates in Freetown not to engage in any act that would cause a breach of peace when they attended political meetings. The appeal followed incidents in East I where stones were thrown at meetings called by Kandeh Bureh. According to Kandeh Bureh, "as far as the Government is concerned, every candidate is equal. It is for the electorate to decide which of the candidates will be elected. I advocate for a fair and just elections. The interest of the country should be first considered before individual interest. Sir Milton has endeavored to establish a peaceful state. Everyone should cooperate to see this continue."[116]

Muslims and Politics

Alhaji Tejan-Jalloh's political alignment with both Alhaji Mustapha and Alhaji Sesay was part of a political strategy by elite Muslim Fula businesspeople to advance Fula interests by forging partnerships with trans-ethnic Muslim politicians. Fula business leaders like Alhaji Bah, Alhaji Allie, Almamy Agibu Jalloh, Alhaji Tejan-Jalloh, Alhaji A. D. Wurie, Alhaji Abdul Jalloh, Alhaji Wuroh Timbo, and Alhaji Ibrahima Sow were key players in this strategic political alliance with non-Fula Sierra Leonean Muslim politicians. The multi-ethnic Muslim collaboration dates back to the colonial period when Fula political leaders such as the well-known Alhaji Almamy Oumarou Jalloh-Jamboria and the legendary Alhaji Momodu Allie worked with Muslims from diverse ethnic and socioeconomic backgrounds in Freetown and elsewhere in Sierra Leone.[117]

The Fula were a large and significant part of the country's Muslim population, as has been shown in previous scholarship. The main Muslim organizations were the SLMC and the Sierra Leone Muslim Brotherhood (SLMB). In fact, a prominent Fula, Alhaji Ahmad Tejan-Sie, was one of the founders of the SLMC in 1931. Smaller Muslim organizations included the Young Men's Muslim Association (YMMA). The role of the SLMC was to guide the spiritual life of Muslims and to advise the government on all Islamic matters. The SLMC also had a Board of Imams, which decided on such issues as the start of Ramadan, the month-long period of Muslim fasting.[118] Important Muslim Fula clerics included Alhaji Ahmadu Sie, who, as chief imam of the Fula mosque, was also a member of the SLMC Board of Imams. Alhaji Sie migrated to Sierra Leone in the early twentieth century and contributed greatly to the spread of Islam in the country. He was an outstanding Islamic scholar whose teachings went beyond the Fula to other communities, including Muslims at Fourah Bay, Foulah (Fula) Town, and Aberdeen in Freetown. Succeeding Alhaji Sie, who died in 1963, as chief imam was the Guinean-born Alhaji Misbahu Bah, who was also a member of the SLMC Board of Imams. Also prominent in the Muslim community was Alhaji Tejan-Jalloh, who besides being a businessman-politician, was treasurer of the SLMB and a member of the SLMRS.[119] Moreover, there was the elite Fula Alhaji Sulaiman Jalloh-Jamboria (son of Almamy Jamboria). He founded the first Fula school that combined Western and Islamic education at his residence on Jenkins Street—where the author was raised—in the east end of Freetown.

The personal friendship between Alhaji Tejan-Jalloh and Alhaji Mustapha that translated into strong political support for each other reflected the close relationship between the Muslim Fula and Muslim Aku communities in Freetown. Alhaji Mustapha was born to an Aku family at Foulah Town in 1903. The Aku were Muslim Krio of mostly Yoruba ancestry who had lived in Freetown since the early nineteenth century as "recaptives," or "liberated Africans," following the British abolition of the slave trade in 1807. Some of the recaptives came from various ethnic groups in the interior of Sierra Leone.[120] From its founding, the Aku community at Foulah Town and Fourah Bay, both in the east end of Freetown, welcomed the Fula, who were primarily responsible for the spread of Islam in Sierra Leone as Islamic educators and imams.[121] As noted above, Imam Alhaji Sie worked with both the Fourah Bay and Foulah Town Muslim communities. He conducted the ordination ceremony of Alhaji Sheikh Sheku Othman, imam of Foulah Town mosque, and that of alfa (Muslim scholar) A. W. Alharazim of Fourah Bay.[122] One prominent Fula merchant-cleric in the Aku community was Chernor (male Muslim cleric) Mohamed Jalloh (Chernor Mamadu Madina), a karamoko (Muslim teacher) on Foulah Street and at the madrasa (Islamic school) in Foulah Town. His karandas (pupils) included Haja Umu Dahniya, daughter of the well-known Fula, Chernor Seray-Wurie of Foulah Town. Chernor Mamadu Madina was also a contemporary of prominent Foulah Town residents such as Alhaji Mustapha. Faced with the prejudice of the British colonial administration and Christian missionaries because of their Islamic faith, the Aku turned to the Fula for support.[123]

Besides helping the Aku build mosques and establish Quranic schools, the Fula traveled with many Aku for advanced studies at Fula Islamic centers like Timbo, where they specialized in Islamic law, theology, and literature. One such Aku was Alfa Muhammad Yadalieu Savage, who left for Futa Jallon in the late 1830s to study Islamic theology, law, and the sciences for several years. At the completion of his studies, Yadalieu was given the title of mugaddam (superior) of the Tijaniyya brotherhood, which gave him the authority to initiate others into the brotherhood. Upon his arrival in Freetown, Alfa Yadalieu embarked on the dissemination of Tijaniyya doctrines in the Aku community. Another noted Aku Tijani was Levally Savage, who studied under Fula Tijani scholars at Dinguiraye for over twenty years before returning to Freetown in the mid-1870s and was appointed as assistant imam of Fourah Bay mosque. By the late nineteenth century, the Aku Muslim community was able to produce its own karamokos, alfas, and imams. One of the outstanding Aku alfas of this period was Mohammad Sanusi of Foulah Town. He received his advanced Islamic education at Timbo and subsequently pursued a career as an Arabic teacher at Fourah Bay and translator of Dr. Edward W. Blyden between 1872 and 1873. He was the chief Arabic translator for the colonial administration from 1873 to 1901 and manager of the Foulah Town madrasa from 1901 to 1907.[124]

For Alhaji Mustapha, his first formal Western education took place at one of the madrasas at Foulah Town, followed by to his secondary school education at the Prince of Wales School, where he was the first senior prefect. The government-owned school was formally opened by the Prince of Wales during a visit to Sierra Leone in 1925. Besides providing cheaper education with a strong emphasis on the sciences, the school represented a departure from the Christian denominational schools in the country. In 1926 Alhaji Mustapha joined the civil service, but after a brief tenure he left for Britain to study law and enrolled at Lincoln's Inn. In the 1930s, Alhaji Mustapha returned to Freetown, and in 1946 he founded Mustapha Brothers and Company, which specialized in the import and export trade. He next entered national politics and became a member of the SLPP. In 1951 Alhaji Mustapha was elected SLPP member of the Legislative Council for Freetown East Electoral District, where he also had his home. Many of the voters were his fellow Aku. Alhaji Mustapha served this constituency until 1969, when he was elected SLPP member to represent Bo North constituency in Parliament; Bo was the most important provincial city. Unlike his Freetown constituents, the vast majority of the voters in the Bo constituency were Mende, the largest ethnic group in the nation. Moreover, Alhaji Mustapha joined with Ahaji Tejan-Jalloh and the Fula community in the spread of Islam. In Foulah Town, Alhaji Mustapha's Fula partners included Alhaji Abdulai Jalloh, who migrated to Foulah Town from Labé in Guinea about 1923. He was popularly known as Modi (a title of respect in Pulaar) Abdulai Foulah Town and was also a successful trader and butcher. And Chernor Mamadu Madina who, as noted earlier, was a famous Koranic teacher at Foulah Street and subsequently at the Amaria School. Meanwhile, in 1958 Alhaji Mustapha was instrumental in launching the SLMC Secondary School in Freetown.[125]

But more than that, Alhaji Mustapha had a good relationship with not only the Muslim Fula in Sierra Leone, but also Muslim Fula politicians in other West African countries such as Senegal. In April 1964, Alhaji Ousmane Sow, a prominent Fula politician in Senegal and a close advisor of President Leopold Sengor, visited Sierra Leone on his way to the hajj. He visited Alhaji Mustapha, who was then minister of social welfare and acting minister of communications, as well as the Fula Speaker of Parliament, Sir Banja Tejan-Sie. In these meetings, Alhaji Sow stated his desire for more understanding and cooperation between Senegal and Sierra Leone. Additionally, he expressed appreciation for the Margai administration's work in the areas of education and industrialization. Alhaji Sow also reiterated Senegal's commitment, like Sierra Leone's, to the promotion of African unity.[126]

Election Results

The 1962 election results for Freetown East I and East II constituencies showed that both independent candidates, Alhaji Tejan-Jalloh and Alhaji Sesay, lost to the incumbent SLPP ministers, Kandeh Bureh and Alhaji Mustapha. In East I, Kandeh Bureh was reelected with 2,667 votes to Alhaji Tejan-Jalloh's 1,255 votes. The APC candidate, Alhaji Abdul Wahid, a Muslim Aku from Fourah Bay, received 1,582 votes. He was a former SLPP member who later joined the UPP before contesting as the APC candidate in the 1962 election.[127] In the wake of his electoral defeat, Alhaji Wahid resigned from the APC because of the "inability of the APC to bring about the kind of progress which the country desires."[128] A second independent candidate, Alimamy B. Sillah, received 803 votes. In East II, Alhaji Mustapha was reelected with 2,781 votes while Alhaji Sesay received 2,543 votes. The APC candidate Alhaji Mucktarru Kallay—a founding member of the APC—received 1,417 votes.[129] According to an influential Sierra Leonean newspaper columnist, Clarence Labor, Sierra Leoneans voted mainly on personality rather than policies.[130]

For Fula candidates elsewhere in the country, the election results showed that in Port Loko North, Alhaji Amadu Wurie (SLPP) was elected with 7,211 votes while S. M. Kabba (APC) received 5,527 votes. In Pujehun West, Hon. Jah (SLPP) was reelected with 5,434 votes; F. S. Anthony (independent) received 5,008 votes; and D. M. Swaray (independent) received 1,672 votes. In Bombali North, Alpha Mohamed Jalloh (SLPP) received 1,779 votes, losing to Edward John Kargbo (APC), who was elected with 4,063 votes; Ibrahim B. Dumbuya (independent) received 1,584 votes; Alpha U. Barrie (independent) received 1,177 votes; and Joseph M. S. Conteh (independent) received 749 votes. In Bombali West, Ibrahim S. Khan (independent) received 3,622 votes but lost to Yankay D. Sesay (SLPP), who was reelected with 5,762 votes; Andrew A. B. Fofana (APC) received 5,488 votes; Usman Sesay (independent) received 1,386 votes; and Kulifa B. Mara (independent) received 580 votes. In Kenema Town, A. G. Umu-Wurie (independent) received 258 votes while B. S. Massaquoi (SLPP) received 3,593 votes; Lansana Turay (APC) received 610 votes; J. B. Francis (independent) received 546 votes; and M. M. Kallon (independent) received 279 votes.

In all, out of the sixty-two election results declared, the SLPP under the leadership of Prime Minister Margai won the plurality of seats in Parliament with twenty-eight. The APC-SLPIM Alliance won twenty seats, independents had fourteen seats, and the UPP won none. Thirteen members of the previous Parliament lost their seats. Four of them were former ministers: Minister of Trade and Industry Ishmael B. Taylor-Kamara; Minister of Education H. . B. John; Resident Minister, Northern Province, Mahmoud Ahmed; and Resident Minister, Southern Province, Charles F. Massally. Also unseated were the former junior minister, S. T. Navo, and the outgoing deputy speaker of Parliament, Arthur J. Massally, who was also the son-in-law of Alhaji Dr. Amadu Wurie (Massally later became the first individual from the Provinces to be appointed as puisne judge in 1966).[131]

Postelection

In the aftermath of the 1962 election, Alhaji Tejan-Jalloh accepted his electoral loss to Kandeh Bureh without recourse to filing petitions in the courts despite strong evidence of widespread violence and intimidation during the election. Moreover, Alhaji Tejan-Jalloh retired from active politics; nevertheless, he remained steadfast in his support of Prime Minister Margai and the SLPP, not only in his East I constituency, but also across Sierra Leone. In addition, Alhaji Tejan-Jalloh maintained and expanded his collaboration with Fula business, political, traditional, religious, and professional elites in promoting broad and varied Fula interests nationwide.[132]

By contrast, Alhaji Sesay pursued a vigorous petition against his opponent, Alhaji Mustapha, which cited charges of violence, intimidation, and rigging during the election. Despite the heated and divisive political struggle, Prime Minister Margai appointed Alhaji Mustapha as minister of trade and industry. In August 1962, Supreme Court Justice S. B. Jones dismissed the election petition filed by Alhaji Sesay against Alhaji Mustapha. As a result, relations between these two prominent

Muslim politicians deteriorated and contributed to the growing rift between their Temne and Aku political supporters in Freetown.[133]

The postelection SLPP cabinet consisted of twenty ministers, including Sir Milton and the government whip. The Fula politicians in the cabinet included Alhaji Amadu Wurie, who was appointed minister of education, and Hon. Jah, who was made ministerial secretary. The Fula MPs included Sir Banja Tejan-Sie, Alhaji Amadu Wurie, Hon. Jah, and Alhaji Kaikai, who represented Pujehun District Council in the 1962 House of Representatives before it was dissolved, was replaced in the post-1962 Parliament by PC B. V. S. K. Kebbie.[134] Writing in a local newspaper, a prominent opposition politician, I. T. A. Wallace-Johnson criticized Dr. Margai's cabinet as too large for a small country with limited resources and further accused the prime minister of nepotism in his cabinet selections. He stated that the SLPP had a total of twenty-three cabinet members, including the first woman, PC Gulama, whose husband PC Koblo Pathbana was defeated in the 1962 election.[135] In response to Wallace-Johnson's newspaper article, the acting permanent secretary in the Ministry of Information, Thomas Decker, pointed out in the same newspaper that the SLPP cabinet consisted of twenty ministers, including Prime Minister Margai and the Government Whip, and not twenty-three, as Wallace-Johnson had stated in his article.[136]

After the 1962 election, the APC and UPP merged under the APC banner. In July 1962, both opposition leaders, Stevens of the APC and Barthes-Wilson of the UPP, issued a joint statement dated July 31, 1962:

> We are of the opinion that this country, like many other countries, now believes in a two-party system, one in power, the other in opposition, one giving way to the other in accordance with the wishes of the people. We also share in that belief, in pursuance of which we have agreed in the interest of the people to effect a union with effect from today between the APC and the UPP both of which parties hold the view that the country needs a two-party system. These two political parties now united would constitutionally continue to fight the people's cause under the APC banner.[137]

Meanwhile, Stevens and APC supporters became increasingly critical of the Fula, especially those Guinean-born. They made repeated allegations that Fula, without distinction between foreign-born and Sierra Leonean–born, were "foreigners" and were registered as voters in previous elections, including the 1962 election. In a veiled threat against the Fula in March 1964, the APC MP Barthes-Wilson warned foreigners to keep off from the country's internal politics or "face deportation when we assume power after the next general election" while addressing an APC meeting at the Queen Elizabeth II Playing Field in Freetown. According to Barthes-Wilson, it was an insult for any foreigner to meddle in the internal affairs of this country. He told the crowd that every foreigner was wholeheartedly welcomed, "but if you want to interfere in our internal matters, we will throw you out of the country." He pointed out that no foreign national should be registered as a voter in the next election. "The fact that a foreigner has stayed in this country for many years is not a guarantee that he should participate in our politics. We in the APC believe in African unity but we will not tolerate any outside interference in our domestic affairs." Other APC speakers at the meeting included Christian Alusine (C. A.) Kamara-Taylor, secretary-general of the APC, and an activist, Borbor Kamara. They both thanked APC followers for their participation during the recent FCC and Kailahun elections. In addition, Kamara-Taylor appealed to them to register for the forthcoming election in 1967.[138]

In spite of the persistent APC political attacks, the vast majority of Fula business leaders maintained their support for Sir Milton and the SLPP. For instance, the Fula chief Alhaji Bah was one of thirteen tribal headmen, chiefs, in the Western Area who passed a vote of confidence for Prime Minister Margai and his cabinet following the 1962 election. The resolution containing the vote of confidence referred to the positive qualities of Dr. Margai and his cabinet ministers. The headmen also pledged unstinted support to the SLPP government. Alhaji Mustapha, minister of finance, was one of the government officials who addressed the group of traditional leaders at the meeting in Gooding Hall in Freetown. When Albert Margai succeeded Sir Milton as head of the SLPP government and party after his death in April 1964, most Fula business elites transferred their political support to him and the SLPP. This is examined in the next chapter.[139]

2

The Administration of Albert M. Margai, 1964–67

Albert Michael Margai, as discussed in the previous chapter, became Sierra Leone's second prime minister following the death of his older brother, Sir Milton, on April 28, 1964. Like his brother, Albert was both the leader of the SLPP and the head of government. He was appointed prime minister on April 29 by the Governor-General Sir Henry J. Light-foot-Boston. Born on October 10, 1910 in Moyamba, he was educated at St. Patrick's School in Bonthe and at St. Edward's Secondary School in Freetown. He first worked as a nurse in the colonial medical department starting in 1931 but resigned in 1944 after becoming a qualified druggist. In 1945 Margai proceeded to Britain to study law at the Inner Temple and was called to the bar in 1949, thus making history as the first lawyer from the Protectorate. In the same year, he returned to Sierra Leone and enrolled as a solicitor and advocate in the Supreme Court, as well as setting up a private law practice.[1]

Albert Margai's political career started in 1949, when he was elected to represent Moyamba in the Protectorate Assembly. In 1951 he became one of the founding members of the SLPP and was elected to the Legislative Council in the country's first general election, which the SLPP won overwhelmingly.[2] Margai played an active role in the debates over the Stevenson Constitution, which for the first time gave the Protectorate an equitable share of representation in the Legislative Council. Also, he was one of the chief spokesmen for Protectorate interests. In 1952 Margai became the first minister of education when he was appointed to the cabinet under the leadership of Sir Milton.[3]

In the 1957 general election, Margai was reelected as an MP representing Moyamba South constituency. Shortly after the election, he challenged Dr. Margai, for the leadership of the SLPP. Although Sir Milton had proven administrative and political skills, the younger members of the SLPP had become impatient with his leadership and looked to Albert as a more dynamic leader. In the leadership election, Albert defeated his brother by one vote. He did, however, step down but refused to serve in a cabinet position under the leadership of Prime Minister Margai. Then, as noted in the previous chapter, Albert—with a number of discontented SLPP members, including Stevens—established a new party, the PNP. According to the PNP leaders, the people were disappointed with the country's progress and with the fact that the SLPP had failed to adopt a nationalist policy. They promised to lead the country to immediate economic independence and political stability. In spite of the dynamism of its leaders, the PNP failed to gain widespread support, particularly in the Protectorate, where people were mainly under the influence of chiefs who were still solidly behind Sir Milton. As the first lawyer from the Protectorate, Albert was highly respected but, unlike Dr. Margai, did not enjoy the support and confidence of all factions of the SLPP.[4]

Despite their political differences, Dr. Margai did appoint Albert as a member of the United Front Coalition that negotiated Sierra Leone's independence from Britain. In 1960 Albert led his PNP into the national front of all parties formed by Milton before independence talks in London. Albert later rejoined the SLPP. In the 1962 general election, which the SLPP won, Albert was reelected as MP for Moyamba South constituency. Prime Minister Margai then appointed him as minister of finance. As finance minister, Albert played a leading role in the establishment of the Bank of Sierra Leone, as well as the introduction of the decimal currency and the "Leone" as the country's new legal tender. Previously, Albert held cabinet positions as minister of agriculture and natural resources before his appointment as prime minister in 1964.[5]

As prime minister, Albert pursued policies similar to those of Sir Milton.[6] However, he dropped from his cabinet some close political allies of Dr. Margai as ministers because they criticized his appointment as prime minister. These included Dr. Karefa-Smart and Alhaji Mustapha. However, he retained the two Fula cabinet members: Alhaji Amadu Wurie as minister of education and Hon. Jah as parliamentary secretary in the Ministry of Trade and Industry.[7] Prime Minister Margai also reduced the number of cabinet positions by merging the ministries of finance and development and by taking over the responsibilities of the ministries of social welfare and health in addition to defense. But Margai's real political challenge was to recapture the enthusiasm of the youths who had seen him as their leader in 1958 when he founded the

PNP, as well as to ensure that ethnic differences did not destroy national unity, for which his brother had fought throughout his political career.[8] In 1965 Prime Minister Margai, like Sir Milton, was knighted by Queen Elizabeth II in recognition of his outstanding services to Sierra Leone, thus receiving the title "Sir."[9]

Immigration

During the prime ministership of Sir Albert, immigration commanded a lot of attention from the SLPP government and divided the citizenry. As a matter of fact, immigration was one of the predominant wedge issues in the country's politics. As the inflow of unauthorized immigrants increased, there grew political pressure to overhaul Sierra Leone's immigration laws. As the national debate over illegal immigration grew more polarized, some Sierra Leoneans pressed for a legislative program that would include a path to citizenship for those who were in the country illegally, while others demanded deportation of illegal immigrants to their homelands. And a section of the population advocated for comprehensive immigration reform legislation that would include non-Africans like the Lebanese. But there was no agreement on solutions to one of the nation's most intractable problems.

As in the course of Sir Milton's rule, the Fula were front and center of the country's political conversations about illegal immigration. Immigration strongly motivated Fula business elites, as well as Fula politicians, professionals, intellectuals, youth activists, and immigration advocates, to participate in national politics. Moreover, it galvanized both the native-born and foreign-born Fula population across the country and energized Fula voters during national elections. While Guinea remained the largest source of illegal and undocumented Fula immigrants, the precise figures for the unauthorized Fula immigrant population during the Margai administration cannot be known.

Like Sir Milton, Prime Minister Margai had a politically tolerant attitude toward foreign-born Fula. Despite the political delicacy of the immigration issue, Margai continued his brother's national immigration policy of ensuring that foreign nationals were properly registered with the government. This was part of the government's efforts to tackle massive immigration challenges, including the influx of illegal immigrants and the crimes committed by them in the country. The prime minister warned foreigners to avoid doing or saying things that would give cause for suspicion of subversive activities. He said that although the SLPP government had been very tolerant toward non–Sierra Leoneans, his government would deport any foreign citizen found guilty of conduct prejudicial to the interest of the state. This reflected the Margai government's tough stance on regulating immigration and a commitment to stop the flow of unauthorized immigrants to Sierra Leone.[10]

Immigration, which was a prickly political subject, was at the core of the national challenge of forging multi-ethnic unity in Sierra Leone. In his first speech to Parliament, Prime Minister Margai promised to uphold the rule of law and the constitution, protect the rights and freedom of individuals, and "above all, may I, Mr. Speaker, take this opportunity to underline again the importance which I attach to maintaining the unity of the peoples of this country and to the achievement of real and true solidarity." He pledged to continue the policies of the previous government, of which he had been a member, into making Sierra Leone a model state in Africa, as envisioned by Dr. Margai.[11] The importance of unifying the country was underscored by PC Gulama, minister without portfolio, who spoke on behalf of the paramount chiefs and women in congratulating Margai on his appointment as prime minister. She said "the new prime minister must try and unite all the different tribes. We know he is a dynamic person and we support him because of that. He must follow the examples of his late brother and other African leaders like Nkrumah of Ghana."[12]

Tribalism, which was linked to immigration, was perhaps the greatest threat to national unity. This was evidenced by political debates and speeches by politicians from diverse ethnic backgrounds. For example, in speeches by the Minister of Works J. Kamanda-Bongay and the minister without portfolio, who was acting minister of information and broadcasting, PC Yumkella II, they appealed to the people of Mambolo and Magbema chiefdoms respectively to promote the love of the country by uniting and ending tribalism for the common good.[13] In addition, the Minister of the Interior Maigore Kallon and PC Gulama also spoke on tribalism during a five-day tour of Bombali.[14] Immigrants not only changed the tribal composition of the country; they also brought about passionate resentment among some local ethnic groups, particularly over illegal immigration and its impact on political voting, jobs, and crime. In particular, the growth of the Fula immigrant population that changed the country's ethnic composition with its political and business implications fueled a large part of the national debate on tribalism. And tribalism would frame Sierra Leone politics for the next several decades.[15]

To regulate immigration, Sir Albert introduced a number of immigration bills. In 1965 the Non-Citizen Registration, Immigration, and Expulsion Act, No. 14, 1965 was passed by Parliament. This law required all noncitizens to register with the Department of Immigration and to renew their registration annually. Under this Act, "every noncitizen belonging to a class of classes prescribed by the prime minister and residing in Sierra Leone shall within three months of the first day of January in each year register and pay such registration fees as shall be prescribed. Any person who fails to comply with this requirement shall be guilty of an offense and shall be liable on conviction to a fine not exceeding twelve months and the court shall recommend that an expulsion order be made against him."[16]

According to the new Act, Nigerians residing in Sierra Leone would now have to register the first day of every year. The only Africans exempted from the provisions of this law were "privileged Africans," which meant "a citizen of any of the countries listed in the Second Schedule or any person, one of whose parents was a citizen of any such country." And the countries listed in the Second Schedule were Guinea, the Gambia, Ghana, Ivory Coast, and Liberia. Until Parliament passed the new Act, Nigerians were treated as "privileged Africans." The privilege was withdrawn, however, because it was not reciprocated in Nigeria.[17] Speaking in Parliament, Prime Minister Margai identified Nigeria as where Sierra Leoneans suffered severe discrimination and stated that those affected had complained bitterly to his government. Furthermore, he said that in 1963 a law was passed by the Nigerian government which adversely affected Sierra Leoneans there in both employment and business undertakings. But he had only come to know about this recently and immediately contacted the Nigerian High Commissioner in Freetown, who later flew to Lagos with the complaint of the government; the effort, however, was fruitless. Speaking on the Act, the opposition leader Stevens expressed regret about the attitude of some neighboring countries towards Sierra Leoneans, particularly Nigeria.[18]

The matter of citizenship, which was related to immigration, was hotly debated in Parliament. In December 1965, A. H. Kandeh, deputy minister in the prime minister's office, stated in Parliament that the SLPP government would grant citizenship to persons of part Sierra Leonean parentage in accordance with the Sierra Leone Nationality and Citizenship Act No. 10 of 1962 when such persons applied in the prescribed manner and were of good behavior. Kandeh, who was replying to a question on behalf of Sir Albert, disclosed that the government had granted citizenship to fourteen persons born of foreign nationals to Sierra Leonean mothers, under sub-section (4) of section 1 of the constitution. S. L. Matturi (MP for Kono West) had asked the prime minister what the government's plans were for granting citizenship to persons born of mixed marriages between Sierra Leoneans and foreign nationals. He also wanted to know whether the government had granted citizenship to any such persons of part Sierra Leonean parentage, and if so how many and under what prevailing ordinances. A. H. Kandeh disclosed that the government had granted citizenship to one person under section 6 of the Sierra Leone Nationality and Citizenship Act of 1962 and to eight under section 3 (1) of that law.[19]

As for the Fula, they were still generally perceived as Guinean-born foreigners by the majority of the Sierra Leonean citizenry. The issue of Guineans, particularly Fula, was politically contentious. In September 1965, Interior Minister Maigore Kallon informed Parliament that Guineans born or resident in Sierra Leone were considered to be aliens if they were not naturalized or registered as citizens of Sierra Leone. He pointed out that they enjoyed no special political privileges. This clarification came in response to a question by the lawmaker Kamara-Taylor, MP for Kambia East and APC secretary-general, who wanted to know from the minister whether Sierra Leoneans who resided and were born in Guinea enjoyed the same political privileges as Guineans who were resident and born in Sierra Leone; for example, could they register as electors and were they eligible to be elected to the central or local governments? Minister Kallon further explained that Sierra Leoneans born and resident in Guinea could not register as electors nor could they be elected to central or local governments in Guinea, but that Sierra Leonean nationals living in some neighboring African countries such as Guinea and Liberia were allowed to enter certain posts in the civil service of those countries.[20]

The Fula were not alone in being perceived as aliens. The Lebanese, too, were in a similar situation; in fact, the Lebanese were legally classified as foreigners. In 1965 Sir Albert told Parliament that children born of Lebanese parents were not Sierra Leoneans. He was replying to a question asked by J. C. Barnett (MP for Kailahun West), who wanted to know whether Lebanese children born in Sierra Leone were Sierra Leoneans or Lebanese, as it was understood that such children were treated as foreigners in Lebanon.[21] Prime Minister Margai also stated, in reply to a question by K. Rashid (MP for Bo Central), that naturalized Lebanese were citizens of Sierra Leone but that children born of Lebanese parents in Sierra Leone were foreigners. Rashid had asked the prime minister what the difference was between naturalized Lebanese and children born of Lebanese parents in Sierra Leone and whether the former enjoyed additional rights and privileges over the latter. Sir Albert made it clear that citizens did indeed enjoy certain privileges over foreigners.[22]

Moreover, in September 1965 Prime Minister Margai stated in Parliament that Lebanese nationals residing in Sierra Leone enjoyed the same privileges and had the same security as other foreigners in the country. He was answering a question put to him by PC Abu Baimba III (MP for Bo District) concerning Lebanese businessmen who had made large-scale investments. The prime minister referred the PC to chapter 16 of the Ten-Year Plan of Economic and Social Development for Sierra Leone for a further clarification of the SLPP government's policy toward foreign investors, including the Lebanese.[23] The Margai administration's position on the Lebanese was challenged by some individuals of mixed Lebanese-Sierra Leonean parentage. One such challenge came from John Akar, an Afro-Lebanese who was secretary to the Hotels and Tourists Board and director of Sierra Leone's National Dance Troupe; Akar resigned from these positions and decided to enter politics even though the constitution regarded him as a foreigner.[24]

Kono

As the national campaign against illegal foreign nationals reignited during Sir Albert's time in office, Kono—the country's diamond mining epicenter—remained front and center of immigration. There was a large immigrant population—many of the immigrants illegal and undocumented—in Kono made up of Fula, Lebanese, and non–Sierra Leonean Africans such as Nigerians, Liberians, and Gambians who had migrated in search of diamond wealth. The diamond industry was dominated by the SLST, but the Fula and many others were also licensed diggers and dealers, as well as illicit miners. The Fula, like the Lebanese, were heavily involved in illicit mining, as were native-born residents. Despite its mineral wealth, which was mostly smuggled out of the District, Kono was faced with infrastructural problems, including inadequate supplies of water and electricity, poor roads, and deforestation. In addition were the related problems of juvenile delinquency and youth unemployment. The bulk of the revenue from diamonds came from the SLST, which paid 60 percent of its profits to the government. However, the government got little revenue, if any, from all alluvial mining. In 1966 non–Sierra Leonean Africans paid Le100 for residential permits while citizens were exempted from such payments.[25]

Speaking at an SLPP rally at the Koidu community center in Kono in December 1964, Prime Minister Margai stated that any foreigners, including Fula, caught smuggling diamonds would now be deported and Sierra Leonean offenders would be banished from the District. Margai was determined to put an end to smuggling and reduce the number of illegal aliens. He said that based on the constitution, his government was committed to protect the life and property of all the nation's residents. He explained the reasons for the Diamond Protection Act, which were chiefly to stop hooliganism in Kono by eradicating the "kaboodo gang," to secure life and property, and to promote Sierra Leonean trade. Sir Albert emphasized that the only aliens who would be allowed to remain in Kono were those who were engaged in profitable business and who were legally in the country. He also warned all foreigners to stop the smuggling of diamonds.[26]

Earlier, in May 1964, J. M. Kamanda (MP for Kenema South) questioned Prime Minister Margai in Parliament as to the total number of non–Sierra Leoneans, including Fula, who were resident in the diamond protection area in Kono. He further enquired how many, if any, were served expulsion notices during the last two months and for what reasons; how many had returned to their former residence within the period; and on what grounds were any eviction notices revoked and on whose recommendation? The prime minister replied that "the particulars of all non–Sierra Leoneans resident in Kono are not readily available. Particulars are available only in respect of those issued with or granted renewal of residential permits in 1964. No expulsion notices were served on anyone, but residential permits of eighty-seven Lebanese and one Briton were revoked in January and March respectively, followed by the issue of exit permits under section 13 (2) of the Diamond Industries Protection rules Cap. 199. The reasons for revoking residential permits were not disclosed as this was a matter within the discretion of the district officer. However, twenty-eight had since returned following successful appeals to the provincial secretary, Eastern Province.[27]

In April 1965, questions were asked in Parliament about the number of prisoners convicted in Kono during the preceding ten months and the cost to the government of maintaining them. In particular M. S. Kanu (MP for Bombali South) asked the minister of social welfare for the total number of prisoners convicted for not possessing residential permits in Kono, with special reference to Sierra Leoneans for the current year and for the total cost incurred by the government. According to the SLPP minister, 767 prisoners, all but 10 of whom were Sierra Leoneans, were convicted and imprisoned for not possessing residential permits in Kono from April 1964 to February 1965.

On the disturbances in Kono, the APC opposition member, Sahr Washington Gandi Capio (MP for Kono North), told Parliament that government troops in Kono were molesting the local people and had arrested more than 650. He alleged that he himself was held at gunpoint and escorted out of his house. Gandi Capio explained that government soldiers came to his village at midnight and held him at gunpoint until they discovered that he was an MP; then they apologized and released him. He stated that this "wicked and outrageous act" in his constituency was meant to reduce the number of registered voters in the area. There were shouts from opposition benches of "shame, shame." A government backbencher Ibrahim Kamanda (MP for Kailahun Central) later challenged Gandi Capio's statements, saying that troops sent to Kono were doing marvelous work in helping to stamp out illicit mining. Minister of the Interior Maigore Kallon further explained that armed troops were stationed at strategic places in Kono to safeguard the security and wealth of the country. He claimed that for many years the gangs of illicit miners in Kono had molested and ravaged the diamond-mining area.[28]

One prominent diamond dealer in Kono was Mohamed W. Jalloh of Koidu, a Fula. In October 1966, the SLPP government deported Jalloh to his homeland in Guinea for suspected illicit diamond and smuggling activities in Kono. He was known to be one of the strongest supporters of the SLPP and had been of great financial assistance to the youth section of the party in Kono. Political considerations aside, and despite his past monetary and in-kind donations to the SLPP and the Margai government, Jalloh was ordered to be deported. Sir Albert dismissed several appeals, including petitions by Jalloh himself, members of the Fula business community—including the Fula chief Alhaji Momodu Alpha Bah—and political friends of Jalloh in the SLPP. The SLPP youths in Kono registered their strong displeasure over Jalloh's deportation. According to one newspaper commentator on the Jalloh deportation case, as far as the present SLPP government under the leadership of Prime Minister Margai was concerned, politics must give way to the national interest.[29]

As further evidence of the Margai administration's tough immigration enforcement policy, in October 1966, 113 persons, many of whom were Fula, were arrested in Koidu on various charges including illicit

in the chapter that follows—to appease his political mentor, Touré. In his fourth monthly press conference, Prime Minister Margai reiterated his government's policy of noninterference in the internal affairs of member states of the OAU, including Guinea.[46]

Following Prime Minister Margai's announcement of a coup against his government in February 1967, President Touré, in a statement broadcast over Radio Guinea, announced that Guinean troops would be stationed in strategic positions along the Guinea–Sierra Leone border based on an agreement for mutual help to end internal subversion aimed at overthrowing either of their governments.[47] The Guinean leader made it clear that his country would help preserve the peace and welfare of Sierra Leone if it were threatened by chaos and disorder.[48] The opposition APC was opposed to Guinea's intervention in Sierra Leone's internal affairs, stating that it "constitutes a grave threat to the liberties of our people and an unparalleled affront to our sovereignty. We consider President Touré's action a naked act of aggression and a flagrant violation of the OAU Charter which specifically prohibits the interference of one state in the internal and domestic affairs of another."[49]

On the question of immigration, Prime Minister Margai and President Touré worked collaboratively to regulate the unlawful flow of Guinean immigrants into Sierra Leone through legislation and better use of law enforcement resources. Many of the illegal Guineans were young Fula immigrants, but the size of the nation's overall illegal Guinean population cannot be precisely known. Determined to show a commitment to stopping the flow of illegal immigration from Guinea, both Margai and Touré deployed police and army manpower at critical areas along the Sierra Leone–Guinea border. Both leaders also supported the criminalization of immigration: that is, making unlawful residence in Sierra Leone a crime subject to arrest and deportation. Under the Margai administration, arrests of unauthorized Fula immigrants increased with tougher law enforcement, and deportations steadily climbed. Getting tougher on Sierra Leone–Guinea border security was one of the few issues on which both the SLPP and the opposition APC agreed in the nations's highly polarized politics. The political cooperation between Sierra Leonean and Guinean authorities on Fula immigration predated independence in both countries, extending back to the colonial era when British and French administrations controlled both territories.[50]

Although opposed to illegal immigration, President Touré was in favor of legal cross-border movement between Guinea and Sierra

Leone. In June 1966, as head of the Guinean delegation at the Guinea-Sierra Leone Relations Commission meeting in Conakry, President Touré announced Guinea's intention to start almost immediately a bus service between Conakry and Freetown. This would facilitate the movement of people and goods between the two countries. Fula legal migrants to Sierra Leone would now have a more convenient and safer route to reach the capital city in search of jobs, business opportunities, and cheap housing. The Fula had a long history of migration and settlement in Freetown, where they were concentrated in various sectors such as livestock, merchandise trade, transportation, and domestic service; they also played a key role in the spread of Islam in the mainly Westernized and Christianized city.[51]

From a business perspective, Prime Minister Margai and President Touré cooperated to expand economic ties between their two countries, thus promoting cross-border trade. At the top of the leaders' political agenda was the issue of smuggling between the two countries that affected key economic sectors such as livestock, diamonds, merchandise, and transport. Guinea was the single largest source of livestock imported into Sierra Leone, and the Fula dominated the multi-ethnic livestock business in both countries. Central to the cross-border business success of the Fula were kinship networks that facilitated both supply and marketing of livestock. Besides livestock, Fula cross-border trade included merchandise such as provisions, textiles, and produce. The motor transport business in which the Fula operated as drivers and owners of commercial vehicles was another important aspect of cross-border Fula business. To be sure, Fula commercial organization and kinship networks that transcended the Sierra Leone–Guinea border contributed greatly to their overall business success in Sierra Leone.[52]

To promote cross-border trade and economic cooperation, Prime Minister Margai collaborated with President Touré, as well as with President Tubman of Liberia and President Félix Houphouët-Boigny of Côte d'Ivoire, to set up a free trade zone among their propinquitous countries.[53] In his opening address on the free trade area in August 1964 in Monrovia, President Tubman stated, "We also propose to seek solutions to problems affecting growth and expansion of trade, commerce, industry and other business in our respective countries in their relation to each other."[54] Prime Minister Margai, in his speech at this initial meeting, referred to Sierra Leone's draft convention, which he said was submitted two days before the start of the conference. He said he had come to Monrovia strongly determined to take concrete steps to bring an economic regional grouping into being. He explained that economic harmonization or integration was their ultimate aim. But this could not be achieved by simple resolution. He stated that its achievement "requires a great deal of study, of different matters and problems. In this study we need to exercise a lot of patience. It is therefore my government's view that in order to ensure success in the long run, permanent machinery should be set up which will undertake this task and which will make specific recommendations from time to time for consideration and adoption of our respective governments."[55]

The Monrovia conference, according to the communiqué signed by the heads of the participating states of Sierra Leone, Guinea, Liberia, and Côte d'Ivoire, resolved to facilitate in the near future the establishment of a multilateral system of regional economic cooperation with a view to encouraging harmonious development of their respective states in every field and removing trade barriers between them. They decided primarily to study the feasibility of establishing a free trade area open to other African states. To this end, they set up a ministerial working commission to convene in Monrovia in December 1964 and agreed that its recommendations would be submitted before January 31, 1965, for the consideration of the four governments with a view to their adoption at the next meeting of heads of state and government to take place in Liberia that April.[56]

In May 1965, a follow-up meeting of representatives of the four countries was held in Freetown. About fifty delegates, including those from Sierra Leone, took part in the conference. Guinea's ten-man delegation included the director of industrial coordination in the Ministry of Economic Development.[57] The conference considered the harmonizing of economic policies as well as the trade and tourist policies of the four countries. Earlier, in February 1965, a meeting in Liberia of the ministerial commission of the proposed organization agreed to set up an interim body charged with making basic studies essential to its establishment of a permament Organization for West African Cooperation. The talks in Freetown covered the possible choice of the organization's first secretary-general and the location of its headquarters.[58] Agreement was reached by the four neighboring countries to form the interim Organization for West African Economic Cooperation, with Donald George, a Sierra Leonean, as its unanimously elected administrative secretary.[59]

Speaking at the opening session of the Sierra Leone–Guinea Relations Ministerial Commission meeting in Freetown in July 1965, Prime Minister Margai stated that the bonds of friendship between Sierra Leone and Guinea had improved, but that for both countries to realize their hopes, "our policies must be harmonized. This is true in the realms of politics as it is in the arena of economics. We have a heavy agenda, but I am confident that with the understanding which has always existed between our two countries, the task will be light. The whole world is watching to see whether we shall bring to practical realization the several agreements signed in October 1964. The agreements have brought us closer together and we are determined to succeed at all costs." Sir Albert emphasized that Sierra Leone and Guinea must continue to provide a shining example of comradeship and fraternity to the rest of Africa and asserted his confidence "that the results we achieved in this commission will go a great way in strengthening African unity."[60]

As a result of the Sierra Leone–Guinea meeting, both governments agreed to expand their economic and commercial relations in accordance with the Trade and Payments Agreements and other accords signed between them in October 1964. Both states were convinced of the necessity of collaboration in order to improve their commercial relations. According to the treaties and agreements, Sierra Leone would export to Guinea large quantities of textiles, fruits, foodstuffs, and building materials, including cement. In return, Guinea would export to Sierra Leone large quantities of cattle and other livestock, as well as palm kernels, fruit juices, beniseed, Guinea corn, unshelled groundnuts, maize, and pigeon peas. Building materials and cement exported from Sierra Leone would be duty free in Guinea and products originating from Guinea to Sierra Leone would be exempt from duties. French would be a compulsory language in all secondary and technical schools in Sierra Leone, and English would be a compulsory language in all secondary and technical schools in Guinea. Scholarships would be awarded to Sierra Leoneans in polytechnic institutes and health schools in Guinea for training as engineers, midwives, and state-registered nurses. Sierra Leone would also award three scholarships to Guineans for study at FBC. In addition, provisions were also made for youth and cultural exchanges.[61]

The long-standing relationship between Sierra Leone and Guinea was further strengthened with the passage of the Sierra Leone–Guinea Relations Act of 1966 by the Sierra Leone Parliament. The Act ratified the agreement signed between both countries in Freetown in July 1965. According to the 1966 Act, in cases of extradition from Sierra Leone of Guinean citizens (or from Guinea of Sierra Leonean nationals), the court or minister responsible for judicial and legal matters had to be fully satisfied that there was sufficient evidence to put the fugitive criminal on trial if the crime of which he or she was accused had been committed in the requesting state. All requests for the extradition of a fugitive criminal had to be addressed through the usual diplomatic channels to the minister responsible for judicial and legal matters. If the minister was satisfied with the authenticity of the warrants for which the request for extradition was made, and the conditions laid down by the relevant treaties were met, and there were no objections on the grounds of public policy, then an order for the apprehension of the fugitive criminal might be issued.[62]

In spite of the warm personal relationship between Prime Minister Margai and President Touré and the close cooperation of their governments, tensions remained between the two neighboring countries, particularly in the business sector, where the Fula were concentrated. In April 1965, for example, lawmaker S. A. Kebe (MP for Kambia Central) asked the minister of external affairs, C. B. Rogers-Wright, "whether Government was aware that immediately following the ratification of the Trade and Transport Agreement between Guinea and Sierra Leone by Parliament, Guineans had ceased coming to trade in Sierra Leone and that Guinean soldiers were guarding all the boundaries against traders who attempted to enter and, if so, what did Government intend to do about this?" According to the minister, "As to the first part of the question, Government is not aware that Guineans have ceased coming to trade in Sierra Leone. With reference to the question of Guinean soldiers guarding the boundaries, it is assumed that the Honorable Member means that the Guinean soldiers are guarding the boundaries within the Guinean territory. The question of what Government intends to do does not therefore arise."[63]

In Parliament, APC opposition lawmaker Edward J. Kargbo (MP for Bombali North) alleged that Guinean troops had sealed off the border with Sierra Leone. He said that these troops had ravaged villages on the border, molested innocent traders, and made away with goods and a large quantity of rice under the pretext that they were smuggled from Guinea into Sierra Leone. Edward Kargbo introduced a motion that read:

> In view of the strong bond of friendship which exists between the Republic of Guinea and Sierra Leone and as further manifested in the speech by the President of the Republic of Guinea to Parliament on March 23, 1965, stating among other things that Guineans and Sierra Leoneans are one and the same people. And in view of the fact that immediately after the ratification by Parliament of trade and transport agreements signed between the two countries. Guinean soldiers and guards have

completely sealed the frontiers against in-coming and out-going traders. Be it resolved that this House urges Government to make suitable representations to the Government of the Republic of Guinea asking for a relaxation of the frontier in order to facilitate the implementation of the trade agreement.

However, when the vote was taken, the motion lost because the majority SLPP lawmakers opposed it along party lines.[64]

Fula Business Elites and Immigration

The political goal of Fula business elites in dealing with the immigration challenge remained focused on responding to the surging Fula immigrant population and Prime Minister Margai's government crackdown on illegal Fula immigrants. Fula business leaders remained the foundation of the Fula interest group that crafted political responses to the Fula immigration question. Though still informal, it had expanded during Sir Albert's rule. But the key businesspeople, traditional rulers, politicians, businessmen-politicians, civil servants, and professionals in the group remained essentially unchanged. Collectively, the Fula lobby continued to work closely with the SLPP leadership and government on immigration legislation and enforcement, as well as explaining immigration policies to the Fula community across the country.

Prominent politicians in the Fula interest group included Alhaji Amadu Wurie, who was now appointed minister of the interior by Prime Minister Margai. Alhaji Wurie also received the Commander of the Most Excellent Order of the British Empire (CBE) in Queen Elizabeth II's birthday honors list in June 1964.[65] Others included Alhaji Kaikai; Speaker Sir Banja Tejan-Sie;[66] Alhaji Tejan-Jalloh, and Parliamentary Secretary in the Ministry of Trade Hon. Jah, who also served as acting minister of trade and industry.[67] These politicians continued to work closely with top Fula civil servants like Alhaji Seray-Wurie;[68] Alim Jallo-Jamboria, who was an architect with the Ministry of Works;[69] Abdul Malik Jalloh-Jamboria,[70] and Alhaji Sidique, who was promoted to permanent secretary, Ministry of the Interior, during the prime ministership of Sir Albert.[71]

Alhaji A. D. Wurie was one of the most influential persons of Fula business elites during the Margai administration. He had one foot in his white-collar world as a business leader and one in his ethnic Fula community, made up of many immigrants. In June 1964, DELCO announced the appointment of Wurie as resident director to succeed

T. W. Harvey, who was promoted to the new post of managing director of Fergusson Wild and Company Ltd. in the United Kingdom. Alhaji Wurie's promotion was significant because this was the first time in the nation's history that a large commercial firm had appointed a Sierra Leonean to a high-level decision-making position.[72] Like many of the Fula business leaders, Alhaji Wurie came from a political family; his ancestral roots were in Senegal. Building on his success as a business executive, he understood the need for community outreach and political participation. As FCC councilor, Alhaji Wurie was elected alderman for the West Ward at the council's monthly meeting in May 1964. He was nominated by Councillor A. B. Paila, a director of the National Construction Company, and was seconded by Mrs. Marie Nelson. Before the election, APC councilors, including Sorie Ibrahim (S. I.) Koroma, whose maternal pedigree was Fula, boycotted the election, saying "it was undemocratic and against the rules of the council." After the election, Mayor A. F. Rahman, and other councilors congratulated Alhaji Wurie on his victory, and Alderman Wurie thanked the FCC for selecting him and pledged his loyalty to the FCC.[73] As alderman, Alhaji Wurie served as chairman of the Finance and General Purposes Committee, which dealt with issues like education, recreational facilities, municipal trading, housing, and water supply.[74] Besides being a member of the business and political elite, Alhaji Wurie served as president of the Sierra Leone Football (American soccer) Association (SLFA).[75] He was a keen footballer and as a young man played for the national team.[76] He also served as vice president of the Sierra Leone Chamber of Mines.[77] In January 1967, having already received the MBE, Wurie was awarded the CBE in recognition of his many years of valued service in commerce and in public life.[78]

Members of the broad-based Fula interest group cultivated a close relationship with Prime Minister Margai through personal, business, and political ties. During his decade-long private legal practice in Freetown, Sir Albert had several Fula clients, including his close personal friend, the Fula chief Alhaji Bah.[79] As a private lawyer in the country's second largest city, Bo, where he won most of his court cases, Prime Minister Margai also had several Fula clients, mainly businessmen involved in various enterprises such as the diamond and merchandise trade.[80] Fula chieftaincy traditions also help to explain the Fula's support for Sir Albert. As prime minister, he promised to protect the institution of chieftaincy. The SLPP leadership showed great respect for traditional rulers, including paramount chiefs who were an integral part of the SLPP since its inception and whose support was central to the party's electoral success in the country.[81] Actually, both Albert and Milton Margai had blood ties and a long association with chiefs, working with paramount chiefs and district councils to gain popular support. Addressing paramount chiefs and the people of Port Loko in June 1964, Prime Minister Margai assured them that the integrity and dignity of chieftaincy would be maintained during his administration and that they would be consulted as often as possible in the future. He further stated, "The question of chieftaincy and chiefs is of great importance, and I hope under my administration, it will continue to be of greater importance than hitherto because I believe very firmly that if anything went wrong in the chiefdoms, it was bound to affect and disrupt the whole administration both local and central."[82] In January 1965, Sir Albert told his monthly press conference that paramount chiefs were entitled to participate in politics and rejected the view that chiefs were meddling in the politics of Sierra Leone.[83]

Despite the strong mutual understanding between Sir Albert and the Fula people, his SLPP government was tough on prosecuting and deporting illegal Fula immigrants. Immigration prosecutions against illegal Fula immigrants in magistrate courts surged during the Margai administration. Key Fula business leaders such as Alhaji Bah, Almamy Agibu Jalloh, Alhaji Ibrahim Allie, and Alhaji Tejan-Jalloh were instrumental in securing legal representation for Fula immigrants in Freetown magistrate courts. They hired Krio lawyers such as Aaron Cole, J. E. Mackay, Johnny Smythe, Livesey Luke, George Gelega-King, and Solomon A. J. Pratt to represent Fula defendants in Freetown courts. To take but a few examples, in September 1965 a Guinean-born Fula, Amadu Wurie Jalloh, was sentenced to three weeks imprisonment by the acting principal magistrate, Mrs. Agnes Macaulay, at the Freetown Police Magistrate Court No. 1. The magistrate also ordered that Jalloh be deported. Jalloh pleaded guilty to a charge of unlawful entry into Sierra Leone. According to the prosecution, Jalloh entered Sierra Leone without a valid passport or any other legal document. It was stated that Jalloh was arrested at Brass Street Lorry Park in the east of Freetown upon information received from the public.[84]

In addition, in September 1966, Principal Magistrate Macaulay sentenced two Guinean Fula, Momodu Barrie and Momodu Bailor Bah, to one month's imprisonment after they pleaded guilty to a charge of entering Sierra Leone without valid traveling documents. They were to be deported in October after serving their sentences at Pademba Road Prison in Freetown.[85] The following month, police arrested thirty-seven Fula at Moa Wharf in the eastern part of Freetown and charged them with being in Sierra Leone without valid entry permits. Only one of the men pleaded not guilty when they were arraigned before Magistrate R. E. Lardner at Freetown Magistrate Court No. 1A. He argued that he was born in Sierra Leone and had been working as a driver in Freetown. According to the police, the crackdown on these illegal immigrants would result in a decrease in the number of armed robberies, burglaries, and thefts in which stolen properties were removed in motor vehicles. The police prosecution also requested the deportation of the thirty-six Fula who were remanded at Pademba Road Prison.[86]

In its efforts to enforce immigration laws, the Margai government deported foreign nationals besides the Fula, including Nigerians and Lebanese, for such crimes as entering the country without valid traveling documents, diamond smuggling, and engaging in political activities considered subversive by the SLPP government.[87] One Lebanese was deported under the Deportation Act, which made it a criminal offense for any person or persons deported to reenter the country without special permission. But this individual was reportedly back in the diamond mining area in Kono, where even the indigenous people were restricted from entering and engaging in mining activities.[88] In addition, a twenty-five-year-old Lebanese national, Mahmoud Mansour of Kabala, was ordered to leave the country because he was allegedly an agent of the APC opposition.[89]

Fula Business Elites and the Politics of Business

The Fula were still an integral part of the national economy, with interests in vital economic sectors such as the diamond trade, livestock, transport, and retail trade. At the 1965 SLPP convention in Kono, Prime Minister Margai stated, "When we were discussing the question of retail trade in Parliament, some people intimated that Foulahs [Fula] were going to leave the country. I am now assuring the Foulahs that I look upon them as an indigenous tribe of Sierra Leone, having equal rights as any other tribe." He further stated that those who circulated rumors about the Fula were only trying to spread propaganda. Cheered by a large group of Fula at the political meeting, Sir Albert spoke of his long-standing relationship with the Fula community through its leaders in Sierra Leone. "I have always admired the Foulahs for one thing," he went on. "When they say yes, they mean yes and when they say no, they mean it. One does not need to campaign for the Foulahs."[90] At the end of the SLPP convention, the Fula delegation contributed twenty cows and Le800 toward the building of the SLPP party headquarters in Freetown.[91]

Some of the Fula business leaders in Kono, including Karim Barrie, had personal business ties with Prime Minister Margai and members of his cabinet, including PC Gulama. Unlike his brother Sir Milton, Sir Albert was a politician-businessman. Like the Fula, he strongly advocated indigenous entrepreneurship. He cultivated relationships with business groups among the Fula and the Lebanese in such sectors as the diamond trade. According to the prime minister, "If I have my way politics would not be a business of money. I have said this over and over again, but I have come to the conclusion from personal experience that if you have no money to spend, then you have no business in politics."[92]

For his politician-businessman lifestyle that resulted in the accumulation of vast wealth in Sierra Leone and overseas, Prime Minister Margai was severely criticized by the public and opposition politicians led by Stevens for corruption.[93] According to the opposition APC, in all civilized countries, elected MPs appointed as ministers would declare their business activities or connections, and those business interests that involved relations with the government would be dispensed with, at least temporarily. Also, once in office a minister was not to use his position or his insider knowledge to enrich himself at state expense. This, in short, was the code of ministerial conduct that the APC claimed should obtain in Sierra Leone.[94] But Sir Albert also had defenders among Sierra Leoneans. One newspaper columnist asked why the prime minister should be deprived of the dual capacity of businessman and politician, as was the case in the United States with Presidents John F. Kennedy and Lyndon B. Johnson. This, the columnist argued, was not stipulated in the Sierra Leone constitution.[95]

Retail Trade

Retail trade was a mainstay of the economy, and one of the priorities of Prime Minister Margai was to increase native-born citizens' participation in the country's commerce, particularly in the retail sector. A central challenge for the Fula business elites remained how to protect the large number of Fula retailers against exploitation and harassment by government officials. In May 1965, Sir Albert introduced in Parliament, the Non-Citizens (Restriction of Retail Trade) Bill that would give legal sanction to a recent decision by the government to ban foreigners from certain aspects of retail trade. Articles of retail trade affected by the new bill were the manufacture of cement blocks for sale; the supply of granite stone or sand; the provision of transport by road, sea, or river, whether for purposes of one's own business or otherwise; a ban on new bakeries or extension of existing bakeries owned by foreigners; and a bar on new mineral water factories or the extension of existing factories. It provided that noncitizens now operating vehicles or vessels in the ordinary course of a private enterprise that was not a transport business could continue to operate such vehicles. The minister of trade would from time to time declare any area in Sierra Leone to be a restricted area for the purpose of the bill.

Contributing to the parliamentary debate, the APC opposition leader Stevens said the legislation was important, but he urged the government to give assurance that MPs and other high-profile officials who had financial interests in certain sectors would not interfere with the restrictions. Another opposition MP, Barthes-Wilson stated that it would be difficult to implement the bill since the necessary machinery to take over retail trade did not exist. He said that 90 percent of retail traders were foreigners. For the SLPP lawmaker Alhaji Mustapha, one way to implement the bill would be to stop all foreign retail traders from opening their shops after 5 pm. In response, Prime Minister Margai said that careful consideration was given to the bill before it was introduced and that every precaution had been taken as to hardship on any company, firm, or individual. The SLPP majority later passed the bill and it became law on May 24, 1965.[96] The Margai administration appointed inspectors to ensure that the provisions of the Act were not violated. In a warning release issued by the Ministry of Trade and Industry in August, the ministry drew particular attention to section 4 (1) of the act regarding penalities.[97]

But the implementation of the Non-Citizens (Restriction of Retail Trade) Act faced challenges. According to a letter by the acting secretary-general of the Sierra Leone Motor Drivers Union (SLMDU),

> Since the announcement by the Ministry of Trade and Industry that foreigners will be completely banned from the transport trade, several reports have reached this Sierra Leone Motor Drivers Union (SLMDU) that a good number of non–Sierra Leoneans have embarked on a very dangerous practice of getting Sierra Leoneans who have not the means to allow their names to be registered as owners of vehicles. These Sierra Leoneans are supposed to be operating the vehicles and pay the proceeds to the foreigners who are the actual owners. The Executive of the SLMDU therefore deem it fit to issue this as a sort of warning to those foreigners and to advise the Sierra Leoneans concerned that it will leave

no stone unturned in bringing to light anybody, whether a Sierra Leonean or not who tries to break this law. To the foreigners we say that this
is our country and retail trade must be left in the hands of indigenous
Sierra Leoneans.[98]

Notwithstanding, Deputy Minister of Trade and Industry Hon. Jah
said that the implementation of the Act was an unqualified success. He
further stated that many commodities were now being handled by Sierra
Leonean traders throughout the country that were formerly sold only
by non–Sierra Leonean traders. He was replying to a question asked
by PC Alikali Modu III of Port Loko, who wanted to know whether the
minister would make a statement in Parliament on the success achieved
since the implementation of the Act on the following: road transport
and retail on articles already declared under Public Notice No. 80 of
1965. According to Minister Jah, "There is evidence that the implementation of the Act was a success and this can be seen in prohibited
goods being sold outside the main stores by Sierra Leoneans."[99]

In February 1966, the Margai government passed new legislation
to restrict certain aspects of retail trade to Sierra Leoneans only, the
Non-Citizens (Restriction of Trade or Business) Act.[100] Non–Sierra
Leoneans participating in retail trade in accordance with the new Act
would have to pay fees ranging from Le100 to Le300. They were to be
restricted from the following: the manufacture of cement blocks for
sale; the supply of granite, stone, or sand; and the provision of transport by sea, road, or river, whether for their own business or otherwise.
The law also limited the opening of new bakeries and the manufacture
of mineral waters to Sierra Leoneans.[101] Some in the business community criticized the Act as a disincentive to foreign investors.[102] But the
vast majority of Sierra Leoneans commended the SLPP government
under Sir Albert for its new commercial legislation. Writing in one of
the local newspapers, one Sierra Leonean stated:

> I wish to comment on the first public appeal made by the Prime Min-
> ister Sir Albert Margai at Regent Village to all Sierra Leoneans to take
> the opportunity of the New Trade Act, which seeks to limit the participa-
> tion of foreigners in the trade and commercial life of this country and
> to boost and encourage the active participation of the indigenous Sierra
> Leoneans in our own trade. Indeed, everyone would agree with me when
> I say that the enactment of that bill is a laudable and commendable ges-
> ture on the part of those concerned, and it goes a great way to show that
> the torch of Sierra Leonean nationalism has been passed on to a new
> generation of Sierra Leoneans. As the prime minister himself said, it is

common knowledge that the greatest proportion of the trade, foreign as well as internal, wholesale as well as retail of this country is in the hands of foreigners, both black and white. This is a sorry and unhealthy state of affairs, because it implies that our economy and consequently the life-blood of our nation is in the hands of foreigners.[103]

Reacting to the SLPP government's trade laws of 1965 and 1966, Fula business leaders crafted a number of strategies, including how to work with government officials such as price inspectors attached to the Ministry of Trade and Industry. A large number of Fula retailers faced constant harassment, and loss of business profits, because these officials expected to receive bribes. As a result, many traders were arrested and prosecuted for crimes such as profiteering and bribery. To take but a few examples, in February 1965 a Fula trader, Amadu Bah of Soldier Street in Freetown, was fined Le60 or four months' imprisonment by Police Magistrate R. E. Larner in Magistrate Court No. 3. The defendant pleaded guilty to the charges of profiteering and bribery. According to the prosecutor, Sergeant A. Nimrod, in January the accused sold one packet of Caroline Rice to Prince Chambers, a price inspector of the Ministry of Trade and Industry, for eighteen cents while the retail price was fifteen cents. He further said that after Prince Chambers had identified himself as a price inspector, Amadu Bah attempted to bribe him not to arrest him.[104] Also in February 1965, a female Fula trader, Fatmata Jalloh of 53 Campbell Street in Freetown, was arrested by a price inspector and charged for selling one packet of 16 oz. Riceland Rice for fifteen cents instead of the controlled price of thirteen cents. She was also charged for bribing a price inspector and special constable connected with the case the sum of Le1. Jalloh pleaded guilty and asked the court for leniency. In granting leniency, Police Magistrate Larner warned the defendant to always adhere to the controlled retail prices of the Declared Goods Order.[105]

Another plan of action of Fula business elites was to encourage Fula retailers to become members of the Sierra Leone Petty Traders Union (SLPTA), which was started in Freetown in 1966. This was a multiethnic organization that included the Temne, Fula, Krio, Limba, and Mende. Members belonged to different political parties, including the SLPP and APC. In fact, the secretary-general of the SLPTA was a Sierra Leonean–born Fula, Mahmoud T. Jalloh. The SLPTA sought to promote unity, self-respect, and understanding among its members, as well as develop business leadership and provide advice on business matters. One of the priorities of the SLPTA was to work with the FCC and government officials in addressing the perennial problem of street trading that affected many of its members.[106]

Livestock

Fula continued to dominate the livestock trade and its related butchering business during the Margai administration. Competition for the meat market in Freetown—the largest in the country—was still mainly among four wholesale butchers: Alhaji Bah, Alhaji Boie Kamara, Alhaji Allie, and Alhaji Mansaray. The Margai government's contract for meat represented about 45 percent of the meat market in Freetown. To handle meat contracting, it retained the Freetown-based Tender Board, which was introduced by the British colonial administration to regulate competition among butchers. However, it appointed Sierra Leoneans as members of the board, which awarded the meat contracts, and at the end of a contract, it would advertise for new tenders in the local newspapers. Interested butchers would obtain the forms, fill them out stating their prices, and send their bids to the board. Board members would then meet to review the applications and make a decision on who would win the contract.

When a government institution wanted to purchase meat, it would issue a requisition that would then be countersigned by a senior government official before being sent out to the meat contractor. In the case of government hospitals, the counter-signatories would include the chief matron or the chief catering officer. After supplying meat to a government institution, the contractor would submit a bill for certification that the meat had been received. The certified bill would then be sent to the headquarters of the institution in Freetown. In the case of government hospitals, the bill would be sent to the Ministry of Health. The ministry would then prepare a voucher for the said amount that would be signed by the meat contractor, and the voucher would be sent to the office of the principal account and to the permanent secretary for their signatures. Next, the voucher would be forwarded to the ministry of finance for payment to the meat contractor.

At the Ministry of Finance, the voucher would be processed at the office of voucher verification, where the yearly budget allocation of the institution involved was verified. The voucher would then be sent to the office of payments, where it was processed by the machine room and given a lodgment number. Then the voucher was sent to the accountant for his signature; to the senior accountant for countersigning; and to the two senior administrative officers and the minister for their signatures. After all this, the voucher would then return to the office of payments before it was sent to the Bank of Sierra Leone, where it was processed and payment was made to the meat contractor's account. The entire process might take between one and two months.

If at the end of a fiscal year a meat contractor was owed money by a government institution because the budget of that institution was insufficient to cover payments, the contractor would submit a list of his debts to the ministry responsible for that institution. The permanent secretary of the institution would prepare a letter stating the debt and would forward it with the vouchers to the financial secretary in the Ministry of Finance who would examine the documents and, if approved, issue an FS (Financial Secretary) letter indicating that the government would pay the meat contractor the money owed him. The FS letter would be sent to the minister of finance for his signature, and then to the governor of the Bank of Sierra Leone, who would authorize payments to the meat contractor. Typically, when processing payments to meat contractors, vouchers were also sent to the income tax department for necessary deductions. However, for payments resulting from the FS letter, taxes were deferred because of the emergency circumstances. A meat contractor was required by the government to continue to supply meat to government institutions even if it was owed money. Otherwise the government would obtain its meat supplies from other butchers and bill the "defaulting" contractor. The debt owed to a meat contractor was considered by the government an "honest debt" that would be repaid.[107]

Under the Margai government, Alhaji Bah, a close personal friend of the prime minister, was the single largest government meat contractor. He was awarded government contracts to supply meat to the Ministry of Social Welfare and Rural Development, the Ministry of Education, the National Dance Troupe, the Remanded and Approved Schools, The King George VI Home, and all government hospitals in Freetown: Connaught Hospital (main referral hospital), Connaught Annex, the National School of Nursing, Kissy Mental Hospital, Princess Christian Maternity Hospital, Princess Christian Maternity Annex, Children's Hospital, Murray Town Convalescence Hospital, Hill Station Hospital, and Lakka Chest Clinic Hospital. Besides meat, Alhaji Bah also supplied fresh produce, palm oil, fish, and firewood.[108] But Alhaji Bah faced strong competition for control of the government and public consumer markets from butchers such as Alhaji Allie. In competing for the government meat-supply contract, Alhaji Allie argued that Alhaji Bah was not a Sierra Leonean and that the contract should be awarded only to Sierra Leonean–born butchers. He made several unsuccessful attempts to get Prime Minister Margai to end Alhaji Bah's government meat contract. Since independence, political patronage has continued to be a major factor in the award of government contracts, including those for meat.[109]

Members of Fula business elites such as Alhaji Bah and Alhaji Allie played a major role in forming the multi-ethnic Sierra Leone Butchers Association (SLBA) in the 1960s. The Association lobbied the Margai administration on broad and diverse issues affecting its members such as government cattle and *woreh* (cattle ranch) taxes, meat prices, facilities to slaughter cattle in hygienic conditions, smuggling of cattle, cattle thefts, and disputes between cattle owners and farmers in the Provinces. Addressing the Association in Freetown in June 1964, Prime Minister Margai described it as a formidable indigenous association that exemplified the ability of Africans to unite as a family. The delegation of the Association which included both Alhaji Bah and Alhaji Allie said that its group was nonreligious, nonsectional, and committed to improving the economy of Sierra Leone. They made a contribution of £50 toward the funeral expenses of the late prime minister, Sir Milton.[110]

Diamond Trade

Fula business leaders intensified their lobbying of the SLPP government on a number of issues related to the diamond trade, including the issuance of more diamond dealer licenses, residential permits, and diggers licenses to the Fula. Some of the Fula business elites like Alhaji Ibrahima Sow, Alhaji Momodu Alpha, and Karim Barrie used their personal connections with Sir Albert and members of his cabinet to lobby for more Fula participation in the diamond business. The granting of diamond dealer and digger licenses remained highly political and competitive.[111] The Fula faced increasing competition from the Lebanese and foreign African nationals.[112] Asians dominated the list of diamond dealers who were granted licenses in 1965 by a ratio of about three to two compared with Sierra Leoneans and other Africans. This fact was disclosed in Parliament during question time by the minister of lands, mines, and labor, A. J. Demby, in reply to M. S. Kanu (MP for Bombali South), who had asked the minister how many diamond dealer licenses had been issued to Sierra Leoneans, other Africans, and Asians, respectively, for the current licensing period. The minister answered that Sierra Leoneans were issued with 64, other Africans 5, and Asians 101 diamond licenses.[113]

Since the 1930s, when diamond mining started in Kono, the Fula had been one of the largest African groups in the diamond trade. However, by the mid-1960s during the Margai administration, many

Fula—like the Mandingo who were also heavily involved in the diamond trade—were now working for Lebanese diamond dealers. By 1966, those Fula who were displeased with the growing Lebanese presence in the diamond trade joined both Sierra Leonean–born and foreign African-born immigrants like the Mandingo and Susu to form the Association of African Diamond Dealers to demand that Lebanese dealers be forced out of the mining areas in Kono. But Prime Minister Margai ordered the group dissolved in spite of his pro-business government statements advocating for more African participation in the commerce of Sierra Leone.[114] Sir Albert had personal diamond business deals with some of the Fula business elites, including Karim Barrie.[115] The findings of the Forster Commission of Inquiry into the Margai administration suggested that Margai connived with his minister of mines, A. J. Demby, and his secretary, George S. Panda, in illicit diamond trafficking.[116] And some of Margai's diamond profits were invested in both domestic and foreign assets.[117] Because of their immigrant status and fear of deportation, some Fula diamond dealers played both sides of the political competition between the SLPP and APC, forging personal ties to important officials in both parties.

Fula business elites were not alone in attempting to influence politicians and political parties. Foreign businesspeople, including Lebanese, Indians, Israelis, and Americans also attempted to lobby Sierra Leonean politicians to advance their business interests.[118] Such foreign businessmen included Joseph Eiger (Israeli), Edmund Murcarzel (Lebanese), Bill Allman (American), Assad Yazbeck (Lebanese), J. Milhem (Lebanese), and A. H. Halloway (Lebanese).[119] The Lebanese had wide-ranging business connections with the Sierra Leonean political class, including Prime Minister Margai. They made financial contributions to the political rallies of the SLPP[120] and supported a variety of projects in the country.[121] Sir Albert praised the Lebanese for their contributions to the nation's development.[122] In a speech to the Lebanese community on his appointment as prime minister, he said, "When people who do not know the amount of investment the Lebanese, at least the majority of them, have made in Sierra Leone in the form of business talk and criticize, I would say that you can't take these beautiful buildings with you, they will be with us for all the time." Referring to Sierra Leone's relations with Lebanon, the prime minister said that there was a common bond between the two countries. They both fought for freedom and democracy and so these relations would remain as always at the best.[123]

The Chamber of Commerce

The Chamber of Commerce was the main business lobby in Sierra Leone.[124] However, only a few Fula business leaders like Alhaji A. D. Wurie were members of this predominantly Western-educated group. The chamber's membership did not reflect the retailers and small businesspeople, including those of the Fula, who dominated the local business environment. Instead, it was dominated by Krio elites including E. D. Morgan, the first Sierra Leonean to be elected president of the Chamber, and H. E. B. John, who was the current president,[125] as well as foreign nationals. Some critics of the Chamber saw it as an advocate for only big business, which included mainly foreign companies and did not consider it representative of the majority of consumers' opinions in the country.[126]

At the 1964 Chamber of Commerce annual dinner, Prime Minister Margai stated that his government would do all that was possible to protect the commercial interests of the country. He urged the commercial sectors to do more and assured them of his government's support. The prime minister reiterated his strong belief in business cooperation. Contrary to his critics, who saw Margai's speech as a declaration of economic war against foreign enterprises operating in the country, the prime minister advocated a more equitable distribution of contracts and expressed the wish that foreign enterprises could help in the training of indigenous personnel in management and better business methods by assigning them more responsible posts within their enterprises.[127]

Sir Albert continued Sir Milton's Open Door Policy that encouraged private investment. In his first press conference as prime minister in May 1964, Sir Albert stated that it had brought great benefits to the country and that its modification was not being considered at the moment. He further noted that the SLPP government would not allow foreigners to exploit Sierra Leoneans through its open business approach,[128] which was aimed at encouraging more foreign investment so long as such investors were prepared to work in cooperation with the people and to abide by the laws of the country. The Open Door Policy was balanced by the prime minister's encouragement of more indigenous participation in Sierra Leone's commerce. In January 1965, Prime Minister Margai told his monthly press conference that a committee had been set up comprising government officials, as well as representatives of the Chamber and indigenous traders, to explore the pathway for greater participation of Sierra Leoneans in the nation's commerce.[129]

The SLPP government's reservation of certain trade sectors for indigenous businesspeople was not a new commercial policy in Africa.

For many local Sierra Leonean businesses, foreign enterprises still exhibited some degree of discrimination and unfair competition against African participation in the commerce of the country. This led the government to commission Professor N. A. Cox-George of FBC to investigate the veracity of the claim and submit a report. He saw the allegations as a change in the pattern of trade generally. He wrote that "all groups are engaged in 'dealer and consumer' trade. The European firms, the Syrian/Lebanese and the Indians entered directly and fully into it since the First World War and have remained in it since." Prime Minister Margai was a strong advocate of the policy of pooling together all of the domestic resources to promote economic, social, and commercial development.[130]

Despite the pro-business attitude of Sir Albert, the country faced serious economic challenges, including poverty, corruption, and the high cost of living.[131] Public opposition to Margai and the SLPP resulted in part from these problems, especially allegations of corruption. Both the SLPP and opposition APC had major disagreements over the 1966–67 proposed budget. Not only did the APC leader Stevens and APC parliamentarians walk out of budget discussions, they also opposed most of the SLPP development programs.[132] In his contribution to the budget debate in Parliament, Stevens stated that people in authority showed no regard for the people when it came to spending public funds. He said that there was a growing gap between the rich and the poor in the country and that gap must be closed in the interest of the nation. Also, he stated that the political system of any country in which a section of the people get lower wages while others earn top salaries should be reviewed. He described the budget as "a couldn't care less budget."[133] Because of the nation's economic difficulties, the International Monetary Fund (IMF) intervened following bilateral discussions and negotiations between the SLPP government finance minister, R. G. O. King, and IMF officials in Washington, DC. But particularly in light of the upcoming 1967 general election, the Margai administration did not implement the Structural Adjustment Program (SAP) signed with the IMF in November 1966 because of the possible negative economic, social, and political consequences.[134]

Fula Business Elites and the 1967 Election

The March 1967 general election was one of the most pivotal in Sierra Leonean history. It cost the SLPP government Le417,699 to hold[135] and was for sixty-six ordinary seats and twelve district council seats held by paramount chiefs.[136] Earlier in February 1967, Governor-General Sir Lightfoot-Boston signed a proclamation that was released by Prime Minister Margai's office to dissolve Parliament and set the general election for March 17.[137] The election was essentially a political contest between the ruling SLPP and the opposition APC. The election manifesto of the SLPP catalogued the main achievements of its five-year rule since the prime ministership of the late Sir Milton. Furthermore, the agenda of the SLPP outlined its future plans to develop Sierra Leone by focusing on such key areas as the economy; foreign policy; communications; infrastructure; agriculture; industrialization; chieftaincy; religion; multi-party politics; women; and social services such as health and education, sports, and employment.[138] In contrast, the APC platform outlined several policies it would implement, including revision of the country's business taxation on the grounds that it was too high, changes in the country's foreign policy, direct government intervention in the diamond sector, significant reduction of government spending, free primary education, the granting of financial incentives to farmers to produce more rice and essential crops for local consumption, and eradication of unemployment. The APC promised to study the institutions of chieftaincy and the judiciary. It called on all Sierra Leoneans to be prepared to make certain "painful sacrifices" because, it claimed, the SLPP had destroyed the economy.[139]

In a political speech on the eve of the election, Sir Albert remarked that "when the time comes in Sierra Leone that Government lacks Opposition, that will be the time that some of us will pack up our bags and baggage and quit politics. This system (multi-party democracy) is one of the best things which we have inherited from our colonial masters."[140] But the opposition leader, Stevens, stated, "Notwithstanding the open declaration of the prime minister to the effect that he welcomed the role of the opposition in Sierra Leone party politics, our experience as a party, especially within the past few months, leaves us in no doubt whatsoever that certain leading members of the SLPP Government are going all out to ruin the APC opposition using all sorts of means including directives and pressures of one kind or another."[141]

The political agenda of most Fula business leaders, such as Alhaji Bah, Alhaji Tejan-Jalloh, Alhaji A. D. Wurie, Almamy Agibu Jalloh, and Alhaji Momodu Alpha Bah, for the election focused on the reelection of the SLPP under the leadership of Prime Minister Margai. The election pushed the issue of the rights of the Fula as citizens and voters toward the forefront of Sierra Leone politics, as the Fula population had increased substantially in the country. The Fula found themselves at the center of a highly charged national public debate over citizenship and voting rights. Sir Albert was a strong supporter of Fula citizenship rights, as evidenced by his speeches in Parliament and political activities across the country. Supporting Fula citizenship rights, Prime Minister Margai hoped, would bring a political payoff for his electoral hopes.

As political battles over Fula citizenship and voting rights continued across the country, opposition APC politicians including Stevens, Barthes-Wilson, and Kamara-Taylor alleged repeatedly that foreign-born Fula, especially from Guinea, were on the list of voters. Prime Minister Margai dismissed this concern at a meeting of the SLPP in Port Loko in April 1965 when he said that such rumors were untrue and that he was determined to deal with any disorder swiftly and effectively in order to maintain peace throughout the country.[142] The APC leaders were critical not only of the voters' registers, but also of the electoral commission appointed by the Margai administration.[143] In Parliament, in June 1966, Kamara-Taylor asked the minister of the interior what percentage of Guinean nationals resident in the country were on the voters' registers. Acting Minister of the Interior S. B. Mara referred him to the definition of the word *alien* under the Franchise and Electoral Registration Act No. 44 of 1961, which clearly precluded the registration of aliens, including Guinean nationals, from registering as voters.[144] For Barthes-Wilson, he inquired from Sir Albert whether the names of aliens could be included in the electoral register. The prime minister replied, "In accordance with the Electoral Registration Act No. 44 of 1961 'aliens' are not eligible to be registered as electors in Sierra Leone. This is the practice which no doubt obtains in other African territories and it is to be hoped that non-citizens of Sierra Leone will strictly abide by them so as not to mar the good and friendly relationship which has always existed between the citizens and non-citizens of this country."[145]

To achieve the political objective of reelecting the SLPP under the leadership of Sir Albert, Fula business leaders pursued a coherent two-part strategy. First, they provided campaign cash and in-kind support such as livestock. Second, they made a well-financed, sustained push to get out the Fula vote. This included registering Fula voters across the country, especially in the Northern Province where they were concentrated, and conducting political campaigns, particularly for Fula candidates. The Fula were a critical part of the electoral base of Sir Albert and the SLPP. Fula chiefs, who were also in the business elite, played an important role in implementing these political strategies. The Freetown-based Fula chief, Alhaji Bah, was the most senior in the hierarchy of Fula traditional rulers in Sierra Leone. In addition to Freetown, the Fula had chiefs in other areas of the country, including Koinadugu, Bo, Kono, Tonkolili, Kenema, and Pujehun. This political alliance between Prime Minister Margai and Fula business elites would make the Fula a political target of the opposition APC.[146]

With an election year approaching, Fula SLPP politicians sought political and material support from Fula business leaders and tried to build bridges among Fula members of their constituencies across the country. In the Northern Province, where the Fula had a large presence, the Fula SLPP politicians included Alhaji Amadu Wurie, minister of education and minister of interior, as well as MP from Port Loko; and A. M. Jalloh, the Fula SLPP candidate for the Bombali South constituency, who ran against Sembu Forna, the APC candidate. Jalloh helped to convince M. S. Kanu (MP for Bombali South) to quit the APC and join the SLPP.[147] In Tonkolili, M. K. Yalloh, an SLPP politician, worked with Fula traditional rulers like PC Alhaji Kulio Yalloh of Bendugu, Sambaia chiefdom, to advance his political interests.[148] In the Southern Province, SLPP Fula politicians included Hon. Jah, acting minister of trade and industry. Fula business elites helped these politicians to raise the electoral deposits, which had been increased from Le200 to Le500 by the 1967 Electoral (Amendment) Act.[149]

Prime Minister Margai successfully assembled various Fula groups, besides Fula SLPP politicians, that included youths and women to expand his electoral coalition for the election. Fula youths such as Alhaji Chernor Sie and Umaru Dumbuya were an important part of the SLPP membership and were active campaigners in the election. Also, Fula youths played a leading role in Freetown and other parts of the country in mobilizing support for Sir Albert Margai and the SLPP.[150] According to Dumbuya, a resident of Freetown Central I constituency, he had been a member of the SLPP since 1964 and chaired the Western Area Youth League of the SLPP in the 1967 election.[151] For Prime Minister Margai, youths represented the future of Sierra Leone and therefore should be helped to actualize their full potential to develop the country.[152] One of the concerns of the Provincial youths was the banishment of traditional rulers. Unlike Sir Milton, Sir Albert was opposed to banishment as a political weapon.[153] The National Youth Movement praised Prime Minister Margai's decision to have all banishment orders now in force revoked.[154] In May 1964, Sir Albert advised the govenor-general to revoke the banishment orders against PC Bai Koblo of Port Loko and PC Mbriwa of Kono, who were restricted to the Pujehun and Kamakwie towns respectively. PC Bai Koblo was a minister without portfolio in Sir Milton's government until 1962. PC Mbriwa was leader of the now defunct SLPIM. The govenor-general ordered that PC Koblo be free to reside anywhere within the country other than Port Loko and that PC Mbriwa be allowed to reside anywhere within the country but Kono.[155] PC Koblo was reelected head of the Marampa-Masimera chiefdom in April 1965.[156]

In addition to Fula youths, Fula women were also an integral part of the SLPP political base. Across Sierra Leone, SLPP women were organized into different groups, including Mammy Queens.[157] Fula women, including Haja Isatu Tejan-Jalloh (wife of Alhaji Tejan-Jalloh), were an important part of this gender political mobilization for the SLPP. She was president of the Fula Women's Association.[158] Some of the female SLPP supporters were also members of the National Congress of Sierra Leone Women.[159] With the introduction of the institution of Mammy Queens, women became more active in politics, organizing their fellow women in sections to provide political support for the SLPP under Prime Minister Margai. In return for the women's support of the SLPP, Sir Albert promised them assistance in the retail trade sector.[160] At the annual SLPP national convention in Makeni in May 1964, Prime Minister Margai appealed to women to take a more active part in the affairs of the country and crowned four female chiefs as Mammy Queens from Kambia in the Biriwa chiefdom.[161]

One-Party State

One of the most politically divisive topics in the months leading up to the 1967 election was the SLPP proposal to introduce a one-party state. It generated a political crisis, threatening to erase political support for the SLPP under Sir Albert's leadership. As for the Fula, they participated in the one-party political debates as politicians, businesspeople, activists, civil servants, and professionals. At a meeting of the Sierra Leone Dock Workers Union in Freetown in December 1966, one of the speakers, M. A. Jalloh, paid glowing tribute to the prime minister, describing him as a natural leader. Jalloh said that political independence without economic stability would be meaningless. He therefore advocated a one-party state as the means to consolidate political unity and advance the nation's economic progress.[162]

Meanwhile, within Margai's administration and the SLPP, there were supportive viewpoints on the one-party proposal. Initially, the Fula minister of the interior, Alhaji Amadu Wurie, suggested caution in introducing one-party rule.[163] But he later joined the Port Loko District Council in passing a resolution in support of the SLPP government's initiative to introduce one-party rule in the country. In his address to the Council, Alhaji Wurie refuted allegations that under a one-party system detention and concentration camps would be set up and chieftaincy abolished. He further stated that it would be financially impossible and impractical to replace chieftaincy by any other form of authority because most of the chiefs were not paid.[164] At the SLPP's third national planning committee meeting in Kambia, nearly five hundred delegates, including Fula business leaders such as Alhaji Momodu Alpha Bah discussed Prime Minister Margai's call for the introduction of one-party rule, but there was no political consensus.[165]

In Parliament, SLPP lawmaker Prince J. Williams (MP for Bo Town II), speaking on the debate on the motion of thanks to the governor-general for the Speech from the Throne, called for a one-party state in the nation. He said, "The day has come when we should have one political flock under one political shepherd." In addition, he said that although he was a firm believer in the two-party system of government, the debate in the House had forced him to that conclusion. The suggestion was stoutly opposed by the APC lawmaker M. O. Bash-Taqui (MP for Tonkolili South).[166] Also opposing the one-party proposal was the leader of the APC opposition, Stevens. Contributing to the debate on the Speech from the Throne, he said that the one-party idea was premature given the country's stage of development. Stevens said that "it tickled him to the bones each time he heard the idea." He further said, "Which party will form this state?" Amidst laughter and cheers from the APC opposition members, he declared, "If the government is pressing on this issue, they should realize that there is a party within their party—a combination of SLPP and the PNP." He again asked which of these two parties would form the one-party state. According to Stevens, the country should first strive for unity and improve the living standard of the people. He added, "When President (Julius) Nyerere had a 90 percent control of the government in his country (Tanzania), he called for a one-party state and he was wholeheartedly supported." The gallery again rocked with laughter when Stevens said, "But with this dubious government, a dependent independence government, now we are entering the fifth year of our dependent independence and yet we are crying for a one-party state." According to Stevens, "Non-alignment, one-party state leave them alone, they will come when they will and it is the electorate that will tell us. We are confident we have the support of the section of the community and we should leave the present government a multi-party government."[167]

Opposition to the proposed one-party rule was also strong outside of Parliament.[168] Critics came from multi-ethnic backgrounds and included professionals, academics, women, and youths across the country.[169] One of the bitterest critics of Prime Minister Margai and the one-party idea was Dr. Easmon, who accepted a nomination by the Medical Practitioners Association to serve on the forty-man one-party committee set up by the SLPP government.[170] Dr. Easmon was a frequent newspaper columnist who wrote extensively on the SLPP one-party proposal, detailing its history and why it was a bad idea for the country.[171] Alongside domestic opponents were Sierra Leoneans overseas, including students in the United States and the United Kingdom.[172]

Meanwhile, Sir Albert tried to educate the public and drum up political support for the proposed one-party system. In Freetown he addressed several groups and held political rallies to explain the one-party idea.[173] Moreover, he made similar political speeches across the Provinces to groups including paramount chiefs, women, youths, and politicians.[174] As a result of mounting public opposition in Parliament and nationwide, as well as among Sierra Leoneans in the diaspora, to one-party rule, the Margai administration eventually decided to abandon the one-party political initiative prior to the 1967 election.[175]

Political Conventions

National party conventions were part of the political landscape leading up to the 1967 election. The SLPP held several conventions before the election. Fula business leaders played major roles as delegates and organizers, as well as contributors of cash and in-kind donations such as livestock and rice. Some of the Fula businessmen who participated at these national political conventions were also traditional rulers and, as such, represented both their constituents and their personal business and political interests. The conventions, which were held in different areas of the country, were colorful affairs with traditional dances, often performed by women, political speeches, free meals, gift exchanges, and a formal ball.[176]

The first national SLPP convention under Sir Albert's leadership was held in June 1964 in Makeni, Bombali. Before the convention, the prime minister visited paramount chiefs in Bombali and addressed the Town Council and members of the Finance and General Purposes Committee of the District Council at the Native Court Barri in Makeni. Among the prominent Fula traditional ruler-business elites who helped to organize the event and welcomed the prime minister were Alhaji Wuroh Timbo and Alhaji Abdul Jalloh. At the Makeni convention, Prime Minister Margai was elected president for life of the SLPP. In his inaugural presidential speech, he outlined the party's achievements and its future plans for the country in several areas, including education, the economy, agriculture, health care, and chieftaincy. He also reaffirmed Sierra Leone's support of the OAU and UN.[177] The prime minister urged delegates to dedicate themselves to the fulfillment of their party's motto: "One country, one people."[178] Three cabinet ministers, M. J. Kamanda-Bongay, Maigore Kallon, and Kandeh Bureh, were elected vice presidents for the Southern Province, Eastern Province, and Western Area, respectively. Two former cabinet ministers, I. B. Taylor-Kamara and Alhaji Mustapha, were reelected vice president for the Northern Province and treasurer, respectively. Besides SLPP delegates, the convention was attended by the commanding officer of the military forces, the commissioner of police, heads of government departments, and senior civil servants.[179]

One of the SLPP's biggest national political conventions was held in Koidu, Kono in May 1965. The diamond wealth of Kono was a primary reason for the SLPP's decision to hold its annual convention in this eastern District.[180] The three-day convention attracted over five thousand delegates, including two from each constituency and three from each chiefdom. Observers included representatives of the diplomatic corps. The local organizing committee was headed by PC Mbriwa, regarded as the "strong man" of Kono, who was participating in the SLPP convention for the first time after declaring for the ruling party earlier in 1965 and dissolving his SLPIM.[181] As national chairman of the SLPP, Prime Minister Margai delivered the annual convention speech in which he outlined the party's program, followed by the election of officers by delegates. Many of the delegates and major financiers of the Kono convention were Fula business elites such as the Freetown-based Fula chief Alhaji Bah, the Kono-based Fula chief Alhaji Momodu Alpha Bah, diamond dealers like Karim Barrie, and businessman-politician Alhaji Tejan-Jalloh.[182] Fula support was complemented by the Kono politician, S. L. Matturi, treasurer of the SLPP, who on behalf of the four host chiefs and people of Kono, presented seventy cows, forty-two bags of rice, and Le2,400 for the SLPP convention.[183]

Replying to the welcome address by Matturi, Prime Minister Margai spoke about possible elections next year. He stated that it was his prerogative to dissolve Parliament and that he would "exercise it without any consultation with any minister or my cabinet. Within a period of eight months I may use my prerogative and advise the governor-general to dissolve Parliament." Sir Albert was optimistic about the SLPP's chances in the next general election. According to him, he had not yet "turned the gun on the opposition APC. I am only getting ready with my cannons to pulverize them." He challenged the APC to make public its program to improve the country and to show that it had the qualified personnel to implement such a program. He announced that the SLPP had a registered membership exceeding one million, of whom many were Fula. He announced that a party office was to be built at Tower Hill with a publishing arm. Speaking about the challenges facing the SLPP, Prime Minister Margai dwelt at length on what he described as lack of faith and warned against selfishness, irresponsibility, indifference, and misrepresentation between nationalism and tribalism among party members. He also strongly criticized some MPs of the SLPP for their negative attitude toward their constituencies and pointed out incidences of intra-party conflicts.[184]

One major issue that Prime Minister Margai addressed at the convention that was of importance to the Fula business elites and delegates was the state of the Sierra Leone economy. On retail trade, Sir Albert stressed that native-born residents must enjoy maximum participation in the retail trade of the country. He described the recent law to regulate retail trade as an opportunity for Sierra Leoneans to participate more fully in the national economy. However, he warned that any citizen who aided a foreigner to sidestep the law would be treated as a criminal. On industry, the prime minister stated that his administration was prepared to give every encouragement to foreign industrialists to set up business in the country as long as they did not interfere with the government. He announced that an industrial bank and sugar industry would soon be set up in the country.[185]

Speaking at a youth rally during the convention, Prime Minister Margai addressed the perennial controversy about the status of the Fula in Sierra Leone. "When we were discussing the question of retail trade in Parliament, some people intimated that Foulahs [Fula] were going to leave the country. I am now assuring the Foulahs that I look upon them as an indigenous tribe of Sierra Leone, having equal rights as any other tribe." He castigated those—particularly members of the opposition APC led by Stevens—who spread rumors about the imminent departure of the Fula from Sierra Leone as political propagandists. Furthermore, Sir Albert told the youth rally of his long-standing association with the Fula through their traditional, business, and political leaders in the country.[186]

After the convention, the Kono branch of the SLPP held its local convention that November. It was attended by about six thousand delegates, one-third of whom were women. Many of the delegates were Fula and were led by their chief, Alhaji Momodu Alpha Bah. They included Fula traditional rulers, merchants, youths, activists, politicians, diamond dealers, and prominent business leaders like Karim Barrie and Mohamed W. Jalloh.[187] This regional SLPP convention was followed by another visit to Kono by Prime Minister Margai in June 1966. While in Kono, Sir Albert addressed a large SLPP political rally that was co-organized and significantly financed by the Fula community under the direction of its business leaders and traditional elites.[188]

The date of the next annual SLPP convention was to be determined by the completion of a new three-story party headquarters in Freetown, whose official opening was planned to coincide with the convention. SLPP members were looking forward eagerly to the convention, which was first announced at a mass rally in Kambia early in 1966. Meanwhile, multi-ethnic and cross-generational SLPP supporters from many parts of the country had been pouring into the capital city to get a glimpse of the new SLPP headquarters under construction—the first of its kind in Sierra Leone. Built on crown land, it had a large assembly hall where the convention would be held. But the convention did not take place in Freetown as planned because construction of the new party headquarters fell behind schedule.[189]

In December 1966 the APC party held its first annual convention since its founding in 1960. Multi-ethnic delegates came from across the country to attend the three-day conference in Freetown.[190] According to some political observers, the APC convention was hurriedly convened for three reasons. First, the party saw the convention as an opportunity to position itself for the upcoming 1967 election and to raise funds for its political campaigns. Second, it was a move to forestall the SLPP convention in Freetown announced in December 1965 in Kambia. Third, the APC wanted to resolve its intra-party leadership conflict before the 1967 election.[191] The left-wing of the APC, which was made up mostly of Temne, had a political goal to replace Stevens as APC leader at the convention. According to one newspaper columnist, the convention was dominated by Temne and Limba delegates, while groups from Freetown and Kono were marginalized; in his view, the convention was a struggle for tribal, not party, supremacy.[192] Political rivalry between the Temne and Limba for leadership in the APC preceded the 1966 convention.[193] In fact, in November 1965, four Temne officers of the youth section of the APC in Lunsar resigned from the party in protest against allegations of an alleged plot by the Limba against the Temne of the north.[194] For the newspaper columnist, if one were not a Temne, one's future in the APC was uncertain; moreover, he believed that Stevens's leadership would be further challenged before the 1967 election. Among the issues discussed at the convention was the possible replacement of the Krio governor-general, Sir Lightfoot-Boston, with a Temne.[195]

The Fula participated in the APC convention as delegates, youths, politicians, and businesspeople. One prominent Fula delegate was A. Wurie, a teacher, who chaired the multi-ethnic APC Eastern Youths Branch in Freetown, one of the largest APC groups nationwide.[196] The APC also had youth branches in other cities across the country. As youth leader in the East where Freetown's population was concentrated, Wurie worked with other youth leaders, including Councillor J. W. Y. Koroma, popularly known as "Mayor of Congo Town," who was leader of the APC youth section and propaganda secretary.[197] Like Sir Albert, Stevens recognized the importance of youths to the political success of the APC. Among the Fula business elites who attended the APC convention was Alhaji Ibrahim Allie, who provided cash and in-kind support including livestock, rice, and lodging for delegates from the Provinces. Despite strong support for the SLPP among Fula business elites, Alhaji Allie was a political maverick who supported the opposition APC. He provided the APC a two-story building to use as office space in the East End of Freetown at no cost for up to seven years. In fact, Ibrahim Taqi, a passionate APC member and newspaper columnist, was one of the occupants. Moreover, on the eve of the 1967 election, Alhaji Allie accompanied the APC opposition leader Siaka Stevens to Kono to meet with wealthy Fula businessmen from Sierra Leone and other West African countries, including Guinea, the Gambia, and Senegal. The Fula chief in Kono, Alhaji Momodu Alpha Bah, a close friend of Alhaji Allie, facilitated these meetings, which raised substantial funds for the APC's election campaigns.[198]

The APC convention was marked by political dissension, with some top executives, mainly Temne, walking out of the discussions. This APC faction, which included lawmakers, threatened to hold its own separate convention after accusing Stevens of tribalism, nepotism, and hypocrisy. They wanted to expel Stevens and pass a vote of no confidence in his leadership, as well as call for fresh election of officers in a mass meeting. For many in this anti-Stevens group, Dr. Karefa-Smart was the best person to lead the APC.[199] Following lengthy negotiations during the convention and interventions by Dr. Easmon and A. Akibo-Betts to settle the internal disputes within the party, the opposing groups were finally reconciled under the leadership of Stevens in preparation for the 1967 election.[200]

Political Fundraising

Political fundraising was an important political activity before the 1967 election. As discussed in Sir Milton's rule, the government did not provide funding for political campaigns and national party conventions. Therefore, political campaigns were financed primarily by party, private, and business contributions. Still, there was no clear boundary between private money and government funds in the financing of political campaigns. Actually, the APC opposition leader Stevens criticized the government under Sir Albert for its extravagant spending of public funds. Speaking during the debate on the 1966–67 budget, Stevens stated, "Money which belongs to the Government belongs to the Government and money which belongs to the party belongs to the party." He further said that the Margai administration should draw a clear line between national and political interests.[201]

On the campaign trail for the highly competitive 1967 election, Prime Minister Margai received large cash and in-kind gifts such as livestock and rice from wealthy Fula business leaders like Alhaji Bah, Almamy Agibu Jalloh, Alhaji Bailor Barrie, Alhaji Momodu Alpha Bah, Karim Barrie, Alhaji A. D. Wurie, and Alhaji Tejan-Jalloh. Some Fula diamond dealers in Kono like Barrie contributed as much as Le50,000 to finance Sir Albert's political campaign. Besides his own personal contributions, the Fula chief Alhaji Bah, working with his sub-chiefs, solicited contributions from individual businesspeople and clan-based groups. In addition, Alhaji Bah collaborated with the SLPP leadership to request donations from wealthy Fula merchants in the Provinces, especially in diamond-rich Kono. Contributions from Fula donors were used mainly for SLPP political organizing across the country. Earlier evidence of Fula support to Sir Albert and the SLPP came in May 1964 when the Fula chief Alhaji Bah led a delegation of the Fula community to Prime Minister Margai's office, where they presented him with a donation of £100 toward the funeral expenses of his brother, Sir

Milton. Sir Albert thanked the Fula after the money was handed over to him by C. B. Rogers-Wright, minister of external affairs.[202] Also, in April 1965 the Fula from Kabala, led by their leader Alhaji Almamy Abdul R. Jalloh, donated several herds of cattle to Prime Minister Margai, whose government spent about Le1,904 to transport the cows from Kabala to the prime minister's hometown in the Southern Province.[203]

In addition to the Fula, the Lebanese business community was an important source of funding for SLPP political activities, including national party conventions and election campaigns.[204] The wealthy Afro-Lebanese diamond dealer Jamil S. Mohamed was a key player in SLPP fundraising campaigns. Jamil, who was based in Kono, was a close personal friend of Prime Minister Margai and contributed generously to the SLPP campaigns for the 1967 election.[205] Before independence in 1961, Jamil was expelled from Kono because he possessed diamonds valued at £8,000. But in 1966, during Sir Albert's rule, he returned to Kono with a dealer's license, a residential permit, and naturalization documents. According to one report, Jamil had a three-story building, seven thousand customers a month, and legal diamond sales of £100,000 a month to the Government Diamond Office (GDO). Other Lebanese financiers of the SLPP under Prime Minister Margai included Assad Yazbeck, whose business was the sole importer of Mercedes-Benz vehicles and who sold such vehicles to the government. Like Jamil, Assad was a close personal friend of the prime minister. The opposition APC led by Stevens criticized the business relationship between wealthy Lebanese like Jamil and Assad and the Margai administration.[206]

On the regional level, Prime Minister Margai and SLPP executives collaborated with traditional elites in the Provinces, including Fula chiefs such as Alhaji Wuroh Timbo and Alhaji Abdul Jalloh, to raise cash and in-kind donations of livestock and rice for the 1967 election. In January 1965, Sir Albert told his monthly press conference that paramount chiefs were free to participate in national politics. To Sir Albert, the fact that the chiefs were lawmakers was an indication of their political responsibility. He was answering a question calling for a clear-cut statement on chiefs and politics. The prime minister rejected "with all the force at my command" that chiefs were meddling in the politics of Sierra Leone.[207] Earlier, addressing paramount chiefs from Tonkolili who called on him to pledge their loyalty to his government, Prime Minister Margai said that his government was working vigorously to improve the stability of chieftaincy in the country. He dismissed speculation that under his administration "chieftaincy would die out." "This is a bad and false rumor. I am from a ruling family and I will one day leave government activities and become a chief. If under my government chieftaincy matters are neglected, I would be going against my conscience and the wish of my people." On behalf of the visiting delegation, PC Alhaji Kulio Yalloh (Jalloh), a Fula, expressed his condolences on the death of the late Prime Minister Margai and congratulated Sir Albert on his new appointment. The paramount chiefs presented the prime minister with £100 as their contribution toward the funeral expenses of the late Sir Milton.[208]

Political rallies were occasions for political contributions for the 1967 election campaign. Such rallies attracted thousands of party supporters and were held across the country. Addressing one SLPP rally attended by more than four thousand members of the Freetown branch of the party and its youth wing at the Brookfields Stadium, Prime Minister Margai said that the SLPP government had no intention of building concentration camps in the country "because under the new government we would embrace all men and women so that we would work together to build a strong nation." He also stated:

> We now have a new Government, a new Sierra Leone and a spirit of undaunted adventure. Let us join together to carry out this work of nation building or die in the battle. It is our policy to move up the party and make it strong so that the opposition party would admire us. In the near future, you cannot distinguish between the Party and the Government. Though not all our party members would become ministers, I assure you all that the voices of each and every one of you would be heard. We have confidence in our supporters and we invite all to join forces and assist in building a new nation.[209]

For the opposition APC, its leader Stevens raised substantial funds at political rallies as well. In one such mass rally at the Queen Elizabeth II Playing Field, Stevens appealed to APC supporters to contribute generously to the party. At the end of the meeting, the party's secretary-general, Kamara-Taylor, announced that Le1,000 had already been collected in less than twenty-four hours after the launching of the fundraising appeal. Reminding his APC supporters that "a general election is fast approaching," Stevens urged them to register to vote and warned that they would not be able to vote if they failed to register their names. The aims of the APC, he reiterated, were to unite the country and raise the living standards of the people. He told party supporters to avoid violence. Members of the APC party executive also spoke to the rally in support of what their leader was saying.[210] In addition to visiting Freetown, Stevens made several fundraising trips to diamond-rich Kono to address APC political rallies. For instance, in 1966 he raised Le30,000, mainly from the business community in Kono, which included Fula and Lebanese diamond dealers. Part of the money was used by the APC to purchase a house in Freetown with the stated goal of providing accommodation to party members from the provinces. But the house was rented to nonparty members under questionable circumstances.[211]

Albert Margai and Muslims

To solidify his electoral coalition for the crucial 1967 election, Prime Minister Margai reached out to the Muslim population for political support. The Fula remained a large and significant part of the country's Muslim community. Like Sir Milton, Sir Albert had a long history of working with the multi-ethnic Muslim population. Although a Catholic, he participated in many Muslim activities, including attending Muslim services inside mosques. Prime Minister Margai's actions reflected the long-standing peaceful and cooperative relationship between Muslims and Christians in Sierra Leone.[212] According to one newspaper editorial in the year of the election,

> In Sierra Leone, nowadays, unlike many years ago, we see Muslims playing an increasingly valuable role in all spheres of our national life. This has helped to create better understanding between our various religions and has helped to create the necessary atmosphere for co-existence which makes any democracy ideal. But the Muslim still has a very important role to play in this country. He must demonstrate, like his counterparts elsewhere, his sense of national discipline.[213]

But some in the Muslim community were opposed to the mixing of politics and religion. Ironically, Alhaji Mustapha, a political rival of Sir Albert and former minister in Sir Milton's administration, warned Muslims not to mingle politics with religion. Addressing more than one thousand Muslims at the groundbreaking ceremony of the Lokko Mosque on James Street in Freetown, Alhaji Mustapha urged Muslims not to focus on politics, which he said catered only to earthly pleasures, but not to the hereafter where all were answerable to Allah. He described religion and politics as two parallel lines that could not meet. He further cautioned against hiding under the religious cloak to participate in politics. He also observed that past misunderstandings between Muslim leaders were often caused by the conflict of politics and religion. He urged Muslims and Christians all over the country to forget their petty squabbles and unite to build a strong country. Donating the land for the Le20,000 Lokko Mosque, Alhaji Mustapha called on Muslims and Christians alike to contribute to the building project. Addressing the Muslim gathering, Dr. Lahai Taylor, a Lokko community leader, said that the mosque would house a school where Arabic would be taught.[214]

In 1966 Prime Minister Margai joined more than one hundred Muslim leaders, such as imams, alhajis, and hajas, at the British Council to inaugurate a new nonpolitical organization, the Sierra Leone Muslim Pilgrims Welfare Association (SLMPWA). The aim of the SLMPWA was to bring together all alhajis and hajas to ensure their general welfare and provide for the needs of future pilgrims to Mecca in Saudi Arabia. The prime minister assured the SLMPWA of his personal support and that of his government. Speaking at the ceremony, Alhaji Sesay, founding president of the SLMPWA, who was also chief imam of the Temne mosque in Freetown and a politician during Sir Milton's prime ministership, stated that Sir Albert had already demonstrated support for the welfare of Muslims.[215] He cited the example of the Margai administration providing the Muslim pilgrims with a doctor to take care of them during their annual hajj. Further evidence of Sir Albert's personal interest was the fact that despite his many duties, he found time to honor their invitation and join with them in inaugurating an organization dedicated to the welfare of Muslim pilgrims. Alhaji Sesay recalled the last hajj when Sir Albert entertained the pilgrims on the eve of their departure and served them with his own hands. He called on the alhajis and hajas to reciprocate the warmheartedness and kindness of the prime minister by offering special prayers for him and the success of his administration.[216] In the same year, Prime Minister Margai offered to sponsor four Muslims to make the hajj. In 1967 the secretary-general of the SLMPWA, Alhaji Abu B. Magba-Kamara announced that Sir Albert had increased the number of sponsorships to five to include a candidate to be elected by the Ahmadiyya Muslim community. Candidates for the awards had to apply and would be interviewed by the SLMPWA, and only those who had never made the pilgrimage would be considered for the prime minister's award.[217]

In addition to religious issues, Prime Minister Margai also worked with the Muslim community on education. In response to the increasing educational needs of the Fula community, in 1965 he provided a large parcel of state land on Guard Street in the east of Freetown for the construction of a school for Fula children. Not only did the Fula chief Alhaji Bah use his good relations with the prime minister to obtain the land, he also personally supervised the building of the school by visiting the site twice daily until it was completed in 1966. The Fula School, which was both an elementary and a high school, played an important role in the socialization of Fula children. Many of the teachers were Fula, who served as role models; donations by Fula business leaders were used as salaries for the teachers. The students received instruction in conventional subjects, such as English and mathematics, as well as in Pulaar, the Fula language. Traditional Fula culture and history were also taught. Some of the students were non-Fula who came from the multi-ethnic population in the eastern part of the city. Besides being used as an educational center, the Fula School became a place for Fula to meet on the last Sunday of every month to raise funds and discuss matters affecting their community.[218]

Also in 1965, Prime Minister Margai told members of the SLMC that its goal to build a secondary school should be regarded as a national project, not just a religious one. He pointed out that his government attached great importance to education and promised its assistance to the SLMC. And he personally promised Le500 to the building fund. Speaking at the event in the East End of Freetown where he laid the foundation stone of an SLMC secondary school, Prime Minister Margai said that the school would teach Arabic and Islam alongside secular subjects. The SLMC expressed gratitude to the Margai government for the land lease and also for the government funding it had received for the erection of the school. To bring about the completion of the school before the next academic year, the SLMC appealed for additional government support.[219] In response to the SLMC fundraising appeal, Muslim Fula politicians such as Alhaji Amadu Wurie donated Le200 and Sir Banja Tejan-Sie gave the same sum. And Alhaji Mustapha contributed Le2,000. A further sum of Le100 was received from each of six mosques in Freetown: Fula, Mandingo, Ahmadiyya, Temne, Foulah Town, and Congo Town.[220]

Despite their cooperation, the Muslim organizations also had differences that undermined unity. In fact, Sir Albert did not attend the Muslim prayers of id ul-fitr (the Muslim feast that marks the end of Ramadan) following advice from his cabinet in regard to a row in the Muslim community. But the leaders of the SLMB and SLMC denied there was a split between the two main Muslim groups in the country. According to the president of the SLMC, Alhaji Mallam Haroun Buhari, there was a "clash" between the two groups only over the use of the Sierra Leone Broadcasting Services (SLBS) and the invitation of Prime Minister Margai to the Muslim id ul-fitr prayers. According to one newspaper editorial, "The country cannot afford disunity in the Muslim community which represents a fair share of its population."[221]

Although Muslims disagreed over the intersection of religion and politics, Muslim organizations did take political positions. For instance, in February 1967, in the aftermath of the alleged coup against the SLPP government under Prime Minister Margai,[222] the SLMPWA issued a resolution that denounced the coup and supported the prime minister. According to the resolution,

> The Association wishes to condemn with all the power at its command the devilish plotters who had contemplated shedding the blood of innocent children, men and women and the peaceful citizens of Sierra Leone in the attempted coup d'etat. In accordance with the teachings of Islam, this Association is pledged to give its unstinted support and loyalty to the duly appointed leader of the nation and to all those in authority. This vote of confidence we today endorse with all the force at our command.[223]

Election Results

The Fula candidates in the 1967 election included Hon. Jah, who ran as an independent candidate against another independent candidate, F. S. Anthony, in Pujehun West constituency. Although a member of the SLPP, Hon. Jah did not run on the SLPP ticket because of technical problems.[224] He received 5,803 votes and Anthony received 5,965. In Tonkolili North, the Fula candidate, M. K. Yalloh (SLPP), received 1,202 votes but lost to the APC candidate, A. K. Koroma, who had 6,375 votes. In Bombali South, A. M. Jalloh (SLPP) received 4,185 votes, losing to Sembu Fornah (APC), who drew 10,618. In Port Loko North, Alhaji Amadu Wurie (SLPP) received 4,023 votes and lost to A. Khazali (APC), who received 10,549 votes.[225]

The March 1967 election was marked by a wave of political violence involving both the SLPP and APC supporters. Evidence suggests that although there was some SLPP violence against APC members, the majority of cases of political violence in the election was committed by APC members against SLPP supporters and those they perceived to be SLPP backers. Since the announcement of the election date by Prime Minister Margai, incidents of political violence by APC supporters against SLPP members occurred frequently across the country, often targeting Fula SLPP supporters. In Freetown, APC supporters made vile abusive statements publicly against SLPP politicians and threw stones at their campaign meetings. The police investigated several threats to dynamite the houses of SLPP supporters, including Fula.[226] In February many Fula retailers were forced to close their shops as rumors of fighting spread in the city.[227] As prime minister and leader of the SLPP, Sir Albert strongly condemned APC political violence across the country.[228] APC opposition leader Stevens countered that the APC eschewed violence and believed in achieving its political objectives by peaceful means.[229]

On election day, Fula mass support for the SLPP made Fula a target of harassment and violence by APC supporters. The vociferous political assaults against the Fula testify to the anti-Fula attitudes prevalent in the APC. According to one witness at the Dove-Edwin Commission of Inquiry into the 1967 election, APC members were told by their leaders to drag Fula voters from queues at polling stations across the country to prevent them from voting for the SLPP.[230] APC supporters intimidated hundreds of SLPP voters, particularly Fula. Several incidents of assault against Fula were reported at almost every police station in Freetown. To take but a few examples, at the Congo Cross Police Station, twenty cases were reported on election day. Army troops had to be called in as APC supporters attacked Fula voters at polling booths, mobbing them and dragging them off. One Fula voter, Mohamed Bah of 55 Sackville Street, was beaten almost to death. At Kroo Town Road, another Fula voter, Umaru Jalloh, had his right ear cut off. Several returning and presiding officers had to seek army protection as APC supporters threatened to beat them up. At a polling station in Kissy, Charles Wyse had to leave his station under army guard. At the polling stations at Dan Street, Jones Street, and Bombay Street, army men had to use the butts of their guns to disperse APC hooligans who raised false alarms that ballot boxes were being stolen.[231]

Moreover, in Kono a key SLPP member and prominent businessman, Alhaji Mahmoud Saccoh, a Mandingo with close ties to the Fula community, was threatened by APC supporters at his residence in Koidu for supporting and recruiting members for the SLPP. Despite the threats, Alhaji Saccoh maintained his support for the SLPP under Prime Minister Margai.[232] Also in Kono, in March 1966, Jamil was also attacked by about 150 APC thugs led by Gborie, the APC branch secretary. Jamil's house was stoned, his car damaged, and verbal abuses were rained on him by APC thugs. The APC members who were reportedly armed also attacked nearby SLPP supporters. Following the attack, the police arrested Gborie who, prior to the March incident, had traveled across Kono threatening SLPP members.[233] In November the Margai government declared a state of emergency in Kono, and the police tried to maintain law and order with round-the-clock checks for permits and by taking culprits to courts.[234] Kono was important in election campaigns because of the large presence of wealthy diamond dealers who gave generously to politicians and political parties, including both the SLPP and APC. Jamil was one of the strongest financial contributors to the SLPP and a business partner of Sir Albert.[235] Jamil sued two journalists of the APC-owned newspaper *We Yone*, Ibrahim Taqi and Samuel Hollist, for alleging that he had attempted to bribe Sir Albert, who was his personal friend. The journalists later retracted their story and apologized to the prime minister and Jamil.[236]

Postelection Situation

In the aftermath of the 1967 election, to the horror of the Fula business community and despite efforts by Fula business leaders to stop APC political violence against the Fula, it continued unabated. The chief reasons why the Fula were singled out by APC partisans centered on Fula support for the SLPP and the prejudicial belief that they had no business participating in national politics and should return to their homelands. Protection of the Fula community had little political appeal among the top leadership of the APC. But there was public pressure to end the political violence against the Fula from diverse groups, including multi-ethnic Muslims and Krio. For many Fula, their biggest weapon against APC political violence was the moral support of broad sections of the country's population.[237]

Fula agitation over mistreatment of their business class by the APC was effectively channeled into political action. Fula business elites understood the significance of popular mobilization. By mobilizing the Fula population to oppose political violence, they sought to transform concerned Fula individuals into a movement of sustained political activism in Sierra Leone. The Fula chief Alhaji Bah led the campaign to stop APC political violence against his people. This campaign energized demands for Fula citizenship rights in Sierra Leone. In addition to drawing support from Fula political activists, postelection violence against the Fula strengthened group solidarity. And this political violence was a strong catalyst for the entry into national politics by some Western-educated, Sierra Leonean–born Fula such as Alhaji Chernor Maju (Sow), Alhaji Ambassador Amadu M. B. Jalloh, Hon. Alpha B. Barrie, Alhaji Ambassador Sulaiman Tejan-Jalloh, and

Alhaji Dr. Hon. Chief Justice Abdullai B. Timbo in the post-1967 election period.[238]

Nothing better illustrates APC-led violence against the Fula than the mayhem at the Kroo Town Road residence of the Fula chief Alhaji Bah on March 20. This incident became an important politicizing moment for the Fula community as politically conservative Fula and activists alike became more politically engaged in the country. APC supporters reportedly attacked the Fula and looted their shops. They accused the Fula chief, a close personal friend of Prime Minister Margai, of stealing ballot papers and mobilizing the Fula people in support of Sir Albert and the SLPP. According to eyewitness reports, unruly APC gangs attacked the Fula chief's residence with intent to loot following an earlier commotion at the Kroo Town Road market. According to Alhaji Bah, APC partisans attacked him and his family after persistent threats. He stated that when they threatened to kill him and started breaking into his house, he grabbed his gun in panic and defended himself. Most of the victims were reported to have been hit by stray bullets from the double-barreled gun. The shooting immediately died down when the army and police officers arrived on the scene and took charge of the situation. Meanwhile, APC supporters attacked scores of other Fula traders, their wives, and children, as well as raided their shops. The Fula traders then armed themselves with matches, knives, and stones to defend themselves. The Fula chief and more than one hundred Fula, including women, alleged to have taken part in the incident were arrested and taken to the Central Police Station. Later that day, a Fula watchman employed by the Freetown Cold Storage Company was attacked by APC thugs and severely beaten. He fled as the attackers made away with his petty wares, mostly cigarettes. As police and army cordoned off a number of streets in the west of Freetown, most of the shops belonging to the Fula business class in the nation's capital were completely deserted.[239]

The police arraigned Fula chief Alhaji Bah and twenty Fula businessmen in Magistrate Court No. 1 before Principal Magistrate Mrs. Agnes Macaulay on charges of wounding and riotous conduct. The Fula were defended by several lawyers, including Solomon A. J. Pratt, Aaron Cole, and Johnny Smythe.[240] In giving evidence for the prosecution, Superintendent of Police Ponsford Benka-Coker told the court that he was on duty along Westmoreland Street when informed that there was shooting and rioting by the house of the Fula chief. On his arrival at the scene, he met some army officers near the Fula chief's residence. He further testified that a small crowd was about one hundred yards from the chief's house and that he was also informed that some Fula had taken refuge in the residence. He then ordered them to surrender to the police and repeated his order, but no one came out. He and his fellow officers then searched the house where they discovered some of the accused, some used cartridge shells, and a loaded double-barreled gun. They found more Fula in the courtyard who, together with those found in the house, were then brought out. Neighboring houses suspected of harboring the Fula were also searched, and a number of additional arrests were made as a result. Superintendent Benka-Coker further said that he collected as many witnesses as possible, and both the witnesses and the accused were sent to the Central Police Station. He said that in all, 138 Fula were arrested and that the street was littered with sticks and stones. Some of the window panes in the Fula chief's house were also damaged. Under cross-examination by defense counsel Pratt, Benka-Coker said that the crowd he saw at Kroo Town Road was small and was about one hundred yards from the Fula chief's house. He denied arresting any Fula he could lay hands on that day, but he admitted arresting those around and inside the chief's house. Benka-Coker said that some of the Fula were injured and that he therefore sent them to the Central Police Station, from where they were sent to the Connaught Hospital for treatment.[241]

Giving further evidence for the prosecution, Police Officer Cyril M. Davies told Principal Magistrate Macaulay that on March 20 he was informed that there was shooting and rioting along Kroo Town Road and that Superintendent of Police Ponsford Benka-Coker had already left with a police unit for the scene. On his arrival at the scene, Officer Davies said he met Superintendent Benka-Coker, who told him that the shooting was from the Fula chief's house. He said he went inside the house with a police unit and discovered about six empty cartridges, a belt loaded with twenty-five cartridges, and a box containing an additional twenty-five cartridges. He discovered, in the presence of the Fula chief, a double-barreled gun hanging on a wall. He removed it and showed it to the chief, who admitted that the gun belonged to him. Officer Davies further stated that he opened the gun and found two cartridges inside. Under cross-examination by the defense counsel, Officer Davies said he informed the Fula chief that he was responsible for the shooting of several people and the Fula chief admitted as much by saying that he did so to defend himself from the angry APC mob that was out to kill him. He then asked the Fula chief to accompany him to the Central Police Station. The Fula chief was granted bail following the intervention of Dr. Easmon, his personal physician and a prominent politician. At the conclusion of the trial, the Fula chief Alhaji Bah and twenty other Fula businessmen were acquitted on grounds of self-defense. The trial did not bring to an end APC violence, ethnic slurs, targeting, and harassment of Fula. Instead, they became exacerbated during APC rule under Stevens—whose party won the watershed 1967 election with thirty-two seats, defeating the SLPP with twenty-eight seats, and independents who captured six seats—which is examined in the next chapter.[242]

1. Second from left: Hon. Abdulai Bum Mikailu Jah (Fula politician, ambassador, member of Parliament, and paramount chief). To the left of Hon. Jah is President William R. Tolbert Jr. of Liberia. Source: Jayne M. Jah.

2. Left to right: Sir Banja Tejan-Sie (Fula politician, speaker of Parliament, hon. justice, and governor-general) and son Malcolm Tejan-Sie. Source: Malcolm Tejan-Sie.

3. Second from right: Alhaji Almamy Dr. Jaia Kaikai (Sidiyankei Barrie) (Fula paramount chief, politician, and businessman) with Dr. Milton A.S. Margai (fourth from right; prime minister, 1961–64) at the Lancaster House conference on Sierra Leone's independence, London, 1960. Source: Sierra Leone Public Archives.

4. Alhaji Almamy Wuroh Jalloh Timbo (Fula business elite and chief). Source: Dr. Babgaleh B. Timbo.

5. Standing: Alhaji Abu Bakarr Tejan-Jalloh (Fula business elite and politician). Sitting: Haja Isatu Tejan-Jalloh (wife of Alhaji Tejan-Jalloh; president of the Fula Women's Association). Source: Alpha O. Tejan-Jalloh.

6. Alhaji Ali Dausy Wurie (Fula politician, top business executive, and sports leader). Source: Alieu D. Wurie.

7. Alhaji Almamy Momodu Bah (Fula business elite, chief, and SLPP benefactor).
Source: Dr. M. Alpha Bah.

8. Alhaji Dr. Amadu Wurie (Fula politician and distinguished educator). Source: Miriam Conteh-Morgan.

9. Alhaji Ibrahim M. Allie (Fula business elite and APC benefactor). Source: Allie family.

10. Alhaji Almamy Abdul R. Jalloh (Fula business elite and chief). Source: Chernor Abdulai Ben Jalloh.

11. Alhaji Momodu Alpha Bah (Fula business elite and chief). Source: Alhaji Salieu Bah.

12. Members of the FYO at the residence of Alhaji Abass Allie (Fula business elite) on Jenkins Street in Freetown. Source: Chernor Abdulai Ben Jalloh.

13. Alhaji Musa Jalloh (FPU president and operations manager at the Sierra Fishing Company). Source: Jalloh family.

14. Alhaji Chernor Maju (Sowe) (Fula politician, educator, and civil servant).
Source: Alhaji Chernor Maju.

15. Alhaji Mohamed Bailor Barrie (Fula business titan and FPU president).
Source: Ijatu Barrie.

16. Standing between those seated: Almamy Agibu Jalloh (Fula business legend and chief). Source: Almamy Agibu Jalloh.

17. Alhaji Abass Allie (Fula business elite and UDP benefactor). Source: Allie family.

18. Alhaji Amadu M. B. Jalloh (Fula politician, educator, and ambassador). Source: Alhaji Amadu M. B. Jalloh.

19. Alhaji Almamy Dr. Hon. Justice Abdullai B. Timbo (Fula politician, hon. justice, and chief). Source: Alhaji Almamy Dr. Hon. Justice Abdullai B. Timbo.

20. Third from left: Alhaji Muhamadu Alieu Seray-Wurie (Fula chief, FPU president, pioneering professional accountant, and high-ranking civil servant). Source: Seray-Wurie family.

21. Alhaji Sanu Barrie (Fula business elite and FPU president). Source: Alhaji Sanu Barrie.

22. Alhaji Monorma Bah (Fula business elite and chief). Source: Algassimu M. Bah.

23. Alhaji Almamy Baba Allie (Fula business elite and chief). Source: Allie family.

24. Hon. Alpha B. Barrie (Fula politician and engineer). Source: Hon. Alpha B. Barrie.

25. Alhaji Mohamed Lamin Sidique (Fula politician, distinguished civil servant, and businessman). Source: Isatu Lamin-Sidique.

26. Alhaji Sajalieu Bah (Fula business elite and philanthropist). Source: Lamin Bah.

27. Meeting of the Fula delegation with President Joseph S. Momoh at State House. Left: Alhaji Seray-Wurie. Right: President Momoh. Source: Seray-Wurie family.

Part 2

The All People's Congress (APC) Era

3

The Siaka P. Stevens Years, 1968–85

Siaka Probyn Stevens, leader, secretary-general, and one of the founders of the APC, was born on August 24, 1905, in Moyamba. He was educated at the Albert Academy in Freetown, and on leaving school, in 1923 he joined the police, where he rose to the rank of a First Class Sergeant and Musketry Instructor by 1930. From 1931 to 1946, he worked on the construction of the DELCO railway linking the Port of Pepel with the iron ore mines at Marampa, where he also served in various capacities, including station manager and stenographer. In 1943 he helped co-found the United Mine Workers Union and served for fifteen years as the Union's first full-time secretary-general. Subsequently, he was appointed to the Protectorate Assembly to represent workers' interests. And in 1947, Stevens won a British Council scholarship to study industrial relations at Ruskin College in Oxford for nine months, and he spent the next six months attending union meetings, working in union branch offices, and visiting mines under the auspices of the British Trades Union Congress in London. Beyond that, he was secretary-general of the Sierra Leone Trades Union Congress from 1948 to 1950. Stevens also served on the Moyamba District Council for seven years.[1]

Stevens was a founding member of the SOS that merged with the PP to form the SLPP in 1951 under the leadership of Sir Milton. In addition, Stevens was elected to the Legislative Council by the Protectorate Assembly in 1951. And he was appointed the country's first minister of lands, mines, and labor in 1952. Moreover, he was the chief negotiator in the SLST–Sierra Leone diamond mining talks of 1956, which brought the country bad publicity and cost taxpayers Le3 million.[2] As minister he oversaw the successful introduction of the program that opened diamond mining to small-scale local miners. But his tenure also witnessed the rapid growth of illicit digging and smuggling and faced the worst strike in the country's history. According to

Stevens, "I sometimes think that the only real division in this country is between those who do and those who do not make money out of illicit diamonds."[3] Stevens's political career suffered a major setback in 1957 when he lost his parliamentary seat after an election petition. As noted earlier, because of disagreements with the SLPP leadership, Stevens joined Sir Albert in resigning from the SLPP and forming the PNP, where he was deputy leader under the leadership of Sir Albert from 1958 to 1960. Additionally, from 1958 to 1960, he was a member of Sierra Leone's delegation to the constitutional talks in London that resulted in the country's independence in April 1961. After refusing to sign the constitutional instruments, Stevens broke away from the then United Front to form Elections before Independence Movement (EBIM), which was later transformed into the APC in 1960.[4]

In the 1962 general election, the APC, in alliance with SLPIM in Kono, campaigned against the SLPP under the leadership of Sir Milton. In the election, the SLPP won twenty-eight seats and the APC and SLPIM twenty, plus fourteen independents. For the next five more years, Stevens led the opposition to the SLPP government. In 1964 the APC won the majority of seats in the FCC municipal elections and Stevens, as opposition leader, was elected mayor of Freetown without contesting the municipal election. The APC made history by having the first mayor without a constituency and mandate.[5] However, the SLPP government under Sir Albert prevented Stevens from running for a second term as mayor by a legal maneuver. During his tenure in the FCC, Stevens worked with the Fula councillor, Alhaji Tejan-Jalloh.[6]

After the March 17, 1967, election, which the APC led by Stevens won, Force Commander Brigadier David Lansana on March 21 declared martial law, which was the first time the military had intervened in Sierra Leone politics. In justifying the military takeover, Brigadier Lansana outlined the irregularities surrounding Governor-General Sir Lightfoot-Boston's appointment of Stevens as prime minister on that same day and further stated that "as custodian of state security, I had decided to protect the constitution and to maintain law and order. Therefore, from now on, we are operating under martial law. From now on the army is in control and will use all its power to see that the constitution is not violated."[7]

However, on March 23, Major Augustine Charles Blake in a public broadcast stated that Brigadier Lansana had been divested of his leadership and was now under protective custody. Also in protective custody were Sir Albert and Stevens. According to Major Blake, "The army and police are now in complete control and the constitution is suspended. The Governor-General Sir Henry Lightfoot-Boston is under house arrest; all political parties dissolved; National Reformation Council (NRC) formed and Lieutenant Colonel Patrick Genda to be its chairman." Major Blake further noted in the broadcast,

> I want to make this quite clear that we the senior officers did not intend to impose a military government on the people of this our beloved country. We had therefore agreed with the Force Commander that since the election results had demonstrated a clearly tribalistic attitude of the country motivated and aggravated by the propaganda campaigning of the two parties, the safest and surest solution for the benefit of our beloved country was to bring both parties to the conference table to discuss the establishment of a national government representative of every section of the country."[8]

The NRC was intended as an interim measure. Besides Lieutenant Colonel Genda, its other members included William Leigh, co-chairman and commissioner of police; Colonel Andrew T. Juxon-Smith; and Major Blake. The NRC was assisted by a National Advisory Council made up of eminent Sierra Leonean civilians.[9] The leadership of the NRC changed on March 28 when Lieutenant Colonel Juxon-Smith arrived from Britain, where he had pursued a military course, to assume the chairmanship of the NRC, replacing Lieutenant Colonel Genda.[10] According to Lieutenant Colonel Juxon-Smith, the chief aim of the NRC was to remove tribalism, bribery, corruption, and nepotism in Sierra Leone.[11]

But the NRC was itself overthrown in a bloodless coup by warrant officers on April 17, 1968. The Anti-Corruption Revolutionary Movement (ACRM) was subsequently formed by junior army officers under the leadership of Captain Patrick Conteh and Warrant Officer, 1st Class Emadu Rogers. The ACRM alleged that the NRC was corrupt and that Juxon-Smith, now a brigadier-general, had wanted to declare a republic and install himself as president. The ACRM was short-lived, replaced by the National Interim Council (NIC) with Colonel John Bangura as leader. On April 29, the NIC handed over power to Stevens as the newly appointed prime minister. Thus, Sierra Leone made history in Africa by being the first country to overthrow a military in order to hand over power to a constitutionally elected government after making history as the first African country where an opposition political party ousted an incumbent government at the polls.[12]

Immigration

With the rise to power of the APC under the leadership of Prime Minister Stevens in April 1968, immigration remained a top political priority in the country. Stevens said that the immediate task of his government was to tighten the immigration laws. He added that it was the responsibility of the government to protect Sierra Leoneans and legal foreign residents. The prime minister was addressing paramount chiefs and chiefdom councilors of the three Kissi chiefdoms and thousands of people who had assembled to welcome him and his entourage at the border town of Koindu in Kailahun. He stressed that stringent measures would soon be taken to control immigration in the country. According to Prime Minister Stevens, "No country can develop without its quota of foreigners, but if there was an influx of foreigners the indigenous people would be deprived of their rights and privileges." He said that Sir Albert's government was responsible for the influx of foreigners in the country. Replying to complaints of interference by Guineans on the Guinea–Sierra Leone border, the prime minister promised to invite President Touré to meet on the border to discuss the matter.[13]

Furthermore, in an address to the staff and students of FBC at the Ajayi Crowther Amphitheater when he visited for the first time as prime minister, Stevens stated that the main challenges facing the government, besides security, was the problem of border control and the illegal immigration.[14] Subsequently, the prime minister made clear that steps were now being taken to make appropriate amendments to Sierra Leone's immigration laws so that commonwealth citizens entering the country would first have entry visas. At the time, commonwealth citizens could enter the country at any time without entry visas.[15]

Commercial immigration involving expatriates was of great concern to the APC government because of corruption allegations against Sir Albert's administration. Responding to the findings of the Wales Commission of Inquiry into the Immigration Quota Committee during the Margai government, the APC administration put out a statement saying that those individuals entering the country on business immigration quotas will in the future come in for a predetermined period and will depart immediately thereafter. This was one way in which the Stevens government attempted to deal with the influx of expatriates into the nation.[16] One newspaper editorial recommended that as a first step, the APC government should require all commercial firms to state the numbers, ages, qualifications, posts held, and duties performed by all expatriate employees. With such information, the administration would be better informed about commercial immigration into the country.[17]

Sierra Leone had long been plagued with the problem of illegal immigrants and the previous SLPP governments had tried unsuccessfully to solve the problem. The unlawful aliens would either go into hiding or return to their homelands for a while only to return after the heat had been turned off by the authorities. A large section of the country's population had repeatedly stressed the need to tighten the country's immigration laws in the face of monthly increases in the number of immigrants. Some suggested that the state emulate Ghana's example in taking bold steps to reduce the number of undesirable aliens. For these Sierra Leoneans, the rising unemployment rate was linked to the many illegal immigrants in the country. Therefore, they called on the APC government to take firm and decisive action to solve the problem of illegal immigration.[18]

Like the previous Margai brothers, Prime Minister Stevens was faced with the challenge of forging national unity, which was shaped by immigration and threatened by tribalism. According to a leading local newspaper editorial, tribalism posed a serious threat to national unity.[19] Prime Minister Stevens spoke against tribalism and nepotism practiced by the Albert Margai regime.[20] Addressing students and nationals at the Sierra Leone High Commission three days before the opening of the Commonwealth prime ministers' conference at Malborough House in London, Stevens said there was no tribalism in his government.[21] In addition, while addressing the people of Kambia, he told them that the present government belonged to all the ethnic groups of the country and that the APC as a political party was different from the government. Stevens further said it was time for a distinct line to be drawn between the party and the government. The prime minister pointed out that public revenues emanated from all parts of the country and that the government would be run in the interest of all Sierra Leoneans. He accused some people of trying to create tribal and sectional conflicts, which would deter progress in the country.[22]

Meanwhile, in Freetown, Stevens urged all students to forget about tribalism and work together in the spirit of oneness and tolerance. He was addressing the staff and students of two secondary schools in Freetown: The Annie Walsh Memorial Secondary School and Bishop Johnson Memorial School.[23] Prime Minister Stevens said that "no one tribe would be able to rule this country." He made this statement during a speech at the ninth anniversary celebration of the National Congress of Sierra Leone Women at the Queen Elizabeth II Playing Field.

The prime minister also stated that the country was too small for tribalism and that unity should be an urgent priority. Moreover, Stevens remarked that his government was inclusive since the country did not belong to one tribe.[24]

Prime Minister Stevens's efforts to end tribalism in the country were complemented by Sierra Leoneans from diverse backgrounds. Delivering a lecture on human rights at the United States Information Services auditorium to mark the end of celebrations of the International Year of Human Rights in Sierra Leone, the acting chief justice, C. O. E. Cole, made an impassioned appeal to all political leaders in the country and worldwide to work collaboratively to end tribalism. He stressed the importance of the rule of law, which he said would enhance progress and create ideal conditions for development. In addition, he warned that there were external forces that interfered in the internal affairs of African countries. And he also stated that Sierra Leoneans should put aside all tribal squabbles and unite against these external threats and interferences.[25]

Beyond that, Principal Max Bailor, addressing Albert Academy students at the annual prize-giving ceremony, said that the task of the school was to train young men and women to live a happy and useful life in the nation. This task, he said, would be made difficult if the adult society failed to provide an atmosphere free from hate, disunity, and greed, as well as fear engendered by tribal affiliations and aspirations.[26] Moreover, Rev. Dr. S. M. Renner of the EUB King Memorial Church in Freetown called for unity and honesty among all Sierra Leoneans at a thanksgiving service organized by the Sierra Leone United Nations Association to mark the end of the UN's twenty-fourth anniversary celebrations in the country.[27] He stated,

> At no time in the history of Sierra Leone has there been such tribal divisions in our communities; tribalism rears its ugly head over all sectors of our national life. While there are signs of progress in various sectors of our national life, such progress is slow, in some cases retarded, because of tribal jealousy. We are not willing to sink our differences for the common good; every attempt to reach our goals is suspended and given a tribal flavoring.[28]

According to one Sierra Leonean, "The slow rate in our political, social and economic progress during the last two decades of the history of Sierra Leone is caused mainly by tribalist or sectional intrigues and devices."[29] A *Daily Mail* newspaper editorial suggested student exchanges, as done earlier, as one way to promote unity and destroy tribalism among the future leaders of the nation.[30]

Citizenship

Central to the public discourse about immigration was still the issue of citizenship. And the Fula remained at the heart of the political controversy over citizenship and immigration. Naturalization was a common pathway for many foreign-born Fula to achieve Sierra Leonean citizenship. But some Sierra Leoneans questioned the circumstances under which some foreigners, especially Lebanese and Indian businessmen, obtained the country's citizenship through naturalization and even asked for the revoking of such doubtful citizenships.[31] Regarding the Fula, a key question was whether they were foreigners or indigenous Sierra Leoneans. In Parliament, during question time, the APC politician Leslie P. Allen (MP for Freetown East II) asked the minister of the interior whether Fula were foreigners or indigenous Sierra Leoneans. According to the minister, "It is presumed that by indigenous Sierra Leoneans the Honourable Member means citizens of Sierra Leone. If so, the Honourable Member is referred to Section 2 of Act 14 of 1965 and Section 1 Sub-Section 3 of the constitution of Sierra Leone. These two provisions deal with citizenship."[32]

Also in Parliament, Prime Minister Stevens, in response to a question by a fellow APC member, A. Khazali (MP for Port Loko North), disclosed that Lebanese and Nigerian nationals topped the list of persons who registered as Sierra Leonean citizens since the country became independent. In all, seventy-five persons had become naturalized citizens of Sierra Leone. Lebanese nationals head the list with twenty-nine, followed by Nigerians with seventeen. The list was as follows: Under Section 2(1) of the Sierra Leone constitution (12 persons)—British 1; Italian 1; Gambian 1; South African 2; Trinidadian 2; Jamaican 2; Guyanan 2; Barbadian 1. Under Sections 3 (1), 3 (2) and 5 of Act 10 of 1962 (27 persons): British 2; Nigerian 17; Ghananaian 4; West Indian 2; New Zealander 1; Indian 1. Under Section 2 (4) of Act 12 of 1962 (24 persons): Lebanese 22; Swiss 1; Norwegian 1. Thirteen persons were naturalized after issue of certificate under Section 6 Act 10 of 1962, and their nationalities were as follows: Liberian 1; Yugoslave 1; Lebanese 7; Togolese 2; Moroccan 1; and Swiss 1.[33]

In 1972, in response to the influx of illegal immigrants, Parliament passed, without dissension, a bill titled the Non-Citizens (Registration, Immigration, and Expulsion) (Amendment No. 2) Act. The bill was proposed by Vice President and Prime Minister Koroma, who stated that although immigration officers had certain powers to deal with illegal immigration, they were constrained when some of these immigrants took illegal refuge in certain areas of the country. The Act now therefore empowered immigration officials to enter homes, shops, offices, and other buildings to carry out their investigations relating to illegal immigration and to arrest illegal immigrants who might take refuge in such buildings. Several MPs, including the SLPP parliamentarian Francis M. Minah (Pujehun South), wanted these powers extended to other law enforcement officials since immigration officers were relatively few.[34]

By 1976 the APC government was expressing grave concern over the large number of immigrants in the country, and the principal immigration officer was instructed not to allow anyone to enter the country without a valid entry visa. According to a government statement, most of the immigrants were without visas and the immigration authorities had difficulty in tracking those who had been given entry visas for visits up to three months. Airlines operating in the country were strongly warned not to allow passengers without valid entry visas to land in Sierra Leone.[35] One local newspaper editorial stated, "We share the growing public concern being expressed over the seemingly endless stream of foreigners into the country."[36] In addition, the government criticized the "influx of illegal foreign cripples, beggars, and notorious law breakers into the country."[37]

Also in 1976, Parliament passed the Sierra Leone Citizenship (Amendment) Act. According to this Act, foreign women married to Sierra Leoneans and people of Negro African descent born in Sierra Leone before April 1971 would now be able to acquire citizenship by naturalization. They would be granted certificates of naturalization after their applications had been approved by the Citizenship Committee. Those who were twenty-one and above whose parents had resided in Sierra Leone for not less than eight years would also be qualified for citizenship by naturalization. Those whose parents were not of Negro African descent but had resided in Sierra Leone for not less than fifteen years would also be qualified for citizenship.

During the debate in Parliament, Attorney-General Solomon A. J. Pratt stated that those applying for citizenship would have to fulfill the following conditions: they should have stayed in Sierra Leone for up to twenty years, speak at least one Sierra Leone language, show that they could contribute to the country's development, renounce their previous citizenship, and be of good behavior. In addition, Pratt said that naturalized citizens would not be exempted from fees under the Business Registration Act, the Non-Citizens Act (registration, immigration, and expulsion), the Payroll Tax Act, the Business Names Registration

Act, the Income Tax Act, and the Alluvial Diamond Mining Act. He explained that those who had acquired citizenship before 1971 would not be affected by the amendment. But he warned that "we are not opening the floodgates by allowing everyone to naturalize. The stringency will continue as set out in this bill." In response to criticisms from backbenchers that the new law had too many loopholes, the speaker, Justice Percy Davies, made it clear that citizenship by naturalization was a concession and not a demand. And that naturalized citizens would not hold public office, serve as diplomats, top civil servants, or serve in the armed forces. Winding up the debate, the Prime Minister and Minister of the Interior, Kamara-Taylor, who introduced the bill, pointed out that naturalized citizens would not enjoy the same rights and privileges as native-born nationals.[38]

According to a State House announcement in 1977, all persons desiring Sierra Leone citizenship by naturalization now had to obtain new application forms from the Office of the President. The announcement stated, "With the exception of all those persons who have actually obtained citizenship by naturalization since the 27th of April, 1961, all other persons desirous of obtaining Sierra Leone citizenship by naturalization, including those whose applications have been pending are now required by law to submit their application on the new forms."[39]

Moreover, in 1980 Vice President Kamara-Taylor informed Parliament that more Lebanese were granted Sierra Leonean citizenship than any other foreign nationals between 1968 and 1978. He said that a total of 135 individuals were granted Sierra Leonean citizenship. Of this number, 73 were Lebanese. The other foreign nationals who were granted Sierra Leonean citizenship included Nigerians, Afro-Lebanese, Ghanaians, West Indians, British, Togolese, and Italians. Vice President Kamara-Taylor was responding to a question from A. B. Sankoh (MP for Kambia South), who wanted to know the number of persons granted Sierra Leonean citizenship from 1968 to 1978 and their former countries of citizenship.[40]

Kono

As in previous governments, Kono was still front and center of the country's immigration challenges. Like diamond-mining areas worldwide, Kono was no exception in attracting citizens as well as both legal and illegal immigrants. An enduring feature of the diamond landscape in Kono was violence. The previous SLPP governments had taken measures to promote peace and order but with little success. The Kono problem was complicated, and there were those, including governmental officials, local authorities, as well as Sierra Leonean and foreign businesspeople, who profited from the continuing unrest relating to diamond mining.[41] In 1968 the APC government began its crackdown on illegal immigrants, with police arrests and prosecutions. In one incident, police arrested more than one hundred strangers, mainly Guinean-born Fula, for being in Kono without valid residential permits. This followed a surprise raid on the premises of the immigrants at about 3:00 am in the towns of Koidu and Sefadu in Kono. Most of those arrested were arraigned in court, convicted, and repatriated at the end of their sentences. A few were allowed to renew their residential permits to enable them stay in the diamond protection area after serving their sentences.[42] Subsequently, the commissioner of police gave a stern warning against illicit mining of diamonds in Koidu which, he said, could result in the loss of life.[43] Despite police warnings, illicit miners, many of whom were Fula, continued their activities and resisted law enforcement, resulting in violence and one death across the mining areas in Kono.[44] Consequently, about 200 illicit diamond miners including Fula, Nigerians, Gambians, Malians, and Senegalese resident in Koidu were arrested and detained by the police.[45] Overall, some 366 foreign nationals were arrested in police raids and were arraigned in court where they faced deportation to their homelands.[46]

Addressing the Lebanese community in Koidu, Minister of the Interior Gandi-Capio warned all Lebanese, and other foreign nationals as well, against interfering in the country's domestic and political affairs. He stated that the APC government was determined to give priority to the interests of the indigenous people and asked all those Lebanese who were in Kono without a residential permit to leave the District before it was too late. However, Minister Gandi Capio assured them that he had no intention of victimizing any law-abiding persons while warning them to abide by the laws of the land and to respect its people.[47]

By 1969 the Stevens administration had intensified its crackdown on foreign nationals without residential permits in Kono. In order to obtain firsthand information on the Kono problem, Prime Minister Stevens visited the District, where he addressed paramount chiefs and chiefdom councilors in Koidu. He warned all foreign nationals who were not in possession of residential permits to leave immediately, since the District was becoming overpopulated. In addition, he stated that his government had set up a joint police and army unit, AMIPOL, to enforce rigid checks on strangers. And he asked for the cooperation of the local authorities. The prime minister further remarked that the army would be increased to two battalions in order to set up border posts to monitor the long frontiers with the country's neighbors, including Guinea, thus helping to check the inflow of illegal immigrants into Sierra Leone.[48]

After Prime Minister Stevens's visit to Kono, the police and army arrested over 150 fifty strangers, the majority of whom were Fula, and brought them down to Freetown, where they were detained at the Central Police Station awaiting repatriation.[49] An additional 74 people, mostly Nigerians, Gambians, and Guineans, were arrested and detained at the Central Police Station before they were deported to their homelands. They were arrested in joint army and police operations in November. By December, an additional over forty-plus strangers who did not have residential permits were arrested and brought to Freetown and detained at the Central Police Station awaiting repatriation.[50] A *Daily Mail* newspaper editorial on the crisis in Kono pointed out that diamond mining had been a long-standing problem because of the profitability of the industry, which attracted many foreign nationals, including Fula. But Sierra Leoneans had to put their national interest first if the country were to benefit from the diamond resources in Kono.[51]

In spite of Prime Minister Stevens's warnings and the police arrests, violence related to illicit diamond mining by foreign nationals including Fula continued in Kono. An eighty-man delegation from the Kono branch of the United Mine Workers Union, led by their president, presented a petition on acts of violence in their homeland to the prime minister. And they complained that gangersterism and thuggery were becoming rampant in the diamond protected areas and that the residents were living in fear. They also reported that illicit diamond miners, about nine thousand strong consisting mostly of foreign nationals, roamed these areas and endlessly molested innocent workers and citizens. Prime Minister Stevens told the delegation that the APC government had been doing all it could to end the violence in Kono since it came to power. In addition, he stated that "it is a very dangerous situation and there are plans to remedy it." The prime minister also said that it was not his government's intention to drive out strangers in the country, "but we must control the inflow and movement of strangers in our midst." Stevens finally appealed to the workers and indigenous people in all the diamond-mining areas to cooperate with his administration in its plans to rid the areas of violence, gangsterism, and unrest.[52]

In December 1969, Prime Minister Stevens instructed the minister of housing and country planning, S. B. Kawusu Konteh, accompanied

by the Fula permanent secretary in the Ministry of the Interior, Alhaji
Sidique, to explain the government's policy on the stranger drives in
the diamond-protected areas in Kono. According to the prime minister, this was necessary because of the misunderstanding resulting from
his recent speech on immigration in Kailahun. According to Minister
Konteh, the APC government was concerned about the influx of illegal
immigrants or strangers, the breakdown of law and order, gangsterism,
and the molestation of chiefs and people in the diamond-protected
areas. And the administration was determined to curb these negative
activities and reduce the number of strangers. Konteh accused foreigners from other African countries of smuggling diamonds and made it
clear that those foreigners without valid traveling documents would
not be allowed to stay in the diamond-protected areas. The minister
stressed that even those with valid traveling documents could stay in
the diamond protected areas only if the Permit Board considered their
stay in the interest of good government. The minister further stated
that there were some foreigners who had obtained Sierra Leone passports and pretended to be Sierra Leoneans, and he appealed to the
local people to bring them to the notice of the police.[53]

Besides Prime Minister Stevens, other APC ministers spoke about the
challenges posed by illegal immigration. For example, Deputy Minister
of Defence Edward Kargbo, addressing the people of Gbanti-Kamaranka
chiefdom in Bombali, said that the APC government was about to review
the diamond-mining agreement in order to increase benefits to Sierra
Leoneans. He assured the people that the government was doing all it
could to alleviate the problem of unemployment. The deputy minister added that for the time being, the government would not be able
to provide jobs for all and advised the people to put more effort into
their farming and emphasized the need for self-help projects. He spoke
at length on government policies of development and on the problem of
controlling the influx of strangers into Sierra Leone.[54]

Meanwhile, in Parliament, S. A. Mansaray (MP for Koinadugu Central) asked Minister of the Interior Gandi-Capio how many foreigners
were evacuated from Kono and how many were subsequently granted
permission to return and reside there. According to the minister, "74
foreigners evacuated the Diamond Protection Area during the recent
drive in Kono District. After careful investigation six of them have been
permitted to return because of insufficient evidence against them. The
question of expelling more undesirable persons from Kono would be
actively pursued when a quota system for the Diamond Protection Area
now being worked out was completed."[55]

In February 1970, more than three thousand strangers, the majority of them Fula, were arrested in several diamond-mining areas in Kono in joint operations by the police and army and brought down to Freetown. By March most of these strangers were repatriated back to neighboring Guinea by armed policemen.[56] This was a continuation of the Stevens administration's efforts to rid the Kono diamond mining areas of strangers without valid permits by arresting and repatriating them to their homeland.[57] In June, following the APC government's tough security measures involving the police and army in Kono that led to the expulsion from the diamond areas of many foreigners, Prime Minister Stevens's office issued a press release stating that any foreigner who was evicted from Kono but who illegally returned to the area would be subject to instant deportation from the country.[58]

However, a former finance minister in the Stevens government, Dr. Mohamed Sorie Forna, criticized Prime Minister Stevens's Kono policies as confusing and wasteful in his letter of resignation on September 12, 1970. According to Dr. Forna,

We all know the repeated use of troops and police for eviction of the stranger elements from Kono, but as the country knows this has become a cyclical exercise. You drive them with fanfare but quietly allow them to return for reasons that you alone can understand. There is no coherence in Government policy, no definitive coordination of Government policies. Your Kono exercise cost this nation Le600,000 extra for the army and police in 1969. The bill for the latest exercise is still to come, In the meantime, most of the Lebanese expelled by this exercise have now been allowed by you to return.

Dr. Forna was subsequently expelled from the APC and later hanged on alleged treason charges in July 1975.[59]

Notwithstanding criticisms, the expulsion of strangers from the diamond areas in Kono continued throughout the Stevens administration. In February 1972, President Stevens stated that the stranger drive in Kono would continue and appealed for cooperation while addressing a delegation from the Alluvial Diamond Mining Licence Holders Union when they presented a petition to him at State House. The Union's membership included parliamentarians, paramount chiefs, elders, and leading businessmen in Kono and Kenema. According to Stevens, "There was no country without strangers but that government must know the number of such strangers in the country." He further stated that he would be sending Vice President Koroma to Kono to make arrangements regarding the stranger drive.[60] On his visit to Kono, Vice

President Koroma discussed the stranger drive and condemned the smuggling of diamonds.[61] On a subsequent visit to Kono, President Stevens said that Sierra Leone had reached a saturation point regarding the influx of strangers in the country. He pointed out that there were about two hundred thousand strangers in Kono and the government would only accommodate about twenty-five thousand to thirty thousand foreign nationals. According to the president, "This free for all immigration which is taking place is also a source of great danger to Sierra Leone both from the point of security and from the fact that it endangers our traditional friendship with neighboring countries."[62] Following Stevens' statements, more than 1,100 foreigners, many of whom were Fula, were arrested during the strangers drive by a combined army, police, and chiefdom police operations in Kono. They were sent to prison after they had been found guilty of not being in possession of Non-Citizen Registration Certificates, of entering Sierra Leone without traveling documents, and for being in the diamond-protected areas without Residential Permits.[63]

In 1977 the new minister of mines, Francis S. Conteh, addressing alluvial diamond miners and dealers, made it clear that it was the responsibility of licensed miners and dealers, including Fula, to help minimize the incidence of illicit mining and smuggling, which were detrimental to the country's economy. The minister noted that because of the limited number of licenses issued, it seemed there was still a good number of miners and dealers who had not renewed or applied for licenses. Therefore, he said that the APC government would strictly enforce the law regarding defaulters. On behalf of the miners and dealers, the Fula chief for Kono, Alhaji Momodu Alpha Bah, thanked the minister for his visit and for his cautionary statements and said that they would cooperate with the minister and his ministry.[64] In a subsequent visit to Kono, President Stevens complemented the minister's remarks by warning all unauthorized strangers in the National Diamond Mining Company's (DIMINCO) leased mining areas to leave immediately or face severe consequences. The president explained how a 145 carat gem was sold at Le500,000 in Sierra Leone, smuggled out of the country and then sold for Le2.5 million in the United States.[65]

In the 1980s, the problem of illegal foreigners continued to plague Sierra Leone.[66] In 1981 the Stevens administration issued a strong warning to undocumented strangers, stating that

contrary to the generally recognized principles regarding the movements of persons in most parts of the world, a considerable number of non–Sierra Leoneans are known to have entered and remained in this country without any valid documents or without reporting to the immigration authorities. While we welcome and appreciate the policies advocated by the Organisation of African Unity for the free movement of persons, we cannot make Sierra Leone a "free for all" area. Non–Sierra Leoneans who have found their way here will therefore do well to take immediate steps to move out or take the necessary measures to legalize their presence in Sierra Leone. For economic, security, and other reasons, no government can allow strangers to pour into its territory ad lib since a very dangerous situation could develop if such a policy is encouraged. This release should serve as a sufficient warning to all concerned so that the forces of law and order will not be blamed when they are forced to take action on the matter.[67]

The problem of undocumented strangers in Sierra Leone was not unique; rather, it was a West African problem.[68] In Ghana, for example, the government ordered that foreigners must obtain permits or leave. In addition, thousands of Nigerians were deported according to Ghanaian immigration laws. In Côte d'Ivoire, the government turned back aliens who did not have work permits although highly qualified workers were permitted into the country.[69] In January 1970, the Ghanaian leader, Dr. Kofi Busia, in an interview with the government-owned newspaper, *Daily Graphic*, defended his government's expulsion of nonresident aliens and said he owed no apology to any country for the decision. He criticized Nigerian press reports on Ghana's "compliance order" that required aliens to obtain permits by December 1969 or leave the country. This government order was also criticized in Côte d'Ivoire, whose citizens constituted a large immigrant population in Ghana. According to Dr. Busia, only forty thousand Nigerians had left since the order and more than half a million still remained in Ghana. He gave no figures of aliens from other countries that were affected by the government order. The serious economic problems, including high unemployment that Ghana faced, influenced the Busia government's immigration policy.[70]

Meanwhile, in Nigeria thousands of Ghanaian immigrants from various backgrounds, including doctors, engineers, teachers, and taxi drivers—almost half of the alien influx—were ordered out of the country in the 1980s. The Nigerian government's position for the expulsion of Ghanaians was that they were illegal aliens. But the evidence suggests that the economic success of the Ghanaian immigrants aroused envy among many Nigerians, as was the case with immigrant Fula merchants in Sierra Leone. The Ghanaian aliens were also accused of taking jobs from local Nigerians. Like Fula immigrants in Sierra Leone, many West African immigrants, including Ghanaians, crossed national boundaries in search of better-paying jobs and commercial opportunities.[71]

Fula Business Elites and Immigration

The political agenda of Fula business elites in dealing with the immigration challenge remained focused on responding to the surging Fula immigrant population and the Stevens government's crackdown on illegal Fula immigrants. Fula business leaders still formed the core of the informal interest group that crafted political responses to the Fula immigration question. The Fula experienced a deterioration in their relationship with the APC government. This is traceable to the period of APC opposition prior to the 1967 election when the Fula chief Alhaji Bah and his wealthy business supporters in the Fula community refused to provide financial support to Stevens despite his many requests and assurances that his APC party would win the 1967 election. The Fula chief also had a personal disdain for Stevens—who, unlike the Margai brothers, did not have chieftaincy pedigree—whom he described as a "gangster" who led a party of "thugs." Not only did Alhaji Bah decline several invitations by Stevens to attend APC political meetings in Freetown, he made it clear that the Fula would not support an opposition party against an incumbent government. This political strategy of supporting the party in power was tried for a period, but it led to difficulties when the NRC entered the political scene in 1967 and condemned tribalism, and especially when the APC took over and saw the Fula as staunchly SLPP.[72]

In a meeting at Parliament in 1969, Prime Minister Stevens told a Fula delegation led by Alhaji Tejan-Jalloh that "Foulah [Fula] immigration into the country is becoming unbearable. On account of this Government has decided that all Foulahs resident in the country should be registered and this will be easy for us to identify any prohibited Foulah immigrant." The prime minister cautioned the Fula to be law-abiding and to have respect for the government. Also, he informed them that his administration was seriously considering reintroducing the office of tribal headmanship or chieftaincy, which was abolished by the previous military regime. And Prime Minister Stevens called on the Fula to forget the past and work for the good of the country. In response, Alhaji Tejan-Jalloh thanked the prime minister for hosting them and for his remarks.

But he pointed out that the Fula had been molested in the country and appealed to the prime minister for security protection of the Fula.[73]

The following year, Alhaji Bah, to protect Fula interests, led a delegation of Fula elders and business elite members across the country, including Imam Alhaji Misbahu Bah, Assistant Imam Alhaji Mohamed Seray Bah, Alhaji Tejan-Jalloh, Alhaji Mohamed Bailor (M. B.) Barrie, Almamy Agibu Jalloh, Alhaji Momodu Alpha Bah, Demba Arch—successful diamond dealer—Alhaji Abdul Jalloh, and Alhaji Kaikai to meet with Prime Minister Stevens at State House to pledge their loyalty to him and the APC Party. As Fula chief, Alhaji Bah told the prime minister there were rumors that the Fula who were resident in Sierra Leone were involved in the foreign invasion of Guinea. He assured Stevens that the rumors were false and that they, as Fula, were prepared to fight for Guinea as it was a sister state of Sierra Leone. He explained that according to Fula customs, they always respected and supported their leaders and as such Fula would not subvert any government of the day. Alhaji Momodu Alpha Bah, Fula chief in Kono, informed Prime Minister Stevens of the situation in Kono and that some people were blackmailing the Fula in the District for selfish reasons.

Addressing the Fula representatives, Prime Minister Stevens called on all Fula residents in Sierra Leone to register with the government and urged them to respect the office of the prime minister. He also pointed out that the APC party was for everybody and assured the Fula that Sierra Leone was their country and that he looked forward to their continued cooperation for its development. The prime minister warned that the APC government would take strict action against anyone who tried to upset the smooth running of the government. He assured the Fula community not to be worried in the wake of the foreign invasion of Guinea but to go about their business and report to the government anyone who tried to subvert it. This meeting with Prime Minister Stevens was part of a broad political strategy involving successful Fula business leaders that would allow Prime Minister Stevens access to Fula wealth through political contributions.[74]

In dealing with the Fula community, many government officials, especially the police, did not discriminate between Sierra Leonean-born and foreign-born Fula in addressing the immigration problem facing the country. This situation compelled the prime minister's office to issue a statement stating that since the APC government's press release about the large number of non–Sierra Leoneans entering the country illegally issued on October 27, 1969, it had been observed that some people, including Policemen had taken upon themselves to molest members of the Foulah [Fula] tribe. Government wishes to make it clear that it has nothing against members of the Foulah tribe who were born in Sierra Leone and who have been resident in this country over the years (many of them for as many as 10 to 20 years). The Government concern is in respect of non–Sierra Leoneans of any tribe or nationality who have entered Sierra Leone within recent months without valid travel documents. A warning having been issued, Government will at the appropriate time take action against persons who have entered Sierra Leone illegally if those persons have not already gone out of the country by then. It must be clearly understood that anyone caught molesting non–Sierra Leoneans who have not entered Sierra Leone illegally will be dealt with severely.[75]

The mistreatment of Fula immigrants and the attacks on Fula citizenship by APC supporters led Western-educated Sierra Leonean–born male and female Fula high school students from diverse backgrounds to spearhead the founding of the Fula Youth Organization (FYO) in August 1967 in Freetown. Many of the founding members were children of Fula immigrants, but their shared experiences and interests gave them the potential to bridge the clan differences that politically separated their parents. The founding members included M. A. Jalloh, M. Alpha Bah (who later became a university professor), Alpha Bundu, Alhaji Musa Jalloh (who later became an accountant), Umaru Dumbuya, Chernor Abdulai Ben Jalloh, Umaru Jalloh, and Kadijatu Jalloh, daughter of the Fula business elite member Alhaji Abdulai Jalloh. In all the FYO had about seventy members whose priorities included protecting their fellow Fula from persecution and working with the elders, especially the Fula chief Alhaji Bah and his long-term political rival Alhaji Allie, to settle their differences. FYO meetings were held at the residence of the Sierra Leonean–born Fula business elite member Alhaji Abass Allie, son of the iconic Alhaji Momodu Allie, on Jenkins Street in Freetown. But the FYO's membership was limited to a small number of students and about thirty taxi drivers. Many Fula businessmen, particularly immigrants, who viewed the FYO with suspicion, and the few Fula university students and professionals who then saw ethnic politics as divisive did not join the organization. But this opposition to the FYO was short-lived, and eventually many Fula, especially business leaders, swung behind the Fula Progressive Union (FPU), which replaced the FYO in 1973.[76]

The FPU was the first formal Fula interest group in Sierra Leone, replacing the earlier informal Fula interest group since the Milton

Margai administration and drawing on the FYO. Western-educated Fula, many of whom were founding members of the FYO, led the effort in forming the FPU. In addition to incorporating the goals of the FYO, the FPU formulated a constitution that created a national governing council comprising well-known Fula dignitaries from the Provinces and the capital city, Freetown. In addition, a national committee with an administrative office in Freetown was also created and availed itself of a variety of methods and channels for communicating Fula interests to the state.

The FPU's membership, which numbered in the thousands, reflected the broad socioeconomic diversity of the Fula community. Because of the widespread and indiscriminate persecution of the Fula during APC rule, the FPU was more successful in its efforts to bring together the different groups among the Futa Jallon Fula and to unite them with Fula from Senegal and elsewhere. In addition, the FPU united Western-educated Sierra Leonean–born Fula and encouraged them to work with the business community, whose wealthy immigrant members had a long-standing distrust of them. During the Stevens years, the FPU presidents who were Sierra Leonean–born, included Alhaji Musa Jalloh, Alhaji Seray-Wurie, and Alhaji Bailor Barrie. In 1981 Alhaji Seray-Wurie was elected national president of the FPU and served until he was elected Fula chief in 1986. Also in 1981, a Freetown branch of the FPU was created with the election of an executive comprising Alhaji Musa Jalloh as regional president, Alhaji Abass Allie as vice president, Abdul Karim Jalloh as secretary-general, Borbor Bah as assistant secretary-general, and Bailor Timbo as financial secretary. An advisory council made up of all sub-chiefs, the Fula imam, and representatives of different sectors of the business community to be chaired by the Freetown-based Fula chief Alhaji Bah was also set up. Speakers at the inaugural meeting included the national president, Alhaji Seray-Wurie, I. M. Jalloh (MP for Freetown East III constituency), and Dr. Abass Bundu of the Commonwealth Secretariat. All the speakers stressed the importance of cooperation and unity in pursuing the goals of the FPU.[77]

With its headquarters in Freetown, the FPU opened branches at the two constituent colleges of the University of Sierra Leone: FBC and Njala University College, as well as in the Northern, Eastern, and Southern Provinces of Sierra Leone. It also founded branches in western Europe and North America. Throughout the Stevens administration, the FPU received financial contributions from its local and overseas branches, as well as from wealthy elite Fula businessmen to lobby the APC government to protect and advance Fula business interests in such areas as government contracts, diamond mining, and the livestock trade. In addition, the FPU fought for better treatment of Fula immigrants by government officials and the police.

From its founding, the FPU undertook nationwide campaigns to educate Fula about their rights and obligations as citizens and resident aliens, the purpose being to integrate immigrant and Sierra Leonean–born Fula more fully into Sierra Leonean society to prevent discrimination and harassment. Moreover, the FPU encouraged Western-educated Sierra Leonean–born Fula to seek political office to protect Fula interests and implored all Fula citizens to participate actively in the political process. The FPU informed the Fula community that increased Fula representation in Parliament would facilitate the passage of legislation to protect Fula minority rights and to promote their commercial interests. Both kinds of legislation were urgently needed because of the increasing unlawful harassment of members of the Fula business class by the police and APC politicians, especially in 1982, when President Stevens expelled a large number of Fula to Guinea, which was sharply criticized by his long-term friend President Touré.[78]

One prominent member of the FPU who took up the organization's challenge was Alhaji Chernor Maju (Sowe). Prior to becoming a politician, Alhaji Maju taught at the Methodist Boys' High School and worked at the Bank of Sierra Leone in Freetown. He joined the APC in 1973 with the express goal of winning a seat in Parliament and securing a ministerial appointment in order to address the concerns of his fellow Fula. In that year, he won the election to represent Freetown East I constituency in Parliament where he served for over a decade. In addition, Alhaji Maju served as minister of state and parliamentary special assistant under Vice President Koroma and as deputy minister of finance.[79] During this period, Alhaji Maju worked with the APC leadership, the Fula chief Alhaji Bah, his advisory group, and prominent Fula businessmen such as Alhaji Bailor Barrie and Almamy Agibu Jalloh, both members of the FPU, to resolve issues affecting the Fula, such as immigration and trade.[80] In October 1973, Alhaji Maju organized a meeting of Fula residents in Freetown at the Fula School on Guard Street that attracted hundreds of Fula. He urged the Fula community to embark on self-help projects and to support the APC government. The keynote speaker was the Guinean ambassador to Sierra Leone, Alpha Camara, who encouraged Guinean-born Fula to be fully involved in the development of Sierra Leone. He stated that Guinea and Sierra Leone were sister countries and called on the Fula to obey the laws of Sierra Leone. Other speakers were Alhaji Seray-Wurie, who was then bursar of FBC,[81] Alhaji Tejan-Jalloh who was the acting Fula chief, and Alhaji Dr. Abdullai B. Timbo, who was a lawyer and nephew of the Fula business elite member Almamy Agibu Jalloh. They all praised the APC government under President Stevens and pledged their loyalty to his administration.[82]

Alhaji Maju worked with an expanded FPU that included many members of the informal Fula interest group during the Margai administrations. These included Almamy Agibu Jalloh who, like Alhaji A. D. Wurie,[83] was a sports enthusiast supporting football teams like Kakuma; Alhaji Bailor Barrie; Demba Arch, who was a sports patron in Kenema;[84] Alhaji Sanu Barrie; and Alhaji Tejan-Jalloh. And the Allie brothers—Alhaji Ibrahim, Alhaji Baba, and Alhaji Abass—remained active in the Fula interest group. Businessmen—traditional rulers such as Alhaji Bah, Alhaji Wuroh Timbo, Alhaji Abdul Jalloh, Alhaji Momodu Alpha Bah, and Alhaji Kulio Yalloh—remained key members of the Fula lobby in Sierra Leone. Fula politicians also remained active in the FPU. Although Alhaji Amadu Wurie lost his parliamentary seat and his SLPP party was no longer in power, he was still politically active in country.[85] This was also true of Hon. Jah from Pujehun.

Outside of the business and political community, FPU members included Alhaji Sidique, who was permanent secretary in the Ministry of the Interior[86] and Alhaji Seray-Wurie, who was appointed by Prime Minister Stevens to chair the commission of inquiry into the general administration of the Sierra Leone Electricity Corporation. The commission submitted its findings to the Stevens administration in February 1971.[87] Emerging figures in the FPU included Alhaji Chernor Sie—son of the well-known Fula Imam Alhaji Ahmadu Sie—who was an employee of the Sierra Leone Ports Authority and team manager of Kakuma and Blackpool football clubs;[88] Alim Jallo-Jamboria, grandson of Almamy Jalloh-Jamboria, who was an architect and deputy professional head in the Ministry of Works;[89] Alhaji U. N. S. Jah, personnel and public relations manager at Bata Shoe Company;[90] the medical doctor, Dr. Ibrahim I. Tejan-Jalloh (son of Alhaji Tejan-Jalloh); and Ibrahim Oponjo Wurie, who was an executive with Mobil Oil, as well as team manager and technical advisor of East End Lions football club and team manager of the national team, Leone Stars.[91]

Fula Deportations

One of the challenges of the FPU was how to deal with Fula deportations relating to immigration. Since the late 1960s, thousands of illegal

Fula immigrants, mainly Guinean born, were deported by the APC government to their homeland because they violated the country's immigration laws. To take but a few examples, in July 1968 a prominent Fula diamond dealer, Mohamed W. Jalloh, was deported to his Guinea homeland for the third time following his arrest in Kono. According to police reports, Jalloh was deported during the Albert Margai administration. Shortly after the military takeover in March 1967, Jalloh returned to Sierra Leone and resumed his diamond business in Kono. Some of Jalloh's assets in Sierra Leone, which he left behind, included six Peugot taxi cabs operating in Freetown.[92] Another prominent Fula businessman deported to Guinea was Karim Barrie. According to a government report,

> Experiences have shown particularly in the Diamond Areas for nearly all Fullahs [Fula] entering Sierra Leone to claim that they are born in the Koinadugu District and the majority of such Fullahs now possess Sierra Leone Passports. A case in point is that of Barrie Karim, who is a Guinean and who was at no time a naturalized Sierra Leonean but possessed a Sierra Leone passport. During the last Operation Exodus in Kono, he together with non–Sierra Leoneans were picked up by the armed Forces and handed over to the Guinea Authorities at the border.[93]

In addition, in 1968 police arrested hundreds of Guinean-born Fula for violating immigration laws; they were prosecuted in court where they received jail sentences and deportation orders. The cases included those of Alusine Jalloh and Gibril Jalloh, who were sentenced to four weeks imprisonment and ordered to be deported after serving their jail terms by the Principal Magistrate Mrs. Agnes Macaulay. According to the prosecuting Police Sergeant I. S. Jalloh, the accused persons were arrested at Cline Town in Freetown and questioned about their traveling documents but failed to produce them and were therefore arrested and prosecuted.[94] In addition, eleven Guinean-born Fula were each sentenced to seven days imprisonment and also ordered deported after serving their jail terms by Police Magistrate D. E. M. Williams in Court No. 6. They pleaded guilty to charges of entering Sierra Leone without valid passports contrary to Non-Citizens Registration, Immigration, and Expulsion Act No. 14 of 1965. According to the prosecution, the accused were arrested at Susan's Bay in Freetown and were questioned about their traveling documents but failed to produce them. They were then arrested and prosecuted.[95] Furthermore, a Guinean-born Fula, Chernor Barrie, who entered Sierra Leone unlawfully, was sentenced to three weeks imprisonment by Principal Magistrate Mrs.

Agnes Macauley and was ordered to be deported to Guinea after serving his sentence. Barrie pleaded guilty to a charge of entering Sierra Leone without a passport or a valid traveling certificate.[96]

Police Magistrate D. E. M. Williams ordered five Guinean-born Fula to be given twelve strokes of the lash each and be deported immediately. According to the police prosecution, the accused persons were arrested along Kissy Street in Freetown, where they were questioned about their traveling documents, which they failed to produce. Before passing sentence, Magistrate Williams said the accused Fula had come to Freetown to molest people and property.[97] In Freetown Magistrate Court No. 5, Principal Magistrate Agnes Macaulay sentenced four Guinean-born Fula to two weeks imprisonment each and ordered that they be deported after their sentence on a charge of entering Sierra Leone without valid permits.[98] In Freetown Court No. 1, Principal Magistrate Donald Macaulay sentenced fifty-six Guinean Fula to one month imprisonment and ordered their deportation after serving their sentence. The Fula had pleaded guilty to charges of entering Sierra Leone without valid permits and also of being within the city for more than twenty-one days without regular employment.[99] Fula deportations continued to increase in 1969. In November alone, forty-one Guinean-born Fula were deported to their homeland. They were arrested following police raids and charged with the offense of being in Sierra Leone without valid traveling documents and were sentenced to a month's imprisonment. The court also ordered their deportation after they served their sentences.[100]

By the 1970s, Fula deportations to Guinea continued as the high number of unregistered Fula immigrants in Sierra Leone became a major concern to the Stevens government.[101] The Fula population had grown to such an extent as to cause public alarm among Sierra Leoneans. A release from the President's Office stated that it had been discovered that many non–Sierra Leoneans at present residing in Sierra Leone had failed to comply with the provisions of the Non-Citizens (Registration, Immigration, and Expulsion) Act No. 14 of 1965, which made it compulsory for all non–Sierra Leoneans to register with the Department of Immigration, which was now under the police after its removal from the prime minister's office,[102] and to renew their registration yearly.[103] A major reason for the growth of the Fula community was the political persecution of the Fula in neighboring Guinea under the government of President Touré who was of Mandingo ancestry. During President Touré's one-party rule under the socialist Parti Démocratique de Guinée (PDG), the Fula, who were the largest ethnic group and whose aristocratic traditional rulers had exercised considerable political power in the precolonial period, were underrepresented and denied political privileges.[104]

Fula immigrants also came to Sierra Leone because of their opposition to the economic ideology of President Touré. The Guinean economy denied enterprising Fula the opportunity to engage in private enterprise. The PDG nationalized banks, insurance companies, and foreign trade companies. In order to consolidate private trade in fewer hands, the PDG also imposed stringent controls on retail trade that required shop owners and merchants to deposit large sums of money in government banks in order to be entitled to engage in commerce. This law severely disrupted the distribution of goods. In 1972 Guinea withdrew from the franc zone and created its own currency, syli. The net result was the creation of a flourishing black market and the smuggling of goods to neighboring countries like Sierra Leone, where prices were higher.[105]

Addressing a visiting Fula delegation at State House in 1971, President Stevens assured the Fula community in Sierra Leone that his government was not out to victimize Fula and that the recent order on strangers was for the repatriation of all foreign nationals without valid documents. The president stressed the need for the registration of the Fula, which he said would be done as soon as the Registration Committee made its recommendations as to how this should be done. He asked the Fula to work toward the development of the country and urged them to cooperate with the government on security matters. The ten-man delegation was led by Alhaji Abdul Jalloh, Fula chief in Koinadugu, and included the Fula chief in Freetown, Alhaji Bah, and the general-secretary of the Fula community, Alhaji Tejan-Jalloh. The Fula delegation was accompanied by Minister of the Interior S. B. Kawusu-Konteh.[106]

In 1975 the Fula chief Alhaji Bah made four recommendations to the APC government on the issue of Fula immigration. They included the proposal that all the Fula resident in Sierra Leone since April 19, 1971, when the country became a republic, should be registered as Sierra Leonean citizens. According to the Republican Constitution Citizenship Act, "Every person who, having been born in Sierra Leone on the eighteenth day of April, 1971, and not the subject of any State shall on the nineteenth day of April, 1971, be deemed to be a citizen of Sierra Leone by birth, provided that his father or his grandfather was born in Sierra Leone or he is a person of negro African descent."

In meetings between the prime minister and minister of the interior, Kamara-Taylor, and Fula delegations led by Alhaji Bah, the prime minister strongly warned against the influx of strangers and reminded them of the forthcoming national registration of foreign nationals in Sierra Leone. The prime minister also outlined the duties connected with the appointment of Alhaji Bah as Fula chief in Freetown. These responsibilities included assisting in the collection of local tax, helping the police and justices of the peace in the discharge of their duties, and serving as a liaison between the Fula community and the APC government on local and national issues.[107]

The following year Alhaji Kaikai, the Fula politician who was acting as prime minister, introduced in Parliament the National Registration (Amendment) Bill, which empowered the minister of the interior to prescribe fees for the issuance of identity cards. The original Act was passed in 1974 to minimize malpractices at elections.[108] Vice President Koroma informed Parliament that the registration would be done yearly and that its purpose was to guard against strangers and protect the rights of indigenous citizens. According to the vice president, "In as much as we tolerate strangers in Sierra Leone, we will like to remind them year in and year out that they are strangers." The MP for Bombali South-East, William Conteh, said that the APC government must ensure that those who were Sierra Leonean by birth or naturalization were registered as citizens and foreigners as foreigners. The MP for Kono South, Sahr R. Fillie-Faboe, told Parliament that since the goal of the registration was to determine the population and raise additional money for development, the government should ensure that it was properly done.[109] The bill was passed, thus becoming the National Registration (Amendment) Act of 1976. Parliament subsequently passed the National Registration (Amendment) Number 2 Act, 1977.[110] After that, in 1978 the APC government established the National Registration Secretariat, with its headquarters in Freetown, to document Sierra Leoneans as well as foreign nationals living in Sierra Leone. Sierra Leonean citizens were required to pay Le1 for a registration card valid for five years and noncitizens Le5 for a card valid for two years.[111]

The 1980s witnessed a substantial return of Guinean-born Fula to their neighboring homeland partly because of improving conditions but, more importantly, as a result of the constant harassment and persecution they faced by the Stevens administration and some members of the public. A front-page commentary in one of the leading Sierra Leone newspapers titled, "Exodus of the Foulahs [Fula]," stated,

By consensus, those Foulahs who consider themselves as foreigners in our community, have decided to call it quits. Their minds are made up, and they are going. In the last few days, the exodus had been so great that by conservative estimates it would be correct to say that some 10,000 of them have already left. The congestion at the lorry parks this week was evidence enough—and that was just Freetown. But every Foulah you talk to nowadays, will tell you the same story: "we are definitely going." Those who have not yet gone, have sent their wives and families ahead of them. Those who can't afford it, are being financed by friends and brothers. The poorest man is being provided with the means of travelling back to his native Guinea. Why this exodus. They will tell you that they have come to the conclusion that they are not liked; that they are being unnecessarily molested; that every time there is trouble, they are the first to be pounced upon—in short, they are fed-up . . . we do not share the view that it will affect relations between Sierra Leone and Guinea.[112]

Subsequently, about one hundred Fula were arrested as illegal immigrants and detained at the Central Police Station in Freetown.[113] Additionally, thirty-four Fula were arrested as illegal immigrants and arraigned in Freetown Magistrate Court No. 1, where they were defended by a group of lawyers led by the Fula Alhaji Dr. Timbo and Alhaji Sulaiman Tejan-Jalloh.[114]

Sierra Leone–Guinea Relations

As during SLPP rule between 1961 and 1967, relations between Sierra Leone and neighboring Guinea continued to shape Fula immigration, business, and politics in Sierra Leone. Guinea remained the single largest source of both legal and illegal Fula immigrants, accounting for over 80 percent of the Fula immigrant population in Sierra Leone. Prior to the 1967 election, President Touré, as part of his Sierra Leone policy, switched his support from Prime Minister Margai to Stevens because the latter was now more popular than the former. It is suggested that President Touré did not make the political switch earlier because his close personal friend, President Nkrumah, had commended Sir Albert to him.[115]

The APC government had a warm relationship with the Guinean government, which was strengthened throughout the Stevens administration.[116] In 1968 Sierra Leone's minister of external affairs, L. A. M. Brewah, expressed admiration for the revolution that was going on in Guinea during a five-day visit in which he led a fifteen-man delegation. Speaking on behalf of the delegation, Brewah praised the Guinean leadership of President Touré and the warmth of the Guinean people through the friendly welcome that was accorded the Sierra Leone delegation. Brewah assured the Guinean people that he would do his utmost to strengthen the relations between the two countries. Before returning home, the delegation watched a Guinean theatrical and cultural presentation, which Brewah described as "exquisitely projecting the African personality."[117] In addition, a six-man delegation from Guinea assured the acting Fula-born Governor-General Sir Banja Tejan-Sie of their country's desire to strengthen already existing cordial relations with Sierra Leone.[118] The following year, a goodwill delegation from Guinea led by two cabinet ministers visited Sierra Leone. The visit followed a similar goodwill mission to Guinea by two Sierra Leonean ministers: Edward Kargbo, deputy minister of defense, and A. B. Janneh, deputy minister of works. The delegation, accompanied by Sierra Leone's ambassador in Guinea, Sorsoh Conteh, was received on arrival by the Guinean ambassador in Sierra Leone, Mohamed Touré. Before its departure, the Guinean delegation called on Prime Minister Stevens and Minister of External Affairs Cyril P. Foray.[119]

Also in 1969, Prime Minister Stevens and President Touré held discussions on Sierra Leone–Guinea relations and African unity when Stevens arrived in Conakry on a short visit on his way to the heads of state conference of the OAU in Ethiopia. He was accompanied by Minister of Information and Broadcasting Ibrahim Taqi and Minister of External Affairs Foray.[120] In an earlier speech, Stevens said that "there is no doubt that to build up African unity neighboring countries should come nearer each other in order to achieve this aim." In addition, he said that he would like to see closer cooperation and relationships between neighboring West African states. He added, "I will do all I can to promote unity, cooperation and closer ties between Sierra Leone and her neighbors." He pointed out that "one of the obstacles to African unity was the language barrier."[121]

Since the APC assumed power in the 1960s and throughout the 1970s, relations between the Fula community and the Stevens government were strained over neighboring Guinea. In 1969 President Touré claimed that a coup was planned against his government involving France. He was addressing an extraordinary meeting of Guinea's ruling National Revolutionary Council in a speech broadcast by Conakry Radio. President Touré also stated that he had photographic copies of letters from some leading Guineans, including Fula, to students preparing to return from abroad advising them to wait because changes were to take place soon.[122] Meanwhile, the allegation of involvement of

Sierra Leone–based Fula in subversive activities in Guinea was denied by the Fula community. In a letter to a local newspaper, key members of the Fula community wrote:

> The Foulah (Fula) Community came to Sierra Leone well over a hundred years ago in pursuance of trade. This country has always treated them well and they in turn have settled peacefully, have married and had children, and become integrated in Sierra Leone society. The Foulahs have always loyally supported the Government of this country, and have never been engaged either collectively or individually in subversive acts. As soon as the present Government was formed we were among the first to pledge our loyalty and support to Honorable Prime Minister and to members of his Cabinet. We wish to stress that as loyal citizens and settlers in this country, it has always been the avowed aim and objective of the Foulah Community to live as peaceable subjects, making our own contribution to the development of the country of our choice and now of birth in the great majority of cases. We categorically deny that the Foulah Community has been collecting any sums of money for any purpose, whether nefarious or otherwise. We wish to assure you and the public that we have the greatest love, admiration and respect for our Prime Minister, the Honorable Siaka Stevens, who may the Great Allah preserve, strengthen and guide in all his undertakings. We wish to add that the sentiments above expressed are endorsed by the entire Foulah Community in Sierra Leone, and we shall be grateful if you can publish this letter to correct the unformidable impression left in the public's mind. (This letter was signed by 35 responsible Foulahs in the Community).[123]

In April 1970, a new Guinean ambassador to Sierra Leone, Souleymane Ben Dauda Touré arrived in Freetown, replacing Mamadu Touré.[124] Welcoming the new Guinean ambassador, Prime Minister Stevens said that they would have to work together on the Fula problem. According to the prime minister, "Some people left Guinea to come to Sierra Leone without travelling documents, and this created a problem." He added that after the Fula problem had been resolved, anyone who wanted to come to Sierra Leone would do so "after all we are all brothers and sisters." Stevens further told Touré that his administration was going to see that a Fula chief was elected to help the APC government in its relationship with the Fula community in the country.[125]

The unsuccessful Portuguese invasion of Guinea to overthrow President Touré's government in November 1970 resulted in the worsening of relations between the Fula and the Stevens administration over President Touré and Guinea. The Guinean administration alleged that besides Portuguese soldiers, there were Guinean fighters, including those in exile in neighboring countries like Sierra Leone. Specifically, it was also alleged that the abortive invasion was organized by the external-based opposition, Front de libération nationale de Guinée (FLNG), and carried out by Guinean exiles, including Fula, who had Soviet-made weapons and had sailed from Sierra Leone. As a result, President Touré not only persecuted his perceived internal enemies, including Fula, but also sought to go after those in neighboring countries, including Sierra Leone. Many Fula, mostly males, left Guinea for neighboring countries like Senegal, The Gambia, and even Sierra Leone. The Fula newcomers who migrated to Sierra Leone were not just from Futa Jallon; a large number came from Conakry, the capital city.[126] Then in 1971 President Stevens arrested and deported the Fula chief Alhaji Bah, a naturalized Sierra Leonean citizen, to face imprisonment at the notorious Camp Boiro in Guinea. This was after the Guinean ambassador in Sierra Leone accused members of the Fula community led by the chief Alhaji Bah of raising money and training mercenaries to overthrow President Touré's government. According to the Guinean ambassador, "Any enemy of Guinea is also an enemy of Sierra Leone."[127] In response to the allegations, the prime minister and minister of the interior, Kamara-Taylor, sent a letter to President Stevens stating that the accusations were "quite alarming" and may have "serious repercussions unless immediate and spectacular action is taken on the matter." He recommended "the immediate suspension of Alhaji Bah from the office of Fullah [Fula] Tribal Headman until further notice."[128] As a result, Stevens created a committee headed by Kamara-Taylor to investigate the charges. The committee uncovered evidence that exonerated the Fula chief of the allegations, but the president disregarded the evidence. This was one of the clearest examples of President Stevens's persecution of the Fula to appease his close personal friend and mentor, President Touré. Not only did relations between Sierra Leone and Guinea involve a mutual defense pact, but President Stevens's personal staff of body guards comprised Guinean soldiers, and a sizable contingent of them protected his residence at Brookfields in the west end of Freetown in the aftermath of the attempted coup of 1971 against the Stevens government.[129]

After the arrest and deportation of the Fula chief Alhaji Bah to Guinea, the Stevens administration appointed Alhaji Tejan-Jalloh as acting Fula chief for the Western Area. A letter from the ministry of the interior stated that his appointment took effect from April 24, 1972. As discussed previously, Alhaji Tejan-Jalloh had served the FCC as a councilor for ten years, from 1957 to 1967. He was secretary of the Fula mosque and registrar of marriages and divorce of the mosque since 1948. He was also treasurer of the SLMPWA, treasurer of the Fula jama'at (Muslim community), treasurer of the SLMB, and treasurer of the FBC Mosque Fund. In addition, Alhaji Tejan-Jalloh was a member of the Sierra Leone Blind Welfare Association, a JP and MBE.[130] Despite the strained relations between the APC government and the Fula community, in 1973 the prominent Fula politician Alhaji Maju, deputy minister and special assistant in the Office of the Vice President,[131] speaking to over one thousand Fula at the formal launching of the Guard Street Self-help School Project, talked of the brotherly ties between Sierra Leone and Guinea that were strengthened by Presidents Stevens and Touré. Alhaji Maju called on the Fula to cooperate with the Stevens administration to promote development, especially through self-help projects.[132]

The Fula chief Alhaji Bah was not the only Fula to suffer at the hands of President Touré. In Guinea, President Touré's Fula political opponents, who included businessmen, professionals, and intellectuals, were arrested, detained, and tortured for alleged involvement in the Fifth Column Plot in 1976. Some, like Barry Diawadou, who served as a government minister and Guinea's ambassador to Egypt before opposing President Touré, as well as Diallo Telli, who was chosen the first secretary-general of the OAU in 1963, died after being tortured at Camp Boiro prison. A few of the Fula detainees, such as Barry Ibrahima, better known as Barry III, a strong opponent of the PDG led by President Touré, were publicly hanged. They were all characterized as counterrevolutionaries and accused of either collaborating with the Portuguese invaders, corruption, subversive activities, or ethnic favoritism.[133] Guinea's ambassador in Sierra Leone, Alpha Camara defended his country's human rights record when questioned by the Sierra Leone press.[134]

The evidence suggests that in persecuting the Fula chief Alhaji Bah, President Stevens was returning earlier political favors by President Touré. After the APC election victory in March 1967, President Stevens and his top leadership were forced into exile in Guinea because of the two military coups by Brigadier David Lansana and the NRC. Although the NRC released Sir Albert and Stevens, both of whom had been detained at Pademba Road Prison, and promised an early restoration to civilian rule, it banned all political activities and any reference to either the SLPP or APC. Not only did President Touré provide asylum to the APC leadership, he allowed them to organize a military group of Sierra Leoneans with the goal of restoring Stevens to power. Some of the members were high-ranking military officers such as Colonel John Bangura. The armed group was trained with the help of the Guinean army, but before it could implement its plan, the NRC was overthrown by noncommissioned officers.[135]

The imprisonment of Alhaji Bah in Guinea resulted in the mobilization of broad sections of the Fula community led by elite business leaders, including Almamy Agibu Jalloh, Alhaji Tejan-Jalloh, and Alhaji Bailor Barrie. They worked collaboratively with Alhaji Maju and Alhaji Seray-Wurie, who as a senior member of the APC played a critical role in lobbying President Stevens and key members of the APC government, like Vice President Koroma, whose mother, as noted earlier, was Fula, to secure the release of the Fula chief in 1975. After Alhaji Bah's release from prison, representatives of the Fula community, including Alhaji Bailor Barrie, Almamy Agibu Jalloh, Alhaji Sidique, Alhaji Maju, and Alhaji Abdul Jalloh,[136] along with Alhaji Seray-Wurie, presented the Fula chief to President Stevens at State House, and they commended the role of President Stevens and his government in securing the release of Alhaji Bah. The Fula spokesman, Alhaji Sidique, stated that they hoped President Stevens would continue to find Alhaji Bah a "true and trusted citizen."[137] As a result, the Stevens administration announced that Alhaji Bah had been reinstated as Fula chief with immediate effect.[138]

The following year, the first secretary of the Guinea Embassy in Sierra Leone, Abdulai Bangura appealed to Guineans, especially Fula, to return to their Guinean homeland and contribute toward the economic development of their country. He stated that there were more than thirty thousand Fula in Freetown alone and called on them to return to Guinea and embark on agriculture, which was the country's economic priority. He said some Guineans in Sierra Leone had been tarnishing the image of their country, especially those involved in robbery, burglary, housebreaking, and prostitution. He called on them to be law-abiding and to respect the government, since Guinea and Sierra Leone were two sister states. The first secretary made these statements on a tour of the Southern and Eastern Provinces in Sierra Leone to acquaint Guinean nationals about recent developments in their homeland.[139] Furthermore, in 1977 the Guinean ambassador to Sierra Leone, Alpha Camara, repeated his appeal to Guineans, especially Fula, resident in Sierra Leone to take advantage of President Touré's offer of unconditional amnesty and return home to help develop their homeland. Ambassador Camara was addressing Guineans at the Railway Union Hall in Freetown.[140]

The Fula community—particularly the business class—greatly welcomed the decision of President Touré to initiate political liberalization in Guinea in 1978. With that, there was an easing of hostility between the two political adversaries as well as an improvement in the relationship between President Stevens and the Fula in Sierra Leone. President Touré also appointed a new Guinean ambassador to Sierra Leone, Sekou Konate, to better improve relations between the two countries. Ambassador Konate encouraged Guinean nationals in Sierra Leone, the majority of whom were Fula, to be law-abiding and reiterated President Touré's call for their return to their homeland to contribute to national development.[141] Indeed, thousands of Fula returned to Guinea. One Guinean-born Fula trader in Freetown summed up the sentiments of the Fula returnees thus:

> Before now all trading (in Guinea) was handled by the government and there was not much scope for private businessmen and traders. Some of us who are traders had to migrate to a number of West African countries—Senegal, Ivory Coast, and Sierra Leone. But the historic broadcast of President Touré opening the door to free trade has stimulated many of us to return home. Apart from that, all our relatives are over there, and we can never really feel at home without them. Some Fula returnees further blamed the APC government's high business tax on their shops, unlike Guinea where they only had to register their businesses.[142]

The ties between Sierra Leone and Guinea were further strengthened when in 1979 President Touré paid a four-day visit to Sierra Leone, where he discussed a broad range of issues with the Stevens administration,[143] including immigration, trade, and the MRU, which was started between Sierra Leone and Liberia in October 1973.[144] It was President Stevens's recommendation that led to the appointment of Alhaji Seray-Wurie as deputy secretary-general of the Mano River Union (MRU) from 1974 until 1977, when he retired for medical reasons.[145] During President Touré's visit, he met with thousands of Guinean nationals, mainly Fula, living in Sierra Leone.[146] After the visit, the Sierra Leone–Guinea Ministerial Commission met in Freetown and decided to reestablish the radio-telephone links between Freetown and Conakry. The commission also explored how to effectively implement the agreements between the two countries in the areas of trade payments, justice, education, agriculture, public health, transport, telecommunications, and public works.[147]

President Stevens subsequently paid a three-day state visit to Guinea.[148] On his return home, he informed the Sierra Leonean people that Guinea would now join the MRU, which Guinea did join in 1980, seven years after it was established by Sierra Leone and Liberia.[149] As OAU chairman, President Stevens paid a subsequent visit to Guinea,[150] and in 1983 he attended a meeting of the Economic Community of West African States (ECOWAS), which was established in May 1975,[151] in Guinea that discussed regional trade.[152] In welcoming the first female Guinean ambassador to Sierra Leone, Tiguidanke Diakhaby, President Stevens said that his administration would continue to work closely with the Guinean government within the MRU and ECOWAS with emphasis on economic cooperation and development.[153] Collectively, these actions, as well as the abolishing of traveling visas; building of bridges;[154] the introduction of bus, airplane, and telephone services between Sierra Leone and Guinea;[155] bilateral sporting activities;[156] student exchange programs between Sierra Leone and Guinea;[157] the activities of the Sierra Leone–Guinea Friendship Society;[158] the Guinea Union in Sierra Leone;[159] and the efforts of APC politicians like Edward Kargbo who represented Bombali North constituency that shared a border with Guinea, facilitated the cross-border movement of the Fula and helped to promote commerce between the two neighboring countries.[160]

Fula Business Elites and the Politics of Business

As discussed in previous chapters, Fula business elites participated in Sierra Leone politics primarily to advance their business interests in key economic sectors such as the retail, livestock, transport, and diamond trades.[161] Issues like residential permits, diamond-mining licenses, stranger drives, and security were of great concern to Fula diamond dealers.[162] Alhaji Bailor Barrie, for example, both as an elite entrepreneur and president of the FPU, played a key role in lobbying the Stevens administration on matters relating to Fula participation in the diamond business. Fula retailers had similar concerns like stranger drives and security, especially during national crises like the student demonstrations in 1977, when they suffered major business losses.[163] As a group, the Fula remained an integral part of the country's economy during the Stevens administration. Unlike trading groups such as the Indians who had a formal business lobby, the Indian Mercantile Association, the Fula did not.[164] The issue of foreign, including Fula, involvement in the Sierra Leone economy remained very politically sensitive and a frequent topic of national debates.[165]

Public discussions centered on economic challenges such as smuggling faced by the APC government.[166] A Fula merchant, for example, found with a large consignment of contraband cigarettes smuggled into the country, received a large fine of Le4,000.[167] Additionally, six Fula traders arrested with large quantities of smuggled cigarettes were each made to pay a fine of Le2,000.[168] In addition, the Stevens government had to navigate problems like increasing government expenditures,[169] tax evasion,[170] profiteering,[171] hoarding of essential commodities like rice,[172] soaring imports,[173] declining exports,[174] foreign exchange shortages,[175] the high cost of living,[176] corruption,[177] high unemployment,[178] large foreign debts,[179] and foreign exploitation and domination of the economy.[180] These difficulties were well-stated in speeches and policy statements on the state of the economy during the annual dinner of the Chamber of Commerce and by the governor of the Bank of Sierra Leone at the Bank's annual banquet, as well as by the minister of finance and minister of development and economic planning.[181] In the early 1970s, the APC government set up the Barthes-Wilson Commission of Inquiry into rising costs of essential commodities in the country.[182] Furthermore, President Stevens periodically announced large salary increases for government workers because of the high cost of living in the country.[183] The president also visited shops in Freetown to find out the prices of consumer goods.[184] The president of the Sierra Leone Employers Federation, David Fraser, and the Chamber urged the Stevens government to take urgent measures to check the rising cost of living in the country.[185]

Earlier as prime minister, Stevens informed the public that "the Government will stand firmly against any kind of commercial activities which will force Sierra Leonean businessmen into economic slavery." He made this statement while addressing foreign and indigenous businessmen at the seventh annual dinner of the Chamber at the Paramount Hotel in Freetown. In addition, the prime minister stated that the APC government was determined to see that the interests of its citizens were placed before all outsiders, though it was not the intention of the government to wage a commercial war on all and sundry. Stevens also said that Sierra Leone seemed to have become an economic free for all, and if this is not dealt with firmly, it would develop into a political free for all. The president of the Chamber, H. E. B. John, who was also the resident director of the Diamond Corporation of West Africa Limited (DICORWAF), observed in his address that no government could command the respect of the citizens of any country if it failed to protect the vital commercial interests of those citizens.[186] Furthermore, in an interview with a German newspaper, Prime Minister Stevens said, "Eighty percent of Sierra Leone's economy is not in our hands at this time. What use is Parliament and Ministers if we cannot determine the economy yourselves."[187]

Retail Trade

During Stevens's rule retail trade was still a key sector of the Sierra Leone economy; it commanded a lot of attention from both Fula business leaders and the APC government. The major challenge for the Fula business elites remained how to protect the large Fula immigrant retailers against exploitation and harassment by government officials. Like the previous Margai administration, a major priority of the Stevens government was to increase Sierra Leonean participation in the country's commerce, particularly in the retail sector. In 1968 the APC government warned foreign nationals against participation in retail trade in a statement issued by the Ministry of Trade and Industry. According to the statement, the government was reviewing its policy on retail trade, including supermarkets and operation of transport by non–Sierra Leoneans. Non-nationals embarking on these enterprises before a policy decision was announced were advised that they would be doing so at their own risk.[188]

The following year, Parliament passed the Non-Citizens (Trade and Business) Act, which came into effect in 1970, to ensure greater participation by Sierra Leoneans in the country's trade and business activities. According to Minister of Trade and Industry D. F. Shears, the Act was a direct response to citizens' demands to have greater participation in the national economy. And he hoped that Sierra Leoneans would avail themselves of the opportunities created by the Act and increase their trading and business activities in the country. The Act, however, was not intended to appropriate businesses operating in Sierra Leone. To ensure and guarantee the continuance of trade, the Act provided that the 51 percent share capital that must be owned by Sierra Leoneans might be paid out of dividends. The APC government also recognized that presently Sierra Leoneans might be unable to provide the management skills necessary for the successful operation of businesses. And the Act did not make any restrictive prohibitions on the management or direction of any companies. However, the government would take steps to see that the 51 percent ownership was real and could be proved. The Act gave expatriate businesses six months within which to comply with the provisions of the Act, which also stated that from August 20 there could be no new branches or new businesses of a retail nature without approval of the minister in writing. Minister Shears said the APC government recognized the situation where an expatriate company would be willing to make 51 percent of its share capital available, but where Sierra Leoneans would be unable to accept the offer. In addition, the minister said that the government was considering that in such cases the National Development Bank (NDB) would be able to act as broker and that the government's decision to found an insurance company was directed toward the same goal and that once in operation, all these sources could be able to provide funds for Sierra Leonean participation in trade and business.[189]

However, President John of the Chamber expressed reservations about the Act, which he considered restrictive, and so he called for amendments.[190] Despite the Act, in 1975 the new president of the Chamber, Tommy Hope, stated that the average Sierra Leonean businessperson was very frustrated that the Act was not strictly enforced to allow his or her participation and growth in the country's economy. And he warned against unscrupulous and selfish trading by foreign nationals. President Hope made these statements in a speech, which dealt with most aspects of the country's economy, at the fourteenth annual dinner of the Chamber at the Cape Sierra Leone Hotel in Freetown that was attended by cabinet ministers, diplomats, MPs, civil servants, and top business executives.[191]

In response to the Non-Citizens (Trade and Business) Act of 1969, Fula business leaders like Almamy Agibu Jalloh continued earlier strategies, including how to work with government officials such as price inspectors and trade inspectors attached to the Ministry of Trade and Industry and the Price Control Board.[192] A large number of Fula retailers faced constant harassment, targeting, extortion, and loss of business profits because government officials like trade inspectors demanded bribes. As a result, many traders were arrested and prosecuted for crimes such as profiteering and bribery.[193] In 1971 Minister of Trade and Industry Bangali Mansaray reprimanded trade inspectors after receiving reports that some of them used the privileges of their office to make money and also help to swell prices of goods to the detriment of the nation and consumers. The minister explained that the intention of the Act was to encourage Sierra Leoneans to participate in the country's commerce and that trade inspectors had an important role to play in the implementation of the Act. He pointed out that any attempt to make money out of the Act would not only kill its spirit but would encourage foreign traders to continue their exploitation of the country. Earlier, a newspaper editorial had accused trade inspectors of using the operations of the Act as a means of extortion and blackmail.[194] In 1973 new Minister of Trade and Industry F. M. Minah also warned trade inspectors to desist from malpractices after receiving several complaints of molestation from traders, including Fula.[195] And in April 1974, the acting president, Koroma, gave a strong warning to trade inspectors because of reported corruption at a meeting at State House.[196]

Another strategy of Fula business elites was to encourage Fula retailers to increase their membership in the Sierra Leone Indigenous Petty Traders Association (SLIPTA) and to join the newly formed Sierra Leone Indigenous Commercial Traders Union (SLICTU), which was nonpolitical and opened to all native commercial traders. The Union's aims included bringing together all indigenous Sierra Leone retail traders for the purpose of strengthening retail trade and its benefits to Sierra Leoneans; to stop foreigners from petty retail trading including produce and transport operation; and to strengthen and promote the economy of Sierra Leone by encouraging indigenous Sierra Leoneans to take active part in commerce. The Union also would encourage and guide traders and businessmen, promote understanding between the members and secure maximum cooperation among them. In addition, the Union would also raise business leadership standards and promote a sense of self-respect among individual traders. The Union had already established branches in the Provinces, including Sefadu, Kenema, Bo, Moyamba, Lunsar, and Makeni.[197]

The secretary-general of the SLPTA was the Sierra Leonean–born Fula Mahmoud T. Jalloh, who played a critical role in mobilizing petty traders and ensuring that foreign nationals did not participate in the retail trade of the country. To achieve its central goal of banning all foreigners from participating in petty and retail trades, the SLPTA submitted resolutions to the Stevens administration and the FCC, staged boycotts, and organized protests and demonstrations. In October 1969, the SLPTA submitted two resolutions to Prime Minister Stevens and the chairman, Committee of Management, FCC, Daniel T. Akibo Betts asking that immediate action be taken to stop foreigners from petty trading. In their ten-point petition to the prime minister, the traders said that all Indians and Lebanese should be asked to remove all foreigners trading outside their shops to make room for Sierra Leoneans. The Association accused Indians, Lebanese, and other foreign businesses of giving employment to foreigners while Sierra Leoneans were unemployed. In an eight-point resolution to the FCC's chairman, the

Association accused the FCC and its security men of favoritism in the allocation of trading spaces in the capital city.[198]

The SLPTA followed these resolutions in November with a massive boycott and demonstration in protest against foreign petty traders in Freetown. Two people were arrested and detained by the police as a result of the demonstration. Two Fula—a driver and a laborer—were attacked and manhandled by some people who claimed to be members of the SLPTA, which called the boycott followed by the demonstration. At Garrison Street in Freetown, a Fula, Alpha Jalloh, was beaten and seriously injured by the demonstrators. Some members and supporters of the Association danced through the main streets of Freetown singing war songs demanding that all Fula should leave the country. Market women and petty traders abandoned their stalls and wares and held a meeting at the Queen Elizabeth II Playing Field. Two people, including a top stalwart of the APC, were asked out of the meeting. Addressing the meeting, the secretary-general of the Association, Jalloh, said that the APC government should ask all foreign petty traders, including Nigerians, Ghanaians, Gambians, and Fula to leave the country and make room for Sierra Leonean petty traders. The traders carried placards that read, "Ban all foreign petty traders," "Ban all immigrants from petty trading." In a subsequent meeting with representatives of the SLPTA, Prime Minister Stevens reiterated his government's call that foreigners in Sierra Leone without valid traveling documents should leave, including Fula who were not of Sierra Leonean origin. He said that it would be improper for some people to take the law into their own hands and demand that all Fula should leave the country or be molested. Stevens said that his administration had taken action to rid the country of illegal immigrants and if those concerned did not heed the government's advice, action would be taken against them in due course. He asked the traders to be patient and not to take the law into their own hands.[199]

Prime Minister Stevens also met representatives of the Fula community in Freetown on the same day after meeting with members of the SLPTA. He asked the Fula elders to consider the appointment of leaders in Freetown and other parts of the country. Among other things, Stevens told the Fula that it was important that they appoint chiefs now in view of the influx of Fula into Sierra Leone and the APC government's steps to check this problem, and also to harmonize relations between Fula resident in Sierra Leone and the government, as well as the Sierra Leonean people. Prime Minister Stevens further told the Fula delegation that only illegal immigrants without valid traveling documents were being asked to leave the country. On behalf of the Fula community, Alhaji Tejan-Jalloh, who served with Prime Minister Stevens in the FCC during the SLPP administration, assured him of the cooperation of the Fula and pledged their support to the APC government.[200]

Some Sierra Leoneans were critical of the tactics of the SLPTA. A *Daily Mail* newspaper editorial captured such sentiments thus:

The Sierra Leone Petty Traders Association yesterday issued a very interesting statement disassociating itself from certain placards and posters displayed at the Association's recent demonstration against foreign petty traders. Notwithstanding the statement, we still think that the Association cannot exonerate itself from the distasteful incidents on that day. We ask: Was there any need for the demonstration? The Association called on Government to ban foreigners from petty trade. Government responding by asking all foreigners without valid traveling documents to leave in their own interest. Quite a number of the immigrants without valid documents were arrested and later deported. The Association was not satisfied. It wanted Government to drive all foreigners with or without valid documents. The General Secretary of the Association Mahmoud T. Jalloh should know better than everyone else that to ban all foreigners engaged in petty trade is to call for trouble. We have had foreigners who have been in petty trade for many years. Many of them have married Sierra Leoneans and have made Sierra Leone their home. Mr. Jalloh should know that. If the Association continues its demands for the expulsion of foreigners, Government should start off by asking Mr. Jalloh a few questions about himself. We are not interested in the Association's claim to be non-political. We are interested in the fact that because of the demonstration by the Association a lot of peaceful people were mobbed and wounded. While we are prepared to support a call and have already for a halt to the influx of strangers, we are certainly not prepared to see a handful of people disrupt the peace and cause chaos in this country. We trust that Mr. Jalloh and his Association will be told by the authorities that no one is above the laws of this country.[201]

A Sierra Leonean–born petty trader wrote this to one of the local newspapers:

Indigenous Sierra Leone petty traders beware! beware! beware of the outcome of your unreasonable demands, chief of which is that Government should ask all foreigners engaged in petty trading to leave the country and make room for you. Stop and think. Think twice before you take the irrevocable step, and listen to reason my dear compatriots. There is no need for all this hue and cry. I am a petty trader myself but I do not endorse your actions. Do not be so ungrateful. These people a long,

long time ago took the initiative to start their little businesses which are only now yielding fruits. They encountered their teething problems and now that they have established themselves and have become a part of our community you want them to leave. . . . By all means, call on Government to restrict the number of people who wish to engage in this type of trade. But don't be so unreasonable as to demand that they all leave. It is all well and good to make demands, but can you guarantee that you will equal their efforts and more. Sierra Leoneans are very lazy. We want to achieve everything and yet do not want to work towards achieving them. We just want to sit back and find everything ready made. Our attitudes to various things are wrong. We are so dishonest and have often times demonstrated that there is nothing like sincerity of purpose amongst us. So I ask the question, can the indigenous petty traders assure us the members of the public that they will render the effective services rendered in the past by the Foulahs (Fula) especially? The Foulahs have been most useful in this our little community. They make a lot of sacrifice to please us. I have never in all my years in Sierra Leone known of any indigenous petty trader who has kept his or her business open till the early hours of the morning to satisfy our needs. Perhaps the officials of the Petty Traders Association in demanding that foreigners leave have under consideration the opening of all night pharmacies, cigarette kiosks, and all. There is no doubt that Government's statements have been misinterpreted by the petty traders. Government's statement was to the effect that foreigners and all Foulahs who are not of Sierra Leone origin at present in Sierra Leone without valid travelling documents should in their own interest leave the country. The incidents which occurred in the Freetown area last Thursday after the mass meeting at the Queen Elizabeth II Playing Field were uncalled for. The action of some of the traders were irresponsible and they must realize that taking the law into their own hands would only lead to more discontent and cause bloodshed.[202]

The secretary-general of the SLPTA, Jalloh, at a general meeting held at the Queen Elizabeth II Playing Field repeated an earlier appeal to the Stevens administration that Sierra Leone's borders with neighboring countries, especially Guinea, be tightened in order to check the inflow of foreigners into the country. He once again called on the APC government to ban all foreigners from petty retail trade and the running of cookery shops in the country. He blamed the high cost of living on the large number of foreigners in the country. He further stated that foreigners should give way to "our jobless brothers and sisters." Secretary-General Jalloh accused the FCC security guards of accepting bribes from foreigners and harassment of indigenous traders. He called on the security guards to desist from corrupt practices and not to allow foreign traders to occupy market stalls.[203] Furthermore, the

SLPTA called on the Management Committee of the FCC to withdraw all hawkers and cookery licenses issued to foreigners in 1970.[204] In addition, the SLPTA renewed its protest against foreign petty traders at a protest meeting at the Queen Elizabeth II Playing field. Their complaints included that Lebanese and Indian businessmen should stop employing foreigners. And that Lebanese and Indian businessmen should remove foreign petty traders in front of their shops.[205]

Responding to persistent complaints by the SLPTA, Shears, the minister of trade and industry, issued a letter to about one hundred owners or occupiers of shops and stores in about fourteen main streets in Freetown asking that they give one month's notice to noncitizen petty traders who carried petty trading in front of their businesses to cease operations. The businesses included G. B. Ollivant, J. T. Chanrai, M. Dialdas, and Chellerams. The streets included Westmoreland Street (now Siaka Stevens Street), Oxford Street (now Lightfoot Boston Street), Rawdon Street, Kissy Street (now Sani Abacha Street), Fourah Bay Road, and Sackville Street. According to the minister, "In consultation with the Sierra Leone Petty Traders Association, suitable arrangements will be made for Sierra Leoneans to replace the non-citizens. It is of course understood that the Sierra Leoneans would have to pay the same level of rent, if any, you now receive from the non-citizens."[206]

In a statement from Secretary-General Jalloh, the Association and the government had not asked the noncitizens petty traders to leave the country. The statement emphasized that foreign petty traders from other countries, particularly Nigeria, Ghana, Guinea, and the Gambia may continue to do their business but on a wholesale basis only. Jalloh assured non–Sierra Leone traders that their goods would be bought by Sierra Leoneans or by the Association.[207] Addressing members of the SLPTA after notices served on noncitizens petty traders to quit shop fronts had expired, Jalloh warned members not to molest or attack any noncitizen petty traders found trading in shop fronts. According to Jalloh, "Anybody caught molesting or attacking the non-citizen petty traders will be arrested, because we have no right to use force on any strangers."[208]

In addition to the SLPTA, a delegation from the SLICTU presented a strongly worded petition to Minister Shears calling for a ban on certain businesses by foreigners. Copies of the petition were sent to the prime minister, the minister of finance, the minister of agriculture and natural resources, the minister of development, the minister of transport and communications, and the minister of lands, mines, and labor. The Union's demands included that the APC government stop all foreign traders from buying, selling, and exporting produce in the country; that all foreigners should be barred from participating in the diamond business; that all foreigners should be barred from operating commercial transport; that all foreigners should be banned from retail trade and that the immigration laws should be tightened. In a brief reply, the trade minister asked for time to act on the petition and suggested a merger between the Union and the SLPTA. Originally, the SLICTU existed and the SLPTA emerged following a split in the Union. According to the trade minister, the APC government was keen to see the country's trade in the hands of indigenous Sierra Leoneans, but warned that politics should be dissociated from business.[209]

Subsequently, a four-man SLPTA delegation led by Secretary-General Jalloh met with Minister Shears to inform him that foreign petty traders had defied his orders to quit shop fronts of Lebanese and Indian businesses. In reply, the minister said that he would discuss with Prime Minister Stevens the question of repatriation of non–Sierra Leoneans without gainful employment as was done in Ghana. He also pointed out that he would recommend to the prime minister the deportation of non–Sierra Leoneans who defied the laws of the country. According to the minister, highway robbery, burglary, and various crimes had been on the increase because of the influx of irresponsible foreigners into the country.[210]

With the appointment of a new minister of trade and industry, Bangali Mansaray, a delegation of SLICTU led by the secretary-general, Abdul K. Kamara, met with the minister and reminded him of an earlier petition sent to his predecessor calling on the APC government to ban foreigners from participating in certain businesses in Sierra Leone. The minister said that he would study the petition and later discuss it with the SLICTU. He also told the delegation that much as the government was doing all it could to help indigenous Sierra Leonean businessmen, they must be prepared to help themselves and the country. He added that they must be prepared to "shoulder the responsibilities now shouldered by foreign businessmen when they are stopped from trading in certain commodities." The trade and industry minister also told the delegation that they must be prepared to pay their direct and indirect taxes regularly as foreign businessmen did since the government derived its revenues from various sources, including taxes paid by businessmen.[211] The minister later signed a notice that taking effect from September 1 1970, foreign traders in Sierra Leone would cease to participate in the retail trade of thirty-eight goods, including sugar and salt. A leading local newspaper commented that

Final effect has given to the Non-Citizen Trade and Business Act, and thirty-eight items have been put on a list which proscribes non-citizens trading in them from September 1. . . . Sierra Leoneans need to be reminded . . . in the grand design for a better and happier life there are bound to be individual hardships. This can be seen in a simple matter as a man buying a tin of Sardines. He may now, hungry as he may be, find himself unable to buy a tin from the Foulah [Fula] trader around his corner. The Foulah himself may find that his origin may be tested. Is he indigenous or foreign?[212]

Some Sierra Leoneans publicly disagreed with the SLPTA and the SLICTU on the issue of foreign traders. In a letter to the editor of a major local newspaper, one Sierra Leonean wrote,

I have been following with keen interest the big fuss being made by our local petty traders about the participation of their foreign counterparts in retail trade. They have often molested and beaten up foreign petty traders to discourage them from continuing their business in Sierra Leone. If all these foreign traders, particularly the Nigerians and the Fullahs [Fula] were to quit our country in disgust, are our local people prepared and able to take up petty trading with the same enthusiasm? Sometime ago the Fullahs in their little shops were molested and beaten up by some irresponsible people who were urging that they (the Fullahs) be ordered to close down and leave the country. But these people soon realized that the Fullahs were a great asset to us, particularly when it comes to buying small quantities of bread, sardines, butter, candles, etc. just down the road. Several families who had been used to getting these things at the moment they wanted to use them suffered great inconvenience when small Fullah shops were forced to close down for a couple of days. . . . Let us be true to ourselves: let us stop being jealous of the success of foreign petty traders when we cannot substitute petty trading on a large scale as they are now doing.[213]

In April 1975, the SLPTA and the SLICTU finally merged into a new organization, the Sierra Leone Indigenous Petty Traders Association (SLIPTA), at a meeting held by the two executives. The executives took the decision to merge the two rival organizations in order to bring all indigenous traders together under one organization. A twenty-six-man executive interim council headed by a chairman was selected to run the affairs of the new association. The secretary-general of the SLIPTA remained Jalloh.[214] In 1978 a delegation of the SLIPTA led by Jalloh met with the new mayor of Freetown, Dr. June Holst-Roness to discuss matters of mutual interest, including street trading and the payment of dues to the FCC.[215] The SLIPTA subsequently formed three branches in the Provinces: Bo in the Southern Province, Kenema in the Eastern Province, and Makeni in the Northern Province.[216]

Despite the passage and implementation of the Retail Trade Act that made provision for active Sierra Leonean participation in the country's private enterprise, foreigners continued to dominate the business sector. Commenting on the Act, a leading newspaper editorial stated,

> Foreigners have never had it so good in the commerce of this country. This is because the average Sierra Leonean lacks that pride and nationalism which should enable him to put the interest of the state above all consideration. The hard fact is that he will be most satisfied with a little money while the state is deprived of thousands through him. It is indeed a very sorry state of affairs. No legislation can be meaningful if through greed and thirst for quick money people are prepared to defeat the provision of the legislation (Act). The Retail Trade Act made necessary provisions for active Sierra Leonean participation. Sierra Leoneans are now more active in business than at any other time because of the provision and incentives made by the Act. Unfortunately, some Sierra Leoneans have turned themselves into commission agents for foreigner (sic) business concerns. In transport business foreigners buy and operate lorries and taxis in the names of Sierra Leoneans. This is equally true for other types of business—diamonds, rice, cement—from which foreigners are prohibited.[217]

Livestock

During the Stevens administration, the Fula continued to dominate the livestock trade and its related butchering business in the Sierra Leone economy. Some of the challenges the Fula faced were the increasing woreh (cattle ranch) taxes, shortage of cattle, the increasing price of meat, competition from imported meat, large-scale theft of cattle in the provinces, cattle diseases, and inadequate slaughtering facilities.[218] However, in 1985 a modern abattoir was opened at Kossoh Town in the Western Area as part of the first phase of a grant-in-aid from the Danish government to Sierra Leone. The facility was to be leased to the newly established Modern Meat Processing and Marketing Company that had about ten indigenous shareholders, including the FCC, as well as the president and vice president of the Sierra Leone Butchers Association.[219]

The Fula chief and livestock entrepreneur Alhaji Bah exemplified Fula business participation in both local and national politics. In contrast, there were those Fula who viewed business and politics as separate. Until his death in 1986,[220] Alhaji Bah dominated the government and public consumer market for meat in Sierra Leone. However, he continued to face strong competition from fellow Fula like Alhaji Allie, and non-Fula like Alhaji Boie Kamara, a Mandingo, who was also president of the Sierra Leone Butchers Association in the 1980s,[221] and Alhaji Kuda Mansaray, Mandingo chief.[222] Alhaji Bah's business career spanned four decades dating back to the 1940s, when he worked under the legendary Fula chief and entrepreneur, Alhaji Momodu Allie, father of Alhaji Allie, who combined business and political leadership in the Fula community to become one of the most successful entrepreneurs in colonial Sierra Leone through his meat supply contract with the colonial state.[223]

As discussed in the preceding chapters, the Fula chief Alhaji Bah developed a close personal relationship with Prime Ministers Milton and Albert Margai. But he was especially close to the latter, which facilitated the award of government meat-supply contracts to him. Besides Alhaji Bah, many Fula merchants prospered during the early years of independence under the SLPP government. As mentioned earlier, the SLPP had an "open door" policy that encouraged investors—foreign and indigenous—to invest in the economy. Alhaji Bah was a strong supporter of Sir Albert. Indeed, he mobilized many wealthy Fula merchants to donate cash, cattle, and rice to the SLPP for Sir Albert's critical election campaign in 1967. For their support of the SLPP, many in the Fula business community were severely victimized by APC supporters.[224]

Even though there was a long-standing Fula political tradition of supporting the government in power, Fula business elites were divided over their support of the APC. This is illustrated by the political and business rivalry between the Fula chief Alhaji Bah and Alhaji Allie. Attempting to influence the political agenda and policy outcomes, Alhaji Bah and Alhaji Allie, acting both independently and collectively, made substantial cash and kind contributions to political candidates and parties. In competing for the meat-supply contract with the government, Alhaji Allie, who was born in Sierra Leone, argued, as he did during Sir Albert's rule, that Alhaji Bah, who was born in Guinea, was not a Sierra Leonean and that the contract should be awarded only to Sierra Leoneans. Alhaji Allie was one of several prominent butchers in Freetown who, as APC supporters, met with Prime Minister Stevens to urge him to terminate Alhaji Bah's meat-supply contract. He alleged that the former prime minister, Albert Margai had favored Alhaji Bah in the competition over the meat-supply contract because of political patronage. In 1970 Alhaji Allie further challenged Alhaji Bah for the Fula chieftaincy.[225]

Since independence in 1961, political patronage has been a major factor in the awarding of government contracts. In 1968, following the general election of 1967, the newly formed APC government led by Prime Minister Stevens terminated Alhaji Bah's meat-supply contract and awarded it to Alhaji Allie, who was a strong APC supporter. Prior to the APC electoral victory, Alhaji Allie had provided Stevens with a two-story building in the east of Freetown to use as an office free of charge for seven years. In addition, on the eve of the 1967 election, he accompanied Stevens to Kono to meet with wealthy Fula diamond businessmen from Sierra Leone, Guinea, Mali, Senegal, and The Gambia in order to raise campaign funds. Alhaji Allie faced a lot of criticism from members of the Fula community, including the Fula chief Alhaji Bah, for supporting an opposition candidate instead of Prime Minister Margai, who had a track record of helping the Fula community. Despite some initial Fula opposition, Alhaji Allie was able to raise substantial funds for Stevens and his APC party. From Kono alone, Stevens collected about Le30,000, but it was alleged that APC officials misused the funds.[226]

In 1969, however, Alhaji Bah regained his meat-supply contract after he developed a rapprochement with Prime Minister Stevens and pledged support for the APC government. In 1971, however, as discussed above, Alhaji Bah was deported to Guinea by the APC government, despite his having become a naturalized Sierra Leonean. This resulted from an accusation by President Touré that the Fula chief had supported Guinean Fula immigrants in Sierra Leone in an attempt to overthrow his government during the Portuguese invasion in 1970. President Touré imprisoned Alhaji Bah until 1975. During this period his business suffered a major decline. Following his return to Sierra Leone in 1975, Alhaji Bah, despite failing health, took over his butchering business and tried to restore it to its former prosperity. In this he received considerable financial assistance from wealthy Fula businessmen, including Almamy Agibu Jalloh, who was also involved in the livestock trade.[227] As a business strategy to retain his meat-supply contract with the APC government, Alhaji Bah cultivated a working relationship with President Stevens and key members of the APC government in spite of the president's role in his deportation to his homeland.[228]

Diamond Trade

Fula business elites, as previously in SLPP administrations, lobbied the APC government on a number of issues related to the diamond trade, including the issuance of more diamond dealer licenses, residential permits, and diggers licenses to the Fula.[229] Prominent Fula diamond dealers included Alhaji Momodu Alpha Bah, Fula chief in Kono; Demba Arch of Kenema;[230] and Alhaji Sanu Barrie. But of all the Fula involved in the diamond business, the most accomplished was Alhaji Bailor Barrie. Until his death in 1989, he was the most successful Fula entrepreneur in postindependence Sierra Leone with a total net worth of millions of dollars and wide-ranging domestic and international businesses from corporations to retail shops. Alhaji Bailor Barrie helped to change the long-standing Sierra Leonean public measurement of elite success from that of academics to entrepreneurialism. The cornerstone of Alhaji Bailor Barrie's business activities was the diamond trade. He was born in 1934 in Koinadugu. After acquiring a basic Western education and with a cattle gift from his Guinean-born father and Fula chief in Koinadugu, Almamy Bademba, to use as start-up capital, Alhaji Bailor Barrie in the 1950s traveled to Bo and then to Kono and Kenema to mine diamonds. He was one of the Fula who started his diamond business career as an illicit miner in Kono. Diamonds were a primary source of capital accumulation among the Fula. Like Almamy Agibu Jalloh, Alhaji Bailor Barrie was a self-taught businessman and his vast knowledge of the diamond trade was derived from many years of experience and on-the-job training. This experience gave Alhaji Bailor Barrie a competitive advantage and set him apart from many Lebanese, who were merely dealers who bought and sold diamonds. The Fula were illicit and licensed diggers, middlemen, and exporters in the diamond business.[231]

With diamond profits in the 1970s, Alhaji Bailor Barrie made history by becoming the first Fula to enter the European-Lebanese-dominated import and retail of motor vehicles when he opened M. B. Barrie Motors, which distributed Daihatsu and Pony vehicles as a division of his parent company, M. B. Barrie Company (Sierra Leone Limited). The company included an import-export subsidiary specializing in consumer goods, rice cultivation and trade, and ownership of a casino hotel in The Gambia.[232] In addition, he realized that he could maximize his diamond profits by eliminating Lebanese middlemen who had created a market niche. Despite his limited Western education, Alhaji Bailor Barrie had gained enough experience to sell his diamonds in Europe without going through Lebanese exporters. He opened a diamond marketing office in Brussels that was managed by a team that included his son, brother, and a Lebanese employee. The evidence suggests that millions of dollars worth of diamonds were sold through this office with profits plowed back into Alhaji Bailor Barrie's businesses in Sierra Leone and foreign countries. This enabled him to compete with elite Lebanese diamond dealers—particularly the popular Afro-Lebanese business tycoon Jamil[233] in the highly politicized diamond business in Sierra Leone. By the 1980s, as Alhaji Bailor Barrie gained greater success in the diamond business and expanded into neighboring Guinea and Liberia, as well as The Gambia, in pursuit of diamond profits, Alhaji Bailor Barrie faced strong competition from the close-knit Lebanese diamond dealers like Jamil who, like Alhaji Bailor Barrie, had strong personal connections to President Stevens and his APC government.[234] According to Jamil's testimony to the Dove-Edwin Commission into the 1967 election, he knew Stevens before Stevens became prime minister in 1968.[235]

In 1982 the Fula community in Sierra Leone faced increased persecution from the Stevens government following a diamond sale dispute between Alhaji Bailor Barrie and Jamil[236] in neighboring Guinea where President Touré reportedly favored Alhaji Barrie. The evidence suggests that after Jamil returned to Freetown after losing out to Alhaji Bailor Barrie in Guinea, he influenced President Stevens to target and harass Fula residents. Some in the Stevens government accused the Fula of committing serious crimes in the country. Reporting on the row, a prominent publication stated, "To say that the Foulahs [Fula] should be blamed for the country's serious increasing crimes is a gross misjudgment, exaggeration and a shift of responsibility. It can open up a lot of debate. However, whatever the motives are, the decision is bound to have some immediate adverse effects on the average low-income Sierra Leonean and the country's stagnated economy as a whole."[237] In response, President Touré accused the Stevens administration of discriminating against the Fula community in Sierra Leone. Speaking on Guinean Radio, President Touré stated that the Stevens government's action was "totally discriminatory against a particular ethnic [Fula] group" and called for an immediate end to such unacceptable behavior.[238]

However, President Stevens assured President Touré and all Fula that his administration did not discriminate against Fula or any ethnic group in Sierra Leone. He emphasized that his government "does not and cannot discriminate against Foulahs [Fula], many of whom were either born here, work here or live in this country for a considerable length of period. What Sierra Leone cannot tolerate or accept is the influx into the country of large number of aliens without identity or valid travelling documents." President Stevens made these remarks while addressing thousands of people at the fortieth-day ceremony of the late Fula PC Alhaji Kaikai in Pujehun.[239] Moreover, in a meeting with the executive of the FPU at State House in 1982, President Stevens made it clear that his APC government did not hate Fula, but that all foreigners, including Fula, living in Sierra Leone must possess the necessary immigration residential documents. Many critics of the Stevens administration, including Fula, had accused the government of targeting Fula residents for expulsion. President Stevens stated that the Fula were part of the ethnic makeup of the country and should therefore contribute to national development since "the country belongs to all of us." Furthermore, the president encouraged members of the FPU to ensure that Fula were registered as citizens and noncitizens. And he also informed them about the forthcoming general elections and solicited their cooperation in maintaining law and order. President Stevens finally called on the Fula business community to help conserve the country's scarce foreign exchange, which was vital to the country's economy.[240]

Motor Transport

Besides Alhaji Bailor Barrie, one of the key Fula business elite persons in the motor transport business was Almamy Agibu Jalloh who was born at Royanka, Sanda Tenraran chiefdom in Bombali in 1917.[241] He was the younger brother of the Fula chief Alhaji Wuroh Timbo. Almamy Agibu's entrepreneurial activities included both large-scale and retail enterprises that included livestock, rice, palm kernels, commercial transportation, and commercial cleaning services.[242] At the end of World War II in 1945, Almamy Agibu was one of the very first to own and operate "Joe Khaki" military Bedford lorries auctioned by the British military, and he developed a fleet under "Jalloh Brothers." He became a successful transporter and maintained his own garage for vehicle repairs and was a fuel contractor with Mobil and Shell. In 1965 Almamy Agibu became a palm kernel agent for the Sierra Leone Produce Marketing Board (SLPMB) and built Banga Store at Kissy Bye Pass. In addition, he opened a modern bakery and later built and operated a jute factory to minimize the importation of sacks for the produce.[243] By the 1970s he had become a large-scale farmer, especially for rice, and was given the title of "master farmer" for Tonkolili and Bombali. Moreover, in 1979 he was awarded a garbage contract by the FCC, and in 1983 he launched a new appeal to keep the city clean. He held the contract for fifteen years and was awarded the Certificate of Honor for Distinguished National Service.[244] Almamy Agibu's Keep the City Clean campaigns were crucial in keeping Freetown clean during the OAU heads of state and governments summit in 1980.[245] Moreover, as noted earlier, Almamy Agibu was also an ardent supporter of football in Sierra Leone.[246]

A major challenge facing Almamy Agibu in the expansion of his transport business was the lack of access to short-term bank loans. Some Sierra Leoneans used the press to call on the Stevens government as a matter of priority to encourage and financially support the establishment of indigenous commercial banks as soon as possible. This would lead to better loan facilities for Sierra Leonean businessmen like Almamy Agibu. It was suggested that the government should provide part of the capital for such banks, and there were native-born citizens who were ready to put up additional capital. Indigenous traders and small businessmen had difficulties in obtaining short-term loans from banks because the securities they were prepared to offer—real estate— were not readily accepted by expatriate banks. Experience elsewhere has shown that a lot of economic activity is generated and immense benefits accrue from the establishment of local commercial banks. One of the disadvantages of expatriate commercial banks was that their interest rates were dictated by external factors, which sometimes had no relation to internal consequences. Another factor was that the policy dictated by the banks' headquarters abroad might be in direct conflict with the policies of the countries in which they operated.[247]

As a close personal friend of President Stevens, Almamy Agibu played an important role in lobbying the Stevens administration on key issues facing transport owners and drivers, including Fula, such as the presence of foreigners in the motor transport business, the high cost of vehicles and spare parts, transport fares, and police harassment of drivers, including the setting up of too many checkpoints. Almamy Agibu worked closely with the Sierra Leone Motor Drivers Union, which staged protests over some of these issues. In 1969, for example, the Union organized a five-hour protest in Freetown that was called off only after a delegation led by the secretary-general of the Union, James Mahoi, and six others called on Prime Minister Stevens in his office and handed him a twenty-point memorandum. Some of the protesting drivers had placards that read, "Ban foreigners in the transport business" and "Too many police checkpoints." In response to complaints from transport owners and drivers, the APC government commissioned the Cox-George Report on vehicles and their spare parts.[248]

The Sierra Leone economy experienced severe difficulties between 1977 and 1979 that affected businesses, including those owned by Fula. Domestic inflation rose sharply, and the balance of payments deficit for 1978 was about $50 million, greatly surpassing the previous year. This situation was worsened by increased imports, which produced a trade deficit of $85 million in 1978, almost double the 1977 figure. The country's international reserves declined 30 percent to $30 million by the end of 1978. These economic challenges were compounded by government's short-term loans, contractor financing, and supply credits. In October 1978, as a response to the growing economic decline and the pressures on the national currency, the Stevens administration decided to delink the Leone from the British Sterling and peg it to the IMF unit of account, the Special Drawing Right (SDR). A rate of exchange was established with a 5 percent devaluation. As a result, the International Monetary Fund (IMF) granted Sierra Leone standby assistance to ease the balance of payments problem. The APC government was required to freeze wages, reduce the budget deficit, and end short-term loans. But President Stevens rejected these measures because of the potential social instability that might arise. Instead, he increased wages from between 10 to 25 percent. The IMF responded by postponing the standby agreement with Sierra Leone. Sierra Leonean–born Fula economist, Mohamed A. Jalloh, an employee of the SLPMB and brother of the author, criticized the country's devaluation in a leading local newspaper.[249]

In spite of the serious economic problems facing Sierra Leone, President Stevens went ahead and hosted the OAU conference in July 1980. This event was an economic watershed, costing the country over Le100 million and resulting in an economic downturn lasting decades.[250] Earlier in 1979, the IMF had approved the Stevens administration's request for a standby arrangement with a key condition of a ceiling of Le100 million expenditure on the proposed hosting of the OAU conference, which was breached.[251] The APC government also failed to introduce financial discipline in its management of the national economy, as had been agreed with the IMF.[252] Despite the many contracts awarded by the APC government regarding the OAU, Fula businesses, as Alhaji Bailor Barrie pointed out, did not benefit compared to foreign-owned, especially Lebanese like Tony Yazbeck, even though in Alhaji Bailor Barrie's case the motor vehicles sold were comparatively more durable and less expensive.[253]

The national economic downturn was compounded by massive government corruption described as "vouchergate" after being exposed by Alfred A. Akibo-Betts, a deputy minister of finance.[254] Following vouchergate, there was also "squandergate," which resulted in massive loss of public funds through corruption.[255] In 1981 the deepening economic crisis resulted in nationwide strikes by workers organized by the Sierra Leone Labor Congress (SLLC). The strikes protested soaring prices and food shortages. The Congress leaders wanted the APC government to cut prices of essential commodities such as rice and meat. Bank officials estimated the country's inflation rate in double digits. Thousands of workers defied a ban on demonstrations and massed at the SLLC headquarters in Freetown to hear speeches attacking the APC government's economic policies. As a result, most businesses were closed, and most main towns in the Provinces were also affected. The SLLC met with the APC government but vowed to continue its walkout despite a promise by authorities to stabilize rice prices.[256] In response, the Stevens political regime declared a state of emergency and arrested and detained several SLLC leaders at Pademba Road Prison.[257] Moreover, the APC government appointed a commission of inquiry into the SLLC.[258] In 1982 the SLLC organized additional strikes that further weakened the country's economy. According to the main government newspaper, "The present state of the economy is naturally the major household talk in Sierra Leone today and as things worsen for the average family member with each waking day, the frustrations bite in deeper and grimaces etch into vivid lines on faces that can no longer hide the physical. . . . That President Stevens had to comment on the situation immediately on his arrival from abroad was no surprise—the situation was a major government matter."[259]

Beyond that, in August 1984, President Stevens assumed the position of chairman of the reconstituted Foreign Exchange Committee, whose creation was one of several new measures adopted by the government to remedy the acute foreign exchange problem facing the country.[260] In September the same year, President Stevens appealed to Britain through the new British High Commissioner to use its international influence to help Sierra Leone deal with its grave economic problems.[261] Faced with enormous and mounting economic problems facing the country, which President Stevens stated at length in Parliament in 1985,[262] the president stepped down from office that year, albeit other factors such as ageing and failing health played a role as well. On balance, although President Stevens achieved some measure of political success, he was not successful regarding the economy in his seventeen-year rule.[263]

Elections under APC Rule

During APC rule under President Stevens, three national elections were held, 1973, 1977, and 1982, to elect a new Parliament. The main opposition party in all three elections was the SLPP. The political agenda of the vast majority of Fula business leaders during these elections was centered on protecting their business interests. But the elections, as in previous national elections under SLPP rule, pushed the issue of the rights of the Fula as citizens and voters toward the forefront of Sierra Leone politics against the backdrop of a substantial increase in the Fula population. Once again the Fula found themselves at the heart of highly charged public debates over citizenship and voting rights. As political battles over Fula citizenship and voting rights continued across the country, some APC politicians and supporters repeatedly alleged that foreign-born Fula, especially from Guinea, were on the list of voters. Nonetheless, some Fula were still active in APC politics such as Alhaji Maju and Dr. Adu Aezick Seray-Wurie, who was national secretary-general of the APC National Youth League and a member of the APC Central Committee.[264]

After its defeat in the 1967 election, the SLPP, with still a large Fula political base, started a reorganization program in 1968 that culminated in the election of a new executive in 1969: Alhaji Mustapha, a former deputy prime minister under Sir Milton and MP for Bo North-East, was unanimously elected as national chairman; Dr. Salia Jusu-Sheriff, MP for Kenema South, was elected parliamentary leader; D. M. Yilla was elected national treasurer; and Julius Cole and Daramy Rogers were elected secretary-general and assistant secretary-general, respectively. The offices were to be held an annual basis. The reorganization of the opposition SLPP continued into the 1970s in the face of intense leadership struggles within the party, involving mainly Sir Albert and Dr. Jusu-Sheriff.[265]

Elections in the 1970s

Prior to the 1973 general election, the Fula community, especially the business class, continued to experience political violence at the hands of APC supporters like Alfred Akibo-Betts across the country. On the eve of the FCC election in March 1970, fighting broke out between APC and SLPP supporters, during which APC supporters threw dynamite at Fula businesses and the homes of Fula and Mende residents in Ginger Hall in the east end of the capital city. These two ethnic groups were targeted because they were perceived to be SLPP supporters. The violent attacks resulted in fatalities, the destruction of homes by fire, and the flight of many residents. Three houses, including that of Mrs. Nancy Koroma, a former Mende chief in the east end of Freetown, were set ablaze before the arrival of the police. As a result, very few SLPP supporters participated in the polls, and the APC had an overwhelming victory.[266]

In the aftermath of the Ginger Hall violence, some high-profile APC members who opposed political violence like the former finance minister, Dr. Forna, resigned from the party and later formed a new party, the United Democratic Party (UDP), which had merged with an earlier party, the National Democratic Party (NDP). The UDP leadership also included the former APC information minister, Ibrahim Basq-Taqi, and the former SLPP external affairs minister, Dr. Karefa-Smart. President Stevens responded by imposing a state of emergency. In addition, the Stevens administration banned the UDP in October 1970 and arrested its leaders and supporters, including a prominent Fula business elite, Alhaji Abass Allie, who was a key benefactor of the UDP.[267]

On April 19, 1971, the APC government declared a Republic and Prime Minister Stevens became the first executive president of the country.[268] In introducing the Republican Constitution of 1971, based entirely on that passed by Sir Albert in Parliament prior to the 1967 elections, Stevens said that "the dignity of Sierra Leone demands that all institutions of government in this country should be in the hands of Sierra Leoneans and based in our country."[269] This was the complete opposite of the view Stevens had expressed when Prime Minister Margai first proposed the idea. Stevens had opposed Margai's proposals because of the "inordinate speed with which the Prime Minister was rushing through a matter of such importance to the state."[270] Stevens added that Margai's republican proposals were not in the national interest in view of the cultural and historical background of Sierra Leone.[271]

As the country prepared for the 1973 general election, the issue of who should be the Fula chief in Western Area, which was connected to national politics, heated up in the Fula community. Previously, Prime Minister Stevens had made it clear his administration was anxious to see the Fula organize and elect a chief. Prominent Sierra Leonean–born Fula including Alhaji Ibrahim Allie said that the Fula chief should only be elected from among their own numbers and no Fula who was only a resident should be recognized as chief. This group of native-born

Fula, including Alhaji Allie, stated that they had held several meetings and passed resolutions and would meet with the Ministry of Interior to explain their position. According to their spokesman, they decided to challenge the eligibility of Guinean-born Fula for chief because of their experience during the 1967 general elections when many Fula were molested because of APC allegations that Fula had been brought from Guinea to vote for the SLPP. He said that although these allegations could not be proved, a lot of people believed them because at the time the Fula chief Alhaji Bah was a Guinean-born Fula, regardless of the fact that the chief was a person of integrity. Alhaji Allie, who hired the Krio lawyer, Cyrus Rogers-Wright, to submit a petition on behalf of himself and his supporters, also pointed out that the country would be facing an even more important election soon, and the Sierra Leonean–born Fula wanted to ensure that there was no public ethnic resentment against the Fula. He further stated that he hoped the Stevens administration would agree with them that only native-born Fula should contest the election for chief.[272] However, another group of prominent Sierra Leonean–born Fula wrote a letter to a leading local newspaper dissociating themselves from the statement that the APC government should only allow Sierra Leonean–born Fula to contest the election for chief. They included Alhaji Seray-Wurie, Almamy Agibu Jalloh, A. M. Cambah, Alhaji Maju, M. S. Seray-Wurie, A. B. Jalloh, and Alhaji M. S. Jalloh.[273]

This was against the backdrop of an earlier press release in June 1970 by the Ministry of the Interior that the APC government was considering the possibility of reviving chieftaincy in the Western Area and the appointment of a Fula chief for Freetown was also contemplated. But before a final decision could be reached on the Fula chieftaincy, every male Fula of the apparent age of twenty-one years and over must be registered. Fula who had recently entered Sierra Leone and were not in possession of valid travel documents would not be registered. Arrangements were made to operate three registration centers: east end of Freetown at the Railway Union Hall; central Freetown at the Cathedral School at Howe Street; and the west of the city at the Reform Club, Mereweather Road. The registration would take place on Sundays from June 21 to July 5. Fula seeking to register were required to give their full names and addresses, the names of their landlords, and the dates they arrived in Freetown. In doubtful cases, the registration officer reserved the right to require the presence of the landlord before an applicant could be registered. The Ministry of Interior release warned members of the public who were not Fula not to present themselves for registration and that any proved attempts at impersonation will be dealt with severely.[274] Hundreds of Fula across Freetown later registered at these centers in preparation for the forthcoming election of a Fula chief.[275] The deputy minister of the interior, A. B. M. Kamara, warned against molestation by anyone during the registration of the Fula.[276]

But before the Fula chieftaincy took place, Alhaji Allie, the main challenger to Alhaji Bah for Fula chief, died in his sleep at his residence in Freetown at the age of fifty-seven in September 1970. Not only was Alhaji Allie an elite member of the Fula business class, he was a JP. It was his brother, Alhaji Almamy Baba Allie, who gave an account of his death to one of the leading local newspapers.[277] The Ministry of Interior later announced that the election of Fula chief would be held on Sunday, October 11, with polling centers in the east, central, and west of Freetown.[278] Four candidates contested for the position: Alhaji Bah, Ahmed Akim Jallo-Jamboria, Mamodou Allie (brother of the late Alhaji Allie), and Amadu Tejan-Jalloh. In spite of strong opposition from Sierra Leonean–born Fula backed by some foreign-born Fula, Alhaji Bah won reelection with strong support from Guinean-born Fula and influential native-born Fula such as Alhaji Tejan-Jalloh, Almamy Agibu Jalloh, and Alhaji Seray-Wurie. Alhaji received 4,598 votes out of the 5,208 votes cast and was declared Fula chief effective October 11, 1970.[279]

The 1973 Election

The May 1973 election was boycotted by opposition SLPP candidates because of widespread intimidation and procedural obstruction by the Stevens administration and its APC supporters. Most APC candidates were returned unopposed to the eighty-five-seat ordinary member Parliament. Some of the Fula candidates in the election included Mohamed Issa Jalloh of Freetown East III constituency (Independent), Alhaji Kaikai of Pujehun (unopposed), and Alhaji Maju of Freetown East I constituency (APC, unopposed). In its fifty-two-page election manifesto, the APC promised, among other things, free primary education in the next five years as well as the development of agriculture and industry. And the platform further proposed to improve the alluvial mining industry.[280] In the wake of the election, Alhaji Maju was appointed as deputy minister in the office of Vice President Koroma. Alhaji Maju also served as special assistant to Vice President Koroma, as well as deputy minister of finance under Koroma, who doubled as minister of finance.[281]

One of the most contentious issues in the 1973 election was over Fula citizenship. Many in the APC continued to label the Fula as Guinean-born SLPP supporters who should not participate in national elections. This had also been the case in the watershed 1967 election that brought the APC under Stevens to power. To address the politically sensitive matter of citizenship, in April 1973 Vice President and Prime Minister Koroma introduced a bill in Parliament that sought to amend and consolidate the law regarding Sierra Leone citizenship consistent with the present republican constitution. This bill was subsequently passed with little opposition as the Sierra Leone Citizenship Act 1973.[282]

The 1977 Election

Against the backdrop of violent students protests in 1977, a general election was held in the same year, which the APC won with an overwhelming majority of the seats in Parliament. Many of their candidates across the country were returned unopposed.[283] Fula APC politicians who were elected to Parliament included Alhaji Maju, who represented Freetown East I constituency,[284] Mohamed I. Jalloh of Freetown East III constituency,[285] and the veteran politician PC Alhaji Kaikai of Pujehun.[286] Some of the Fula politicians who contested the election but were unsuccessful included Mahmoud T. Jalloh, secretary-general of the SLPTA, who was an independent candidate in Freetown Central I constituency, and Hon. Jah, who was the APC candidate in Pujehun East constituency. In the new cabinet, President Stevens appointed Alhaji Kaikai, the longest serving PC to serve as MP, as minister of state. In this position, he acted as first vice president in the absence of the substantive holder, Koroma.[287] And President Stevens also appointed Alhaji Maju, former deputy minister in the Ministry of Finance, as parliamentary special assistant to the vice president's office. In this capacity, Alhaji Maju also served as acting minister of development and economic planning.[288] In addition, the president appointed Hon. Jah as Sierra Leone's ambassador to Liberia.[289] Moreover, President Stevens, in his efforts to unite the country, appointed the longtime member of the Fula business elite, Alhaji A. D. Wurie, a close personal friend, as a nominated MP.[290]

As for Alhaji Wurie, as discussed earlier, he served as resident director of DELCO, which he joined in 1941 and from which he stayed from

1964 until the company was closed in 1975. Earlier in 1963, Alhaji Wurie received the MBE and received the CBE in 1967. Between 1962 and 1964, he was a councilor and alderman in the FCC. Beyond that, Alhaji Wurie was appointed a member of the Court of the University of Sierra Leone in 1975. And he also served as the president of the Western Area Football Association (WAFA), president of the Sierra Leone Basketball Association, and first national president of the reconstituted Sierra Leone Amateur Football Association (SLAFA). In 1984 he donated Le3,000 to the national football team, the Leone Stars, after their performance in the West African Zone II football tournament held in Freetown. In addition, Alhaji Wurie was a consultant to the Sierra Leone Ports Authority (Waportman International), chairman of the Western Area branch of the Old Bo Boys Association (OBBA), president of the Young Men's Muslim Association (YMMA), and president of the Sierra Leone Employers Federation (SLEF). Furthermore, Alhaji Wurie served as interim chairman of the Board of Directors of Ports Authority and chairman of Mining and General Services. After more than three decades of service to football in Sierra Leone, Alhaji Wurie resigned as president of SLAFA in 1980.[291]

The political collaboration between Alhaji Wurie and President Stevens was emulated by Fula business leaders led by the Fula chief Alhaji Bah. Collectively, they recognized that they would have to work with President Stevens and his government despite his poor record in dealing with the Fula community. So rather than oppose the president, the Fula restated their public support for him and the APC. As the chief power broker and intermediary between the Fula community and the government, Alhaji Bah now sought to incorporate the Fula community into the national political system through a process of coalition formation and bargaining. In addition, the Fula chief promoted efforts by the elite Fula businessmen to make monetary and in-kind donations to the APC. On the strong advice of the Fula chief, the Fula people also resolved to avoid any appearance of interference in the political affairs of neighboring Guinea.

After the 1977 election, there were calls for a one-party system in Sierra Leone.[292] Some of the politicians who supported a one-party state included Alhaji Maju, parliamentary special assistant in the vice president's office, and Mohamed I. Jalloh, who spoke at a political meeting in Kambia.[293] Alhaji Maju urged his constituents at Railway Union Hall in Freetown East I constituency to support fully the one-party constitution.[294] Addressing the APC National Delegates Conference in Kaffu Bullom, Port Loko, President Stevens urged delegates to legalize the one-party system. He explained that although he believed in the evolutionary path to a one-party state, he was now convinced that in the absence of an opposition, it was necessary to legalize the de facto one-party state.[295]

Notwithstanding political opposition, the APC government introduced a one-party state in 1978.[296] In defending the one-party system, which he had opposed during Sir Albert's rule, President Stevens argued that the decision came "at the right time in the history of my people."[297] For Vice President Koroma, a one-party government had several advantages, and, in fact, the country had had a de facto one party system over the preceding ten years.[298] In introducing the proposed one-party republican constitution bill in Parliament, Koroma described it as one that would promote unity, prosperity, peace, and progress.[299] Prime Minister Kamara-Taylor, speaking in the parliamentary debate on the one-party republican constitution, described it as the "people's constitution" that would stand the test of time. Moreover, PC Alhaji Kaikai outlined the disadvantages of the multiparty system and stated that the one-party system would bring about unity in the country.[300] Another Fula politician, Mohamed I. Jalloh, organized a mammoth mass rally in his Freetown East III constituency in support of the one-party system. One of the speakers at the rally was the APC secretary-general, E. T. Kamara.[301]

Addressing a cross-section of the Fula community that included prominent business elite members such as Almamy Agibu Jalloh, Alhaji Tejan-Jalloh, and Alhaji Bailor Barrie when they visited him at State House after the introduction of the one-party constitution, President Stevens explained that the one-party system had many benefits and expressed appreciation to the Fula for their contributions to the development of the country. Speaking on behalf of the Fula delegation, Alhaji Seray-Wurie praised President Stevens for uniting Sierra Leoneans under the one-party system. The delegation thanked the president for appointing Alhaji Maju, who pioneered the Children's Hospital extension in his constituency as parliamentary special assistant in the first vice president's office[302] and Alhaji A. D. Wurie as a Nominated MP.[303] However, in 1980 President Stevens suspended Alhaji Maju for unstated reasons. As a result, a high-level delegation led by the Fula business elite members Alhaji Bah, Almamy Agibu Jalloh, and Alhaji Bailor Barrie, as well as the notable Fula civil servant Alhaji Seray-Wurie and the Fula Imam Alhaji Seray Bah, who was also a merchant, lobbied President Stevens to reinstate Alhaji Maju in his previous position, which Stevens subsequently did the same year.[304]

The 1982 Election

The 1982 general election, the first under the one-party system, saw more than two hundred candidates in over eighty constituencies in different parts of the country. The election was marked by widespread political violence, which should be seen as part of a broader culture of political violence under APC rule.[305] According to one senior APC minister, Dr. Sama Banya, the election "proved to be the most vicious and violent in the history of the country."[306] Fula candidates contested parliamentary seats in the Western Area, Port Loko, Bombali, and Koinadugu. In that area, the Fula candidates were Alhaji Maju (incumbent), a member of the APC Central Committee, who was challenged by Mohammed M. King and Sorsoh I. Conteh to represent East I constituency in Parliament.[307] In East III constituency, Mohammed I. Jalloh (incumbent) faced Emeric B. Kargbo and Morlai Bai Kamara. In Central I constituency, Mahmoud T. Jalloh, secretary-general of the SLPTA, was among several candidates seeking nomination to contest the by-election. In Port Loko West II constituency, the Fula candidate and businessman Bai Sheka Wurie, a relative of Alhaji A. D. Wurie, contested against Dr. Moses Dumbuya and S. A. Fofana (incumbent). In Bombali Central constituency, the British-trained lawyer and Fula candidate Dr. Timbo faced two Temne British-trained lawyers: Thaimu Bangura (incumbent) and Edward (Eddie) M. Turay. In Koinadugu North constituency, the incumbent A. B. M. Kamara was challenged by the Fula politician Alpha B. Barrie, brother of the iconic Fula businessman, Alhaji Bailor Barrie. And in Koinadugu North West constituency, the incumbent Philipson H. Kamara was challenged by the Fula politician Alhaji Amadu M. B. Jalloh and Alhassan H. Kandeh.[308]

For the Fula candidates, Bai Sheka Wurie was elected to represent Port Loko West II constituency. However, the incumbent, Mohammed I. Jalloh, was unseated by newcomer Morlai B. Kamara in Freetown East III constituency. Elections in the following constituencies were rescheduled because of violence and voting irregularities: Freetown East I, Bombali Central, Koinadugu North East, and Koinadugu North. The Fula candidates and their opponents were required to go through a second time the procedures of primary elections, nominations, and elections according to the Electoral Commission. In the subsequent by-elections, in Koinadugu North constituency, the APC Central Committee approved only one candidate, Philipson Kamara; in Freetown East I constituency, Alhaji Maju contested alongside Abdul Mansaray and Tejan Savage; in Bombali Central, Alhaji Dr. Timbo faced his former opponent Thaimu and a newcomer, Abdul M. Kamara; and in Koinadugu North, it was a political fight between two former adversaries: A. B. M. Kamara and Alpha B. Barrie. In the by-election in Freetown East I constituency, the incumbent Alhaji Maju won with 11,056 votes while his opponents Tejan M. Savage received 875 votes and Abdul Kamara 6,241 votes. Alhaji Maju received broad support from the Fula community, including business elite members like Alhaji Tejan-Jalloh.[309]

The election in Bombali Central constituency, Sanda, that included Rokulan, Mateboi, Royanka, and Sanda Tenraran chiefdom experienced some of the worst political violence during the elections.[310] Thaimu Bangura was one of the young, Western-educated elite individuals elected to Parliament in the 1977 general election. He represented Bombali Central constitutency and served in the Stevens administration as, first, minister of information and broadcasting, then as minister of social welfare and rural development, and in addition was responsible for sports.[311] For Alhaji Dr. Timbo, as noted earlier, he was the son of the Fula chief Alhaji Wuroh Timbo of Rokulan, who was the older brother of the well-known Fula business elite person Almamy Agibu Jalloh.[312] In the 1980s, Alhaji Dr. Timbo, a well-established lawyer and justice, played a key role in the establishment of the first law school in Sierra Leone.[313]

Almamy Agibu Jalloh was instrumental in launching Alhaji Dr. Timbo's political career. He played an important role in the Sanda election, including mobilizing material and human resources to ensure the victory of his nephew, Alhaji Dr. Timbo. Moreover, Almamy Agibu recruited Fula across the country, particularly in the Northern Province, to bolster the campaign efforts. Almamy Agibu also drew on his close personal friendship with President Stevens, whose government he had supported in cash and kind to advance his nephew's political interests.[314] The political competition between Thaimu and Alhaji Dr. Timbo degenerated into open warfare and massacres between the Fula and Temne on the eve of the nomination of candidates, resulting in the cancelation of the election. In the by-election, the incumbent Thaimu won with 12,221 votes; Alhaji Dr. Timbo received 7,690 votes, and Kamara's total was 6,241.[315] Despite his election victory, Thaimu was not appointed to the new cabinet. He instead set up a private business, T. D. Y. Enterprises in Freetown, that provided legal and political services. He was also managing director of Agro Dynamics and Union Trading Companies.[316] After the election, Almamy Agibu and eight others were prosecuted in a Freetown magistrate court on allegations of looting, raping, and eventually setting on fire an entire village in

Thaimu's Bombali Central constituency. As a matter of fact, Thaimu and Gershon Collier, a former senior member of Sir Albert's government, led the prosecution team. However, Almamy Agibu and other defendants who were represented by six lawyers including, Alhaji Dr. Timbo and Alhaji Sulaiman Tejan-Jalloh, were freed after a successful defense.[317]

The political conflict between the Fula and Temne in Sanda was rooted in large measure in a row between Fula cattle owners and local Temne crop farmers who had long complained about the destruction of their crops by Fula-owned cattle. Indeed, such disputes were widespread between Fula immigrants from Guinea with their cattle and local farmers in Bombali. But they were often resolved at the chiefdom level without central government intervention. Additionally, there was the issue of the large-scale theft of Fula cattle in the Bombali Central constituency, which was brought to the attention of the APC government for speedy resolution.[318] As far back as 1963, a resident of the District published a complaint on this matter in a leading newspaper and requested the Ministry of Internal Affairs to investigate the local complaints against the Fula herdsmen in the District.[319] In 1972, however, the acting Fula chief for Freetown, Alhaji Tejan-Jalloh, told the Barthes-Wilson Commission of Inquiry into the high cost of living that one of the reasons for the scarcity of meat in the country was the exodus of Fula herdsmen and cattle from grazing areas like Bombali to barren areas of the country because of molestation and heavy fines levied on them by local administration authorities. Alhaji Tejan-Jalloh also cited cruelty to Fula cattle as another factor. He gave the example of an incident where over six hundred cows were killed indiscriminately by angry residents who claimed that the animals encroached on their farms and destroyed their crops. He further quoted two instances when in Bombali a Fula was fined Le1,600 and in Koinadugu another Fula was fined Le800 for destruction of farms by their cattle. Alhaji Tejan-Jalloh added that most of the meat consumed in Sierra Leone were from local cattle and that if the Fula and other herdsmen were allowed to rear cattle on a large scale as in other countries without such fines and destruction, the country would have cheaper and better meat supplies. He urged the APC government to give land settlements to cattle owners for nominal fees, as was done during the British colonial era.[320] Notwithstanding, Fula-Temne relations were not always marked by political conflicts in Bombali. Both groups had a long history of cross-ethnic marriages that produced children who were fluent in both languages. Some of the offspring of such unions occupied prominent positions such as medical doctors, educators, lawyers, politicians, businesspeople, and accountants in Sierra Leonean society. Furthermore, there was business cooperation between both groups in such areas as livestock, retail, farming, and transportation.[321]

Besides Bombali, political violence involving Fula and other ethnic groups occurred elsewhere in Sierra Leone during the 1982 general election, particularly in Koinadugu North constituency, where the election was canceled twice because of widespread violence and irregularities.[322] The political aspirations of the United States–educated Fula engineer Alpha B. Barrie, brother of the business titan, Alhaji Bailor Barrie, to contest the parliamentary seat for Koinadugu North led to conflicts with the dominant Yalunka group, although the area also had Mandingo, Limba, and Koranko residents. Alpha B. Barrie himself was the result of a cross-ethnic marriage in which his father was Fula but his mother was Mandingo. He faced A. B. M. Kamara, a Yalunka political incumbent who mobilized his ethnic group in Koinadugu and across the country in opposing Barrie's candidacy. According to Alpha Barrie, Kamara and his Yalunka supporters spread vicious propaganda that he was a Guinean-born Fula, just like his supporters, and therefore should not contest the election. The political conflict, which included fist fights, spilled over into Guinea and resulted in the intervention of President Stevens and First Vice President Koroma, as well as elders from both ethnic groups and paramount chiefs from across Koinadugu. According to one top APC minister then, Dr. Sama Banya, he was instructed by President Stevens to prevent the two Fula candidates in the District, Barrie and Alhaji Amadu Jalloh, from being nominated to contest the election.[323] In 1984 a peace agreement was reached in which the constituency was divided into two: Fula and Yalunka, with Barrie and Kamara declaring that they would contest future elections in these newly drawn constituencies respectively.

Alpha Barrie's decision to become a politician was inspired by the earlier political careers of Fula politicians such as Alhaji Maju and Alhaji Amadu Jalloh.[324] Earlier in 1977, Alhaji Jalloh had contested for a parliamentary seat to represent Koinadugu North-West constituency but lost the election to the APC candidate. When Barrie returned to Sierra Leone from the United States, his focus was to start a private business as a civil engineer. However, he faced a lot of pressure from key members of the Fula community, including business elite personages like his brother, Alhaji Bailor Barrie, and politicians like Alhaji Jalloh, to enter politics. As a result, he decided to contest for a parliamentary seat for Koinadugu North constituency in the 1982 general election. As a politician, Barrie traveled to many areas outside of his constituency where Fula were in large numbers, including Freetown along with Bombali, Kenema, Kono, and Pujehin.[325]

The iconic Alhaji Bailor Barrie, like the legendary Almamy Agibu Jalloh, played a key role in the campaigns to elect his brother, mobilizing material and human capital, particularly Fula. One of his closest allies was the Fula business leader, Alhaji Sanu Barrie, a fellow diamond dealer and business partner, who was also from Koinadugu. One successful strategy of Alhaji Bailor Barrie was to recruit Fula from elsewhere in Sierra Leone to provide both financial and logistical support in the election. Furthermore, he introduced his politician brother to key Fula business elite persons like Almamy Agibu Jalloh, and Alhaji Tejan-Jalloh, Alhaji Momodu Alpha Bah, as well as the FPU in order to broaden political support among the Fula in the country. But Alhaji Bailor Barrie was unsuccessful in his efforts to convince the Fula politician Alhaji Jalloh to join his brother in contesting for parliamentary seats in Koinadugu.[326]

In the postelection cabinet, President Stevens appointed the veteran Fula politician Alhaji Maju as minister of state in the first vice president's office headed by Koroma. Following the appointment, representatives of Alhaji Maju's East I constituency called on President Stevens at State House to express their appreciation for the appointment. Speakers included Paul Sesay, secretary of the constituency, who commended President Stevens for the peaceful conduct of the election. And a strong constituency supporter, D. W. Decker, gave the vote of thanks. In reply, President Stevens praised the one-party system as the best method to utilize human, social, and other resources to develop the state.[327] Alhaji Maju, together with the Kenema-based Fula politician M. A. Jalloh,[328] was later appointed a member of the APC Central Committee, which, together with the Governing Council, made the key decisions in the APC.[329] However, President Stevens dropped Alhaji Maju from his cabinet in August 1984.[330]

In addition to Alhaji Maju, President Stevens reappointed the long-term Fula business executive Alhaji A. D. Wurie to serve another five-year term in the fourth Parliament. As a Nominated MP, Alhaji Wurie, given his broad business background, including resident director of DELCO and member of the Board of Management of the SEF, made significant contributions to wide-ranging and often heated debates on the country's deepening economic crisis. He called for a reintroduction of the railway and improving the quality of rice grown in the country. Moreover, speaking on The Motion of Thanks for the Presidential

Address in Parliament, Alhaji Wurie recommended the creation of a permanent negotiating board comprising a legal expert, an economist with an accounting background, and a seasoned businessperson to assist the government in fast-tracking negotiations with would-be investors since in the past such discussions had been very slow.[331]

The APC and Muslims

As in previous SLPP governments, Fula political strategy during the Stevens administration included aligning, not only with Muslim Fula politicians like Alhaji Maju Alhaji A. D. Wurie, Hon. Jah,[332] and PC Alhaji Kaikai, but also with non-Fula Muslim politicians and Muslim organizations: the SLMC;[333] SLMB (Alhaji Sidique was elected secretary-general of the SLMB in 1979);[334] the Board of Imams of the SLMC; the Sierra Leone Muslim Pilgrims Welfare Association (SLMPWA);[335] the Sierra Leone Supreme Islamic Council (SLSIC); the YMMA (Alhaji Wurie served as president of the YMMA and was made honorary life president in the 1980s);[336] the Sierra Leone Muslim Union (SLMU); the Sierra Leone Islamic League (SLIL); the Sierra Leone Muslim Women Benevolent Organization (SLMWBO); the Sierra Leone Islamic Society (SLIS); the Sierra Leone Pilgrims Movement (SLPM); the Sierra Leone Women Pilgrims Movement (SLWPM); the Sierra Leone Muslim Men and Women's Association (SLMMWA), Kankalay; the Sierra Leone Muslim Women's Association (SLMWA); the Sierra Leone Muslim League (SLML); the Hanafiyatu Muslim Organization (HMO), founded by a female Fula, Haja Kadi Bah;[337] the Sierra Leone Muslim Pilgrims Movement (SLMPM); the United Muslim Jamaat (UMJ); Sierra Leone Pilgrims to Mecca (SLPM); and the Sierra Leone Pilgrims Welfare Association (SLPWA).[338]

Like his predecessors, the Margai brothers, President Stevens collaborated and worshiped with Muslims, many of whom were Fula, as part of his political strategy. Over 50 percent of the Sierra Leonean population was Muslim.[339] Stevens included in his cabinet Muslim Fula like PC Alhaji Kaikai, who served as minister of state, as well as acting vice president and prime minister,[340] and Alhaji Maju, as well as Muslims like Vice President Koroma and Dr. Forna. In 1968 Alhaji Gibril Sesay, president of the SLPWA and founding member of the APC, joined by hundreds of alhajis and hajas at State House, described Prime Minister Stevens as "the popular choice of the people."[341] Alhaji Sesay, who worked closely with Muslim Fula business leaders, was also a JP, chief imam of Temne Central Mosque in Freetown, and organizing secretary of the SLMB.[342] Prime Minister Stevens later joined the Fula acting governor-general, Sir Banja Tejan-Sie, and thousands of Muslims at id ul-fitr prayers marking the end of the month-long fasting, Ramadan, at Cline Town in Freetown. Also present at the ceremony were Alhaji Mustapha and Alhaji Haroun Buhari, president of the SLMC.[343] Among the APC Muslim politicians who members of the Fula business elite like Almamy Agibu Jalloh and Alhaji Tejan-Jalloh worked with was Dr. Forna who, as noted earlier, served as minister of finance and occasionally as acting prime minister. In May 1969, Acting Prime Minister Dr. Forna told thousands of Muslims, including Fula, on the occasion to mark the fourteenth annual celebrations of the birthday of the Holy Prophet Muhammad, *mawlid ul-nabi*, at Leone Memorial Gardens in Freetown, that Sierra Leone at that time faced problems not dissimilar to those the Holy Prophet faced in Mecca. He called on Muslims to speak against social evils and promote unity as the Prophet did. The birthday message for the occasion was delivered by Alhaji Sesay. Other speakers were Alhaji Abdul Gadri Saccoh, national vice president of the SLMB. The chairman of the occasion was the Muslim politician I. B. Taylor-Kamara.[344]

Besides President Stevens, Fula business elites worked with the Muslim Vice President Koroma whose mother, as noted previously, was Fula. As discussed earlier, Alhaji Maju greatly facilitated the relationship between Vice President Koroma and the Fula people.[345] Vice President Koroma was born in 1929 and educated at the Bo Government Secondary School, joined the Cooperatives in 1952, and served there for six years before entering active politics in 1959. He was a private businessman and first secretary of the Sierra Leone Motors Union. In 1962 Koroma first entered Parliament representing Freetown Central I constituency, which also voted him councilor of the FCC. In addition, Koroma served as alderman and acting mayor. In the 1967 general election, Koroma was reelected to Parliament and was appointed a cabinet minister after the APC assumed office in 1968. As a cabinet minister, Koroma served as minister of trade and industry, as well as minister of agriculture and natural resources, before his appointment as vice president and prime minister when Sierra Leone became a Republic in 1971. He also served as minister of the interior. In 1975 a constitutional amendment separated the office of prime minister from that of vice president, and Koroma became not only the vice president but was also assigned the Ministry of Finance. When the country became a one-party state in 1978, Koroma was appointed first vice president.[346]

Addressing Muslims while deputizing President Stevens at the celebration of Prophet Muhammad's birthday at the Queen Elizabeth II Playing Field in 1971, Vice President Koroma stated, "As a nation we in Sierra Leone have just been celebrating our tenth independence anniversary as well as the birth of a new republic. The task that lies ahead of us is to build a stable and united Sierra Leone where all can live in peace. This is a task in which every true citizen of Sierra Leone without distinction as to tribe or religion must take an active part."[347] Vice President Koroma retired from active politics in 1986, a year after his political mentor, President Stevens, resigned from office. Until his death in 1994, Koroma maintained a close relationship with the Fula community.[348]

One aspect of President Stevens's political strategy, although a Christian like his political predecessors the Margai brothers, was to provide governmental support to Muslims, including members of the Fula business class, to make the annual pilgrimage to Mecca. Such assistance included waiving the Le1 airport tax per passenger and having a government medical officer accompany the pilgrims.[349] The APC government worked primarily with the SLPWA, which was now headed by the Muslim Fula, Alhaji A. S. Tejan-Sie.[350] In 1969 a total number of 216 Muslim men and women—the largest in five years—left Freetown for the hajj. Before their departure, Acting Governor-General Sir Banja Tejan-Sie urged the pilgrims to pray fervently for the government and people of Sierra Leone while addressing them at State House at a party he gave in their honor. He told the Muslims that every true Muslim should believe that God had chosen those that should be in authority in the country. Introducing the acting governor-general, the secretary-general of the SLPWA, Alhaji Magba Kamara described that year's reception as historic, adding that this was the first time that a Muslim was holding the high office of governor-general.[351] The SLPWA played a key role in welcoming Muslim pilgrims, including a prominent businesswoman, Haja Isha Rahman.[352] Addressing Sierra Leone pilgrims passing through Egypt to Mecca in 1971, the chargé d'affaires in Cairo, Alhaji Gibril Sesay, said that the only way the country would progress was for the people to accept and respect their leaders. He further stated that God had chosen Prime Minister Stevens to lead the country and "any one group of people challenging his leadership to benefit their own selfish needs would definitely face destruction."[353]

In 1972 President Stevens, in an address to the people of Bonthe, said that his government would now play an active role in the hajj and that the Ministry of Social Welfare would be responsible for all future

Muslim pilgrims. The president said that the government could not take an active interest before now because some Muslims, especially those of the SLMC, were opposed to state interference in religious affairs. The APC government's decision came in the wake of Saudi Arabia's arrest and detention on allegations of drug trafficking of two Muslim leaders who led a hajj delegation of Muslim pilgrims. The Stevens administration had to intervene to provide aid to stranded pilgrims and repair the country's image.[354] Moreover, addressing a representative group of alhajis and hajas of the SLMPWA at State House, President Stevens promised that his government would continue to assist Sierra Leonean Muslim pilgrims in whatever way it could.[355]

In a subsequent meeting at State House with multiethnic Muslim leaders across the country, including Alhaji Seray-Wurie, Alhaji Mohamed B. Kebbay, and Haja Dankay Kabia, President Stevens stated that the government's decision to make arrangements for the hajj did not mean that it was trying to interfere in Islamic matters.[356] The Stevens administration's position on the hajj was reiterated by the Muslim Vice President Koroma while addressing Muslims at Limba Mosque in Freetown to mark the first anniversary of the Republic of Sierra Leone.[357] In 1973 President Stevens further informed a large group of Muslims at State House that the APC government would do everything possible to reduce the cost and increase the number of pilgrims going on the hajj.[358] In 1974, according to Minister of Social Welfare A. B. S. Janneh, that year's pilgrimage of five hundred Sierra Leoneans—the largest to date—was the best organized under the APC government.[359]

Beyond that, in 1974 President Stevens appointed a prominent Sierra Leonean–born Fula, Alhaji Seray-Wurie, to serve as chairman of the Pilgrimage Committee.[360] As noted earlier, he was also the deputy secretary-general of the MRU and a Member of the Order of the Rokel (MOR), an award he received from President Stevens for distinguished public service. Alhaji Seray-Wurie was also an active member of the SLMC and sometimes chaired its meetings.[361] As chair of the government-appointed Pilgrimage Committee, he accompanied the first group of 175 Muslim pilgrims to Mecca. The APC government provided a medical officer, nursing sister, dispenser, and two pilgrim aides to accompany the Muslim pilgrims.[362] In all, a total of 350 Sierra Leonean Muslims performed the hajj in 1975.[363]

Moreover, in 1976 the Stevens administration issued a release through the Ministry of Education, Social Welfare, and Rural Development that the SLMPM would now be the sole body to organize pilgrimages. This followed an earlier appeal to President Stevens by a delegation representing the national executive of the SLMPM led by Haja Dankay Kabia that pilgrimage affairs be handed over to it. President Stevens continued to express concerns but informed the delegation that a decision would be made after consultations within the government. The delegation assured the president of their financial and logistical readiness to undertake the annual Muslim pilgrimage, which numbered about 250 pilgrims in 1977.[364]

By 1978 several Muslim organizations, such as the newly formed SLMWA and the SLML, were in the forefront of advocates for a one-party system for Sierra Leone. The president and founder of SLMWA, Haja Isha Sasso, told members at an inaugural meeting that as women they had an important role to play in developing the country. She therefore urged the women to support the APC government under President Stevens in its efforts to bring about unity through a one-party system.[365] Writing in one of the leading local newspapers, Alhaji Sheikh Al-Farid Ibrahim Cole of the SLML drew extensively on Islam to explain the parallels between Islam and the proposed one-party system, as well as to solicit public support for a one-party state on Islamic grounds.[366] The SLPM also pledged strong support for the APC government's move to introduce a one-party system of government. The SLPM's secretary-general, Alhaji A. Mackie, stated in a press release that the group's executive fully supported the one-party initiative and praised the APC for creating an environment that allowed Muslims freedom of worship.[367] The Freetown-based Council of Imams and Muslim Leaders, which included Fula business elites like Alhaji Tejan-Jalloh, also pledged their support for the one-party system in a meeting with President Stevens at State House. Speaking on behalf of a cross-section of the Muslim community, Alhaji A. F. Rahman pledged the full support of the Council for a one-party system of government. President Stevens reminded the Muslims that it was in the house of one of the Muslim leaders present, Alhaji Gibril Sesay, Sierra Leone's former ambassador to Egypt, that the APC was formed in 1960.[368] In return for their political support, President Stevens strengthened his collaboration with Muslims despite their many organizations and competing interests. Some of the Muslim groups were led by women such as Haja Dankay Kabia, Haja Isha Rahman, and Haja Isha Sasso. To address the challenge of the proliferation of Muslim organizations, the Muslim minister of social welfare and rural development, Thaimu Bangura, called for an all-embracing body similar to the United Christian Council to facilitate government assistance to the country's large Muslim population.[369]

In 1985 the eighty-year-old President Stevens retired after seventeen years in office and handed power to his army chief, Momoh, whose rule I discuss in the next chapter. Thus, President Stevens made history as the first civilian African leader to hand over power to a military head.[370] At this time, Stevens's relationship with the Fula community—particularly its business elites of Guinean nationality—showed marked improvement, in contrast to the earlier and prolonged, difficult tensions. A primary explanation was the fact that his close personal friend and political mentor, President Touré, the arch nemesis of the Sierra Leone–based Guinean-born Fula, died in 1984 after twenty-six years as president of Guinea. In the same year, a small group of military officers led by Colonel Lansana Conté, the Army Chief of Staff, staged a bloodless coup against the late President Touré's government. Col. Conté then became the new president of Guinea.[371] In March 1985 President Conté, on the invitation of President Stevens, came to Sierra Leone on a one-day working visit. According to a communiqué signed by both leaders at the end of the visit, they agreed to set up committees in both countries to improve the existing friendly relationship, especially in economic matters. Moreover, they stated their determination to advance the mission of the MRU in efforts to improve living standards in both countries. The communiqué further noted that both countries would reactivate the joint commissions for cooperation and explore new areas of cooperation, which would now occur during the Momoh presidency.[372]

4

The Joseph S. Momoh
Presidency, 1985–92

Joseph Saidu Momoh was born on January 26, 1937, at Binkolo in Bombali, but the Momoh family migrated to Freetown and then settled at rural Wilberforce in the early 1940s.[1] Momoh attended the West African Methodist Collegiate School in Freetown between 1951 and 1955, when he earned the Cambridge school Certificate. Next, Momoh enrolled at the Government Clerks School, Technical Institute. On graduation, Momoh joined the Civil Service in 1956 and worked as a third grade clerk until his resignation in 1958. In that year, Momoh enlisted as a private in the then Royal West African Frontier Force (RWAFF)—officially disbanded in 1960—thus starting a long distinguished military career. In the 1950s and 1960s, Momoh received military training at the Regular Officers Training School in Tieshi, Ghana; the Nigerian Military Training Academy in Kaduna, where he won the Baton of Honor; and in the United Kingdom both in the School of Infantry in Hythe and the Mons Officers Cadet School at Aldershot, where he was awarded the Sword of Honor as the most exceptional overseas cadet. In 1963 Momoh was commissioned as second lieutenant in the then Royal Sierra Leone Military Forces and promoted to major while he was commanding Moa Barracks at Daru in Kailahun.

In the wake of Momoh's brief imprisonment at Pademba Road Prison after the military coup that ousted the NRC, he continued to serve in the military and was made lieutenant colonel and commanding officer of the First Battalion in 1969. This was followed by promotion to full colonel in 1970. Then, in September 1971, President Stevens appointed Colonel Momoh, deputy force commander, as acting force commander following an attempted military coup led by Force Commander Brigadier John Bangura earlier in March 1971; Momoh was confirmed in his new position in November the same year.[2] Moreover,

Momoh received the insignia of Officer of the Most Excellent Order of the British Empire (OBE) in the same year. And in 1973, President Stevens promoted Momoh to Brigadier of the Republic of Sierra Leone Military Forces (RSLMF). Beyond that, in 1974 President Stevens named Brigadier Momoh as a Nominated MP and minister of state with cabinet status. By including Momoh in political decision making, President Stevens was influenced by the Tanzanian model of governance, which he admired. President Stevens justified the appointment on the grounds that his government now "recognized the necessity and expediency of involving every section of the nation in the running of the government."[3] For Vice President Koroma, the president's decision was a throwback to the colonial era: "In the colonial days the Commissioner of Police and the Commanding Officer for Sierra Leone and the Gambia were members of the Legislative Council." And Koroma also noted that there were instances when "the Commanding Officer had even acted as Governor."[4] Also in 1974, Brigadier Momoh was awarded the Order of the Rokel (OR) in recognition of his decades-long distinguished service. And in 1983, President Stevens promoted Brigadier Momoh to the rank of major-general.[5]

Prior to becoming president, Major-General Momoh, besides his military career, also served in various sporting and civic capacities, including president of the Sierra Leone Amateur Boxing Association (SLABA); executive member of WAFA; vice president and president of SLAFA; chairman, board of governors, West African Methodist Collegiate School in Freetown; chief patron of the Blackpool football team; and chairman, board of governors, Services Secondary School, also in Freetown. In his earlier years, President Momoh played competitive football for Young Stars of Makeni and subsequently for Blackpool in first division league matches in Freetown. In addition, he played tennis, volleyball, and basketball. As a sports enthusiast, Momoh worked with notable Fula sports leaders, including the business executive and politician Alhaji A. D. Wurie, who served in several positions, including president of SLAFA and the Sierra Leone Amateur Basketball Association; Mobil Oil executive Ibrahim Oponjo Wurie, who was team manager and technical advisor of the East End Lions football club, as well as team manager of the Leone Stars, the national team; and Sierra Leone Ports Authority employee Alhaji Chernor Sie, who was manager of the Kakuma and Mighty Blackpool football clubs. Moreover, Major-General Momoh strongly supported army participation in competitive sporting activities locally, such as the annual inter-unit athletic programs; the Forces Football League involving the police, fire forces, and prison;

and against the Young Sportsmen Club, which was mainly Lebanese. Furthermore, the army took part in overseas tournaments like the ECOWAS and Commonwealth Games. Under Momoh's leadership, the army also embarked on several self-help projects involving the construction of hospitals, bridges, roads, and schools, as well as rice cultivation in many areas of the country such as Port Loko, Kambia, Kailahun, and Bombali.[6]

Major-General Momoh succeeded Stevens as president on November 28, 1985, in a peaceful transfer of power in Parliament[7] following his election as secretary-general and leader of the APC in August; both positions were previously held by President Stevens. Next, he was nominated as the sole presidential candidate in September and won a landslide electoral victory in October.[8] President Stevens was among many top APC and government leaders who campaigned for Momoh. In a campaign rally in Kambia witnessed by a massive crowd, President Stevens presented Momoh as a "son of the soil," like him, and asked the crowd to give Momoh maximum support because he would bring prosperity to the country. He told the masses to work with Momoh in advancing national development since foreigners with external loyalties would not develop the country. The political campaign meeting was chaired by the former foreign minister, Dr. Abdulai Conteh, who was from Kambia.[9]

In January 1986 Momoh, at age forty-nine, was inaugurated as president and received strong support from Sierra Leoneans across the country. The three-day events marking the inauguration were witnessed by over forty delegations from several areas of the world, including the United States, Europe, and Asia. In his inaugural speech, President Momoh laid out a vision for a new political philosophy, Constructive Nationalism, and introduced a New Order underpinned by eight policies addressing such issues as taxation, foreign exchange, inflation, foreign investment, and small businesses. As described by President Momoh,

Constructive nationalism involves putting the interests of the nation above all else, above all others, at all times; above but without neglecting the legitimate needs and interests of individuals and groups. In other words, it is a political philosophy that seeks to unify the whole without destroying the single components. It seeks to give a sense of awakening to the people of this country—to have them realize that the nation to which they belong can only be built through their own hard work and dedication and that, at best, the outside world can only be of assistance in that task. Above all, it requires a brand new political system in which the emphasis will be on the freedom of the individual: freedom to develop his capabilities and talents so as to contribute effectively to the development of the nation; freedom to choose his own political leaders so as to ensure that the path chosen by those leaders in the conduct of the affairs of the State is in conformity with the desires of those they are said to represent.[10]

Immigration

As with previous administrations, immigration was still a challenge during the Momoh presidency, and tribalism continued to influence national debates on immigration and politics.[11] The seventeen-year-rule of President Stevens was marked by frequent stranger drives (expulsion of undocumented immigrants) that often targeted Fula, but this was less so during the Momoh presidency. To take but one example, in December 1987, a joint army and police operation in diamond areas in Kono led to the arrest of 103 illegal aliens, many of whom were Fula; they were detained at Mafanta Prison in Tonkolili, Northern Province.[12] Kono, as discussed in the preceding chapters, was the centerpiece of diamond mining activities in the country.[13] Earlier in 1986, the minister of finance, Joe Amara Bangali, in an interview on the Sierra Leone Broadcasting Services (SLBS) radio, stated that the Momoh administration was to embark on a stranger drive in the diamond-mining areas, particularly Kono and Tongo Field in Kenema to curb illicit mining and stop the parallel foreign exchange market, which affected the foreign exchange rate. A large number of Fula were involved in both illicit diamond mining and trading foreign currencies on the parallel market.[14]

Both Inspector-General of Police James Bambay Kamara and Minister of Mines Birch M. Conteh put the number of illicit diamond miners and dealers in Kono at over ten thousand. And they both promised harsh penalties for those who did not secure licenses or leave the mining areas in Kono. For the inspector-general of police, "Illicit miners and dealers have been having a field day, cheating the government and the people of this country in the process. These are strangers who have been living in the (Kono) district for five, ten, fifteen and upwards to forty years. Therefore, they must be made to pay now, obtain their licenses to operate legally, or quit Kono immediately."[15] In a meeting with diamond dealers, including Fula, in Freetown, the minister of mines informed them that diamond dealers' licenses were abolished with immediate effect and that mining licenses would only be issued to native-born citizens, excluding naturalized citizens, under the Mining Act. .[16] In addition, the Momoh government resorted to an earlier practice of deporting foreigners in the Kono diamond areas because of economic crimes, particularly the smuggling of diamonds. A prominent businessman, the Fula diamond dealer Alhaji Habibu Sowe, was deported.[17]

One solution to the problem of illegal immigration was the registration of citizens and noncitizens, a practice of earlier governments that the Momoh administration perpetuated. Announcing the activation of the national registration and identification (I.D.) card program, the Fula minister of internal affairs, Alhaji Sidique, stated the advantages for both individual citizens and the government. For citizens, an I.D. card would facilitate "(a) admission to higher institutions of learning, employment, issuance of driving license, processing of national passport, claim on insurance companies, retirement and other benefits, collection of parcels from the post office and withdrawal of money from the bank (b) identification of accident victims and (c) easing immigration formalities when crossing national boundaries to neighboring countries."[18] Furthermore, identity cards would assist the state in the process of democratic elections and minimize electoral malpractices, as well as enhance state security. Alhaji Sidique called on all residents, citizens and noncitizens, to cooperate with the APC government to ensure the success of the program. He explained that the exercise would help promote national awareness and identity and also advance the integration of the different ethnic groups, including Fula, in the country. As with previous governments, the Fula chief Alhaji Bah and prominent members of Fula business elites, including Almamy Agibu Jalloh, Alhaji Tejan-Jalloh, Alhaji Momodu Alpha Bah, and Alhaji Bailor Barrie, played a key role in educating and mobilizing native-born and foreign-born Fula to register with the Momoh government. By August 1987, about 50,000 had been registered since the exercise started earlier in the year. And it was projected that about 2.5 million people would have been issued with identity cards by the time of the next general election, planned for 1991.[19]

The FPU remained actively involved in Fula immigration issues during the Momoh presidency. The death of the Fula chief Alhaji Bah in March 1986 brought about a change in the leadership of the FPU.[20] The FPU President Alhaji Seray-Wurie succeeded the late Fula chief whose funeral in Freetown was attended by thousands of mourners, including high-profile Fula businesspeople such as Almamy Agibu Jalloh, Alhaji Bailor Barrie, Alhaji Momodu Alpha Bah, Alhaji Sanu Barrie, Alhaji Tejan-Jalloh, and Alhaji Sorie Bailor Bah, vice president of the FPU in the Eastern Province that included Kono. APC government officials who paid tributes and visited the bereaved family included Acting President Francis M. Minah, Acting First Vice President A. B. Kamara, Acting Second Vice President and Minister of Education Dr. A. F. Joe-Jackson, and Minister of the Interior Kawusu Konteh. As discussed in previous chapters, the late Alhaji Bah had been Fula chief since 1956 and in 1971 was extradited to Guinea by President Stevens after the abortive Portuguese invasion on charges by the late President Touré that the Fula chief had trained Fula mercenaries in Sierra Leone to overthrow the Guinean government. Alhaji Bah was detained for several years but the charges were never proved. He was later released and returned to Freetown, where he continued to serve as Fula chief despite health problems that worsened during his imprisonment.[21]

At age seventy-nine, Alhaji Seray-Wurie was the first Sierra Leonean–born Fula chief of the Western Area. His crowning ceremony in which he received the title of Almamy was attended by a large crowd drawn from a cross-section of the Freetown community at the Siaka Stevens Stadium.[22] Prior to this position, Alhaji Seray-Wurie, as discussed earlier, worked as a civil servant and was an accomplished professional accountant and auditor. He was the first native-born national to be appointed deputy director of the Audit Department. After he retired in 1965, Alhaji Seray-Wurie worked as chief accountant and deputy registrar at Ahmadu Bello University in Nigeria. Following his return to Sierra Leone, Alhaji Seray-Wurie served as bursar at FBC. And he was later appointed as the first deputy secretary-general of the MRU.[23]

Replacing Alhaji Seray-Wurie as FPU president was the Fula business titan, Alhaji Bailor Barrie, who was elected national president in 1986 and served until his death in April 1989.[24] In the wake of the death of Alhaji Bailor Barrie, a prominent Fula civil servant Alim Jallo-Jamboria, professional head in the Ministry of Works,[25] served as interim president until another successful diamond dealer, Alhaji Sanu Barrie, close personal friend of Alhaji Bailor Barrie, was elected president at the first national convention of the FPU held in Makeni in Bombali in January 1990. The event was attended by President Momoh, cabinet ministers, and hundreds of Fula, including elite businesspeople Almamy Agibu Jalloh, Fatmata Binta Jalloh, and Mohamed "Texaco" Bah. To advance their broad interests, Fula business elites, working collaboratively with Fula professionals, political leaders, and religious leaders, crafted a political strategy to mobilize the Fula community to organize national conventions, which was the culmination of many years of political organizing by the FPU in Sierra Leone.[26]

At the opening of the first FPU national convention, President Momoh said that "anybody who is not proud of his origin is not fit to live." He encouraged more Fula participation in the economy as entrepreneurs, especially in the mining sector, and urged them to guard against smuggling. The chairman of the event, Alhaji Sidique, who was also a cabinet minister in President Momoh's government, admonished the Fula to be law-abiding. In his welcome address, the Fula chief for Bombali, Alhaji Alpha Mamadu Jalloh Timbo, commented on efforts to resolve the differences between Fula cattle owners and indigenous crop farmers. The professional head of the Ministry of Works and interim chair of the Fula convention, Alim Jallo-Jamboria, presented a paper on the origins of the Fula. The two-day convention ended with the election of a national executive that included prominent members of the Fula business class: Alhaji Sanu Barrie, president; Alim Jalloh-Jamboria, first vice president; Mohammed "Texaco" Bah, second vice president; Abu B. Jalloh, secretary-general; Mohamed Wurie Jalloh, assistant secretary-general; Hon. Alpha Barrie, social secretary; Abdul Karim Jalloh, assistant social secretary; Hassan Barrie, organizing secretary; Fatmata Binta Jalloh, assistant organizing secretary; and Ibrahim Jalloh, financial secretary. The following were elected regional vice presidents: Musa Jalloh, Western Area; Sori Bah, Eastern Province; Usman Sawaneh, Northern Province; and Abdul Jalloh, Southern Province.[27] Fatmata Binta Jalloh was the founder of the National Women's Cooperative Society, which was multi-ethnic and had members in all the country's districts. Besides business activities, the Cooperative was an important political mobilizing instrument for the APC among women.[28] Collectively, the earlier efforts of the FPU and the Fula convention in Makeni contributed significantly to Fula political visibility in the country.

As discussed in previous chapters, Fula immigration was affected by Sierra Leone–Guinea relations. However, after the death of President Touré and the presidency of Lansana Conté, cross-border movement of Fula increased with less harassment and restrictions. President Momoh built on the long-established ties between the two neighboring countries. In June 1986, President Momoh visited Guinea and held wide-ranging talks with President Conté, including the topics of immigration, trade, sports, education, and security between the two countries.[29] Following this visit, the capitals Freetown and Conakry became sister cities to strengthen existing ties between the two neighboring countries and to deal with problems of urban growth such as pollution, electricity, and water. According to the chairman of the FCC Committee of Management (FCCCM), Alfred Akibo-Betts, Guinea and Sierra

Leone shared cultural and linguistic backgrounds. He expressed the hope that both states, in keeping with the principles of unity and cooperation of the MRU, OAU, and ECOWAS, would work toward eliminating the artificial boundaries between them.[30]

In November 1986, President Momoh joined President Conté and President Samuel Doe of Liberia in signing a tripartite treaty of nonaggression and security cooperation within the MRU. The three heads of state agreed "to respect the territorial integrity of each other, renounce the use of force or threats in all their relations and to resolve all their differences by peaceful means." Moreover, they consented "not to engage directly or indirectly in any acts of forceful nature against the interests of each other's countries and they promised to prevent all covert or overt actions in the military, paramilitary or political fields and not to allow the use of each other's territory as bases for subversive activities against the other." Furthermore, "that both state controlled and independent media be discouraged to create insurrection against the parties in the treaty." The treaty also made clear "that any military or paramilitary personnel found in each other's territory without proper travel documents should be arrested, investigated and extradited upon the request by his country of origin." Finally, the three leaders agreed to set up a "joint liaison commission to study the questions of dissidents, criminals, and fugitives and the exchange of information to promote peaceful co-existence among the three countries."[31]

Beyond that, in November 1987, President Momoh welcomed a twenty-member Guinean delegation in Freetown, which was to reciprocate a similar visit by the chairman of the FCCCM, Akibo-Betts, on the twinning of the cities of Freetown and Conakry.[32] Subsequently, in July 1989, President Conté made a return visit to Sierra Leone, where the two leaders further discussed bilateral issues, including an ongoing border crisis; immigration; trade; health care; aviation; the use of both countries as transit routes for drugs from Asia and Africa to the United States and Europe; the smuggling of gold, diamonds, produce, and stolen cars; and the regional organization, MRU. As a result of the talks between the two leaders, ministers of the interior of both countries agreed to meet in Guinea to follow up on the broad range of issues between the two neighbors.[33] In February 1990, President Momoh made a second visit to Guinea, where he engaged President Conté on a number of bilateral matters including immigration, cross-border trade, sports, the nonaggression and security cooperation treaty among the MRU members, as well as the largest regional body, ECOWAS.[34]

The well-established bilateral relations between the two neighboring countries were further highlighted by the Guinean ambassador to Sierra Leone, Ibrahim Cherif Maidara in his remarks celebrating his country's thirty-first independence anniversary in Freetown. The ambassador spoke about the shared cultures and history of both nations and the past efforts of Sierra Leone governments to strengthen the relationship with his homeland. In his statement, the foreign minister of Sierra Leone, Dr. Abdul Karim Koroma, stated that relations between the two countries predated independence, and that the two societies shared common cultures, languages, and history.[35]

Fula Business Elites and the Politics of Business

Decades after independence in 1961, Fula business elites expanded their participation in national politics during the Momoh presidency largely, as previously, to advance their business interests in core economic sectors such as the diamond trade, transport, livestock, and retail trade. Issues like diamond mining and export licenses, residential permits, and security were of great concern to the Fula business community, particularly diamond dealers and retailers.[36] Addressing the first national convention of the FPU, President Momoh stressed that Fula businesspeople were an important group in the national economy and encouraged them, especially the elites, to work with his government in dealing with the country's worsening economic difficulties. Moreover, the president urged them to desist from economic crimes such as smuggling, tax evasion, and currency hoarding.[37] This was especially in the context of the Momoh government's deportation of prominent foreign-born Fula businessmen found guilty of tax evasion and smuggling, particularly Mohamed Sall in 1985[38] and Alhaji Habibu Sowe in 1986;[39] the seizure of millions of Leones owned by Fula businesspeople, particularly elites, in violation of the Economic Emergency Act;[40] and the unlawful activities of Koindu-based Fula in Kailahun in cross-border trading between Sierra Leone and Liberia.[41] In one noted case involving the Fula business elite Alhaji Umaru Monorma Bah, the Momoh government seized and confiscated a large quantity of Alhaji Bah's imported cigarettes over allegations of smuggling and tax evasion. However, Alhaji Bah disputed the charges, insisting that he received the administrations's approval to bring foreign cigarettes into the country and had paid all the requisite taxes. Despite Alhaji Bah's protests, the Momoh government did not return the cigarettes or compensate Alhaji Bah.[42] In February 1992, the APC secretary-general, Edward M. Turay (MP for Bombali Central I), in a seven-page "Position Paper on Mining" called for the expulsion of foreigners, including Fula, from the diamond areas because their activities, which included smuggling, were inimical to the interest of the state.[43]

Retail Trade

With their increasing and visible business success in key sectors like the merchandise, diamond, transport, livestock trade, and real estate, the Fula faced mounting challenges such as the demands by the newly formed National Association of Indigenous Businessmen (NAIB) "that foreigners and naturalized citizens be restricted from participating in sensitive areas of the retail trade to be reserved for indigenous businessmen" and "that no foreign or naturalized citizens be allowed to reside and deal in diamond or gold in the mining areas." The Association also demanded from the Momoh government "that the relevant provisions of the Non-Citizens Trade and Business Act No. 9 of 1969 restricting the participation of non-citizens in certain key areas of the retail trade be more vigorously enforced for the benefit of the indigenous Sierra Leoneans." Many of the concerns of the NAIB had earlier been presented to previous governments in efforts to solve the country's serious economic problems.[44] Beyond that, Fula business elites still had a key challenge of how to prevent the large Fula immigrant and Sierra Leonean–born retailers from being exploited and harassed by government officials such as price and trade inspectors, as well as law enforcement. As earlier, in partial response to these problems, Fula business leaders encouraged Fula retailers to broaden their membership in the several multi-ethnic traders' associations, including the United Indigenous Commercial and Petty Traders Association (UICPTA) and the SLPTA, where the secretary-general of the latter was still Jalloh.

As previously, during the Momoh presidency, Secretary-General Jalloh—although a Sierra Leonean–born Fula—continued his efforts to advance the SLPTA's main goal of banning all foreigners, including Fula, from participating in petty and retail trades. He still played a key role in presenting resolutions to the Momoh government and the FCC, staging boycotts, and organizing protests and demonstrations that sometimes became violent. The Association continued to maintain that Lebanese, Indians, and other foreign businesses were hiring foreigners rather than Sierra Leoneans, a sore point particularly given the massive economic problems facing the country.[45] A perennial problem between the FCC and the traders' associations was over street trading. Just after President Momoh became president in November, the FCC announced that it would move most of the traders at Guard Street to a Le300,000 one-storey market at the abattoir (Cow Yard) after its completion at the end of the month. Most of the funding for the market was provided by the US embassy. According to the director of the US Peace Corps, Dr. Habib Khan, the money came from the American embassy's Small Project Assistance to help developing countries implement small projects. For the FCC, it provided local materials and labor estimated at Le45,000. Although the secretary-general of the UICPTA, Bai H. K. Bangura, praised the US embassy and the FCC for the new market, he made clear that it was inadequate given the large number of traders. Moreover, he stressed that difficulties would arise if one group of traders were forced to use the market and others were left to continue street trading. According to him, "What we need is a large central market that could be built in a place like Sewa grounds for all traders."[46] The *Daily Mail* newspaper in one editorial described street trading as a "cancer" and stated that "Government must look immediately into the insidious element of street trading in the capital Freetown. . . . Today street trading in Freetown has become a cancerous affair. . . . As President Momoh's new administration continues to set the pace of house cleaning, it is vital that this deplorable situation be arrested and contained once and for all."[47]

Additionally, the traders clashed with the FCC over market dues and licences. For example, in 1986 thousands of petty traders marched to the City Hall to protest against the FCC's increase in licences, fees, and market dues. Led by Bangura of the UICPTA, the traders presented an eleven-point petition stating that the FCC had reneged on its 1985 agreement when market dues were increased from eight cents to twenty cents per day. Under the agreement, the FCC was to repair all existing markets in Freetown, including the provision of electricity, toilets, water stand pipes, and the weekly cleaning of all markets. The petition also mentioned the poor conditions of FCC schools and the lack of uniforms and identification cards for FCC security and market dues collectors. The dispute between the FCC and the traders led to the intervention of the second vice president, A. B. Kamara, and the minister of internal affairs, Alhaji Sidique. Vice President Kamara informed the traders that the Momoh government was in the process of restructuring the FCC to be more efficient and responsive in its responsibilities, including those to traders. He made clear that an increase in market dues should have a corresponding increase in amenities, including water and toilet facilities. In addition, he advised the traders to pay their charges to provide the necessary funding for the FCC.[48] As the new chairman of the FCC Committee of Management, Alfred Akibo-Betts stated in November 1986 that traders had to register with the FCC and would be issued a trading license only after they had submitted the required paperwork. He stressed that a key priority was to end indiscipline by street traders who were responsible for the poor environment in Freetown.[49] For instance, in May 1987, eleven petty traders including three Fula, Mohamed Barrie, Mohamed Jalloh, and Abdul Bah, were arrested with their goods on charges of trading in Freetown's prohibited areas and were brought to Magistrate Court No. 1A presided over by Magistrate Catherine Martyn. They all pleaded guilty and were each fined Le100 or an alternative two-month prison sentence. The magistrate also gave them a stern warning against engaging in illegal street trading. They all paid their fines and were subsequently released from custody.[50]

In November 1987, Parliament approved a bill, the Freetown Municipality Amendment Act of 1987, which transferred certain responsibilities of the president regarding the approval of budget estimates, as well as administrative supervision and approval of the bylaws of the FCC, to the minister of internal affairs. The bill would give the minister better oversight over the finances of the FCC, as well as the authority to supervise the FCC as a government corporation, consistent with other local bodies in the country. Introducing the bill in Parliament, Internal Affairs Minister Alhaji Sidique pointed out excesses in the collection of market dues, which brought about late payment of salaries of FCC's workers. Moreover, the Act empowered the president to appoint six councilors to the FCC in addition to the councilors required to be elected under the Act, which amended the Freetown Municipality Act of 1973 in restoring the principle of government-appointed councilors. Additionally, the new Act stated that the FCC shall not, without the consent of the internal affairs minister, terminate the appointment of the town clerk, the deputy town clerk, the medical officer of health, the treasurer, the accountant, the town engineer, the chief sanitary superintendent, the valuer, or the city bailiff.[51]

Livestock

During the Momoh presidency, the Fula were still at the core of the livestock business of Sierra Leone. However, the death of Almamy

Bah—the preeminent Fula meat contractor—in March 1986 created a void that his family tried to fill by continuing his meat supply contracts. One of his wives, the Sierra Leonean–born Fula Iye, who was Western-educated, played a central role in sustaining the Bah meat supply business. She closely worked with the stepchildren including Mamadu and Kanja to keep the business profitable and competitive. Yet, over time, they suffered loss of market share from long-established competitors like Alhaji Boie Kamara. The Allie family business in the cattle and butchering was continued by Alhaji Baba Allie, brother of Alhaji Ibrahim Allie, with whom he had partnered in the family business. Drawing on the long-established networks of his father and late brother in both the Fula community in Sierra Leone and beyond, as well as outside the Fula population, Alhaji Baba Allie achieved considerable success in the butchering business. He was a key member of the Sierra Leone Butchers Association, which was still an important bridge between the butchers and both the central government and local governments like the FCC. Political patronage remained a significant factor in the awarding of government meat contracts.[52]

As for Almamy Agibu Jalloh, he remained a major supplier of cattle to multi-ethnic butchers, especially those in Freetown. He maintained an area in Kissy where his cattle were temporarily housed before distribution to buyers in the capital city. Almamy Agibu's hometown of Rokulan in Bombali was still a vital part of his cattle business where cattle were raised. Almamy Agibu's cattle business was only one aspect of his diversified business portfolio, which included commercial transportation and agriculture. He developed a business model in which he had his livestock on his Provincial lands and employed kinsmen to help manage them with raising, grazing, and transporting when the livestock were fully grown in his vehicles to various market centers, including the largest—Freetown.[53]

Fula livestock business faced many challenges, some of which predated the Momoh era. For example, conflicts between Fula cattle owners and local crop farmers such as the Temne who had persistently complained about the destruction of their crops by Fula-owned cattle remained, and in some instances worsened. This was especially so in the Northern Province, particularly Bombali and Koinadugu where there were a large number of Fula cattle owners. Furthermore, the supply of meat to major markets like Freetown was seriously impacted by the large-scale departure of Fula herdsmen and their cattle from grazing areas such as Bombali because of constant harassments and hefty fines levied on them by local authorities. As previously, the Momoh government intervened to help resolve such disputes, largely because they had political implications. In doing so, it worked closely with the Fula chiefs in Freetown and the Northern Province, as well as non-Fula traditional rulers in those areas. Moreover, the large-scale theft of Fula-owned cattle remained a serious problem, particularly during periods leading up to general elections. The worsening economy under the leadership of President Momoh compounded the financial difficulties that Fula faced in the livestock sector, including reduced cattle, goats, and sheep sales; expensive transport costs; and a high cost of living.[54]

Motor Transport

By President Momoh's presidency, the Fula had broadened their involvement in the country's transport sector, owning commercial transport vehicles such as long-haul lorries, taxis, and minivans (*poda-poda*), as well as selling imported preowned vehicles mainly from Europe and America. Many were immigrants from neighboring Guinea, where they had acquired a wide range of skills needed in the transport business. In addition to being owners, the Fula were drivers, apprentices, auto mechanics, and providers of tire repair and replacement service. Alhaji Bailor Barrie remained the single largest Fula investor in the transport business sector as an importer and retailer of foreign vehicles. This was one aspect of those businesses of his grouped under M. B. Barrie Co. (SL) LTD.[55] In addition, Almamy Agibu Jalloh continued as a major businessman in the transport sector. He still operated commercial vehicles that transported goods and passengers between the Provinces and Freetown. Beyond his business activities, in 1991 Almamy Agibu Jalloh was appointed Fula chief for Bombali. His social contributions included establishing the Wuroh Memorial Secondary School at Roku-lan and providing the foundation for construction of a modern hospital, also at Rokulan. Moreover, Almamy Agibu Jalloh used some of the profits from his vast transport business to continue supporting football in Sierra Leone.[56]

The severe economic problems during the Momoh presidency compounded the challenges facing the transport sector. The Fula, like others in this business, contended with very short-term, high interest loans that hampered the expansion of their businesses. Moreover, there were the high cost of vehicles and spare parts; increasing transport fares that affected consumer demand; competition from the Road Transport Corporation (RTC) and foreigners in the motor transport business; and the persistent traffic police harassment of drivers, including the setting up of too many checkpoints and demands for bribes that impacted negatively their profitability. Writing about the transport challenges in 1985, one newspaper columnist stated, "Transportation became almost a privileged aspect of social life. Taxi drivers touted their fares to Le4 per city trip while they crammed their cars with passengers packed like sardines. Sierra Leoneans were daily losing their dignity. At this juncture, a word of praise is appropriate for poda-poda owners and operators who, many a time tried not to exceed fifty cents on their city fares. If they had followed the general trend, the country would simply have erupted."[57] One newspaper editorial stated,

> The transportation situation remains one of the biggest problems confronting the nation and the Momoh administration. The long lines of weary, dispirited people waiting endlessly at bus halts and improvised poda poda stations tell the sordid story with each waking day. Scores of frustrated commuters, some of them aged people narrate heart-rending stories of their daily tramping to work in the centre of Freetown from distances as far away as Waterloo and Goderich. . . . The crux of the entire problem is that at a time when the population in the metropolis has soared, there is an acute shortage of buses which should provide this vital utility service. The Road Transport Corporation has complained for long about the unavailability of spare parts for dozens of Mercedes Benz and other buses lying idle at their depot. The RTC also complains about the difficulty in obtaining the foreign exchange to purchase these necessary spare parts. . . . As a newspaper, reflecting the views and mood of the public to such a well meaning government, we stress that a conference be held as a matter of urgency involving the RTC, private transporters, thinking members of the public and the government to work out a comprehensive and speedy programme for a solution to this dominant problem.[58]

As for Almamy Agibu, he sustained his earlier efforts in working with the Sierra Leone Motor Drivers Union—who staged frequent protests over the issues highlighted above—and the Momoh government to find solutions to these difficulties.[59]

Diamond Trade

During the Momoh presidency, the Fula remained important participants in the diamond trade as licensed dealers and diggers, but many were not licensed. With increased opportunities, the Fula faced many challenges, most predating the Momoh presidency. They centered on the issuance, renewal, and revocation of residential permits; corruption surrounding such permits; the high cost of the permits; law enforcement harassment and bribery demands; violence tied to illicit mining; taxing demands from traditional rulers and local authorities; issuance, renewal, and revocation of dealers' and diggers' licenses; corruption involved in connection with such licenses; the increasing cost of these licenses; and competition from Sierra Leoneans and African and non-African foreign nationals in the diamond business. The acute economic problems faced by the Momoh administration, which are discussed in detail below, exacerbated these difficulties with which the Fula had to contend in the diamond sector of the national economy.[60]

The death of the business icon Alhaji Bailor Barrie in April 1989 deprived the Fula business class of leadership, particularly in the diamond sector. He was the single largest and wealthiest Fula involved in the country's diamond business. Moreover, he mentored many Fula businesspeople not only in the diamond trade, but in other areas of the Sierra Leone economy and beyond, including, for example, the Guinean and The Gambian economies. By the time of his death, Alhaji Bailor Barrie had expanded his business portfolio in areas such as real estate both within and without the country, commercial agriculture, and motor transport. This was fueled in large measure by diamond profits. Given Alhaji Bailor Barrie's long entrepreneurial experience and vast business and political networks in both Sierra Leone and abroad, he was a valuable bridge builder in the Fula community.[61]

Furthermore, Alhaji Bailor Barrie worked tirelessly in collaboration with Fula elites in the diamond business to engage the APC government, law enforcement, the Guinean ambassador in Sierra Leone, and traditional rulers and local authorities in the diamond areas to find solutions to difficulties faced by Fula in the diamond business. Although Alhaji Bailor Barrie's death left a huge vacuum to fill, Fula businessmen such as Alhaji Sanu Barrie, who was a close friend and business partner of Alhaji Barrie, stepped up their efforts to provide leadership, not just in the diamond sector, but the Fula business class as a whole. He continued working with Fula business leaders such as Alhaji Momodu Alpha Bah, Alhaji Chewtor Jalloh, Almamy Agibu Jalloh, Almamy Alhaji Seray-Wurie, Alhaji Tejan-Jalloh, and Fula religious heads and traditional rulers in the Provinces to provide collective responses to Fula challenges in post-Alhaji Bailor Barrie Sierra Leone.[62]

President Momoh inherited a host of economic challenges from the Stevens era that would significantly define his presidency. As president, Momoh prioritized and used different mediums such as independence and presidential anniversaries, press conferences, Christmas messages, APC conventions and rallies, and parliamentary speeches to identify and propose solutions to the country's pressing economic problems.[63] In a broadcast to the nation on the occasion of its twenty-sixth independence anniversary, President Momoh stated,

> Fellow citizens, on this day of reckoning, as your President, I am the first to admit that the performance of our economy is still far from satisfactory. In the past, we have made a number of sacrifices in the hope of arresting the downward trend. Within our capability and even under extremely difficult circumstances, we have gone a long way in not only negotiating an International Monetary Fund programme but also in implementing a variety of measures prescribed by that Institution such as a full adoption of a floating monetary exchange rate system which resulted in a massive and rapid deterioration of our currency, the Leone. Far-reaching increases in the prices of petroleum products, rice our staple food, as well as many other essential items that account for our basic subsistence are a direct consequence of the Leone's depreciating value in the last few months. With the high cost of living consequent upon the floating of the Leone, the population has endured all the hardship that it entails with equanimity. For this, my Government would like to register its profound gratitude to the nation as a whole for their understanding and maturity.[64]

Moreover, in a presidential address to Parliament in June 1987, Momoh outlined some of the key economic issues. The president acknowledged,

> I am aware of the recent acute shortage of cash in our banking system, a situation that has caused some discomfort and inconvenience to the general public particularly to businessmen and wage earners. More than ever, this strange phenomenon exemplifies the glaring and unpatriotic manner in which certain members of the business community have been treating the citizens of this country. In order to prevent a further deterioration of the situation, my government is considering three key policy measures geared to firstly, strict control of the circulation of the Leone, our national currency, to prevent abuse; secondly, enforcement of greater financial discipline by the Ministry of Finance to ensure that government only spend what it earns; and thirdly, introduction of other measures designed to ensure the release of our currency by those holding large quantities of it.

President Momoh further stated that the details of these measures would be made available by the minister of finance.[65] In addition, in 1989 President Momoh informed the public at a mass rally in Kenema to be ready for tougher economic measures in the coming financial year.[66]

Beyond that, President Momoh, as well as Minister of Finance Hassan Gbassay Kanu, in explaining the country's growing economic difficulties, also partially blamed the IMF.[67] Besides government officials, many private citizens also questioned IMF prescriptions and their dire economic and social consequences for ordinary citizens. Notwithstanding, in 1986 the IMF made available to the Momoh government special drawing rights in the amount of more than $60 million. This was a response to the administration's request for a twelve-month standby agreement to deal with balance of payment problems resulting from foreign exchange scarcity. The IMF support also included three-year structural adjustment aspects to tackle the country's myriad economic obstacles, including infrastructure.[68] Meanwhile, in November 1988, Parliament unanimously approved a six-month extension of the Economic Emergency Regulations declared by President Momoh in November 1987.[69] In a nationwide broadcast to mark the country's twenty-eighth independence anniversary in April 1989, President Momoh announced that he had set up a committee of financial experts to recommend how to solve the mounting economic troubles.[70] The president also established an anti-corruption squad with wide-ranging powers to curb business crimes such as tax evasion and smuggling.[71]

Three years after his presidential victory, Momoh announced a new set of measures to arrest the deteriorating economy. These economic reforms, according to the president, had the full support of the IMF and World Bank. He stated,

> Apart from halting the decline of the economy, the measures will improve our export performance and bring back bank transactions into the formal sector. . . . We Sierra Leoneans have all witnessed the fact that over the last several years the economic and financial situation in our country deteriorated significantly. This fact is evident from many instances of increasing poverty, malnutrition, deplorable health standards, inadequately equipped schools and hospitals, poor roads, inadequate public transportation and telecommunications, and ineffective public institutions. The decline in all these areas is an indication of the brute fact that the entire economy and social infrastructure has fallen into disrepair. This sad state of affairs did not arise overnight. The slide downhill started since before the mid-seventies and Sierra Leone lost the greater part of two decades because we failed to retrieve the economy

from the collapse which was so clear to everyone. The agriculture sector remained weak, we have still not been able to produce enough rice—our staple food. The fledging manufacturing sector is in decline, our exports do not earn much foreign exchange, at least through the formal banking system. Public debt, both external and internal, continued to rise. . . . Over the last three years we have witnessed an undesirable lack of monetary and financial discipline. Money supply has risen significantly because Government itself has borrowed far more than it should from the banking system. The direct effect of this excessive spending has pushed up prices, led to high inflation and people have needed increasing sums of money to buy the same unit of goods and services. Every one of us has been affected by the problem of getting cash from the banks. Government has made every effort to provide currency notes and has spent a great deal of foreign currency to ensure that supply but still shortages have persisted. This crisis has contributed to the public's lack of faith and confidence in the banking system, and in the credibility of our public institutions. The time has come to make a complete break with the past, a past which has been marked by overspending and inflation of Government contracts and several irregularities. We are implementing measures to stabilize the economy, to revitalize the banking sector by bringing the informal sector back into the mainstream, to build trust and confidence in Government's capacity to run the economy efficiently, and even more importantly, to create a conducive environment which will attract our friends and partners in development.[72]

Despite the difficult relationship with the IMF, in 1990 the Momoh government started implementing a three-year, IMF-supported Economic Recovery Program (ERP) to arrest the plummeting of the Leone's value against foreign currencies and revamp the declining economy.[73] Specifically, Sierra Leone's GDP was only $300 per capita, the economic growth rate was less than one percent—one of the lowest in West Africa—and the country was heavily indebted. By contrast, from the 1950s to 1972, the country had one of the fastest-growing economies in West Africa at an average of 7 percent per year. In the mid-1970s, however, there was economic slowdown mainly because of oil price increases and the country's dependence on fuel imports. By the 1980s, the economic slowdown had worsened significantly as a result of the OAU summit, as discussed in the previous chapter. This period was marked by an acute shortage of foreign exchange, a sharp decline in mining revenues, rising imports, and low agricultural exports. To stimulate the depressed economy, the Momoh government, in addition to implementing the ERP, had Parliament repeal the Currency Control and Economic Sabotage Act.[74]

To the APC government under the leadership of President Momoh, the main economic challenges included smuggling, particularly diamonds, gold, produce, petrol, cattle, cigarettes, and rice;[75] profiteering;[76] foreign exchange shortages;[77] tax evasion;[78] high unemployment;[79] corruption,[80] including scandals such as "contractgate,"[81] "milliongate,"[82] and "Die-Man" (ghost workers);[83] the hoarding of essential commodities like rice and petrol along with currency;[84] the high cost of living;[85] exploitation by foreign businesspeople;[86] the poor and late payment of salaries;[87] the currency liquidity crisis;[88] and large foreign debts.[89] These problems were repeatedly discussed in budget and policy speeches by the minister of finance[90] and in the annual address on the state of the economy by the president of the Chamber of Commerce.[91] To address the thorny problem of the smuggling of foreign currency, the minister of finance, Dr. Sheka Kanu, in presenting the country's mini-budget announced the establishment of the Economic Intelligence Unit (EIU) headed by the retired Fula senior police officer in charge of the Criminal Investigations Department (CID), Frank Jalloh, under the Ministry of Finance. According to the finance minister, the Unit would have experienced individuals with proven integrity to ensure that foreign exchange went through the banking system. He blamed certain business owners for the persistent foreign exchange shortages, claiming they colluded and manipulated foreign exchanges rates to the detriment of the country. Illustrative of the Momoh government's crackdown on foreign businesspeople because of tax evasion, smuggling, and hoarding of foreign currencies was the arrest of a Lebanese businessman, N. Z. Nassar, and a Cape Verdian businesswoman, Flora Da Silva Viegers, by the EIU and their subsequent deportation.[92]

The grave national economic crisis inherited from the Stevens era led President Momoh to declare a State of Economic Emergency in November 1987 and to announce the Public Economic Emergency Regulations (PEER), which Parliament enacted as the Public Emergency Act. President Momoh made it clear in his press conference that he alone could not solve the economic problems facing the nation and that he needed the support of the public to actualize the goals of the emergency regulations. According to President Momoh,

> Hoarding of our currency, diamonds and essential commodities such as rice and petrol will all soon become crimes to be punished severely by law. The Police and the Armed Forces will be empowered to enter into premises and search for these items. . . . In the case of our currency, henceforth, no one will be allowed to keep above one hundred

and fifty thousand Leones (Le150,000) in his premises for more than three days. . . . All diamond exporters licences will be suspended and the export of diamonds until further notice, will be done only by the Government Gold and Diamond Office (GGDO). . . . Smuggling of our commodities and precious minerals from Sierra Leone will henceforth be a criminal offence to be severely punished by law. . . . Corruption will now be a crime to be severely punished by law. . . . The new regulations also provide for the deportation, exclusion, restriction or detention of persons whose activities are considered to be inimical to the good administration of Sierra Leone. . . . For the first time, persons involved in crimes against the state will now be tried in absentia. . . . As and when necessary a freeze will be imposed on the prices of our basic and essential commodities so as to protect the vast majority of the masses of this country.[93]

And in December 1989, Parliament passed the Currency Control and Economic Sabotage Act, which imposed stricter control over business transactions and prohibited the hoarding of currency. In addition, the Act prescribed heavy monetary fines ranging from Le250,000 to Le500,000 and prison terms from two years to five years for those convicted of economic crimes such as smuggling and corruption.[94]

Several Sierra Leoneans and foreign nationals, including high-ranking public officials and major businesspeople were arrested for violating the new Act. The foreign businessmen included Fula, Lebanese, Indians, Nigerians, Gambians, and Israelis with businesses ranging from the mining of diamonds to merchandise. Penalties included the seizure and public sale of goods, monetary fines, imprisonment, and deportation. A prominent case was that involving the Israeli national, Nir R. Guaz, head of the multinational N. R. Scipa group of companies, whose activities included diamond mining, and top state employees such as James Sanpha Koroma, managing director of the National Development Bank, in what came to be known as "Scipagate." Guaz was arrested for allegedly possessing Le57 million and was detained for one month at Pademba Road Prison. He was released only after the intervention of President Momoh, in consideration of the enormous and diverse investments of the Scipa companies in the national economy. In April 1990, a Freetown High Court found two of Scipa's executives, Colonel Joseph Noy and business manager Offir Hagay guilty of economic sabotage under the terms of the Act. Each defendant was fined Le1.6 million, which they paid, or the alternative of a prison term of sixteen to eighteen years at Pademba Road Prison.[95] In another instance, the defense attorneys of some government officials such as the former deputy minister of development and economic planning,

Shamsu Mustapha, challenged provisions of the Act in court when he, alongside the Lebanese Adel Osman of the Maisa group of companies, was charged on ninety-two counts of conspiracy to defraud the government, thus violating provisions of the Act. Mustapha's defense lawyer, Terrence Terry, argued in the Supreme Court that the president was not authorized by the 1978 constitution to declare a state of public economic emergency. Instead, the constitution only allowed the president to declare a state of public emergency.[96] To many Fula businesspeople, the Act brought hardship. In March 1988, for example, the joint Army and Police Economic Emergency Squad arrested Fula businessmen in three vehicles traveling from Koindu—one of the busiest border trading towns connecting Sierra Leone, Guinea, and Liberia—in Kailahun to Koidu in Kono with a total amount of Le4.599 in various denominations and a large quantity of essential goods. In all, twenty Fula businessmen in both Koindu and Koidu helped the squad with its investigations. The liquid cash and goods were subsequently impounded by the police, although there is no indication that the state benefited from the seizure and forfeiture. The evidence suggests that there was repeated police confiscation of goods and cash from not just elite Fula businesspeople, but also ordinary Fula, without accounting for such actions to the Ministry of Finance regarding revenue generation. Instead, the police were accused of theft by many Fula businesspersons.[97] Faced with mounting economic problems, Parliament repealed the Act in May 1990, as well as many of the country's import and export licenses. The state of the national economy was summed up by the new finance minister, Tommy Taylor-Morgan, thus: "Simply put, our economy is sick."[98]

Delivering the annual dinner address of the Chamber of Commerce, Industry, and Agriculture, the Chamber's President Donald Smythe-Macauley—managing director of the National Petroleum Company Sierra Leone Limited—proposed that the Momoh government abandon a "crisis management" approach and instead set up a task force that would recommend both short-term and long-term measures to reverse the economic downturn. On the theme, "Rapid Sustainable Economic Growth," Smythe-Macauley outlined major vulnerabilities in the economy, including the absence of managerial competence; fiscal controls; the near collapse of the once highly profitable SLPMB; extrabudgetary expenditures; and poor energy, road, and communications infrastructure. He implored the government to have more consultations and collaboration with the business sector in the implementation of domestic economic programs and IMF prescriptions in efforts to solve the country's deepening economic crisis. In response, the minister of finance, development, and economic planning, J. S. Funna, stated that the road to economic recovery would be slow and difficult. According to the minister,

> As regards the on-going negotiations with the IMF, we have made considerable progress on the content of the programme. Most of the policy actions expected of us are already in place. The one area of concern, which is worth highlighting is the budget. As you all know, Sierra Leone is in effect engaged in fighting two wars: there was firstly the military conflict whose cost in terms of human lives lost and properties destroyed continued to be very high indeed. By the same token, the financial cost of prosecuting the war also has serious budgetary implications. This means that the government's ability to meet its other obligations as originally intended in 1991–1992 estimates has been adversely affected. However, the choice is not between prosecuting the military war or the war on the economy; the only option open to us is to prosecute both wars simultaneously. This requires a delicate balance between defeating Charles Taylor's forces and having an economic recovery programme in place with the support of the donor community.[99]

The 1986 Election

The first and only national election held during the Momoh presidency was in May 1986, five months after the formal transfer of power in November 1985. President Momoh wanted a new mandate from Sierra Leoneans that would pave the way for urgently needed political and economic reforms. Prior to the election, the APC announced a twenty-page manifesto that centered on "constructive nationalism through self-reliance, discipline, accountability, and grassroots participation." In a Foreword to the platform, President Momoh, leader and secretary-general of the APC, called for a new sense of patriotism that would prioritize the national interest. For the APC, constructive nationalism "aims at welding together our disparate ethnic elements into a united and cohesive whole. This would dispose of the tendency for diverse groups in our society to view their relationships to one another in an antagonistic way. Through constructive nationalism we hope to build a healthy political community by engendering a fellow feeling in the heart of our citizens; a sense of public duty and self-reliant attitude."[100]

The previous elections during the Stevens years were marked by extreme violence, intimidation, and fraud, but this was less so in the 1986 election. Prior to the vote, the Momoh government set up a seven-man committee headed by Dr. Abdulai Conteh to draw up a code of conduct for the election campaigns. In April the Electoral Commission announced the code, which had been approved by the APC Central Committee. And President Momoh made it clear that any candidate who engaged in violence would be disqualified, as was the case with his close personal friend and minister of mines and labor, Sanie Sesay (Bombali East Constituency), as well as a minister of state, Ibrahim Sorie, and former secretary to the president, Abdul Karim (Kambia Central constituency). And two additional candidates—former MP Musa Y. Komeh (Tonkolili Central constituency) and Paul A. Bangura (Tonkolili North constituency)—were also disqualified because of election violence.[101] According to one political commentator, President Momoh "injected sanity into the political process when, for the first time, he ensured the 1986 general election was free to a large extent from the thuggery that had characterized previous ones."[102] Candidates included veteran politicians from previous Margai and Stevens administrations such as Alhaji Mustapha, Mana Kpaka, Dr. Salia Jusu-Sheriff,[103] Edward Kargbo, Thaimu Bangura, Dr. Sama Banya, and Sembu Forna, as well as those contesting for parliamentary seats for the first time like Dr. June Holst-Roness, Alhaji Sulaiman Tejan-Jalloh, and Mohamed Bockarie Ngele.[104]

Fula Candidates

Fula candidates were drawn from diverse regions, as well as professional and political backgrounds. They included the veteran politician Alhaji Maju and relatively newcomer Alhaji Sulaiman Tejan-Jalloh (Freetown East I constituency); retired senior police officer and chairman of the Blackpool Social Club, Frank Jalloh (Tonkolili West II constituency); Alpha B. Barrie (Koinadugu North constituency); Alhaji Sidique (Makeni Town); Alhaji Dr. Timbo (Bombali Central II constituency); Bai Sheka Wurie (Port Loko West II constituency); Dr. Abass Bundu (Port Loko North East I constituency); Mohamed Ibrahim Jalloh (Kailahun East constituency); and Patrick Jaia Modibo Kaikai (Pujehun West I constituency). Successful Fula candidates included Alhaji Sidique and Alpha B. Barrie. However, those who lost the election included both Fula candidates in Freetown East I constituency, Alhaji Maju and Alhaji Sulaiman Tejan-Jalloh; Mohamed Musa King was the winner.[105]

As a result of the 1986 electoral reforms, the area of the Bombali Central constituency was now divided into Bombali Central I and II. In

Bombali Central II, the long-standing political rivalry between Thaimu Bangura and Alhaji Dr. Timbo continued with intensity. The election was marked, as earlier elections, by violence between Fula and Temne supporters of opposing candidates, leading to the cancelation of the election results. A third candidate who competed alongside Alhaji Dr. Timbo and Thaimu Bangura was Mohamed Munu. The violence was such that the father of Dr. Timbo, Alhaji Wuroh, left Rokulan for Makeni, where he was hosted for several months by Alhaji Sidique. As in previous elections, the legendary Almamy Agibu Jalloh continued to play a critical role in financing and mobilizing cross-country Fula support for his nephew, Alhaji Dr. Timbo, in the latter's attempt to win the election. In spite of the best efforts of Alhaji Dr. Timbo and Almamy Agibu's countrywide Fula political and financial networks that included prominent Fula businesspeople, the former lost the election to Thaimu Bangura. To many Fula, it appeared that the electoral loss was primarily due to the intimidation and violence of Thaimu Bangura and his Temne supporters.[106]

In Koinadugu North Constituency, the Fula politician Alpha B. Barrie contested the general election and was successful against two candidates, Musa Y. Turay and D. B. Samura, thus becoming the parliamentary representative. He worked closely with his brother Alhaji Bailor Barrie, who was national president of the FPU. In fact, Alpha Barrie was the first president of the FYO, which preceded the FPU, in the Americas when the organization was formed in Washington, DC in 1970. According to Alpha Barrie, his brother introduced him to many Fula dignitaries across the country to aid his electoral contest. In opposing Alpha Barrie's candidacy, the Koindaugu-based Yalunka spread propaganda that he was a Guinean-born Fula and therefore not qualified to contest for political office. Beyond that, they mobilized Yalunka across the country, including those in Freetown, Kono, Kenema, Bo, and Makeni, as well as the three Yalunka chiefdoms, Solima, Sinkunia, and Dembelia, to oppose his candidacy. In response, Alpha Barrie helped to mobilize Sierra Leonean–born Fula to support him and counter the Yalunka propaganda against his citizenship status. Meanwhile, the Guinean-born Fula were kept out of the political conflict although they provided material support.[107] For Alpha Barrie, a motivating factor in entering politics was to help change a core aspect of Fula behavior regarding government officials and law enforcement, which was to pay bribes rather than challenge injustices; face arrest, jail, or embarrassment; or disrupt their business activities. Even when Fula had rights, many exhibited this behavior. Both government officials and law enforcement were aware of this behavior and took advantage of it. It was a long and difficult struggle for native-born Fula to fight against this pernicious behavior both inside and outside of the Fula community.[108]

Post-1986 Election

Following the 1986 elections, President Momoh appointed a new cabinet that included Minister of Internal Affairs Alhaji Sidique. In November 1988, President Momoh reshuffled his cabinet, transferring Alhaji Sidique to head the Ministry of Labor, a position he held until the cabinet changes of September 1991. He was highly respected by President Momoh and the Fula community. Prior to entering politics in 1986 and winning the Makeni Town Council seat before becoming a minister, Alhaji Sidique had a long, distinguished career in the country's civil service. His great grandfather was a Torodo Fula from Senegal with a family name Sie who had earlier migrated to Sierra Leone. The Sie name was later changed to Sesay and then replaced by Sidique—the name of Alhaji Sidique's father. Alhaji Sidique was one of a privileged few who was recruited from high school to work for the colonial government as a clerk and Temne interpreter. He assisted in the founding of district councils in the Provinces, first at Port Loko. He received rapid promotion and was appointed acting assistant district commissioner (DO). Next, the colonial administration sponsored him to pursue one year of administrative training at a university in northern Nigeria in 1957–58. On returning home and with independence and the departure of colonial administrators, Alhaji Sidique was appointed as DO to Pujehun and later as senior district officer in Kono. He subsequently served as the first African DO in Kono. Alhaji Sidique was next transferred to Freetown, where he held various positions including development secretary in Sir Milton's government. With the restructuring of the civil service under Sir Albert, Alhaji Sidique was promoted to provincial secretary in Bo and then to Kenema. In 1971 he retired at age forty-five as secretary to the cabinet and head of the Civil Service. Alhaji Sidique then went into private business, opening a supermarket in Freetown, which he later transferred to Makeni. He also was a distributor for the Aureol Tobacco Company for parts of Bombali and Port Loko before entering national politics.[109]

In addition to Alhaji Sidique, President Momoh appointed Alpha Barrie as minister of energy and power. By contrast, President Momoh, earlier in his presidency in 1985, relieved two veteran Fula politicians of their political appointments: Alhaji A. D. Wurie as a Nominated MP and Alhaji Maju as parliamentary special assistant, First Vice President's Office.[110] No official reasons were given for President Momoh's decision. And the evidence suggests that the Fula community, including business elites, tried to lobby President Momoh to reverse this political change affecting two high-profile Fula political patrons of the Fula people. Ethnic politics was a significant factor that shaped not only elections but also representation in the cabinet. The challenge for President Momoh, as for previous leaders, was how to balance the ethnic composition of the government given that there were more than a dozen ethnic groups in the country. And also doing so without marginalizing minority ethnic groups, especially if they had not traditionally supported the ruling party, as was the case with the Fula.[111]

In spite of the low representation of Fula in the postelection cabinet of President Momoh, Fula business elites continued to lobby the APC government on key issues centered on business and immigration. In particular, the Economic Emergency Act and its implementation by the police and army, resulting in the harassment, arrest, as well as confiscation of large quantities of goods and vast amounts of cash in local and foreign currencies, were serious concerns to the Fula business class. As noted earlier, the evidence suggests that law enforcement officials did not properly account for such seizure and forfeiture that would have boosted revenues to help the country's struggling economy. Instead, there was the likelihood of corruption, as indicated by the Fula who were affected by such law enforcement activities. Furthermore, Fula business leaders made repeated representations to the Momoh administration over the deportation of Fula businesspeople who were accused of economic crimes such as smuggling, tax evasion, and profiteering. Leading Fula lobbying efforts were business leaders like Alhaji Bailor Barrie, Almamy Agibu Jalloh, Alhaji Sanu Barrie, Alhaji Momodu Alpha Bah, Alhaji Jalloh Timbo, and Alhaji Hamidu Jalloh (Fula chief of Bo District) in collaboration with the Freetown-based Fula chief Alhaji Seray-Wurie, who had a long association with the APC since its founding in the 1960s under the leadership of Stevens.[112]

Momoh and Muslims

As discussed in preceding chapters, Fula business elites were important members of the Muslim community in Sierra Leone. As a group—the largest in the country—Muslims had great influence in the nation's politics. As in previous administrations, both SLPP and APC, President Momoh continued the political practice of working collaboratively with the broad and diverse Muslim organizations such as the SLMB, SLMC, YMMA, SLSIC, SLMMWA, and SLPM. As influential members of the Muslim population, Fula business leaders worked closely with the Momoh government on a variety of issues, including the annual pilgrimage to Mecca; resolving disputes among Muslim organizations; and monitoring assistance from Muslims countries like Saudi Arabia to fund Islamic education, the building of mosques, and Islamic centers in the country. Additionally, they collaborated with foreign Muslim organizations such as the Association of Religious Families based in Senegal, which was the ancestral homeland of some of the Fula business leaders, such as the legendary Allie family, in the promotion of Islam in Sierra Leone.[113]

The country's Muslim leadership included members of Fula business elites like Alhaji Tejan-Jalloh, Alhaji Bailor Barrie, Almamy Agibu Jalloh, Alhaji Momodu Alpha Bah, Alhaji Sanu Barrie, and Alhaji Alpha Mamadu Jalloh Timbo, the last being national president of the SLSIC. They were an influential lobby in the country's politics, particularly during political campaigns and elections. For instance, they contributed greatly to President Momoh's efforts to mobilize widespread support for his election as head of state in 1985. Many traveled with the president across the country, including to Bombali and Koinadugu, where many Fula resided, to solicit their political support. In particular, Almamy Agibu Jalloh, Alhaji Jalloh Timbo, and other Fula traditional rulers in the Northern Province made great efforts to get fellow Muslim Fula to support President Momoh and his administration. To unite Muslims in the Northern Province, the chief imams of the five Districts in the Province met at the Makeni Central Mosque, where they unanimously elected Sheikh Mohamed Bundu Kamara as the regional chief imam of the entire Northern Province. Sheikh Kamara was described as an outstanding Muslim leader and a strong advocate for unifying Muslims not only in his native Bombali, but the northern region as a whole. Present at the meeting were Alhaji Jalloh Timbo and the assistant district officer, who chaired the event.[114]

Alhaji Tejan-Jalloh—registrar of marriages and divorce at the Fula mosque in Freetown since 1948—contributed immensely to Parliament's amendment of the Mohammedan Marriage Act in 1988, which received strong general support, to benefit Muslim wives in the country. The Muslim attorney general and minister of justice, Dr.

Abdulai Conteh, introduced the bill, stating that the word *Moham-mehdan* that was in the original Act was being replaced by the word "Muslim in order to bring the Act in line with current Islamic thinking." He explained that the term *Mohammedan* was offensive to Muslims. And that the provision of wills did not contradict Koranic laws of inheritance. Dr. Conteh pointed out that the main goal of the bill was to empower Muslims to make wills under the country's laws, as Christians already did in the country. Thus, beneficiaries of Muslims would be legally protected against earlier insidious actions by relatives of deceased male Muslims to deprive surviving families—particularly women—of material inheritance. Moreover, Dr. Conteh informed Parliament that the proposed amendment was the result of work carried out by the country's Law Reform Commission, which was reexamining the nation's postindependence laws in order to modernize them. A female MP praised the amendment, particularly as it related to women in the Northern Province, where they faced deep discrimination and could not contest local, chieftaincy, and parliamentary elections because of traditions, customs, and Koranic laws of inheritance. Another female backer of the bill was Mrs. Regina Tucker-James (MP for Bonthe Urban South), who spoke about the difficulties women faced in the Southern Province in inheriting the properties of their deceased Muslim husbands because of Koranic laws and traditional practices. The bill also received support from male Muslims in Parliament, including Thaimu Bangura (MP for Bombali Central I), who lamented the injustice against women on the issue of inheritance under the old Act. And he called for the Momoh government to set up a review committee to harmonize the Koranic and Western laws in the implementation of the proposed Act. Also supportive of the bill was the Muslim minister of tourism, Abdul Iscandari who spoke about the challenges women encountered under the old Act and said that the new bill will remedy those problems.[115]

In the realm of Muslim education, President Momoh, like his SLPP and APC political predecessors, supported Muslim education alongside Western education in such ways as providing state lands for the construction of classroom buildings, Ministry of Education grants and study leave for teachers. In addition to the earlier schools such as the SLMC and SLMB, a relatively new type was the government-assisted Ansarul (the name is derived from the Arabic word, *Ansar*, for "helpers") primary and secondary schools in Kono and elsewhere in the country that were open to both boys and girls. The first Ansarul school was founded and funded by the Fula business elite persons Alhaji Mohamed Chewtor

Jalloh and Alhaji Sajalieu Bah—who were close friends and business partners—in Koidu in Kono in 1974. A core mission of the school was the teaching and propagation of Islam alongside Western education. The school drew on Fula administrators and teachers, including founding Education Secretary Sheikh Abu Bakarr Bah, who studied in Egypt. Both Alhaji Chewtor Jalloh and Alhaji Sajalieu Bah were involved in the diamond trade in Kono, where diamond profits made them wealthy. They were part of a group of elite Fula diamond businessmen that included Alhaji Unduru Bah, Alhaji Ibrahim Sow, Alhaji Sanu Barrie, Alhaji Ndireh Bah, Alhaji Sorie Bailor Bah, and Alhaji Bailor Barrie. Although having a shared ethnic heritage, this business class was characterized by internal competition as well as partnerships in the pursuit of diamond profits.

Regarding Alhaji Sajalieu Bah, he migrated from Maasi in Pita, Guinea, to Sierra Leone at an early age and stayed with his uncle in Freetown, a petty trader selling items such as bread. For a short while Alhaji Bah assisted his uncle in his business, but the former later branched out on his own, trading small items like chewing gum in the business district of the capital city. In pursuit of better opportunities, he left for the Provinces and settled in Tongo Field, where he was introduced to the diamond business. While at Tongo Field, Kenema, Alhaji Bah cultivated a friendship with Alhaji Chewtor Jalloh, who was already in the diamond trade. Recognizing that there were greater prospects in Kono, Alhaji Bah traveled there in 1969 to pursue his diamond business. He next invited Alhaji Jalloh to join him. Both became highly successful diamond businessmen. With well-established businesses, these friends now decided to invest their time and resources in educational philanthropy, first approaching Alhaji Sulaiman Bah, who already had a school in Kono teaching exclusively Islamic studies, about broadening the curriculum to include Western education. However, Alhaji Bah declined their request. It was then, with the firm conviction that Fula children in Kono and beyond should be exposed to both Islamic and Western education, that both Alhaji Bah and Alhaji Jalloh started the Ansarul School with their own resources. With the assistance of Sheikh Bah, they opened a coeducational primary and secondary school, although the genders were later separated. According to one source, it was Sheikh Bah who suggested the name Ansarul. During the Momoh presidency—in addition to the expansion of primary and secondary schools in Kono and the opening of new schools in Kenema—both Alhaji Bah and Alhaji Jalloh used their private wealth to purchase ten acres of land in the east end of Freetown, where they build an Islamic college, a mosque, and a primary school. By this time they had also taken over the earlier Fula School at Guard Street, which was now a secondary school offering both Western and Islamic education.[116]

Although a Christian—like previous political leaders—President Momoh maintained earlier practices such as attending and supporting Muslim ceremonies like *id ul-fitr* marking the end of the month-long fasting of Ramadan and the birthday of the Holy Prophet Muhammad, *mawlid ul-nabi*, and *id ul-adha*. Moreover, top Muslim cabinet members in President Momoh's administration—First Vice President A. B. Kamara and Second Vice President Dr. Jusu-Sheriff—also participated in Muslim rites such as id ul-fitr, encouraging Muslims to uphold the spiritual values of Islam and working collaboratively with the APC government to advance the country. Both Muslim leaders showed President Momoh's commitment to Muslims.[117] In another example, President Momoh, through the Ministry of Rural Development, Youths, and Social services that was responsible for the annual hajj, ensured that Muslim pilgrims were assisted with their annual rites in spite of the mounting economic challenges facing the nation. However, in 1986, four hundred pilgrims were unable to make the annual trip to Mecca mainly because of the acute scarcity of foreign exchange, as explained by a top official of the SLPM organizers, Alhaji Mohamed B. Kebbay. The intervention of the minister of state, health, and social services, Morlai Bai Kamara, who worked collaboratively with Alhaji Kebbay to bring about the trip, was unsuccessful. Only ten pilgrims led by Alhaji Gibril Sesay and sponsored by the Muslim World League (MWL) through the SLSIC made the pilgrimage. Beyond that, the MWL presented a check of $10,000 to President Momoh at State House to help complete the construction of a mosque at the president's hometown, Binkolo. The MWL's director, Sheikh Abdul Salam Bashyouni, who made the donation, praised President Momoh for his commitment to religious tolerance and nation building. The director also commended the support given to the MWL by the minister of rural development, social services, and youths, Alhaji Musa Kabia. The MWL also had a track record of donating Holy Korans and Islamic literature, as well as supporting the building of Muslim schools. Besides the WLO, Sierra Leone received assistance from the Organization of the Islamic Conference (OIC), which it joined in 1972 under the leadership of President Stevens. The OIC is an international organization that brings together states to safeguard and promote the interests and well-being of Muslims worldwide.[118]

As discussed previously, the Muslim landscape was marked by too many organizations, often in competition for members and resources.

And there were also differences in policies and ambitions. The SLSIC was born out of the need to unify Muslims, as was the UCC in the case of Christians, and to serve as a bridge between the government and the country's Muslim groups. Yet the SLSIC faced challenges from the proliferation of Muslim groups, which was criticized by Alhaji S. A. Kabba in one of the nation's elite newspapers.[119] Responding to the perennial disunity among Muslims, a new group—the Federation of Sierra Leone Muslim Organizations (FSLMO)—was created; it was headed by the Fula chief Alhaji Seray-Wurie. In 1987 President Momoh, in a meeting with the FSLMO at State House, made it clear that his government now recognized it as the supreme body of all Muslim groups in the country and would serve as the link between the government and Muslim organizations, as well as coordinate all Muslim activities with foreign governments and entities. And President Momoh also encouraged all Muslim bodies to operate now under the FSLMO. In his address, Alhaji Seray-Wurie emphasized the urgency and importance of forging unity among the nation's Muslims. Also present was First Vice President A. B. Kamara, an ex officio member of the FSLMO and the executive secretary of the FSLMO, Alhaji Mallam Haroun Buhari, who gave the vote of thanks.[120]

Welcoming alhajis and hajas who had just returned from the hajj at State House, President Momoh spoke about his government's commitment to remain an advisor on religious issues. However, he criticized the corruption of individuals who exploited religious organizations to acquire quick wealth. Specifically, the president expressed his disappointment that some individuals had deprived the Muslim pilgrims of the foreign exchange his government had provided them, especially given the strenuous efforts of the administration to secure the foreign currency. Moreover, President Momoh informed the Muslims that a major reason for his government's recognition of the FSLMO was to help promote unity among the many Muslim groups and to prevent the bad planning of pilgrimage trips to Mecca. In his remarks, Alhaji Burahi praised President Momoh for his strong interest in the welfare of Muslims. In particular, he requested that President Momoh investigate the alleged misappropriation of $47,000 meant for the Muslim pilgrims.[121]

The following year, 1989, President Momoh reiterated his call for Muslim unity and urged collaboration among the many Muslim bodies in order to take over from the government the organizing of the annual pilgrimage to Mecca, which was becoming burdensome given the economic challenges facing the country. The president made these remarks at State House in welcoming First Vice President Alhaji A. B. Kamara and his wife, Haja Sadia, and other pilgrims who had returned home from the hajj. One of the pilgrims, PC Alhaji Sahr Mohamed Thollie praised the APC government for the success of that year's pilgrimage and hoped that this would continue in the future. In his statement, the minister of rural development, social services, and youths, Alhaji Kabia, informed the gathering of plans to construct a Pilgrims Village at Lungi Airport. This facility would also be used as an induction center for prospective Muslim pilgrims.[122] In advocating for Muslim unity, President Momoh was not alone. For instance, the imam of the FBC Muslim Jam`at, Sheikh Ibrahim Kamara, called for unity among Muslim youths across the country. He was speaking at the luncheon ceremony of the Foulah Town United Association of Muslim Youths held at the Amaria Primary School in Freetown. He further stated that it was high time Muslim youths got involved in what he described as "Constructive Islamic Organization."[123]

In 1991 the minister of rural development, social services, and youths, Alhaji Musa Kabia—who was also the minister responsible for religious affairs—informed the public that the annual pilgrimage to Mecca might not take place because of the Gulf War.[124] However, Muslim pilgrims were able to make the hajj with strong support from the Momoh government. Welcoming the returning pilgrims at State House, President Momoh called on them to "always set examples which can be emulated." In his remarks, the Fula executive secretary of the SLSIC, Alhaji U. N. S. Jah disclosed that only sixty-three Sierra Leoneans were able to perform the hajj, a small number compared to previous years. He praised President Momoh for appointing Dr. A. N. D. Koroma, who chaired the meeting, as the new minister responsible for religious affairs. The vote of thanks was given by Alhaji Abdul K. Wahab.[125]

In the aftermath of the invasion of Sierra Leone by the Revolutionary United Front (RUF) led by Foday S. Sankoh and backed by the forces of Charles G. Taylor's National Patriotic Front of Liberia (NPFL),[126] the country's Muslim population further demonstrated their collaboration with the APC government. For instance, in April 1991, the Board of Imams of the SLMC expressed its support and loyalty to President Momoh at State House in the face of the rebel incursion that led to the brutal massacre of civilians and the destruction of properties. This backing was contained in a statement read by the secretary to the board, Alhaji A. K. Zubairu. President Momoh thanked the imams for their kind gesture and extended his appreciation to the entire Muslim community for its support. The president also stated that the rebel invasion was unprecedented in the modern history of the nation. Moreover, he sympathized with the group for the loss of Alhaji Jalloh Timbo, who was killed by the rebels, describing him as a man who was committed to Islam.[127] In another example, the SLMC donated Le50,000 to President Momoh for the National Refugee Coordinating Committee at State House to help victims of the Liberian civil war who were in the country. The president said that the war was raging on in spite of all efforts to prevent it, and he called on religious leaders to pray for peace. The secretary-general of the SLMC, Alhaji K. A. D. Swaray, praised the Mediation Committee of ECOWAS for sending a peace-keeping force to Liberia.[128]

The NPRC Military Coup

The NPRC military coup of April 29, 1992, led by Captain Strasser, brought to an end the Momoh government and twenty-four-year APC rule in Sierra Leone. It was a political watershed, though repeating the country's postindependence history of military intervention, which brought hope to a country that was on the brink of economic collapse, political chaos, as well as a devastating civil war that started in March 1991 and caused the deaths of thousands of people, widespread destruction of property worth millions of Leones, closure of schools, starvation, malnutrition, and disruption of agricultural and economic activities. By March 1992, it was estimated that two hundred thousand Sierra Leoneans were in refugee camps in southern Guinea, about three hundred thousand were internally displaced, and almost four hundred thousand were behind rebel lines. The root causes of the civil war and the NPRC takeover such as corruption, weak economy, and bad governance are traceable to earlier governments, particularly the Stevens era, which has been examined in the previous chapter. According to one political commentator, "The Sierra Leone coup of April 30 was arguably a long time in coming. All the preconditions for a political upheaval had been in place for the past two years or more."[129] To many multi-generational Sierra Leoneans, the coup was a revolution and was widely celebrated across the country.[130] But to President Momoh, the coup organizers were "malcontents and misguided people" who "made a desperate bid to disrupt the public peace and tranquility we know and have enjoyed as a nation. . . . I want to pledge again that no force will disrupt our programme towards multi-party democracy."[131] In spite of the president's strong assurance to the country, his combined police and military forces were unable to foil the military overthrow.

In a radio broadcast justifying the coup, the NPRC Chairman, Captain Strasser stated:

> Fellow citizens for over 23 years, we have been misruled by an oppressive, corrupt, exploitative and tribalistic bunch of crooks and traitors under the umbrella of the APC. Government. This regime has perpetuated nepotism, tribalism, gross mismanagement, total collapse of our economy, education, health, transport, and communication system. This regime has brought permanent poverty and a deplorable life for most Sierra Leoneans. This regime has failed us woefully. For Sierra Leone the past 23 years can only be described as the lost decades. It is all over now. Fellow countrymen and women, today marks the end of the APC regime forever. Today marks the beginning of a new era in the history of our country. We the patriotic officers and men of the Sierra Leone Armed forces have overthrown the doomed APC government. The two constitutions by which the tyrannic APC government had been manipulating and creating complete chaos in our country have been suspended with immediate effect. A full State of Emergency is declared throughout the country. We have initiated this clean up exercise to eradicate from our country the destructive, exploitative, and oppressive regime of the APC Government hitherto under the misguided leadership of the so-called Major General J. S. Momoh.[132]

By the end of the Momoh presidency, Fula business elites had expanded and deepened their presence in the national economy. Moreover, they had vastly broadened their political participation, outreach, representation, and visibility in the country. As financial contributors to Fula political candidates, private donors to political parties, voters, political contestants, and lobbyists, Fula business leaders, particularly Sierra Leonean–born, were now an important part of the political landscape. With business success, Fula political giving increased substantially across the nation. And Fula political followers and networks widened as well. Meanwhile, the evidence suggests that the political identity of the Fula business class, despite APC twenty-four-year rule and the one-party state, remained largely pro-SLPP. Although the political intervention of Fula business leaders in some parts of the country such as Bombali and Koinadugu exacerbated ethnic resentment against the Fula, it contributed significantly to changing their traditional political marginalization. Moreover, the issues of Fula immigration and citizenship—which had been deeply controversial throughout the postindependence period—were less of a fault line in the political discourse. Finally, the trajectory of the Fula population in the political history of postindependence Sierra Leone reveals a long, painful struggle characterized by tenacity, resilience, perseverance, fortitude, and eventual triumph.

Conclusion

This book has reconstructed why and how Muslim Fula business elites participated in the politics of postindependence Sierra Leone. Focusing on the years 1961 to 1992, the study covers the political administrations of Prime Ministers Milton and Albert Margai of the SLPP as well as the Prime Minister Siaka Stevens, and later, Presidents Stevens and Momoh of the APC. The book has successfully argued that although there were varied reasons for Fula business elites' involvement in national politics, they centered on immigration and business, which were interconnected. Vivid collective portraits of the prominent Fula business leaders are contained in the work. In pursuit of their goals in Sierra Leone's political landscape, the book has documented that Fula business leaders demonstrated political pragmatism by focusing on strategies centered on building and expanding intra-group collaboration involving traditional, political, and business leaders, as well as Western-educated Sierra Leonean–born public officials and professionals. Moreover, the Fula forged bipartisan political alliances and served in important leadership positions in multiethnic Muslim organizations such as the SLMC, SLMB, SLPWA, and SLSIC, which provided platforms to work with government officials, politicians, business elites, religious leaders, and both police and army law enforcement on policies relating to the Fula population.[1]

For four decades after independence in 1961, the FPU—which brought together foreign-born and Sierra Leonean–born Fula—evolved into an effective interest group that advocated and defended broad Fula interests, particularly those relating to immigration and business. The FPU was successful in bridging political, generational, class, religious, and ancestral homeland divides among the Fula people. Among its members were Fula business elites, politicians, traditional rulers, top government employees, religious leaders, highly skilled professionals, students, housewives, and grassroots individuals in the Fula community. The Stevens era witnessed the largest growth of the FBU's membership in response to the APC government's repressive actions against the Fula people, as clearly evidenced in the study. With highly placed Sierra Leonean–born leadership, the FPU was largely successful in navigating the country's political landscape in dealing with Fula immigration and business challenges. Moreover, the FPU leadership played a pivotal role in resolving long-standing intra-Fula mistrust and disputes between native-born and foreign-born Fula, as well as between Western-educated and non–Western educated Fula. Also, deeply rooted rivalry between the minority Fula of Senegalese heritage and the majority from neighboring Guinea was reconciled. By the Momoh presidency, the FPU was much more unified and had put down deep roots across the country. In contrast to earlier years, many Fula now self-identified as FPU members. Additionally, the FPU was now integrated into the political fabric of the nation as shown in the watershed Makeni convention that was addressed by President Momoh in 1990.

I have explored immigration from the dual prism of domestic politics and Sierra Leone–Guinea relations. In doing so, I have shown that immigration was both a unifying and radicalizing factor in the Fula community, serving as a catalyst for the birth of the FPU and a primary motivation for Sierra Leonean–born Fula to enter national politics. Furthermore, over four decades, the Fula were front and center of immigration- and citizenship-connected public controversies and policy debates. In dealing with immigration matters, Fula business elites collaborated to push a political agenda that addressed the surging Fula immigrant population and both the SLPP and APC governments' crackdowns on illegal Fula immigrants. Both Sir Milton and his brother, Sir Albert, were politically tolerant toward foreign-born Fula. Although immigration was a prickly political issue, both prime ministers ensured that foreign nationals, including Fula, were properly registered with the government to deal with the influx of illegal immigrants and crimes committed by them in the country. Both politicians made it clear that, despite their accommodation of non–Sierra Leoneans, their governments, as documented in the study, would deport any foreign citizen found guilty of conduct inimical to the state. Indeed, many noncitizens, including Fula, were deported for violating the country's immigration laws.[2]

For President Stevens, who pledged a new political course while attacking the SLPP political record, he maintained continuity in the country's immigration legislation and enforcement, especially in regard to registration and deportation of foreign nationals, including Fula. Actually, the Non-Citizens (Registration, Immigration, and Expulsion) Act No. 14 of 1965, which was enacted under the administration of Sir Albert, was carried over into the Stevens era. One innovation by the APC government, however, was the establishment of the National

Registration Secretariat in 1978, with its headquarters in Freetown, to document Sierra Leoneans as well as foreigners, including Fula, living in the country. However, there was a marked difference, as the book reveals, in relation to the extent of Fula arrests, detentions, and deportations to their homelands, particularly Guinea, during the Stevens administration. There were far more stranger drives, especially impacting the Fula community, in this period compared to the SLPP era. The varied reasons, including the APC perception of the bulk of the Fula population as being SLPP supporters and anti-APC, are discussed in detail in the book.

By contrast, the Momoh presidency that promised to revive the hope of many Sierra Leoneans—although APC like the previous administration—witnessed less frequent stranger drives affecting the Fula community. The factors accounting for this political reversal are also examined in detail in the study. Immigration, however, as in previous governments, remained a challenge, although less so regarding immigrant Fula, particularly those from neighboring Guinea. Another continuity from the SLPP era was the involvement of illegal Fula immigrants, as well as other illegal African and non-African foreign nationals, in illicit diamond mining, prompting public and governmental demands for their arrests and expulsions from the country. Moreover, the Momoh government maintained and expanded the national registration and identification card program, which brought benefits to both the public and the state such as ease of processing the national passport and revenue income, but anxiety to many illegal foreign citizens, including Fula. The well-regarded Fula civil servant who later became a successful politician, Alhaji Sidique, played an important role in these accomplishments as minister of the interior in the Momoh administration.[3]

The book has clearly shown that Kono—the country's diamond mining epicenter—was at the heart of the immigration conversations in the postindependence politics of Sierra Leone. The area attracted Sierra Leoneans across the country and foreign nationals from several West African countries including Mali, Liberia, Senegal, The Gambia, and Guinea. Outside of the subregion, citizens from abroad, particularly the Lebanese, flocked to the diamond-rich District. To all the four governments in the study, Kono posed serious challenges, such as massive loss of alluvial diamond revenues through smuggling, clashes between indigenous Kono peoples and both foreigners and Sierra Leoneans from others parts of the country, armed violence, corruption regarding residential permits to non-Kono residents, lawlessness, the question of who was a stranger or citizen in Kono, partisan political disagreements, police and army human rights abuses, infrastructural problems such as poor supplies of water and electricity, bad roads, deforestation, youth employment, juvenile delinquency, and the high cost of stranger drives and expulsions of noncitizens to their homelands. And the Fula—although one of several African and non-African groups in the diamond-rich area—featured prominently in governmental efforts to curb illegal immigration in Kono. The Kono problem was complicated, and many—including local authorities, indigenous and foreign businessmen, law enforcement, and government officials—profited from the continuing unrests connected to diamond mining. The book argues that the problem of undocumented strangers was not unique to Sierra Leone, but was a West African problem, drawing on examples from such countries as Ghana, Nigeria, and Côte d'Ivoire.

Although there were policy and law enforcement consistencies throughout SLPP and APC rule such as the Diamond Protection Act, Aliens (Expulsion) Act, the Alluvial Diamond Mining Scheme, stranger drives against the growing illegal immigrant population, arrests and deportations of illegal Fula immigrants in Kono, there was a clear contrast during the Stevens regime, as shown in the study, when Fula, regardless of native-born or foreign status, faced the most stringent immigration policies and enforcement. Moreover, they were subjected to mass arrests, detentions, and deportations to their homelands, particularly Guinea. By the end of the Stevens era in 1985, there was some degree of relaxation of the tough immigration crackdowns compared to previous years. The reasons are discussed in detail in the book. However, a primary explanation was the strong and effective lobbying efforts of the Fula business elites, particularly Alhaji Bailor Barrie, Alhaji Momodu Alpha Bah, Alhaji Sanu Barrie, Almamy Bah, Alhaji Ibrahima Sow, Alhaji Mohamed Chewtor Jalloh, Alhaji Sajalieu Bah, Almamy Agibu Jalloh, and Alhaji Seray-Wurie. The Kono-based Fula diamond businessmen also worked with organizations such as the Alluvial Diamond Mining Licence Holders Union, whose members included key businessmen in Kono and Kenema, as well as parliamentarians and paramount chiefs in their efforts to lobby the government on issues affecting Fula miners.[4]

From the perspective of Sierra Leone–Guinea relations, immigration was mainly shaped by the outbound and return migration of Fula to their neighboring Guinean homeland. During both SLPP administrations, the government did not victimize the Fula immigrant community for political reasons connected to President Touré. Sir Milton, a conservative politician who was pro-Western and practiced multiparty democracy, had ideological differences with the Guinean leader, a radical pan-Africanist who had one of the most vibrant one-party systems in Africa. Unlike Sir Milton, Sir Albert had a warm relationship with President Touré, whom he admired and considered a political mentor. In fact, Guinea's one-party state inspired Prime Minister Margai to propose the idea, which he later withdrew in the face of fierce widespread public opposition in Sierra Leone. By contrast, the Stevens era, although sustaining and strengthening the bilateral friendship between Sierra Leone and Guinea, was characterized by strained relations between the Fula community and the Stevens government over Guinea. President Touré, a close ally and political mentor of President Stevens, made several allegations implicating Sierra Leone–based Fula led by Almamy Bah in coups and subversive attempts to overthrow his government. Although such charges were not conclusively proven, Stevens took punitive actions against Fula, as examined in the book. The Momoh presidency, in contrast, witnessed a warm relationship between the Fula community and the APC government over Guinea. Although several factors contributed to this new reality, a primary explanation was the death of President Touré in March 1984, which ushered in a military regime with a less adversarial posture towards the Fula people, including those across the border in Sierra Leone. President Momoh, like his predecessors, maintained and expanded political, economic, cultural, military, and social ties between Sierra Leone and Guinea, as shown in the book.[5]

I have looked at Fula business elites' approach to the politically contentious immigration question over the course of the study that shows considerable continuity despite the differences between the SLPP and APC leaderships. For instance, Fula business leaders hired Western-trained lawyers, particularly Krio who dominated the legal profession because of their long history of Western education, to defend Fula immigrants in immigration court cases. By the Stevens and Momoh administrations, there was a small but growing number of Fula lawyers who worked alongside Krio attorneys to represent Fula defendants. In addition, Fula business leaders provided substantial financial support to cover Fula immigration legal bills. As Fula graduated from overseas law schools—particularly those in Britain—and started practicing law in the country, such legal expenses declined considerably since the Fula lawyers provided pro bono service to their community, as was the case of Dr. Timbo and Ambassador Tejan-Jalloh, as documented in the book. Furthermore, Fula business leaders conducted sensitization drives across the country to educate Fula people about their rights and obligations as native-born and immigrants. This was especially the case during periods of national elections when immigration and citizenship became front and center public questions. Throughout the period under study, Fula business elites consistently engaged the SLPP and APC governments on immigration legislation and enforcement, as well as explaining immigration policies to the Fula people nationwide. Discussions centered on deportations, as well as on the rights and obligations of Sierra Leonean–born and foreign-born Fula in the face of the public indiscriminate lumping together of both groups of Fula as foreign nationals who should not participate in national politics. Fula meetings with government officials often involved the prime minister or president and his cabinet members. The Fula community was usually represented by business and religious leaders, professionals, politicians, top civil servants, and traditional rulers.[6]

The book has covered the significant increase in the number of Sierra Leonean–born Fula political contestants, elected officials, parliamentarians, and cabinet ministers from across the country from 1961 to 1992. Their constituents were not exclusively Fula; on the contrary, they were multiethnic with varied religious and socioeconomic backgrounds. Many of the Fula politicians also had cross-ethnic backgrounds such as Mende and Temne—the two largest ethnic groups—that contributed to their political success. The reasons for the increased Fula political representation included a strong motivation to advance and defend Fula interests—especially immigration and business, greater political awareness among the Fula, an expanding Western-educated Fula population, strong support from the Fula business community, increased Fula voter turnout during nationwide elections, effective political outreach by Fula politicians to non-Fula groups, and the governments' recognition of the Fula as an integral part of the country. Also, the Fula, though an ethnic minority, played an important role in the national economy, as documented in the book. Of the four political administrations under study, the evidence suggests that Fula participation in national politics as election candidates, MPs, and cabinet appointees was greatest during the Stevens years between 1968 and 1985.[7]

I have discussed, from a business standpoint, the fact that the Fula were an integral part of the national economy, particularly in the livestock, merchandise, diamond, and transport sectors. Although Fula businesses evolved into successful private enterprises during the SLPP and APC rule, there was no umbrella mercantile association that brought together the different parts, as well as Sierra Leonean and foreign-born Fula. Arguably, this constrained the effectiveness of the Fula business lobby in influencing government economic policies affecting Fula activities. By contrast, foreign businesses such as those of the Indians had formal business organizations such as the Indian Mercantile Association. One issue that was at the core of business-government relations throughout the SLPP and APC administrations was the participation of immigrants, especially those who were illegal, in the country's economy. This was politically contentious and divisive, resulting in the passage and implementation of several trade laws as documented in the study, to address this long-standing challenge. Over the period of the study, local business organizations such as the SLPTA, NAIB, SLICTU, and SLIPTA, were front and center of advocating for the exclusion of immigrants and the protection and expansion of indigenous rights and opportunities in the business landscape of the country.

The Fula dominated the livestock sector under both the SLPP and APC administrations. They controlled most of the cattle supply networks originating in Guinea and the Northern Province, particularly in Bombali and Koinadugu. And through extensive kinship networks, they also dominated the meat retail distribution networks across the country. Despite intra-Fula rivalry between Sierra Leonean–born and foreign-born Fula, as well as cross-ethnic competition to secure the government meat contracts and to sell meat to the public, the Fula consistently held government contracts to supply meat to public institutions, as well as dominated the retail meat market. Partisan national politics did not diminish their pivotal role in the livestock trade and the related butchering business. Yet as shown in the study, political patronage was a constant factor in the awarding of meat contracts regardless of the government in power. Another aspect of the livestock business that remained the same under both the SLPP and the APC governments were the long-standing feuds between Fula cattle herders and owners, many of whom were immigrants from Guinea, and indigenous farmers, especially in the Northern Province, over grazing lands. Throughout the period under study, Fula business elites and traditional rulers such as Alhaji Tejan-Jalloh and Alhaji Wuroh Timbo played key roles in working collaboratively with government leaders, local authorities, and both parties involved in resolving these problems. Since its inception in the 1960s, the Sierra Leone Butchers Association was an effective interest group in working with both the SLPP and APC governments in addressing challenges such as the cattle and woreh (cattle ranch) taxes, cattle thefts, meat prices, smuggling of cattle, facilities to slaughter cattle in hygienic conditions, and disputes between cattle owners and farmers in the Provinces.

In the realm of retail trade, Fula diverse participation, including petty traders, shopkeepers, and wholesalers remained important and expanded in the course of the study. During both SLPP and APC administrations, the Fula faced similar challenges: their blanket classification as foreigners, who therefore should not be involved in retail, and, moreover, persistent harassment, exploitation, and victimization from trade inspectors and police officers. In addition, Fula business elites continuously intervened to resolve these long-standing problems by engaging Ministry of Trade officials, as well as SLPP and APC government leaders. Over time communication between the Fula business community and the ministry improved, particularly when permanent secretaries such as the Fula named Hon. Jah worked in the government institution.

As for the diamond business, Fula business elites, as the book has documented, were competitive and highly successful during both SLPP and APC rule in Sierra Leone. Their success can be attributed to many factors, including entrepreneurship, hard work, highly developed kinship networks, active collaboration with local authorities and traditional rulers, as well as to networking with multi-racial and multi-ethnic groups involved in the diamond business from mining to marketing both local and abroad. In contrast to the Fula business leaders who had both diamond dealer and digger licenses, many Fula in the diamond business engaged in illicit activities throughout the period under study. Despite changes in political administrations from SLPP to APC, the Fula faced challenges such as police harassment, illicit mining, deportations, difficulties in securing permits to enter Kono, and the highly political and divisive issue of granting diamond dealer and digger licenses. In response, Fula business leaders such as Alhaji Bailor Barrie and Alhaji Sanu Barrie worked cooperatively to help address these problems.

On the transport sector, it also witnessed continuities and changes in the course of the study. Fula business leaders like Almamy Agibu Jalloh and Alhaji Bailor Barrie were the dominant players. The sources of capital to finance commercial transport ownership did diversify, more so with the expanding diamond trade. Continuities in the transport sector during both SLPP and APC rule that affected Fula transport owners and commercial drivers included the high cost of spare parts and vehicles, the shortage of commercial loans with low interest rates, political interference in transport fares, and police harassment of drivers.

Fula business elites worked with both SLPP and APC governments to address the long-standing and politically sensitive issue of foreign, particularly Fula, participation in the transport sector.

One significant change over the course of the study was the growth in the number of Fula-owned commercial vehicles, particularly taxis, which created problems such as frequent traffic violations and arrests that led to Fula business leaders engaging law enforcement authorities and the Motor Drivers Union to resolve these challenges. Fula transport business was mainly based in Freetown, which was the hub of the transportation network of Sierra Leone. The reasons included the city's port, being the seat of government, and the concentration of economic and utility services in the city. Freetown, therefore, became the focus of modernization in the country, which impacted significantly the transport sector. In addition to the use of motor vehicles to move goods between Freetown and the Provinces, they transported rural migrants from the Provinces to the capital city, attracted by its many amenities. The transport sector was a key source of socioeconomic development in Sierra Leone.[8]

Regarding Fula business elites in government-Islamic interactions, the book reveals that they forged political partnerships with cross-ethnic Muslims as part of their political strategy to advance their interests. The Fula were founders, leaders, and members of the many Muslim organizations such as the SLMB, SLMC, and SLSIC that emerged in the postindependence period. For centuries Fula businesspeople played an important and expanding role in shaping the religious landscape of the country. As I argued in a previous study, not only was there a close link between trade and Islam in Sierra Leone, but this relationship was found across West Africa. The Fula business class and Islam support each other: Islam provides eternal salvation and social recognition; in return, the businesspeople gave financial support. Moreover, Fula business elites contributed greatly to Islamic organizations that worked collaboratively with both the SLPP and APC governments in support of such activities as the annual pilgrimage to Mecca. As key members in the various Islamic groups, Fula business leaders like Almamy Agibu Jalloh, Alhaji Tejan-Jalloh, and Alhaji A. D. Wurie were able to leverage their influence to help shape government policies towards the Fula community, particularly regarding immigration and private enterprise.

With a strong belief in the importance of education based on their faith, Fula business elites played important roles in founding and funding Islamic educational institutions such as the SLMC Secondary School, Fula School at Guard Street in Freetown, as well as Ansarul schools and colleges in Kono, Freetown, Kenema, and other areas in Sierra Leone. The Fula business class and Islam support each other: Islam assures eternal salvation and social recognition; in return, the Fula business leaders provide financial support. In pursuit of their educational goals, Fula business elites worked closely with both SLPP and APC administrations. Governmental support included providing public land for school construction and financing that included teacher salaries, construction costs, and subsidies for students. As this work and my earlier book demonstrate, the Fula have a long history of introducing, expanding, and strengthening Islamic educational institutions across Sierra Leone.[9]

Although all the SLPP and APC political leaders were Christians, the Fula worked collaboratively with them, reflecting the long-standing peaceful and cooperative relationship between Muslims and Christians in the country. Indeed, Sierra Leone was a model of religious pluralism and tolerance in Africa. Moreover, by the Stevens era, Muslim women, including Fula, were founders of Muslim groups that partnered with multi-ethnic Christian women in addressing various challenges such as girls' education, women's participation in politics, and inheritance laws that were biased against Muslim women. Both the SLPP and APC governments sustained a long tradition of providing governmental support to Muslim pilgrims such as travel grants, the waiving of travel-related taxes, the accompanying of medical personnel and government ministers, and taking care of stranded Muslims on the hajj in Saudi Arabia. In addition, there was bipartisan participation by the Christian political elite in the celebration of Muslim holidays such as id ul-fitr. The diverse Muslim community reciprocated with strong political support for Sierra Leonean prime ministers and presidents and their respective political parties in the postindependence period. This was especially evidenced during political campaigns and elections. Both Muslim religious and traditional rulers were often enlisted by the political leadership to serve as bridge builders in their efforts to explain their political programs and seek electoral support in the diverse political landscape of the country.[10]

With their proliferation in the postindependence era, Muslims organizations were faced with significant differences over such issues as the role of government in religious affairs, Islamic theology, financial resources, leadership styles, the practice of Ramadan, organization of the annual pilgrimage to Mecca, relationships with outside Islamic bodies, and whether Muslims should contest for elected political office. Partisan politics between the SLPP and APC divided the Muslim community, and in some instances, as shown in the study, Muslim leaders competed against each other for political office. During both SLPP and APC rule, political leaders implored the fragmented Muslim community to unite in the larger interest of the country. Fula business leaders like Alhaji Bailor Barrie, Almamy Agibu Jalloh, Alhaji Momodu Alpha Bah, Alhaji Tejan-Jalloh, Alhaji A. D. Wurie, Alhaji Sanu Barrie, Alhaji Mohamed Chewtor Jalloh, and Alhaji Sajalieu Bah contributed greatly toward resolving intra-Muslim problems and promoting trans-ethnic Muslim unity. However, despite the best efforts of both SLPP and APC political leaders, as well as the multi-ethnic Muslim leaders, Muslim unity remained a challenge throughout the period under study as Muslim groups competed over local resources, political access and influence, members, partnerships with overseas-based Muslim organizations, and Islamic aid to Sierra Leone.[11]

Not only does this book contribute to the important yet under-studied intersectionality of business and politics in postindependence Sierra Leone, the issues it explores—such as the interconnections among African minority business groups, governments, and political parties; immigration; ethnic political behavior; the intersection of ethnicity and politics; the political relationship between immigrant communities and host societies; political networking; minority business elites; political mobilization; the interactions between immigrants and their homelands; political parties; interest groups; political leadership; political fundraising; elections; party politics; political culture; political traditions; political violence; and the intergenerational relations within minority communities—will be useful to researchers investigating the subject from a comparative African and global perspective as well. The present work also illustrates the range of possibilities for innovative and interdisciplinary research on the fascinating but under-researched postcolonial era in Sierra Leone.

Notes

Acknowledgments

1. Alhaji is a title used by Muslim men who have made the hajj or pilgrimage to Mecca in Saudi Arabia.

2. Jamboria or Jamburia is a village in Dalaba, a town in Futa Jallon. Dalaba was once an important regional market and center of cattle production. Some Fula in Sierra Leone add their place of birth to their family name.

3. Alimamy or Almamy designates a political leader of high rank. In Sierra Leone, the person is referred to as a Tribal Headman.

Introduction

1. The Fula, who are mostly nomads, are also known elsewhere in West Africa as Fulbe, Fulani, or Fulatta. Their language, Pulaar, belongs to the West Atlantic group of the Niger-Congo family, which also includes Wolof and Temne. Variants of the spelling of Fula in Sierra Leone are Foulah, Fullah, Fulah, and Fulla.

2. For descriptions of the Sierra Leone economy, see Emmanuel S. E. Leigh, *The Sierra Leone Financial System* (Freetown, Sierra Leone: Author House, 2004); Kelfala M. Kallon, *The Economics of Sierra Leonean Entrepreneurship* (Lanham, MD: University Press of America, 1990); R. G. Saylor, *The Economic System of Sierra Leone* (Durham, NC: Duke University Press, 1967); Daniel T. Jack, *Economic Survey of Sierra Leone* (Freetown, Sierra Leone: Government Printer, 1958); N. A. Cox-George, *Finance and Development in West Africa: The Sierra Leone Experience* (London: D. Dobson Books, 1961); J. B. Ridell, *The Spatial Dynamics of Modernization in Sierra Leone: Structure, Diffusion, and Response* (Evanston, IL: Northwestern University Press, 1970); and A. T. Beresford Taylor, *Money and Banking in Sierra Leone* (Milan, Italy: Finafrica, Cassa di Risparmio delle Provincie Lombarde, 1980).

3. The Mandingo are also known elsewhere in West Africa as Mandinka or Maninka. In this study, Mandingo also refers to the Jahakanke and Sarakule.

4. See Alusine Jalloh, *African Entrepreneurship: Muslim Fula Merchants in Sierra Leone* (Athens: Ohio University Press, 1999); Alusine Jalloh and David E. Skinner, eds., *Islam and Trade in Sierra Leone* (Trenton, NJ: Africa World Press, 1997); Alusine Jalloh, "African Muslim Business in Postcolonial West Africa," in *Black Business and Economic Power*, ed. Alusine Jalloh and Toyin Falola (Rochester, NY:

University of Rochester Press, 2002), 311–30; H. L. van der Laan, *The Lebanese Traders in Sierra Leone* (The Hague: Mouton, 1975); H. V. Merani and H. L. van der Laan, "The Indian Traders in Sierra Leone," *African Affairs* 78 (1979): 240–50; Allen M. Howard, "The Role of Freetown in the Commercial Life of Sierra Leone," in *Freetown: A Symposium*, ed. Christopher Fyfe and Eldred Jones (Freetown: Sierra Leone University Press, 1968), 38–64; A. B. Zack-Williams, "Merchant Capital and Underdevelopment in Sierra Leone," *Review of African Political Economy* (1982): 74–82; Vernon R. Dorjahn, "African Traders in Central Sierra Leone," in *Markets in Africa*, ed. Paul Bohannan and George Dalton (Evanston, IL: Northwestern University Press, 1962), 61–88; Barry L. Isaac, "Business Failure in a Devloping Town: Pendembu, Sierra Leone," *Human Organization* 30 (1971): 288–94; A. Zack-Williams, *Tributors, Supporters, and Merchant Capital: Mining and Underdevelopment in Sierra Leone* (Brookfield, VT: Ashgate, 1995); William Reno, *Corruption and State Politics in Sierra Leone* (Cambridge: Cambridge University Press, 1995); Abner Cohen, *The Politics of Elite Culture: Explorations in the Dramaturgy of Power in a Modern Society* (Berkeley: University of California Press, 1981).

5. See Jalloh, *African Entrepreneurship*; M. Alpha Bah, *Fulbe Presence in Sierra Leone: A Case History of Twentieth-Century Migration and Settlement Among the Kissi of Koindu* (New York: Peter Lang, 1998); B. E. Harrell-Bond, Allen M. Howard, and David E. Skinner, *Community Leadership and the Transformation of Freetown (1801–1976)* (The Hague: Mouton, 1978); Steve Tonah, *The Fulani in Ghana: Migration History, Integration and Resistance* (Accra: University of Ghana, 2005); C. Magbaily Fyle, "Fula Diaspora: The Sierra Leone Experience,' in *History and Socio-Economic Development in Sierra Leone*, ed. C. Magbaily Fyle (Freetown: SLADEA, 1988), 101–23; Mahdi Adamu and A. H. M. Kirk-Greene, eds. *Pastoralists of the West African Savanna* (Manchester: Manchester University Press, 1986); Victor Azarya, *Aristocrats Facing Change: The Fulbe in Guinea, Nigeria, and Cameroon* (Chicago: University of Chicago Press, 1978).

6. See Bankole Thompson, *The Constitutional History and Law of Sierra Leone (1961–1995)* (New York: University Press of America, 1997).

7. For more information on Fula business activities in Sierra Leone, see Jalloh, *African Entrepreneurship*; Bah, *Fulbe Presence in Sierra Leone*; Alusine Jalloh, "Muslim Fula Business Elites and Politics in Sierra Leone," *African Economic History* 35 (2007): 89–104; Alusine Jalloh, "Informal Credit and Politics in Sierra Leone," *African Economic History* 31 (2003): 91–110; Alusine Jalloh, "The Fula and the Motor Transport Business in Freetown, Sierra Leone," *African Economic History* 26 (1998): 63–81; Alusine Jalloh, "Alhaji Momodu Allie: Muslim Fula Entrepreneur in Colonial Sierra Leone," in Jalloh and Skinner, *Islam and Trade in Sierra Leone*, 65–86; Alusine Jalloh, "Muslim Fula Merchants and the Motor Transport Business in Freetown, 1961–78," in Jalloh and Skinner, *Islam and Trade in Sierra Leone*, 119–36; Alusine Jalloh, "The Fula Trading Diaspora in Colonial Sierra Leone," in *The African Diaspora*, ed. Alusine Jalloh and Stephen E. Maizlish (College Station: Texas A & M University Press, 1996), 22–38; C. Magbaily Fyle, "Fula Diaspora."

8. See Scott Kennedy, *The Business of Lobbying in China* (Cambridge, MA: Harvard University Press, 2005); Franco Amatori and Geoffrey Jones, eds. *Business History around the World* (Cambridge: Cambridge University Press, 2003); Alusine Jalloh and Toyin Falola, eds. *Black Business and Economic Power* (Rochester, NY: University of Rochester Press, 2002); Hideaki Miyajima, Takeo Kikkawa, and Takashi Hikino, eds. *Policies for Competitiveness: Comparing Business-Government Relationships in the "Golden Age of Capitalism"* (New York: Oxford University Press, 1999); Alfred Chandler Jr., Franco Amatori, and Takashi Hikino, eds., *Big Business and the Wealth of Nations* (New York: Cambridge University Press, 1999); Steven W. Tolliday, ed. *Government and Business* (Brookfield, VT: Ashgate, 1992).

9. See Anita Spring and Barbara E. McDade, eds., *African Entrepreneurship: Theory and Reality* (Gainesville: University Press of Florida, 1998); Reno, *Corruption and State Politics in Sierra Leone*; Tom Forrest, *The Advance of African Capital: The Growth of Nigerian Private Enterprise* (Charlottesville: University Press of Virginia, 1994); Bruce J. Berman and Colin Leys, eds., *African Capitalists in African Development* (Boulder, CO: Lynne Rienner, 1994); Paul Kennedy, *African Capitalism* (Cambridge: Cambridge University Press, 1988).

10. See Jalloh, *African Entrepreneurship*; Jimmy D. Kandeh, Ricardo René Larémont, and Rachel Cremona, "Ethnicity and National Identity in Sierra Leone," in *Borders, Nationalism, and the African State*, ed. Ricardo René Larémont (Boulder, CO: Lynne Reinner, 2005), 179–229; Kelfala M. Kallon, *The Political Economy of Corruption in Sierra Leone* (New York: The Edwin Mellen Press, 2004); Jimmy D. Kandeh, "Politicization of Ethnic Identities in Sierra Leone," *African Studies Review* 35 (1992): 81–99; Earl Conteh-Morgan and Mac Dixon-Fyle, *Sierra Leone at the End of the Twentieth Century: History, Politics, and Society* (New York: Peter Lang, 1999); Bah, *Fulbe Presence in Sierra Leone*; Jalloh and Skinner, *Islam and Trade in Sierra Leone*; Reno, *Corruption and State Politics in Sierra Leone*; Sahr John Kpundeh, *Politics and Corruption in Africa: A Case Study of Sierra Leone* (Lanham, MD: University Press of America, 1995); Sheikh Batu Daramy, *Constitutional Developments in the Post-Colonial State of Sierra Leone, 1961–1984* (New York: The Edwin Mellen Press, 1993); Fyle, "Fula Diaspora"; Fred M. Hayward, and Jimmy D. Kandeh, "Perspectives on Twenty-Five Years of Elections in Sierra Leone," in *Elections in Independent Africa*, ed. Fred M. Hayward (Boulder, CO: Westview Press, 1987), 25–59; Gustav H. K. Deveneaux, *Power Politics in Sierra Leone* (Ibadan, Nigeria: African Universities Press, 1982); Arthur Abraham, *Mende Government and Politics under Colonial Rule* (Oxford: Oxford University Press, 1978); S. T. Cox, *Civil-Military Relations in Sierra Leone: A Case Study of African Soldiers in Politics* (Cambridge, MA: Harvard University Press, 1976); John R. Cartwright, *Politics in Sierra Leone, 1964–1967* (Toronto: University of Toronto Press, 1970); John R. Cartwright, *Political Leadership in Sierra Leone* (Toronto: University of Toronto Press, 1978); Gershon Collier, *Sierra Leone: Experiment in Democracy in an African Nation* (New York: New York University Press, 1970); Martin Kilson, *Political Change in a West Africa State: A Study of the Modernization Process in Sierra Leone* (Cambridge, MA: Harvard University Press, 1966).

Chapter One

1. For a profile of Dr. Milton Margai, see author's interview with Dr. John A. N. Karefa-Smart (a contemporary of Dr. Margai and a founding member of the SLPP), Arlington, Texas, March 29, 2005; and author's interview with Dr. Peter L. Tucker, Freetown, Sierra Leone, December 17, 2012. See also Dr. Karefa-Smart's memoir, *Rainbow Happenings: A Memoir* (self-pub., Xlibris, 2010); *Daily Mail*, June 30, 1961, 2; *Daily Mail*, December 8, 1961, 1, 12; *Daily Mail*, March 18, 1965, 1; Sierra Leone Government, *Sierra Leonean Heroes: Fifty Great Men and Women Who Helped to Build Our Nation* (Freetown: Government Printer, 1988), 74–75; C. Magbaily Fyle, *Historical Dictionary of Sierra Leone*, new ed. (Oxford: The Scarecrow Press, 2006), 122–23; Cyril P. Foray, *Historical Dictionary of Sierra Leone* (London: The Scarecrow Press, 1977), 134–35; Cartwright, *Political Leadership in Sierra Leone*; and Christopher Fyfe, *Sierra Leone Inheritance* (Oxford: Oxford University Press, 1964), 316–43.

2. Author's interview with Dr. Karefa-Smart, Arlington, Texas, March 29, 2005; *Sierra Leonean Heroes*, 82–83.

3. For more information on the origins of the SLPP, see *Daily Mail*, January 10, 1961, 1; *We Yone*, December 14, 1963, 1; *Unity*, June 11, 1966, 3; Peter L. Tucker, *Origin and Philosophy of the Sierra Leone People's Party* (Freetown, Sierra Leone: Mount Everest Publishing House (MEPH), 2001; Cartwright, *Political Leadership in Sierra Leone*; Kilson, *Political Change*; Cartwright, *Politics in Sierra Leone*; Collier, *Sierra Leone*; Kelfala M. Kallon, *The Political Economy of Corruption in Sierra Leone* (New York: The Edwin Mellen Press, 2004); For profiles of many of the early leading SLPP politicians, see *Sierra Leonean Heroes*; Christopher Allen, "Sierra Leone Politics since Independence," *African Affairs* 67 (1968): 305–29; Christopher Allen, "Sierra Leone," in *West African States: Failure and Promise: A Study in Comparative Politics*, ed. John Dunn (London: Cambridge University Press, 189–210; David Harris, *Sierra Leone: A Political History* (New York: Oxford University Press, 2014); Peter A. Dumbuya, *Reinventing the Colonial State: Constitutionalism, One-Party Rule, and Civil War in Sierra Leone* (self-pub., iUniverse, 2008); Gustav H. K. Deveneaux, *Power Politics in Sierra Leone* (Ibadan, Nigeria: African Universities Press, 1982).

4. For details about Fula immigration in colonial Sierra Leone and during the Milton Margai administration, see Jalloh, *African Entrepreneurship*, 1–30; Jalloh and Skinner, *Islam and Trade*; Fyle, "Fula Diaspora"; Bah, *Fulbe Presence in Sierra Leone*; Michael Banton, *West African City: A Study of Tribal Life in Freetown* (London: Oxford University Press, 1957); Harrell-Bond, Howard, and Skinner, *Community Leadership and the Transformation of Freetown (1801–1976)*.

5. See Alusine Jalloh, "Informal Credit and Politics in Sierra Leone," *African Economic History* 31 (2003): 91–110. See also articles on unity in Sierra Leone by John Gbla in *Daily Mail*, 1960, July 13, 5, and July 16, 6; and *Daily Mail*, December 16, 1963, 3, 9; Kandeh, "Politicization of Ethnic Identities in Sierra Leone"; Deveneaux, *Power Politics in Sierra Leone*.

6. Hon. A. B. M. Jah became a paramount chief on October 22, 1983.

7. For more on the parliamentary citizenship debates, see *Daily Mail,* January 18, 1962, 1, 12.

8. *Daily Mail,* January 8, 1962, 3.

9. Author's interview with Dr. Raymond Sarif Easmon, Freetown, August 3, 1992. See also *Daily Mail,* January 18, 1962, 1.

10. *Daily Mail,* January 18, 1962, 1, 12.

11. *Daily Mail,* January 12, 1962, 1, 2. See also Harrell-Bond, Howard, and Skinner, *Community Leadership and the Transformation of Freetown (1801–1976).*

12. *West Africa,* January 25, 1958, 78.

13. For more information on diamond mining in Kono, see *Daily Mail,* November 4, 1961, 3; *West Africa,* January 25, 1958, 78; June 14, 1958, 560; October 18, 1958, 986; October 25, 1958, 1012, 1108; April 1, 1961, 341; July 1, 1967, 870; July 8, 1967, 855; August 19, 1967, 1090. See also H. L. van der Laan, *The Sierra Leone Diamonds: An Economic Study Covering the Years 1952–1961* (London: Oxford University Press, 1965); Zack-Williams, *Tributors, Supporters, and Merchant Capital*; Reno, *Corruption and State Politics*; Zack-Williams, "Merchant Capital and Underdevelopment in Sierra Leone"; A. B. Zack-Williams, "Sierra Leone: Crisis and Despair," *Review of African Political Economy* 49 (1990): 22–33; Christopher Clapham, *Liberia and Sierra Leone: An Essay in Comparative Politics* (Cambridge: Cambridge University Press, 1976).

14. *Daily Mail,* June 23, 1970, 13, 15, 17, 18; *We Yone,* February 26, 1972, 19. See also van der Laan, *The Sierra Leone Diamonds*; Zack-Williams, *Tributors, Supporters, and Merchant Capital.*

15. *Daily Mail,* December 18, 1962, 3.

16. *Daily Mail,* December 4, 1962, 3.

17. *Daily Mail,* August 6, 1962, 3.

18. *Daily Mail,* August 7, 1962, 3; Reno, *Corruption and State Politics in Sierra Leone.*

19. *Daily Mail,* March 20, 1964, 1.

20. *Daily Mail,* April 3, 1964, 1; April 16, 1964, 3; March 25, 1964, 4.

21. *Daily Mail,* February 12, 1963, 1, 3.

22. *Daily Mail,* May 7, 1963, 1, 7.

23. *Daily Mail,* April 3, 1964, 1.

24. *Daily Mail,* December 20, 1962, 1, 7.

25. Author's interview with Alhaji Sanu Barrie (a prominent Fula diamond dealer in Sierra Leone), Freetown, Sierra Leone, August 4, 1990.

26. For more information on Fula business elites in Sierra Leone, see Jalloh, *African Entrepreneurship*; Bah, *Fulbe Presence in Sierra Leone*; Jalloh, "Alhaji Momodu Allie"; A. Wurie, "The Bundukas of Sierra Leone," *Sierra Leone Studies* 1 (1953): 14–25; Jalloh, "Fula Trading Diaspora"; Fyle, "Fula Diaspora"; Alusine Jalloh, "The Fula and the Motor Transport Business in Freetown, Sierra Leone," *African Economic History* 26 (1998): 63–81; Harrell-Bond, Howard, and Skinner, *Community Leadership and the Transformation of Freetown (1801–1976).* For a profile of Alhaji Abu Bakarr Tejan-Jalloh, see author's interview with Alhaji Abu Bakarr Tejan-Jalloh, Freetown, Sierra Leone, June 21, 1990; author's interview

with Ambassador Alhaji Sulaiman Tejan-Jalloh (son of Alhaji Tejan-Jalloh), Freetown, Sierra Leone, October 25, 2008; and author's interview with Honorable Justice Umu Hawa Tejan-Jalloh (daughter of Alhaji Tejan-Jalloh and first Sierra Leonean female chief justice), Freetown, Sierra Leone, December 17, 2010. See also *Unity*, January 8, 1966, 1, 8; Jalloh, *African Entrepreneurship*, 188–218. For a profile of Alhaji A. D. Wurie, see author's interview with Bai Sheka Wurie (a relative of Alhaji Wurie), Lungi, Sierra Leone, September 28, 2008. See also Wurie, "Bundukas of Sierra Leone," Godwin Samba, "Response: Lunsar Descendants in Sierra Leone Blast Gbinti Wuries," *Awareness Times* (Freetown, Sierra Leone), June 1, 2006.

27. For a profile of Alhaji Dr. Amadu Wurie, see author's interview with Bai Sheka Wurie (relative of Alhaji Wurie), Lungi, Sierra Leone, September 28, 2008; *Sierra Leonean Heroes*, 86–87, 34–35; Ahmadu Wurie and Elizabeth Hirst, *Rassin* (London: University of London Press, 1968); Wurie, "Bundukas of Sierra Leone"; Foray, *Historical Dictionary of Sierra Leone*, 234; Fyle, *Historical Dictionary of Sierra Leone*, 223.

28. Alhaji Jaia Kaikai became paramount chief on April 20, 1947.

29. For a profile of Sir Banja Tejan-Sie, see author's interview with Alhaji Chernor Sie (a relative of Sir Banja Tejan-Sie), Freetown, Sierra Leone, October 31, 2010; *Sierra Leonean Heroes*, 90–91; Foray, *Historical Dictionary of Sierra Leone*, 210; Fyle, *Historical Dictionary of Sierra Leone*, 205.

30. Author's interview with Alhaji Muhamadu Alieu Seray-Wurie, Freetown, Sierra Leone, June 17, 1990.

31. *Daily Mail*, May 1961, 1.

32. Author's interview with Alhaji Mohamed Lamin, Sidique, Freetown, Sierra Leone, October 27, 2008. See also Jalloh, *African Entrepreneurship*; Bah, *Fulbe Presence in Sierra Leone*.

33. Author's interview with Alhaji Tejan-Jalloh, Freetown, June 21, 1990. See also Mohamed N'fah-Alie Conteh, *Paramount Chieftaincy in Sierra Leone: History and Electoral Process* (Saarbrücken, Germany: Lambert Academic Publishing, 2016); Walter Barrows, *Grassroots Politics in an African State: Integration and Development* (New York: Africana Publishing, 1976); Cartwright, *Political leadership in Sierra Leone*; Kilson, *Political Change*.

34. Author's interview with Alhaji Tejan-Jalloh, Freetown, June 21, 1990. See also Jalloh, *African Entrepreneurship*, 1–31; Bah, *Fulbe Presence in Sierra Leone*; Solomon A. J. Pratt, *An Autobiography: Jolliboy: "A Most Un-Ordinary African Boy" From Street Starch Hawker to United Nations Debate Champion* (self-pub., Lulu, 2010); Akintola J. G. Wyse, *The Krio of Sierra Leone* (London: Hurst, 1989); Gibril R. Cole, *The Krio of West Africa: Islam, Culture, Creolization, and Colonialism in the Nineteenth Century* (Athens: Ohio University Press, 2013); Mac Dixon-Fyle and Gibril Cole, eds. *New Perspectives on the Sierra Leone Krio* (New York: Peter Lang, 2006); Cohen, *Politics of Elite Culture*.

35. *Daily Mail*, August 9, 1962, 2.

36. *Daily Mail*, December 21, 1962, 1.

37. *Daily Mail*, December 27, 1963, 1.

38. *Daily Mail*, March 16, 1964, 2.

39. *Daily Mail*, April 9, 1964, 1.

40. *Daily Mail*, October 18, 1962, 1. See also Harrell-Bond, Howard, and Skinner, *Community Leadership and the Transformation of Freetown (1801–1976)*.

41. *Daily Mail*, November 24, 1962, 1, 2.

42. *Daily Mail*, December 31, 1962, 1, 12. See also van der Laan, *Sierra Leone Diamonds*; Zack-Williams, "Merchant Capital and Underdevelopment in Sierra Leone."

43. *Daily Mail*, December 29, 1962, 1, 16.

44. *We Yone*, October 5, 1963, 2. See also André Lewin, *Ahmed Sékou Touré (1922–1984): Président de la Guinée* (Paris: L'Harmattan, 2009); Elizabeth Schmidt, *Cold War and Decoloniztion in Guinea, 1946–1958* (Athens: Ohio University Press, 2007); John Straussberger, "Storming the Citadel: Decolonization and Political Contestation in Guinea's Futa Jallon, 1945–61," *Journal of African History* 57 (2016): 231–49; Thomas S. Cox, *Civil-Military Relations in Sierra Leone: A Case Study of African Soldiers in Politics* (Cambridge, MA: Harvard University Press, 1976); Robert H. Jackson and Carl G. Rosberg, *Personal Rule in Black Africa: Prince, Autocrat, Prophet, Tyrant* (Berkeley: University of California Press, 1982).

45. Author's interview with Bai Sheka Wurie, Lungi, Sierra Leone, September 28, 2008. See also *Daily Mail*, April 30, 1964, 1, 9.

46. Author's interview with Alhaji Sidique, Freetown, Sierra Leone, October 27, 2008; *Daily Mail*, August 14, 1961, 1; Straussberger, "Storming the Citadel."

47. Author's interview with Alhaji Sidique, Freetown, Sierra Leone, October 27, 2008; *Daily Mail*, September 12, 1961, 7. For a detailed examination of Fula chieftaincy in Sierra Leone, see Jalloh, *African Entrepreneurship*, 188–218; Harrell-Bond, Howard, and Skinner, *Community Leadership and the Transformation of Freetown (1801–1976)*, 28–108; Baton, *West African City*, 96–161.

48. Author's interview with Alhaji Sidique, Freetown, Sierra Leone, October 27, 2008. See also Cartwright, *Political Leadership in Sierra Leone*; Harrell-Bond, Howard, and Skinner, *Community Leadership and the Transformation of Freetown (1801–1976)*; Barrows, *Grassroots Politics in an African State*.

49. See Lewin, *Ahmed Sékou Touré (1922–1984)*; Ladipo Adamolekun, *Sékou Touré's Guinea: An Experiment in Nation Building* (London: Methuen, 1976); Barrows, *Grassroots Politics in an African State*; Straussberger, "Storming the Citadel."

50. *Daily Mail*, April 6, 1964, 1, 5. See also Talabi A. Lucan, *The Life and Times of Paramount Chief Madam Ella Koblo Gulama* (Freetown: Sierra Leone Association of Writers and Illustrators, 2003); Tucker, *Origin and Philosophy*; John Gbla, "Temnes Should Stand Solidly Behind Their Leaders," *Daily Mail*, March 11, 1964, 13; Conteh, *Paramount Chieftaincy in Sierra Leone*; Barrows, *Grassroots Politics in an African State*.

51. *Daily Mail*, March 10, 1961, 2.

52. *Daily Mail*, December 16, 1960, 1, 16.

53. *Daily Mail*, December 15, 16, 1960, 1. See also *Sierra Leone Year Book 1961* (Independence ed.) published by the *Daily Mail* for pictures of President

Sékou Touré's visit to Sierra Leone in December 1960; Lewin, *Ahmed Sékou Touré (1922–1984)*.

54. *Daily Mail*, January 20, 1961, 12. See also Lewin, *Ahmed Sékou Touré (1922–1984)*; Claude Riviere, *Guinea: The Mobilization of a People* (Ithaca, NY: Cornell University Press, 1977).

55. *We Yone*, December 28, 1963, 3; *Daily Mail*, January 8, 1964, 1, 2; *Daily Mail*, January 9, 1964, 1.

56. *Daily Mail*, January 19, 1962, 1.

57. *Daily Mail*, January 23, 1962, 1.

58. *Daily Mail*, March 13, 1962, 1, 16.

59. *Daily Mail*, March 16, 1962, 1.

60. *Daily Mail*, March 19, 1962, 1. For more information on smuggling between Guinea and Sierra Leone, see *Daily Mail*, August 17, 1961, 8; August 18, 1961, 5.

61. *Daily Mail*, December 17, 1962, 1, 4. See also Straussberger, "Storming the Citadel"; Lewin, *Ahmed Sékou Touré (1922–1984)*.

62. *Daily Mail*, January 18, 1964, 3.

63. *Daily Mail*, December 5, 1962, 3.

64. *Daily Mail*, January 7, 1961, 7; *We Yone*, November 30, 1963, 3. See also Lewin, *Ahmed Sékou Touré (1922–1984)*; Straussberger, "Storming the Citadel"; Hakim Adi and Marika Sherwood, *Pan-African History: Political Figures from Africa and the Diaspora since 1787* (New York: Routledge, 2003); P. Olisanwuche Esedebe, *Pan Africanism: The Idea and Movement 1776–1963*, 2nd ed. (Washington, DC: Howard University Press, 1994); and A. B. Assensoh, *African Political Leadership: Jomo Kenyatta, Kwame Nkrumah, and Julius K. Nyerere* (Malabar, FL: Krieger Publishing, 1998).

65. *Daily Mail*, June 8, 1961, 8.

66. *We Yone*, December 7, 1963, 1; *Daily Mail*, May 2, 1964, 9, 11; *Unity*, January 23, 1967, 2; see also Lewin, *Ahmed Sékou Touré (1922–1984)*; Elizabeth Schmidt, *Cold War and Decolonization in Guinea, 1946–1958* (Athens: Ohio University Press, 2007); Cartwright, *Political Leadership in Sierra Leone*; and Elizabeth Schmidt, *Mobilizing the Masses: Gender, Ethnicity, and Class in the Nationalist Movement in Guinea, 1939–1958* (Portsmouth, NH: Heineman, 2005).

67. *Daily Mail*, October 19, 1963, 5; *We Yone*, November 9, 1963, 3.

68. *Daily Mail*, May 4, 1961, 1, 3.

69. *Daily Mail*, May 12, 1961, 1.

70. *Daily Mail*, May 10, 1961, 1, 4.

71. *Daily Mail*, March 11, 1961, 1, 3.

72. *Daily Mail*, December 16, 1961, 1.

73. *We Yone*, August 24, 1963, 2. See also Jalloh, *African Entrepreneurship*, 76–112.

74. *Daily Mail*, September 3, 1963, 3; *We Yone*, November 9, 1963, 1. See also Jalloh, *African Entrepreneurship*, 76–112.

75. For more information on the livestock trade in Sierra Leone, see Jalloh, *African Entrepreneurship*, 31–75; Josie A. Beckley, "The Northern Province: The

Livestock in the Northern Province of Sierra Leone" (BA thesis, Fourah Bay College, University of Sierra Leone, 1978); R. A. A. Kumpayi, "The Livestock Industry in Sierra Leone" (BS thesis, Fourah Bay College, 1966); *Aerial Survey of Livestock and Resources in Sierra Leone* (London: Hunting Technical Services, 1979); *Sierra Leone Livestock Development Study*, vol. 1 (London: Hunting Technical Services, 1979); *National Livestock Policy and Programme Workshop* (Freetown, Sierra Leone: Ministry of Agriculture, Forestry, and Fisheries, 1991); Bah, *Fulbe Presence in Sierra Leone.*

76. See Jalloh, *African Entrepreneurship*, 31–75; Kevin Waldie, "'Cattle and Concrete': Changing Property Rights and Property Interests among the Fula Cattle Herders around Kabala, North East Sierra Leone," in *Property, Poverty, and People: Changing Rights in Property and Problems of Pastoral Development*, ed. P. T. W. Baxter and R. Hogg (Manchester: University of Manchester, Department of Social Anthropology and International Development Centre, 1989), 229–39; Abner Cohen, "The Social Organization of Credit in a West African Cattle Market," *Africa* 35 (1965): 8–20.

77. *Daily Mail*, September 3, 1963, 7.

78. Author's interview with Alhaji Baba Allie (a butcher and brother of Alhaji Ibrahim A. Allie), Freetown, Sierra Leone, June 20, 1990. See also Jalloh, *African Entrepreneurship*, 76–112; Vernon R. Dorjahn and Christopher Fyfe, "Landlord and Stranger: Change in Tenancy Relations in Sierra Leone," *Journal of African History* 3 (1962): 391–97; Harrell-Bond, Howard, and Skinner, *Community Leadership and the Transformation of Freetown (1801–1976).*

79. Author's interview with Alhaji Tejan-Jalloh, Freetown, Sierra Leone, June 21, 1990. See also Mohamed N'fah-Alie Conteh, *The Management of Sierra Leone's Electoral Process—An Introduction* (Saarbrüucken, Germany: Lambert Academic Publishing, 2016); Cartwright, *Political Leadership in Sierra Leone*; Kilson, *Political Change in a West African State*; Collier, *Sierra Leone: Experiment in Democracy*; Daramy, *Constitutional Developments in the Post-Colonial State of Sierra Leone*; Allen, "Sierra Leone Politics since Independence"; Harrell-Bond, Howard, and Skinner, *Community Leadership and the Transformation of Freetown (1801–1976)*; Kallon, *Political Economy of Corruption in Sierra Leone*; Allen, "Sierra Leone"; Harris, *Sierra Leone: A Political History*; Cyril Foray, *The Road to the One-Party State: The Sierra Leone Experience* (Edinburgh: Center of African Studies, University of Edinburgh: Africanus Horton Memorial Lecture, 1988); E. D. A. Turay and A. Abraham, *The Sierra Leone Army: A Century of History* (London: Macmillan, 1987); Cox, *Civil-Military Relations in Sierra Leone.*

80. *Daily Mail*, May 17, 1962, 3, 5; May 18, 1962, 3, 9.

81. *Daily Mail*, May 18, 1962, 3, 9.

82. *Daily Mail*, May 4, 1962, 5.

83. *Daily Mail*, May 19, 1962, 7, 9. See also Harrell-Bond, Howard, and Skinner, *Community Leadership and the Transformation of Freetown (1801–1976).*

84. Author's interview with Alhaji Tejan-Jalloh, Freetown, Sierra Leone, June 21, 1990; author's interview with Dr. Karefa-Smart, Arlington, Texas, March 29, 2005. See also *Daily Mail*, March 11, 1961, 1, 3; May 21, 1962, 1, 12; April 3, 1964, 14.

85. *Daily Mail,* May 8, 1961, 4, 8. See also Harrell-Bond, Howard, and Skinner, *Community Leadership and the Transformation of Freetown (1801–1976).*

86. See article by Salieu Sesay on the 1962 general election in *Daily Mail,* June 14, 1961, 5.

87. See article by A. S. Bangura on the 1962 general election in *Daily Mail,* July 6, 1961, 5.

88. *Daily Mail,* April 28, 1962, 1, 5.

89. *Daily Mail,* July 14, 1961, 3; Barrows, *Grassroots Politics in an African State;* Cartwright, *Political Leadership in Sierra Leone.*

90. Author's interview with Alhaji Tejan-Jalloh, Freetown, Sierra Leone, June 21, 1990. See also Cohen, *Politics of Elite Culture;* Cartwright, *Political Leadership in Sierra Leone.*

91. *Daily Mail,* May 21, 1962, 1, 3, 4, 5; August 15, 1961, 1; August 22, 1961, 4; Harrell-Bond, Howard, and Skinner, *Community Leadership and the Transformation of Freetown (1801–1976).*

92. *Daily Mail,* March 10, 1961, 2; April 5, 1961, 1; Harrell-Bond, Howard, and Skinner, *Community Leadership and the Transformation of Freetown (1801–1976);* Cartwright, *Political Leadership in Sierra Leone.*

93. Author's interview with Dr. Karefa-Smart, Arlington, Texas, March 29, 2005. See also Cartwright, *Political Leadership in Sierra Leone;* Kilson, *Political Change in a West African State;* Collier, *Sierra Leone: Experiment in Democracy.*

94. See Cartwright, *Political Leadership in Sierra Leone,* 150–51.

95. See Kilson, *Political Change in a West African State,* 250.

96. See Akintola J. G. Wyse, *H. C. Bankole-Bright and Politics in Colonial Sierra Leone, 1919–1958* (Cambridge: Cambridge University Press, 1990); Kilson, *Political Change in a West African State.*

97. *Daily Mail,* April 28, 1962, 5.

98. Author's interview with Alhaji Tejan-Jalloh, Freetown, Sierra Leone, June 21, 1990. See also *Daily Mail,* June 5, 1990, 3, 5; David Skinner, Barbara Harrell-Bond, Allen Howard, "A Profile of Urban Leaders in Freetown, Sierra Leone 1905–1945," *Tarikh* 7 (1981): 11–19; Harrell-Bond, Howard, and Skinner, *Community Leadership and the Transformation of Freetown (1801–1976),* 41–104; *Sierra Leonean Heroes: Thirty Great Men and Women.*

99. Title used by Muslim women who have made the pilgrimage to Mecca in Saudi Arabia.

100. Author's interview with Alhaji Tejan-Jalloh, Freetown, Sierra Leone, June 21, 1990. See also "Statement by Hon. Justice Umu Hawa Tejan-Jalloh at the Launch of the Fatima Club," Freetown, Sierra Leone, March 29, 2009.

101. Author's interview with Alhaji Tejan-Jalloh, Freetown, Sierra Leone, June 21, 1990. See also *Daily Mail,* December 15, 16, 1960. 1.

102. Author's interview with Alhaji Chernor Sie (son of Alhaji Ahmadu Sie), Freetown, Sierra Leone, October 31, 2010; author's interview with Alhaji Tejan-Jalloh, Freetown, Sierra Leone, June 21, 1990. See also Harrell-Bond, Howard, and Skinner, *Community Leadership and the Transformation of Freetown (1801–1976).*

103. Author's interview with Alhaji Tejan-Jalloh, Freetown, Sierra Leone, June 21, 1990; author's interview with Chief Justice Umu Hawa Tejan-Jalloh, Freetown, Sierra Leone, December 17, 2010. See also *Unity*, September 21, 1966, 1, 4; Filomina Chioma Steady, *Women and Leadership in West Africa: Mothering the Nation and Humanizing the State* (New York: Palgrave, 2011).

104. See Umu Kultumie Tejan-Jalloh, *Telling It As It Was: The Career of A Sierra Leonean Woman in Public Service: A Memoir* (Freetown: Sierra Leone Writers Series, 2016).

105. Author's interview with Alhaji Tejan-Jalloh, Freetown, Sierra Leone, June 21, 1990; *Daily Mail*, October 3, 1963, 5. See also Assanatu Jalloh, "Problems and Challenges of an Educated Fullah Woman," BA thesis, Fourah Bay College, University of Sierra Leone, 1986; Harrell-Bond, Howard, and Skinner, *Community Leadership and the Transformation of Freetown (1801–1976)*.

106. Author's interview with Alhaji Tejan-Jalloh, Freetown, Sierra Leone, June 21, 1990. See also *Daily Mail*, November 14, 1963, 1; Jalloh, "Informal Credit and Politics in Sierra Leone"; Harrell-Bond, Howard, and Skinner, *Community Leadership and the Transformation of Freetown (1801–1976)*.

107. Muslim leader who heads prayer.

108. For the activities of Alhaji Gibril Sesay as president of the Sierra Leone Muslim Reformation Society, see author's interview with Alhaji Tejan-Jalloh, Freetown, Sierra Leone, June 21, 1990; *Daily Mail*, August 26, 1961, 6.

109. For more information on the work of Alhaji Gibril Sesay as secretary of the Sierra Leone Muslim Congress, see author's interview with Alhaji Tejan-Jalloh, Freetown, Sierra Leone, June 21, 1990; *Daily Mail*, September 13, 1961, 1.

110. For Alhaji Gibril Sesay's ties with the Fourah Bay Muslim community, see author's interview with Alhaji Tejan-Jalloh, Freetown, Sierra Leone, June 21, 1990; *Daily Mail*, September 11, 1961, 5.

111. Author's interview with Alhaji Tejan-Jalloh, Freetown, Sierra Leone, June 21, 1990. See also *Daily Mail*, May 5, 1961, 3; Joseph J. Bangura, "The Temne in Freetown History: Rethinking the History of the Sierra Leone Colony, 1890–1961" (PhD diss., Dalhousie University, 2006); Harrell-Bond, Howard, and Skinner, *Community Leadership and the Transformation of Freetown (1801–1976)*, 41–202; Joseph J. Bangura, *The Temne of Sierra Leone: African Agency in the Making of a British Colony*, Cambridge: Cambridge University Press, 2017.

112. Author's interview with Alhaji Tejan-Jalloh, Freetown, Sierra Leone, June 21, 1990. See also *Daily Mail*, April 28, 1962, 5; Bangura, "The Temne in Freetown History"; Bangura, *The Temne of Sierra Leone*.

113. Author's interview with Alhaji Tejan-Jalloh, Freetown, Sierra Leone, June 21, 1990; see also *Daily Mail*, May 1, 1962, 1, 8.

114. Author's interview with Alhaji Tejan-Jalloh, Freetown, Sierra Leone, June 21, 1990; see also *Daily Mail*, April 25, 1962, 1.

115. Author's interview with Alhaji Tejan-Jalloh, Freetown, Sierra Leone, June 21, 1990; author's interview with Ambassador Sulaiman Tejan-Jalloh, Freetown, Sierra Leone, October 25, 2008. See also Harrell-Bond, Howard, and Skinner, *Community Leadership and the Transformation of Freetown (1801–1976)*.

116. Author's interview with Alhaji Tejan-Jalloh, Freetown, Sierra Leone, June 21, 1990. See also *Daily Mail*, May 18, 1962, 1, 2; Harrell-Bond, Howard, and Skinner, *Community Leadership and the Transformation of Freetown (1801–1976)*.

117. See Jalloh, *African Entrepreneurship*, 151–218; Harrell-Bond, Howard, and Skinner, *Community Leadership and the Transformation of Freetown (1801–1976)*.

118. For more on the Fula and Islam in Sierra Leone, see Jalloh, *African Entrepreneurship*, 151–87; Jalloh and Skinner, *Islam and Trade*; Alusine Jalloh, "The Fula and Islamic Education in Freetown, Sierra Leone," *American Journal of Islamic Social Sciences* 14 (Winter 1997): 51–68; David E. Skinner, "Islam and Education in the Colony and Hinterland of Sierra Leone, 1750–1914," *Canadian Journal of African Studies* 10 (1976): 499–520; Bah, *Fulbe Presence in Sierra Leone*; M. Saif'ud Deen Alharazim, "The Origin and Progress of Islam in Sierra Leone," *Sierra Leone Studies* 21 (1939): 13–26; K. G. Dalton, "A Fula Settlement in Mendeland," *Sierra Leone Geographical Association Bulletin* 6 (1962): 3–17; Christopher Fyfe and J. S. Trimingham, "The Early Expansion of Islam in Sierra Leone," *Sierra Leone Bulletin of Religion* 2 (1960): 3–24; Harrell-Bond, Howard, and Skinner, *Community Leadership and the Transformation of Freetown (1801–1976)*; Leslie Proudfoot, "Mosque-Building and Tribal Separatism in Freetown," *Africa* 29 (1959): 405–15; Omar Jalloh-Jamboria, "The Story of Jihad or Holy War of the Fulah," *Sierra Leone Studies* 3 (1919): 10–17; Leslie Proudfoot and H. S. Wilson, "Muslim Attitudes to Education in Sierra Leone," *Muslim World* (1960): 86–96; Leslie Proudfoot, "Towards Muslim Solidarity in Freetown," *Africa* 31 (1961): 147–56; David E. Skinner, "The Incorporation of Muslim Elites into the Colonial Administrative Systems of Sierra Leone, The Gambia, and the Gold Coast," *Journal of Muslim Minority Affairs* 29 (2009): 91–108.

119. For more on Alhaji Ahmadu Sie, see author's interview with Alhaji Chernor Sie, Freetown, Sierra Leone, October 31, 2010; author's interview with Alhaji Tejan-Jalloh, Freetown, Sierra Leone, June 21, 1990. See also *Daily Mail*, July 19, 1963, 7; Harrell-Bond, Howard, and Skinner, *Community Leadership and the Transformation of Freetown (1801–1976)*.

120. For more information on the Krio, see Cole, *The Krio of West Africa*; Wyse, *The Krio of Sierra Leone*; Dixon-Fyle and Cole, eds., *New Perspectives on the Krio of Sierra Leone*; Cohen, *The Politics of Elite Culture*; Harrell-Bond, Howard, and Skinner, *Community Leadership and the Transformation of Freetown (1801–1976)*; Bangura, *The Temne of Sierra Leone*.

121. Author's interview with Alhaji Tejan-Jalloh, Freetown, Sierra Leone, June 21, 1990. See also Jalloh and Skinner, *Islam and Trade*; Bah, *Fulbe Presence in Sierra Leone*; Harrell-Bond, Howard, and Skinner, *Community Leadership and the Transformation of Freetown (1801–1976)*; Gibril R. Cole, "Religious Plurality and Economic Sustainability: Muslim Merchants in the Colonial Economy of Nineteenth Century Freetown," *African Economic History* 36 (2008): 79–92.

122. Author's interview with Alhaji Tejan-Jalloh, Freetown, Sierra Leone, June 21, 1990. See also *Daily Mail,* July 19, 1963, 7; Harrell-Bond, Howard, and Skinner, *Community Leadership and the Transformation of Freetown (1801–1976).*

123. See Jalloh, *African Entrepreneurship;* Cole, *Krio of West Africa;* Bah, *Fulbe Presence in Sierra Leone;* Harrell-Bond, Howard, and Skinner, *Community Leadership and the Transformation of Freetown (1801–1976).*

124. Author's interview with Alhaji Tejan-Jalloh, Freetown, Sierra Leone, June 21, 1990. See also Jalloh, *African Entrepreneurship;* Bah, *Fulbe Presence in Sierra Leone;* Jalloh and Skinner, *Islam and Trade in Sierra Leone;* Skinner, "Islam and Education in the Colony and Hinterland of Sierra Leone," 499–520; Harrell-Bond, Howard, and Skinner, *Community Leadership and the Transformation of Freetown (1801–1976);* Edward W. Blyden, *Christianity, Islam, and the Negro Race* (Baltimore: Black Classic Press, 1994); Hollis R. Lynch, *Edward Wilmot Blyden: Pan-Negro Patriot, 1832–1912* (London: Oxford University Press, 1967).

125. Author's interview with Kadijatu Jalloh (daughter of Alhaji Abdulai Jalloh), Freetown, June 3, 1990; author's interview with Alhaji Tejan-Jalloh, Freetown, Sierra Leone, June 21, 1990. See also Jalloh, *African Entrepreneurship;* Bah, *Fulbe Presence in Sierra Leone;* Harrell-Bond, Howard, and Skinner, *Community Leadership and the Transformation of Freetown (1801–1976); Sierra Leonean Heroes.*

126. *Daily Mail,* April 13, 1964, 7. See also Harrell-Bond, Howard, and Skinner, *Community Leadership and the Transformation of Freetown (1801–1976).*

127. For information on the political activities of Alhaji Abdul Wahid, see *We Yone,* November 2, 1963, 3.

128. *Daily Mail,* October 11, 1963, 1, 3.

129. *Daily Mail,* May 28, 1962, 1.

130. *Daily Mail,* May 28, 1962, 4.

131. *Daily Mail,* May 28, 1962, 1, 3, 8; Mohamed N'fah-Alie Conteh, *The Management of Sierra Leone's Electoral Process—An Introduction* (Saarbrücken, Germany: Lambert Academic Publishing, 2016).

132. Author's interview with Alhaji Tejan-Jalloh, Freetown, Sierra Leone, June 21, 1990.

133. *Daily Mail,* August 1, 1962, 1. See also Harrell-Bond, Howard, and Skinner, *Community Leadership and the Transformation of Freetown (1801–1976).*

134. *Daily Mail,* May 30, 1962, 1.

135. *Daily Mail,* June 6, 1962, 4.

136. *Daily Mail,* June 7, 1962, 5.

137. *Daily Mail,* September 3, 1962, 1. See also Harrell-Bond, Howard, and Skinner, *Community Leadership and the Transformation of Freetown (1801–1976).*

138. *Daily Mail,* March 3, 1964, 1, 6; *We Yone,* February 15, 1964, 3. See also Harrell-Bond, Howard, and Skinner, *Community Leadership and the Transformation of Freetown (1801–1976).*

139. *Daily Mail,* February 23, 1964, 2. See also Harrell-Bond, Howard, and Skinner, *Community Leadership and the Transformation of Freetown (1801–1976).*

Chapter Two

1. Sir Albert Margai died in the United States in 1980. For a profile of Prime Minister Margai, see author's interview with Dr. Karefa-Smart, Arlington, Texas, March 29, 2005; author's interview with Dr. Tucker, Freetown Sierra Leone, December 17, 2012. See also *Daily Mail*, January 21, 1965, 1, 3; *Unity*, January 16, 1967, 2; *The Tablet*, December 20, 1980, 1, 6; *The Tablet*, January 7, 1981, 1, 8; *The Tablet*, January 17, 1981, 2, 3; *Sierra Leonean Heroes*; Fyle, *Historical Dictionary of Sierra Leone*, 121–22; Cartwright, *Political Leadership in Sierra Leone*; Foray, *Historical Dictionary of Sierra Leone*, 132–34; *The Rising Sun: A History of the All People's Congress Party of Sierra Leone* (Freetown, Sierra Leone: APC Secretariat, 1982), 62; Siaka Stevens, *What Life Has Taught Me* (London: Kensal Press, 1984), 228–29, 233; Mohamed M. Bangura, *Sierra Leone and the Legacy of Failed Leaderships: Essays from Asylum* (Laurel, MD: African Renaissance Books, 2003), 17–35; Harris, *Sierra Leone: A Political History*.

2. For a history of the SLPP, see author's interview with Dr. Karefa-Smart, Arlington, Texas, March 29, 2005; author's interview with Dr. Tucker, Freetown, Sierra Leone, December 17, 2012. See also Karefa-Smart, *Rainbow Happenings*; *Unity*, June 11, 1966, 3; Tucker, *Origin and Philosophy*; Collier, *Sierra Leone* (Collier served in the Albert Margai administration); Kilson, *Political Change*; Allen, "Sierra Leone Politics since Independence."

3. *Unity*, August 20, 1966, 6. See also Collier, *Sierra Leone*.

4. For the earlier political career of Albert Margai, see *Daily Mail*, May 20, 1964, 1, 3; *Unity*, July 2, 1966, 2, 7; *Daily Mail*, March 10, 1961, 2; *Unity*, January 16, 1967, 2; Cartwright, *Political Leadership in Sierra Leone*; Collier, *Sierra Leone*; John R. Cartwright, *Politics in Sierra Leone, 1964–1967* (Toronto: University of Toronto Press, 1970).

5. *Unity*, August 20, 1966, 6. See also Cartwright, *Political Leadership in Sierra Leone*; Collier, *Sierra Leone*; Cartwright, *Politics in Sierra Leone*; Harris, *Sierra Leone: A Political History*.

6. *Daily Mail*, July 21, 1964, 3. See also Cartwright, *Political Leadership in Sierra Leone*; Kilson, *Political Change*.

7. For a complete list of Prime Minister Margai's new cabinet, see *Daily Mail*, May 2, 1964, 3; May 5, 1964, 1.

8. Author's interview with Dr. Karefa-Smart, Arlington, Texas, March 29, 2005. See also Cartwright, *Political Leadership in Sierra Leone*; Collier, *Sierra Leone*; Kilson, *Political Change*; Allen, "Sierra Leone Politics since Independence." Harris, *Sierra Leone: A Political History*; Dumbuya, *Reinventing the Colonial State*.

9. Author's interview with Dr. Karefa-Smart, Arlington, Texas, March 29, 2005. See also *Daily Mail*, January 8, 1965, 1; Cox, *Civil-Military Relations in Sierra Leone*.

10. On immigration, see *Daily Mail*, February 21, 1966, 1; Jalloh, *African Entrepreneurship*; Harrell-Bond, Howard, and Skinner, *Community Leadership and the Transformation of Freetown (1801–1976)*.

11. *Daily Mail,* May 6, 1964, 1. See also Kandeh, "Politicization of Ethnic Identities in Sierra Leone"; Deveneaux, *Power Politics in Sierra Leone;* Harrell-Bond, Howard, and Skinner, *Community Leadership and the Transformation of Freetown (1801–1976).*

12. *Daily Mail,* May 6, 1964, 3; June 12, 1965, 10; May 20, 1964, 1, 3; July 24, 1965, 1. See also Harrell-Bond, Howard, and Skinner, *Community Leadership and the Transformation of Freetown (1801–1976).*

13. *Daily Mail,* June 23, 1965, 8.

14. *Daily Mail,* June 26, 1965, 2.

15. For more information on tribalism in Sierra Leone, see *Unity,* November 13, 1965, 2, 6; *We Yone,* June 11, 1966, 1, 7; June 18, 1966, 1, 2, 8; *Unity,* October 19, 1966, 3, 6; *We Yone,* October 8, 1966, 2, 7, 8; *Unity,* May 24, 1966, 2; *We Yone,* July 2, 1966, 5; June 18, 1966, 1, 2, 8; *Unity,* April 11, 1967, 1; Collier, *Sierra Leone,* 67–77; Harrell-Bond, Howard, and Skinner, *Community Leadership and the Transformation of Freetown (1801–1976);* Kandeh, "Politicization of Ethnic Identities in Sierra Leone."

16. For additional information on the 1965 Non-Citizen Registration, Immigration, and Expulsion Act, see *Daily Mail,* June 14, 1965, 24; *We Yone,* December 4, 1971, 2; *West Africa,* November 26, 1971, 140.

17. *Daily Mail,* June 16, 1965, 8.

18. *Daily Mail,* May 14, 1965, 1.

19. *Daily Mail,* December 8, 1965, 8.

20. Author's interview with Alhaji Tejan-Jalloh, Freetown, Sierra Leone, June 21, 1990. See also *Daily Mail,* September 9, 1965, 8; *Daily Mail,* September 30, 1965, 8; Harrell-Bond, Howard, and Skinner, *Community Leadership and the Transformation of Freetown (1801–1876).*

21. *Daily Mail,* September 1, 1965, 8.

22. On the Lebanese in Sierra Leone, see *Daily Mail,* March 21, 1966, 2; Lina Beydoun, "Lebanese Migration to Sierra Leone: Issues of Transnationalism, Gender, Citizenship, and the Construction of a Globalized Identity" (PhD diss. Wayne State University, 2005); Neil O. Leighton, "Lebanese Emigration: Its Effect on the Political Economy of Sierra Leone," in *The Lebanese in the World: A Century of Emigration,* ed. Albert Hourani and Nadim Shehadi (London: I. B. Tauris, 1992), 579–601; van der Laan, *Lebanese Traders in Sierra Leone.*

23. *Daily Mail,* October 1, 1965, 1.

24. *Unity,* October 19, 1966, 1, 8.

25. For more information on diamond mining in Kono, see author's interview with Alhaji Sanu Barrie, Freetown, Sierra Leone, August 4, 1990. See also *We Yone,* September 26, 1964, 1; *Unity,* December 11, 1965, 3, 6; *Unity,* September 3, 1966, 8; October 29, 1966, 8; van der Laan, *Sierra Leone Diamonds;* Reno, *Corruption and State Politics in Sierra Leone;* Zack-Williams, *Tributors, Supporters, and Merchant Capital.*

26. *Daily Mail,* December 9, 1964, 1, 6; *We Yone,* October 3, 1964, 3; Reno, *Corruption and State Politics in Sierra Leone.*

27. *Daily Mail,* May 8, 1964, 3.

28. *Daily Mail*, April 24, 1965, 12; Reno, *Corruption and State Politics in Sierra Leone*.

29. Author's interview with Alhaji Sanu Barrie, Freetown, Sierra Leone, August 4, 1990. See also *Unity*, October 26, 1966, 1, 4; December 19, 1966, 2.

30. *Unity*, October 11, 1966, 8; *We Yone*, April 11, 1964, 1.

31. *Unity*, November 18, 1966, 1, 2, 4; *We Yone*, April 11, 1964, 1; *Unity*, September 23, 1966, 1, 8.

32. *We Yone*, May 28, 1966, 2; Reno, *Corruption and State Politics in Sierra Leone*.

33. *Daily Mail*, September 8, 1965, 1; *Unity*, December 11, 1965, 8; Reno, *Corruption and State Politics in Sierra Leone*.

34. *Unity*, December 4, 1965, 5.

35. *We Yone*, August 22, 1964, 1; Reno, *Corruption and State Politics in Sierra Leone*.

36. *We Yone*, October 22, 1966, 1; Reno, *Corruption and State Politics in Sierra Leone*.

37. See Jalloh, *African Entrepreneurship* 1–30; Harrell-Bond, Howard, and Skinner, *Community Leadership and the Transformation of Freetown (1801–1976)*.

38. Harrell-Bond, Howard, and Skinner, *Community Leadership and the Transformation of Freetown (1801–1976)*, 272.

39. *Daily Mail*, May 20, 1964, 1, 3. See also Straussberger, "Storming the Citadel"; Turay and Abraham, *Sierra Leone Army*; Cox, *Civil-Military Relations in Sierra Leone*.

40. *Daily Mail*, June 30, 1964, 3.

41. For more information on Sékou Touré, see *Daily Mail*, July 7, 1965, 1, 8; Lewin, *Ahmed Sékou Touré (1922–1984)*; Adamolekun, *Sékou Touré's Guinea*; Ibrahima B. Kaké, *Sékou Touré: Le héro et le tyran* (Paris: Jeune Afrique Livres, 1987); Ahmed Sékou Touré, *L'Action politique du Parti démocratique de Guinée*, 18 vols (Conakry, Guinea: INRNG, 1958–72); Claude Riviere, *Guinea: The Mobilization of a People* (Ithaca, NY: Cornell University Press, 1977); Schmidt, *Cold War and Decolonization in Guinea*; and Mohamed Saliou Camara, *Political History of Guinea since World War Two* (New York: Peter Lang, 2014).

42. *Daily Mail*, June 15, 1964, 1, 4, 13; Harrell-Bond, Howard, and Skinner, *Community Leadership and the Transformation of Freetown (1801–1976)*.

43. On the OAU, see *Daily Mail*, June 16, 1964, 1; Esedebe, *Pan-Africanism*; Adi and Sherwood, *Pan-African History*; and A. I. Asiwaju, Michael Crowder, and P. Olisanwuche Esedebe, eds., *Tarikh: Pan-Africanism* 6, no. 3 (London: Longman, 1980).

44. *Daily Mail*, June 23, 1964, 1.

45. *Daily Mail*, August 4, 1964, 2. See also Lewin, *Ahmed Sékou Touré (1922–1984)*; Lansiné Kaba, "From Colonialism to Autocracy: Guinea under Sékou Touré, 1957–1984," in *Decolonization and African Independence: The Transfer of Power, 1960–1980* (New Haven, CT: Yale University Press, 1988), ed. P. Gifford and W. R. Louis, 225–44; Kaké, *Sékou Touré: le héro et le tyran.*; V. D. Du Bois, *The Rise of an Opposition to Sékou Touré. Part 6: The Activation of the Guinean Exiles: The*

Front de Liberation Nationale de Guinée (FLAG); AUFS reports, West African Series 9, no. 6 (New York: AUFS, 1966); Straussberger, "Storming the Citadel."

46. *Daily Mail*, June 8, 1964, 2; *Daily Mail*, February 10, 1965, 3.

47. *Unity*, February 9, 1967, 3; *We Yone*, February 7, 1967, 1. See also Turay and Abraham, *Sierra Leone Army*.

48. *Unity*, February 10, 1967, 3. See also Turay and Abraham, *Sierra Leone Army*.

49. *We Yone*, February 8, 1967, 1. See also Turay and Abraham, *Sierra Leone Army*; Cox, *Civil-Military Relations in Sierra Leone*; Esedebe, *Pan-Africanism*.

50. See Jalloh, *African Entrepreneurship*, 1–30; Harrell-Bond, Howard, and Skinner, *Community Leadership and the Transformation of Freetown (1801–1976)*.

51. *Unity*, June 4, 1966, 8; July 2, 1966, 1, 4, 5. See also Jalloh, *African Entrepreneurship*, 1–30; Howard, "The Role of Freetown," 38–64; J. Mckay, "Commercial Life in Freetown," in *Freetown: A Symposium*, 65–76; Harrell-Bond, Howard, and Skinner, *Community Leadership and the Transformation of Freetown (1801–1976)*.

52. For more information on Fula business activities in Sierra Leone, see Jalloh, *African Entrepreneurship*; Jalloh, "Alhaji Momodu Allie"; Jalloh, "Fula Trading Diaspora"; Jalloh, "Fula and the Motor Transport Business"; Bah, *Fulbe Presence in Sierra Leone*; Jalloh and Skinner, *Islam and Trade*; Harrell-Bond, Howard, and Skinner, *Community Leadership and the Transformation of Freetown (1801–1976)*.

53. *Daily Mail*, August 17, 1964, 1.

54. *Daily Mail*, August 21, 1964, 1, 7.

55. *Daily Mail*, August 22, 1964, 1, 3.

56. *Daily Mail* August 24, 1964, 1.

57. *Daily Mail*, May 26, 1965, 8.

58. *Daily Mail*, May 8, 1965, 12; May 29, 1965, 12.

59. *Daily Mail*, May 31, 1965, 16.

60. *Daily Mail* July 28, 1965, 1.

61. *Daily Mail* October 15, 1965, 1, 4.

62. *Daily Mail* March 21, 1966, 12.

63. *Daily Mail*, April 7, 1965, 3.

64. *Daily Mail*, May 12, 1965, 8.

65. *Unity*, December 8, 1966, 1; *We Yone*, December 10, 1966, 2.

66. *Unity*, January 1, 1967, 1.

67. *Daily Mail*, June 14, 1965, 2.

68. Author's interview with Alhaji Seray-Wurie, Freetown, Sierra Leone, June 17, 1990. See also *Unity*, September 17, 1966, 3.

69. Alim Jallo-Jamboria left a lucrative job as an architect in London to return to Sierra Leone in the 1960s to contribute to national development. See Peter Tucker, *The Mission Boy from Shebar: An Autobiography* (self-pub., Author-House, 2011), 142; *Daily Mail*, February 21, 1966, 1.

70. *Daily Mail*, April 8, 1986, 5.

71. Author's interview with Alhaji Sidique, Freetown, Sierra Leone, October 27, 2008. See also *Daily Mail*, April 14, 1965, 8.

72. *Daily Mail,* June 2, 1964, 1.

73. *Daily Mail,* May 13, 1964, 3; Harrell-Bond, Howard, and Skinner, *Community Leadership and the Transformation of Freetown (1801–1976).*

74. *Daily Mail,* August 12, 1964, 1.

75. *Daily Mail,* April 1, 1965, 6.

76. *Unity,* September 10, 1966, 8.

77. *Daily Mail,* January 19, 1966, 1, 8.

78. *Unity,* January 1, 1967, 1.

79. Author's interview with Alhaji Tejan-Jalloh, Freetown, Sierra Leone, June 21, 1990.

80. Author's interview with Alhaji Sanu Barrie, Freetown, Sierra Leone, August 4, 1990. See also *Unity,* November 19, 1966, 4.

81. For more information on chieftaincy and politics in Sierra Leone, see *Unity,* April 9, 1966, 2; *Daily Mail,* April 21, 1965, 1; Conteh, *Paramount Chieftaincy in Sierra Leone;* Collier, *Sierra Leone,* 78–95; Abraham, *Mende Government;* C. Magbaily Fyle, *The Solima Yalunka Kingdom: Pre-Colonial Politics, Economics and Society* (Freetown, Sierra Leone: Nyakon, 1979); Kenneth Wylie, *The Political Kingdoms of the Temne: Temne Government in Sierra Leone, 1825–1910* (New York: Africana, 1977).

82. *Daily Mail,* June 1, 1964, 1.

83. *Daily Mail,* January 13, 1965, 1. See also Conteh, *Paramount Chieftaincy in Sierra Leone;* Harrell-Bond, Howard, and Skinner, *Community Leadership and the Transformation of Freetown (1801–1976);* Barrows, *Grassroots Politics in an African State.*

84. *Daily Mail,* September 9, 1965, 2.

85. *Unity,* September 29, 1966, 8.

86. *Unity,* October 13, 1966, 1.

87. On Nigerians, see *Unity,* May 14, 1966, 1; on Lebanese, see *We Yone,* December 17, 1966, 1.

88. *We Yone,* July 24, 1965, 2.

89. *Unity,* December 19, 1966, 2.

90. *Daily Mail,* May 24, 1965, 8; Harrell-Bond, Howard, and Skinner, *Community Leadership and the Transformation of Freetown (1801–1976).*

91. *Daily Mail,* May 25, 1965, 2.

92. Author's interview with Alhaji Sanu Barrie, Freetown, Sierra Leone, August 4, 1990. See also *Unity,* August 13, 1966, 2, 4, 8; Kallon, *Political Economy of Corruption,* 152–53.

93. For more information on the domestic investments of Prime Minister Margai, see *We Yone,* August 20, 1966, 2–8; *Unity,* September 3, 1966, 2; *We Yone,* August 27, 1966, 1, 2, 6; *Unity,* August 27, 1966, 3; Cartwright, *Politics in Sierra Leone;* Collier, *Sierra Leone.* On Sir Albert's overseas investments, see *We Yone,* October 1, 1966, 1, 12; February 18, 1967, 4; *We Yone,* January 8, 1966, 2; February 26, 1966, 2, 8; Cartwright, *Politics in Sierra Leone;* Collier, *Sierra Leone.* For more information on corruption allegations against Albert Margai, see *We Yone,* June 4, 1966, 1; *Unity,* October 21, 1966, 1, 3, 8; *We Yone,* November 5,

1966, 3, 7; *Daily Mail,* March 20, 1968, 1, 8. See also *Report of the Forster Commission of Inquiry on the Assets of Ex-Ministers and Ex-Deputy Ministers* (Freetown, Sierra Leone: Government Printer, 1968); Cox, *Civil-Military Relations in Sierra Leone*; Kallon, *Political Economy of Corruption*; Cartwright, *Political Leadership in Sierra Leone*; Collier, *Sierra Leone*; Cartwright, *Politics in Sierra Leone*; Allen, "Sierra Leone."

94. *We Yone,* April 3, 1965, 3.

95. *Unity,* August 20, 1966, 2.

96. *Daily Mail,* May 14, 1965, 16.

97. *Daily Mail,* August 14, 1965, 16.

98. *Daily Mail,* April 22, 1965, 5.

99. *Daily Mail,* March 17, 1965, 8.

100. *Unity,* December 11, 1965, 3.

101. *Unity,* March 5, 1966, 12.

102. *Unity,* December 23, 1966, 1, 3.

103. *Daily Mail,* May 19, 1965, 4, 9.

104. *Daily Mail,* February 6, 1965, 2.

105. *Daily Mail,* February 9, 1965, 2.

106. Author's interview with Alhaji Tejan-Jalloh, Freetown, Sierra Leone, June 21, 1990. See also *Unity,* April 30, 1966, 3; October 22, 1966, 6.

107. Author's interview with Alpha Amadu Bah (employee of Alhaji Momodu Bah), Freetown, Sierra Leone, August 5, 1990. See also Jalloh, *African Entrepreneurship.*

108. Interview with Alpha Amadu Bah. See also the business papers of Alhaji Momodu Bah, held by the Bah family in Freetown.

109. Author's interview with Alhaji Baba Allie, Freetown, Sierra Leone, June 20, 1990. See also author's interview with Mohammed Cham (close personal friend of Alhaji Ibrahim Allie), Freetown, Sierra Leone, June 10, 1990.

110. *Daily Mail,* June 6, 1964, 3.

111. Author's interview with Alhaji Sanu Barrie, Freetown, Sierra Leone, August 4, 1990.

112. For more on the Indian population in Sierra Leone, see *We Yone,* January 28, 1967, 4; *Unity,* May 28, 1966, 6; H. V. Merani and H. L. van der Laan, "The Indian Traders in Sierra Leone," *African Affairs* 78 (1979): 240–50.

113. *Daily Mail,* April 8, 1965, 3.

114. Author's interview with Alhaji Sanu Barrie, Freetown, Sierra Leone, August 4, 1990. See also Reno, *Corruption and State Politics,* 75; Peter Greenhalgh, *West African Diamonds, 1919–83: An Economic History* (Manchester: Manchester University Press, 1985).

115. Author's interview with Alhaji Sanu Barrie, Freetown, Sierra Leone, August 4, 1990. See also Zack-Williams, *Tributors, Supporters, and Merchant Capital.*

116. *Unity,* March 19, 1968, 1; Kallon, *Political Economy of Corruption,* 150–51.

117. On the domestic and overseas assets of Albert Margai, see *We Yone,* January 8, 1966, 2; February 26, 1966, 2, 8; *Unity,* August 27, 1966, 3; *We Yone,*

August 20, 1966, 2–8; August 27, 1966, 1, 2, 6; *Unity*, September 3, 1966, 2; *We Yone*, October 1, 1966, 1, 12; February 18, 1967, 4.

118. For more information on the relationship between foreign businesses and the SLPP government, see *Unity*, October 10, 1966, 5; *We Yone*, March 11, 1967, 1; June 4, 1966, 1.

119. *We Yone*, January 21, 1967, 4; December 31, 1966, 3, 8; January 28, 1967, 4.

120. *We Yone*, February 19, 1966, 6; *Unity*, January 7, 1967, 8.

121. *We Yone*, February 19, 1966, 6; *Unity*, January 7, 1967, 8.

122. *Daily Mail*, May 29, 1964, 3.

123. *Daily Mail*, June 11, 1964, 4.

124. *Unity*, December 17, 1966, 2; December 16, 1966, 2.

125. *Unity*, January 22, 1966, 6.

126. *Unity*, December 23, 1966, 1, 3.

127. *Daily Mail*, January 7, 1965, 4, 6.

128. *Daily Mail*, May 20, 1964, 1, 3; Allen, "Sierra Leone Politics since Independence."

129. *Daily Mail*, January 13, 1965, 1.

130. *Daily Mail*, January 7, 1965, 4, 6.

131. For more information on poverty in Sierra Leone, see the newspaper articles by Julius Cole titled "Why we are poor," *Unity*, September 23, 1966, 2; and "We must fend for ourselves," *Unity*, September 27, 1966, 2. On corruption during the Albert Margai administration, see *Unity*, October 21, 1966, 1, 3, 8; *We Yone*, October 15, 1966, 1, 2; June 4, 1966, 1; *We Yone*, September 3, 1966, 1; November 5, 1966, 1; October 8, 1966, 2; November 5, 1966, 3, 7; December 1, 1966, 1, 3, 4, 6, 8; December 17, 1966, 3; Cartwright, *Political Leadership in Sierra Leone*; Kallon, *Political Economy of Corruption*; Cartwright, *Politics in Sierra Leone*; and Reno, *Corruption and State Politics*. For more on the state of the Sierra Leone economy, see *We Yone*, June 11, 1966, 1; *Unity*, September 21, 1966, 2; *We Yone* September 24, 1966, 5, 6; *We Yone*, October 15, 1966, 2; *Unity*, November 24, 1966, 2, 5; Cox-George, *Finance and Development*; Saylor, *Economic System*; Kallon, *Economics of Sierra Leonean Entrepreneurship*; J. B. Riddell, *The Spatial Dynamics of Modernization in Sierra Leone: Structure, Diffusion, and Response* (Evanston, IL: Northwestern University Press, 1970); Taylor, *Money and Banking*; Leigh, *Sierra Leone Financial System*.

132. For more on APC's reactions to the SLPP 1966/1967 budget, see *Unity*, June 18, 1966, 1, 4, 5, 6; *Unity*, June 25, 1966, 3; July 9, 1966, 1, 2, 6.

133. *Daily Mail*, April 10, 1965, 16.

134. On the IMF in Sierra Leone, see *We Yone*, November 12, 1966, 8; Kallon, *Political Economy of Corruption*, 147–48.

135. *Unity*, December 19, 1968, 1. See also Stevens, *What Life Has Taught Me*, 233, 267; Hayward and Kandeh, "Perspectives"; Cartwright, *Politics in Sierra Leone*; Allen, "Sierra Leone Politics since Independence."

136. *Unity*, February 11, 1967, 1. See also Conteh, *Management of Sierra Leone's Electoral Process*; Conteh, *Paramount Chieftaincy in Sierra Leone*; Allen,

"Sierra Leone Politics since Independence." Kallon, *Political Economy of Corruption in Sierra Leone*; Harris, *Sierra Leone: A Political History*.

137. *Unity*, February 17, 1967, 1. See also Conteh, *Management of Sierra Leone's Electoral Process*; Fred M. Hayward and Jimmy D. Kandeh, "Perspectives on Twenty-Five Years of Elections in Sierra Leone," in *Elections in Independent Africa*, ed. Fred M. Hayward (London: Westview Press, 1987), 25–59; David Dalby, "The Military Takeover in Sierra Leone, 1967," *World Today* 23 (1967): 354–60; Humphrey J. Fisher, "Elections and Coups in Sierra Leone, 1967," *Journal of Modern African Studies* 7 (1969): 611–36; Harrell-Bond, Howard, and Skinner, *Community Leadership and the Transformation of Freetown (1801–1976)*; Dumbuya, *Reinventing the Colonial State*; Foray, *Road to the One-Party State*; Turay and Abraham, *Sierra Leone Army*; Cox, *Civil-Military Relations in Sierra Leone*.

138. For more information on the SLPP manifesto, see *Unity*, March 11, 1967, 2–6; March 13, 1967, 2, 3; March 8, 1967, 1; Dalby, "Military Takeover in Sierra Leone, 1967"; Fisher, "Elections and Coups in Sierra Leone, 1967"; Cartwright, *Politics in Sierra Leone*; Kilson, *Political Change*; Barrows, *Grassroots Politics in an African State*; Cartwright, *Political Leadership*; Collier, *Sierra Leone*; Allen, "Sierra Leone Politics since Independence."

139. On the APC platform, se*e Unity*, March 10, 1967, 1, 2, 3; March 11, 1967, 2; March 8, 1967, 2; *We Yone*, March 11, 1967, 4, 8; March 16, 1967, 2, 6; Dalby, "Military Takeover in Sierra Leone, 1967"; Fisher, "Elections and Coups in Sierra Leone, 1967"; Barrows, *Grassroots Politics in an African State*; Cartwright, *Politics in Sierra Leone*; Deveneaux, *Power Politics*; Allen, "Sierra Leone Politics since Independence."

140. *Daily Mail*, April 8, 1964, 1.

141. *Daily Mail*, July 17, 1964, 3; Hayward and Kandeh, "Perspectives on Twenty-Five Years of Elections in Sierra Leone"; Harrell-Bond, Howard, and Skinner, *Community Leadership and the Transformation of Freetown (1801–1976)*.

142. *Daily Mail*, April 24, 1965, 12; Harrell-Bond, Howard, and Skinner, *Community Leadership and the Transformation of Freetown (1801–1976)*.

143. *We Yone*, September 3, 1966, 3; November 5, 1966, 1; December 17, 1966, 4.

144. *Daily Mail*, June 28, 1966, 2; Harrell-Bond, Howard, and Skinner, *Community Leadership and the Transformation of Freetown (1801–1976)*.

145. *We Yone*, April 11, 1964, 1; July 2, 1966, 6; Harrell-Bond, Howard, and Skinner, *Community Leadership and the Transformation of Freetown (1801–1976)*.

146. Author's interview with Alhaji Tejan-Jalloh, Freetown, Sierra Leone, June 21, 1990. See also *Daily Mail*, November 19, 1965, 16; Jalloh, *African Entrepreneurship*, 188–218; Bah, *Fulbe Presence in Sierra Leone*; Harrell-Bond, Howard, and Skinner, *Community Leadership and the Transformation of Freetown (1801–1976)*.

147. *Daily Mail*, June 13, 1964, 1.

148. *Daily Mail*, June 25, 1964, 2.

149. *We Yone*, January 28, 1967, 1. See also Jalloh, *African Entrepreneurship*; Bah, *Fulbe Presence in Sierra Leone*; Harrell-Bond, Howard, and Skinner, *Community Leadership and the Transformation of Freetown (1801–1976)*.

150. Author's interview with Alhaji Chernor Sie, Freetown, Sierra Leone, December 31, 2011. See also *Unity*, November 6, 1965, 5.

151. *Concord Times*, June 8, 2010, 1; *Unity*, June 25, 1966, 1, 8.

152. *Unity*, July 9, 1966, 2.

153. *Daily Mail*, August 14, 1964, 4.

154. *Daily Mail*, April 6, 1965, 2.

155. *Daily Mail*, May 14, 1964, 1. See also Barrows, *Grassroots Politics in an African State.*

156. *We Yone*, April 3, 1965, 4. See also Barrows, *Grassroots Politics in an African State.*

157. For the history of Mammy Queens, see *We Yone*, July 31, 1965, 3.

158. Author's interview with Hon. Justice Tejan-Jalloh, Freetown, Sierra Leone, December 17, 2010. See also "Statement by Hon. Justice Umu Hawa Tejan-Jalloh at the launch of the Fatima Club." For more on women in Sierra Leone politics, see Laray Denzer, "Women in Freetown Politics, 1914–61: A Preliminary Study," *Africa* 57 (1987): 439–56; Filomina C. Steady, *Female Power in African Politics: The National Congress of Sierra Leone* (Los Angeles: California Institute of Technology Munger African Library Notes, 1975); Filomina C. Steady, "Women's Associations and Female Education in Sierra Leone," in *New Perspectives on the Sierra Leone Krio,* ed. Mac Dixon-Fyle and Gibril Cole (New York: Peter Lang, 2006), 267–85; and Steady, *Women and Leadership in West Africa.*

159. *We Yone*, September 4, 1965, 2.

160. *We Yone*, August 7, 1965, 1.

161. *Daily Mail*, June 22, 1964, 1, 3.

162. *Unity*, December 11, 1965, 1, 8. See also Cartwright, *Politics in Sierra Leone;* Collier, *Sierra Leone;* Cartwright, *Political Leadership in Sierra Leone;* Daramy, *Constitutional Developments in the Post-Colonial State of Sierra Leone;* Foray, *Road to the One-Party State;* Cox, *Civil-Military Relations in Sierra Leone.*

163. *We Yone*, October 9, 1965, 1.

164. *Daily Mail*, January 18, 1966, 8; Allen, "Sierra Leone Politics since Independence."

165. Author's interview with Alhaji Tejan-Jalloh, Freetown, Sierra Leone, June 21, 1990. See also Allen, "Sierra Leone Politics since Independence."

166. *Daily Mail*, March 26, 1965, 16. For APC debates and opposition to the one-party system, see *Unity*, November 6, 1965, 3, 6; *We Yone*, November 13, 1965, 4, 5; December 24, 1, 5, 6; January 1, 1966, 2, 4; July 2, 1966, 1; February 18, 1967, 2. See also Cartwright, *Politics in Sierra Leone.*

167. For more information on Stevens's views on one-party rule, see *We Yone*, November 20, 1965, 1; January 1, 1966, 1; *Daily Mail*, March 30, 1965, 8; Foray, *Road to the One-Party State.*

168. For public opposition to the SLPP-proposed one-party state, see *We Yone*, January 22, 1966, 1, 8; February 12, 1966, 1; February 19, 1966, 5; February 26, 1966, 4, 5, 8; March 19, 1966, 1, 5, 6; March 26, 1966, 1, 3; May 14, 1966, 4, 5, 6; May 28, 1966, 2, 3, 6; June 18, 1966, 2.

169. On FBC faculty and administrators' stance on the one-party proposal, see *We Yone*, February 12, 1966, 7; February 26, 1966, 5, 6; October 15, 1966, 5, 6. For women's protests against one-party rule, see January 8, 1966, 4; January 15, 1966, 2, 5, 6. For more on youth opposition to one-party rule, see June 11, 1966, 1, 8; June 18, 1966, 4; Allen, "Sierra Leone Politics since Independence."

170. *Unity*, May 21, 1966, 1, 4.

171. For the political writings of Dr. Easmon on the one-party idea, see *We Yone*, February 12, 1966, 4, 5, 6; March 19, 1966, 2; March 26, 1966, 4, 5, 6; April 9, 1966, 4, 5, 6; May 14, 1966, 3, 7, 8; July 2, 1966, 3, 6; October 22, 1966, 3, 7, 8.

172. *We Yone*, October 16, 1965, 5.

173. *Unity*, January 29, 1966, 1, 8; *We Yone*, January 29, 1966, 1; February 5, 1966, 1, 2, 3, 5, 6; *Unity*, May 14, 1966, 1, 3, 4; *We Yone*, November 20, 1965, 5, 6.

174. *Unity*, February 19, 1966, 1, 4, 5, 6.

175. *We Yone*, February 11, 1967, 1.

176. *Unity*, May 20, 1968, 3.

177. *Daily Mail*, July 17, 1964, 5.

178. *Daily Mail*, June 22, 1964, 1, 3.

179. *Daily Mail*, June 19, 1964, 1, 9; June 20, 1964, 1; *We Yone*, July 4, 1964, 1; July 11, 1964, 1; February 26, 1966, 3.

180. For more information on Kono's diamond wealth, see van der Laan, *Sierra Leone Diamonds*; Reno, *Corruption and State Politics*.

181. *Daily Mail*, May 20, 1965, 8.

182. *Daily Mail*, May 20, 1967, 1, 4; *Unity*, October 26, 1966, 4.

183. *Daily Mail*, May 25, 2.

184. *Daily Mail*, May 20, 1965, 8.

185. *Daily Mail*, May 24, 1965, 1, 4.

186. Ibid., 8.

187. Author's interview with Alhaji Sanu Barrie, Freetown, Sierra Leone, August 4, 1990. See also *Unity*, November 13, 1965, 4.

188. *Unity*, June 25, 1966, 5, 6.

189. *Unity*, December 20, 1966, 1; *We Yone*, April 9, 1966, 3.

190. Author's interview with Dr. Karefa-Smart, Arlington, Texas, March 29, 2005. See also *Unity*, December 10, 1966, 8.

191. *Unity*, December 9, 1966, 1.

192. *Unity*, December 28, 1966, 2.

193. For more information on Temne-Limba rivalry within the APC, see *Unity*, February 26, 1966, 8; October 21, 1966, 6; December 24, 1966, 11; and *We Yone*, November 5, 1966, 7. On the Temne and politics in Sierra Leone, see *We Yone*, August 28, 1965, 3; November 5, 1966, 5; Bangura, "Temne in Freetown History: Rethinking the History of the Sierra Leone Colony, 1890–1961"; Wylie, *Political Kingdoms of the Temne*; Bangura, *The Temne of Sierra Leone*.

194. *Unity*, November 6, 1965, 1.

195. *Unity*, December 28, 1966, 2.

196. *We Yone*, October 1, 1966, 2; February 12, 1966, 6; *Unity*, February 5, 1966, 8.

197. *Unity*, November 12, 1966, 1.

198. Author's interview with Alhaji Baba Allie (brother of Alhaji Ibrahim Allie), Freetown, Sierra Leone, June 20, 1990. See also Jalloh, *African Entrepreneurship*, 31–75.

199. *Unity*, December 16, 1966, 1; December 17, 1966, 1, 4, 5.

200. For an analysis of the 1966 APC convention, see the newspaper editorial by Frank Blunt in *Unity*, December 14, 1966, 2. See also *We Yone*, December 10, 1966, 1, 8; December 17, 1966, 1; December 17, 1966, 6, 7.

201. *Daily Mail*, April 10, 1965, 16.

202. Author's interview with Alhaji Tejan-Jalloh, Freetown, Sierra Leone, June 21, 1990. See also *Daily Mail*, May 13, 1964, 4.

203. *We Yone*, April 3, 1965, 1. See also Siaka Stevens, *What Life Has Taught Me* (London: Kensal Press, 1984), 220; Reno, *Corruption and State Politics*, 75.

204. *We Yone*, December 17, 1966, 1. See also *Report of the Forster Commission*, 1, 12.

205. *Unity*, February 19, 1966, 1; December 16, 1966, 1.

206. *We Yone*, September 4, 1966; December 31, 1966, 3, 8; Reno, *Corruption and State Politics*.

207. *Daily Mail*, January 13, 1965, 1. For more on chiefs and politics in Sierra Leone, see *Unity*, April 9, 1966, 2; *Daily Mail*, January 29, 1965, 4; *We Yone*, August 28, 1965, 3; Conteh, *Paramount Chieftaincy in Sierra Leone*; Collier, *Sierra Leone*, 78–95.

208. *Daily Mail*, May 16, 1964, 3.

209. *Daily Mail*, May 21, 1964, 3.

210. *Daily Mail*, March 12, 1965, 1.

211. *Unity*, August 13, 1966, 1; October 11, 1966, 1; *We Yone*, December 17, 1966, 1. See also Reno, *Corruption and State Politics*.

212. *Unity*, February 14, 1967, 1; Harrell-Bond, Howard, and Skinner, *Community Leadership and the Transformation of Freetown (1801–1976)*.

213. *Unity*, January 13, 1967, 2.

214. *Daily Mail*, April 12, 1965, 8.

215. For more on Alhaji Gibril Sesay, see *We Yone*, August 28, 1965, 3; *Daily Mail*, August 5, 1964, 3; Bangura, "Temne in Freetown History"; Bangura, *The Temne of Sierra Leone.*"

216. *Unity*, November 1, 1966, 4, 5; *We Yone*, November 5, 1966, 5; Harrell-Bond, Howard, and Skinner, *Community Leadership and the Transformation of Freetown (1801–1976)*.

217. *Unity*, February 15, 1967, 1.

218. Author's interview with Alhaji Tejan-Jalloh, Freetown, Sierra Leone, June 21, 1990. See also Jalloh, *African Entrepreneurship*; Harrell-Bond, Howard, and Skinner, *Community Leadership and the Transformation of Freetown (1801–1976)*.

219. *Daily Mail*, March 29, 1965, 12; Harrell-Bond, Howard, and Skinner, *Community Leadership and the Transformation of Freetown (1801–1976)*.

220. *Daily Mail,* May 22, 1965, 12; Harrell-Bond, Howard, and Skinner, *Community Leadership and the Transformation of Freetown (1801–1976).*

221. *Daily Mail,* February 4, 1965, 1.

222. For more on the alleged coup against Albert Margai's government, see *Unity,* February 10, 1967, 2; *Unity,* February 7, 1967, 1; Cartwright, *Politics in Sierra Leone.*

223. *Unity,* February 15, 1967, 2; Harrell-Bond, Howard, and Skinner, *Community Leadership and the Transformation of Freetown (1801–1976).*

224. *Unity,* March 2, 1967, 4.

225. *Unity,* March 20, 1967, 2, 3; Allen, "Sierra Leone since Independence."

226. *Unity,* March 15, 1967, 1.

227. *Unity,* February 28, 1967, 1; *Rising Sun,* 77, 152, 306; Stevens, *What Life Has Taught Me.*

228. *Unity,* March 10, 1967, 1; March 8, 1967, 4. See also Allen, "Sierra Leone since Independence." Dalby, "The Military Takeover in Sierra Leone, 1967"; Fisher, "Elections and Coups in Sierra Leone, 1967"; Turay and Abraham, *Sierra Leone Army*; Cox, *Civil-Military Relations in Sierra Leone.*

229. *Unity,* February 14, 1967, 2. See also Hayward and Kandeh, "Perspectives on Twenty-Five Years of Elections in Sierra Leone"; Dalby, "Military Takeover in Sierra Leone, 1967"; Fisher, "Elections and Coups in Sierra Leone, 1967"; Allen, "Sierra Leone Politics since Independence"; Turay and Abraham, *Sierra Leone Army*; Cox, *Civil-Military Relations in Sierra Leone.*

230. *West Africa,* August 5, 1967, 1032. For more information about APC violence against the Fula during the 1967 election, see author's interview with Alhaji Tejan-Jalloh, Freetown, Sierra Leone, June 21, 1990; Tucker, *Mission Boy from Shebar,* 180, 187.

231. *Unity,* March 20, 1967, 1. See also Bah, *Fulbe Presence in Sierra Leone*; Jalloh, *African Entrepreneurship*; Tucker, *Mission Boy from Shebar,* 180, 187; Daramy, *Constitutional Developments in the Post-Colonial State of Sierra Leone,* 44, 49, 85; Kandeh, "Politicization of Ethnic Identities in Sierra Leone"; Harrell-Bond, Howard, and Skinner, *Community Leadership and the Transformation of Freetown (1801–1976).*

232. Author's interview with Alhaji Sanu Barrie, Freetown, Sierra Leone, August 4, 1990. See also *Unity,* December 10, 1966, 8.

233. *Unity,* December 19, 1966, 1; March 13, 1967, 1, 4; *Daily Mail,* July 14, 1967, 8.

234. *Unity,* November 22, 1966, 8.

235. For Jamil S. Mohamed's business activities and his relationship with Albert Margai, see *Unity,* February 19, 1966, 1; December 16, 1966, 1; Reno, *Corruption and State Politics in Sierra Leone.*

236. *Unity,* February 19, 1966, 4.

237. Author's interview with Alhaji Tejan-Jalloh, Freetown, Sierra Leone, June 21, 1990. See also C. M. Tejan-Jalloh (son of Alhaji Tejan-Jalloh), "Why This Campaign of Hate Against Foulahs?," *Unity,* March 21, 1969, 2; Daramy, *Constitutional Developments in the Post-Colonial State of Sierra Leone,* 44, 49, 85;

Jalloh, *African Entrepreneurship*; Bah, *Fulbe Presence in Sierra Leone*; Harrell-Bond, Howard, and Skinner, *Community Leadership and the Transformation of Freetown (1801–1976)*.

238. Author's interview with Alhaji Chernor Maju (Sow), Freetown, Sierra Leone, November 14, 1991; author's interview with Honorable Justice Alhaji Dr. Abdulai B. Timbo, Freetown, October 30, 2008; Tejan-Jalloh, "Why This Campaign of Hate Against Foulahs"; Jalloh, *African Entrepreneurship*; Bah, *Fulbe Presence in Sierra Leone*; Harrell-Bond, Howard, and Skinner, *Community Leadership and the Transformation of Freetown (1801–1976)*.

239. Author's interview with Almamy Agibu Jalloh, Freetown, June 29, 1990; author's interview with Alhaji Tejan-Jalloh, Freetown, Sierra Leone, June 21, 1990. See also *Unity*, March 21, 1967, 1, 2; *Daily Mail*, March 21, 1967, 1, 8; Jalloh, *African Entrepreneurship*; Daramy, *Constitutional Developments in the Post-Colonial State of Sierra Leone*, 44, 49, 85; Abdul K. Koroma, *Sierra Leone: The Agony of a Nation* (Freetown, Sierra Leone: Andromeda Publications, 1996), 22; Hayward and Kandeh, "Perspectives on Twenty-Five Years of Elections in Sierra Leone"; Bah, *Fulbe Presence in Sierra Leone*; Harrell-Bond, Howard, and Skinner, *Community Leadership and the Transformation of Freetown (1801–1976)*.

240. *Daily Mail*, April 13, 1967, 2; *Unity*, January 17, 1967, 7. See also Pratt, *An Autobiography*; Cohen, *Politics of Elite Culture.*

241. *Daily Mail*, April 7, 1967, 1, 2. See also Jalloh, *African Entrepreneurship*; Bah, *Fulbe Presence in Sierra Leone*; Harrell-Bond, Howard, and Skinner, *Community Leadership and the Transformation of Freetown (1801–1976)*.

242. Author's interview with Dr. Easmon, Freetown, Sierra Leone, August 3, 1992; author's interview with Alhaji Tejan-Jalloh, Freetown, Sierra Leone, June 21, 1990; and author's interview with Almamy Agibu Jalloh, Freetown, Sierra Leone, June 29, 1990. See also *Daily Mail*, May 11, 1967, 2; Tejan-Jalloh, "Why This Campaign of Hate against Foulahs"; Jalloh, *African Entrepreneurship*; Bah, *Fulbe Presence in Sierra Leone*; Harrell-Bond, Howard, and Skinner, *Community Leadership and the Transformation of Freetown (1801–1976)*; Conteh, *Management of Sierra Leone's Electoral Process.*

Chapter Three

1. President Stevens died on May 28, 1988. Author's interview with Egerton T. (E. T.) Kamara, Dallas, Texas, November 13, 2011. E. T. Kamara was the APC national secretary-general and later assistant to the APC secretary-general, President Stevens, as well as national administrative secretary of the APC. See also *Daily Mail*, August 24, 1968, 1; August 24, 1976, 12, 13; *The Tablet*, August 24, 1978, 1, 3; September 27, 1980, 2, 5, 6; Daily Mail, June 4, 1988, 1–4; June 9, 1988, 1, 3; June 15, 1988, 1, 2, 3, 4, 16; *West Africa*, May 4, 1968, 509, 511; Siaka Stevens, *What Life Has Taught Me* (London: Kensal Press, 1984), 5–153; *The Rising Sun: A History of the All People's Congress Party of Sierra Leone* (Freetown, Sierra Leone: APC Secretariat, 1982), 10, 24, 156, 163. One of the founders of the

APC, alongside Stevens, was Alhaji Sheikh Gibril Sesay. See *The Rising Sun*, 51, 55, 207, and Bangura, *Sierra Leone and the Legacy of Failed Leaderships*, 36.

2. *Unity*, August 13, 1966, 7; *Sunday We Yone*, August 26, 1973, 2, 5.

3. *West Africa*, May 4, 1968, 530. See also *Unity*, May 10, 1968, 2, 3, 6, and Stevens, *What Life Has Taught Me*, 97, 137.

4. *Unity*, December 24, 1966, 11; May 10, 1968, 3, 6; *Daily Mail*, June 15, 1978, 1, 8; January 12, 1984, 5, 11. See also Stevens, *What Life Has Taught Me*, 177–79, 182–92, 203–7; *Rising Sun*, 55; and Allen, "Sierra Leone Politics since Independence."

5. *Unity*, October 10, 1966, 3. See also Deveneaux, *Power Politics in Sierra Leone*; Reno, *Corruption and State Politics in Sierra Leone*; Harrell-Bond, Howard, and Skinner, *Community Leadership and the Transformation of Freetown (1801–1976)*.

6. *Unity*, September 14, 1966, 8. See also Stevens, *What Life Has Taught Me*, 213–22; *Rising Sun*, 61; Daramy, *Constitutional Developments in the Post-Colonial State of Sierra Leone*; Allen, "Sierra Leone Politics since Independence"; Harrell-Bond, Howard, and Skinner, *Community Leadership and the Transformation of Freetown (1801–1976)*.

7. *Daily Mail*, March 23, 1967, 1. See also *The Tablet*, September 13, 1978, 1, 4; *The Tablet*, November 15, 1980, 3; *Rising Sun*, 61–81, 152, 306; Dalby, "Military Takeover in Sierra Leone, 1967"; Fisher, "Elections and Coups in Sierra Leone, 1967"; Turay and Abraham, *Sierra Leone Army*; Cox, *Civil-Military Relations in Sierra Leone*; Cartwright, *Politics in Sierra Leone*; Deveneaux, *Power Politics in Sierra Leone*; Daramy, *Constitutional Developments in the Post-Colonial State of Sierra Leone*; Harrel-Bond, Howard, and Skinner, *Community Leadership and the Transformation of Freetown (1801–1976)*; Kallon, *Political Economy of Corruption in Sierra Leone*; Allen, "Sierra Leone Politics since Independence." Harris, *Sierra Leone: A Political History*.

8. *Daily Mail*, March 25, 1967, 1.

9. *Daily Mail*, March 31, 1967, 1.

10. *Daily Mail*, March 29, 1967, 1.

11. *Daily Mail*, March 31, 1967, 1; *The Tablet*, December 15, 1980, 3, 4. See also Dalby, "Military Takeover in Sierra Leone, 1967"; Fisher, "Elections and Coups in Sierra Leone, 1967"; Turay and Abraham, *Sierra Leone Army*; *Rising Sun*, 83; Stevens, *What Life Has Taught Me*, 262; Cox, *Civil-Military Relations in Sierra Leone*; Bangura, *Sierra Leone and the Legacy of Failed Leaderships*, 38–39, 43; Allen, "Sierra Leone Politics since Independence"; Harrell-Bond, Howard, and Skinner, *Community Leadership and the Transformation of Freetown (1801–1976)*; Kallon, *Political Economy of Corruption in Sierra Leone*.

12. *Sunday We Yone*, April 19, 1981, 7; *The Tablet*, July 9, 1980, 6, 8. See also Dalby, "Military Takeover in Sierra Leone, 1967"; Fisher, "Elections and Coups in Sierra Leone, 1967"; Turay and Abraham, *Sierra Leone Army*; *Rising Sun*, 95–96, 99–106; Stevens, *What Life Has Taught Me*, 6, 267, 279–80; Daramy, *Constitutional Developments in the Post-Colonial State of Sierra Leone*; Cox, *Civil-Military Relations in Sierra Leone*; Allen, "Sierra Leone Politics since Independence";

Harrell-Bond, Howard, and Skinner, *Community Leadership and the Transformation of Freetown (1801–1976)*; Kallon, *Political Economy of Corruption in Sierra Leone*; Allen, "Sierra Leone"; Harris, *Sierra Leone: A Political History*; Dumbuya, *Reinventing the Colonial State*; Foray, *Road to the One-Party State*.

13. *Daily Mail*, September 24, 1968, 2. See also Jalloh, *African Entrepreneurship*; Bah, *Fulbe Presence in Sierra Leone*; Harrell-Bond, Howard, and Skinner, *Community Leadership and Transformation in Freetown (1801–1976)*.

14. *Daily Mail*, October 14, 1968, 1. See also Harrell-Bond, Howard, and Skinner, *Community Leadership and the Transformation of Freetown (1801–1976)*.

15. *Daily Mail*, December 7, 1968, 1.

16. *Unity*, December 19, 1968, 3; May 22, 1968, 1; *Daily Mail*, August 5, 1968, 2.

17. *Daily Mail*, December 18, 1968, 8; December 30, 1968, 1. See also *Sierra Leone: 12 Years of Economic Achievement and Political Consolidation under the APC and Dr. Siaka Stevens, 1968–1980* (Freetown, Sierra Leone: Office of the President, 1980), 37.

18. *Daily Mail*, December 4, 1969, 1; *We Yone*, April 1, 1972, 2, 8. See also Harrell-Bond, Howard, and Skinner, *Community Leadership and the Transformation of Freetown (1801–1976)*.

19. *Daily Mail*, December 6, 1969, 1, 12. For more discussions about tribalism, see also *We Yone*, December 18, 1971, 1, 4, 6, 8; *We Yone*, March 4, 1972, 1, 8; March 11, 1972, 2, 7, 8; *Sunday We Yone*, February 18, 1973, 1, 2, 6; May 25, 1977, 5, 6; June 28, 1978, 6, 7, 8; *Sunday We Yone*, August 6, 1978, 7; *We Yone*, January 3, 1979, 9; *The Tablet*, March 5, 1978, 1, 2; *The Tablet*, June 24, 1978, 1, 7, 8; March 31, 1979, 4; June 26, 1979, 4, 5; January 5, 1980, 3, 4; April 30, 1980, 7; May 28, 1980, 6; Collier, *Sierra Leone*, 23, 50, 53; *Rising Sun*, 142; Stevens, *What Life Has Taught Me*, 234, 267, 285, 316, 371.

20. *Daily Mail*, March 1, 1969, 1, 2.

21. *Daily Mail*, January 6, 1969, 1, 2.

22. *Daily Mail*, October 26, 1968, 1. See also Harrell-Bond, Howard, and Skinner, *Community Leadership and the Transformation of Freetown (1801–1976)*; Kandeh, "Politicization of Ethnic Identities in Sierra Leone."

23. *Daily Mail*, November 27, 1969, 1.

24. *Daily Mail*, February 3, 1970, 1.

25. *Daily Mail*, December 16, 1968, 8.

26. *Daily Mail*, December 6, 1968, 12.

27. *Daily Mail*, October 27, 1969, 12.

28. *Daily Mail*, October 28, 1969, 1.

29. *Daily Mail*, March 21, 1970, 2, 4.

30. *Daily Mail*, November 27, 1969, 1, 8.

31. *Daily Mail*, February 28, 1970, 1, 3; March 2, 1970, 1; *We Yone*, March 21, 1973, 1.

32. T2/8, MP 141, Question 0.77, 17.7.1968. See also *Daily Mail*, July 18, 1968, 2, 6; Harrell-Bond, Howard, and Skinner, *Community Leadership and the Transformation of Freetown (1801–1976)*, 270. For more information on the

problems of citizenship in Africa, see Jalloh, *African Entrepreneurship*, 1–30; Bronwen Manby, *Struggles for Citizenship in Africa* (London: Zed Books, 2009); William A. Shack, "Open Systems and Closed Boundaries: The Ritual Process of Stranger Relations in New African States," in *Strangers in African Societies*, ed. William A. Shack and Elliot P. Skinner (Berkeley: University of California Press, 1979), 37–47; and A. I. Asiwaju, ed., *Partitioned Africans: Ethnic Relations across Africa's International Boundaries, 1884–1984* (New York: St. Martin's Press, 1985).

33. *Daily Mail*, December 16, 1969, 5; *We Yone*, February 26, 1972, 8.

34. *We Yone*, September 20, 1972, 8. See also Harrell-Bond, Howard, and Skinner, *Community Leadership and the Transformation of Freetown (1801–1976)*.

35. *Daily Mail*, September 23, 1976, 1, 6.

36. *Daily Mail*, January 14, 1977, 1, 3. See also Harrell-Bond, Howard, and Skinner, *Community Leadership and the Transformation of Freetown (1801–1976)*.

37. *Daily Mail*, January 25, 1977, 6.

38. *Daily Mail*, August 11, 1976, 1, 4; *We Yone*, August 11, 1976, 2. See also Pratt, *An Autobiography*; Harrell-Bond, Howard, and Skinner, *Community Leadership and the Transformation of Freetown (1801–1976)*.

39. *We Yone*, March 22, 1977, 2.

40. *Daily Mail*, January 11, 1980, 2; *The Tablet*, August 11, 1979, 1, 8.

41. *Daily Mail*, November 22, 1969, 1; *We Yone*, September 4, 1971, 3; December 11, 1971, 3; April 8, 1972, 1, 2; May 27, 1972, 6; *Daily Mail*, February 16, 1985, 1, 8; *We Yone*, March 12, 1975, 3; *Sunday We Yone*, January 12, 1975, 1, 2, 5, 10; *Sunday We Yone*, August 3, 1975, 12; August 10, 1975, 12; July 27, 1980, 1; June 21, 1981, 3, 4; August 30, 1981, 1, 16; *We Yone*, June 3, 1981, 8; *Sunday We Yone*, July 24, 1983, 2; *We Yone*, October 24, 1984, 1, 3; *Sunday We Yone*, October 28, 1984, 3, 4; *The Tablet*, January 6, 1979, 4, 6; February 9, 1979, 6, 7; July 4, 1981, 5. See also Collier, *Sierra Leone*, 24, 25, 54, 57, 58, 59, 60, 66, 67, 81, 84, 123, 127, 128, 158, 176, 234, 354, 358, 414; Stevens, *What Life Has Taught Me*, 69, 70, 88–92, 164–72, 186–202, 218–19; Zack-Williams, "Sierra Leone: Crisis and Despair"; Jalloh, *African Entrepreneurship*; Bah, *Fulbe Presence in Sierra Leone*; Deveneaux, *Power Politics in Sierra Leone*; Reno, *Corruption and State Politics in Sierra Leone*; Turay and Abraham, *Sierra Leone Army*; Harris, *Sierra Leone: A Political History*; Dumbuya, *Reinventing the Colonial State*.

42. *Daily Mail*, August 21, 1968, 8. See also Jalloh, *African Entrepreneurship*; Bah, *Fulbe Presence in Sierra Leone*.

43. *Daily Mail*, September 7, 1968, 1. See also Jalloh, *African Entrepreneurship*; Bah, *Fulbe Presence in Sierra Leone*.

44. *Daily Mail*, September 9, 1968, 1; October 2, 1968, 10; October 4, 1968, 10. See also Jalloh, *African Entrepreneurship*; Bah, *Fulbe Presence in Sierra Leone*; Reno, *Corruption and State Politics in Sierra Leone*.

45. *Daily Mail*, October 4, 1968, 12. See also Jalloh, *African Entrepreneurship*; Bah, *Fulbe Presence in Sierra Leone*.

46. *Daily Mail*, October 14, 1968, 8. See also Jalloh, *African Entrepreneurship*; Bah, *Fulbe Presence in Sierra Leone*.

47. *Unity,* June 13, 1968, 4. See also Reno, *Corruption and State Politics in Sierra Leone.*

48. *Daily Mail,* November 22, 1969, 20. See also Turay and Abraham, *Sierra Leone Army;* Reno, *Corruption and State Politics in Sierra Leone;* Cox, *Civil-Military Relations in Sierra Leone.*

49. *Daily Mail,* November 25, 1969, 1. See also Turay and Abraham, *Sierra Leone Army.*

50. *Daily Mail,* December 2, 1969, 1; Turay and Abraham, *Sierra Leone Army.*

51. *Daily Mail,* November 22, 1969, 1.

52. *Daily Mail,* November 20, 1969, 8; Reno, *Corruption and State Politics in Sierra Leone.*

53. *Daily Mail,* December 9, 1969, 2; Reno, *Corruption and State Politics in Sierra Leone.*

54. *Daily Mail,* September 17, 1969, 8.

55. *Daily Mail,* January 23, 1969, 2.

56. *Daily Mail,* March 3, 1970, 2; March 6, 1970, 8.

57. *Daily Mail,* February 17, 1970, 3.

58. *Daily Mail,* June 17, 1970, 1; June 22, 1970, 1. See also Jalloh, *African Entrepreneurship;* Bah, *Fulbe Presence in Sierra Leone;* Reno, *Corruption and State Politics in Sierra Leone.*

59. *Daily Mail,* September 14, 1970, 1, 8. See also Aminatta Forna, *The Devil That Danced on the Water: A Daughter's Quest* (New York: Atlantic Monthly Press, 2002), 185–86, 395–403; Reno, *Corruption and State Politics in Sierra Leone.*

60. *Daily Mail,* February 5, 1972, 1, 2; Reno, *Corruption and State Politics in Sierra Leone.*

61. *Daily Mail,* February 12, 1972, 1, 9; February 14, 1972, 1, 4.

62. *Daily Mail,* March 23, 1972, 1, 2; May 17, 1972, 1, 2, 4; *We Yone,* February 19, 1972, 2; Reno, *Corruption and State Politics in Sierra Leone.*

63. *Daily Mail,* May 19, 1972, 1; May 23, 1972, 1; May 26, 1972, 12; September 7, 1972, 8; *We Yone,* January 8, 1975, 1, 2; Reno, *Corruption and State Politics in Sierra Leone.*

64. *Daily Mail,* June 27, 1977, 1. In 1977 illicit miners caused severe damage to roads and bridges in diamond areas in Kono. See *Daily Mail,* October 25, 1977, 2.

65. *Daily Mail,* October 12, 1978, 1, 8; October 13, 1978, 2; October 16, 1978, 1, 8; Reno, *Corruption and State Politics in Sierra Leone.*

66. *Daily Mail,* December 10, 1982, 1, 8; January 10, 1983, 1, 7; April 25, 1983, 1, 7; *We Yone,* May 13, 1981, 3, 4. In March 1985, President Stevens, speaking at the Kambia District Convention, stated that his government's current move to rid the diamond areas of Kono and Kenema of illegal aliens or strangers would be extended to Freetown. See *Daily Mail,* March 22, 1985, 1, 8; *We Yone,* March 21, 1985, 1, 2; *Sunday We Yone,* July 12, 1981, 16; July 26, 1981, 1; *We Yone,* January 28, 1981, 1, 3, 4; *Sunday We Yone,* May 23, 1982, 1; March 17, 1985, 1; *Rising Sun,* 149, 213, 484–85; Stevens, *What Life Has Taught Me,* 287.

67. *Daily Mail,* January 28, 1981, 1, 8. See also *Daily Mail,* January 31, 1981, 1, 8; November 23, 1981, 1, 8; July 14, 1982, 1, 5; October 11, 1982, 1, 7; *Sunday We Yone,* February 1, 1981, 1.

68. *We Yone,* January 31, 1979, 3, 10; *Sunday We Yone,* September 7, 1980, 4; March 29, 1981, 3, 4; *We Yone,* March 11, 1981, 2; May 13, 1981, 3, 4; *Sunday We Yone,* December 2, 1984, 3; May 12, 1985, 8; *The Tablet,* May 26, 1979, 4; June 9, 1979, 6.

69. *Daily Mail,* February 11, 1969, 1; December 9, 1969, 2.

70. *Daily Mail,* January 20, 1970, 8; June 10, 1972, 1, 2.

71. *Daily Mail,* January 26, 1983, 1, 7; January 28, 1983, 1, 8; January 31, 1983, 1, 4; February 2, 1983, 2; February 4, 1983, 1, 4; February 14, 1983, 4; February 28, 1983, 4; March 16, 1983, 1, 12; March 23, 1983, 4; November 11, 1983, 4. See also O. Aluko, "The Expulsion of Illegal Aliens from Nigeria: A Study of Nigeria's Decision-Making," *African Affairs* 84 (1985): 539–60; and P. Nugent and A. I. Asiwaju, eds. *African Boundaries: Barriers, Conduits, and Opportunities* (New York: Pinter, 1996); and K. C. Zacharia and Julian Conde, "Crossing Borders in West Africa," *West Africa,* April 27, 1981.

72. Author's interview with Dr. M. Alpha Bah (relative of Alhaji Bah), Washington, DC, March 9, 1991; See also Tejan-Jalloh, "Why This Campaign of Hate against Foulahs"; Jalloh, *African Entrepreneurship;* Bah, *Fulbe Presence in Sierra Leone;* Harrell-Bond, Howard, and Skinner, *Community Leadership and the Transformation of Freetown (1801–1976);* Conteh, *Paramount Chieftaincy in Sierra Leone.*

73. Author's interview with Alhaji Tejan-Jalloh, Freetown, Sierra Leone, June 21, 1990; T2/5/12; MI/1/34, MP 11–12, 5-6-1969; MI/Q/34, MP 14–15, CP (69), 579, 12-11-1969; "Memorandum Submitted on the Story of the Fullahs in Sierra Leone by the Delegates to the Meeting with the Honorourable the Prime Minister on Wednesday 5th March, 1969" (signed by Alhaji A. B. T. Jalloh). A copy is with the author. See also *Daily Mail,* March 6, 1969, 1, 2, and Jalloh, *African Entrepreneurship;* Bah, *Fulbe Presence in Sierra Leone;* Harrell-Bond, Howard, and Skinner, *Community Leadership and the Transformation of Freetown (1801–1976).*

74. Author's interview with Alhaji Tejan-Jalloh, Freetown, Sierra Leone, June 21, 1990. See also *Daily Mail,* February 7, 1970, 8; December 17, 1970, 2; Collier, *Sierra Leone,* 77; Jalloh, *African Entrepreneurship;* Bah, *Fulbe Presence in Sierra Leone;* Harrel-Bond, Howard, and Skinner, *Community Leadership and the Transformation of Freetown (1801–1976).*

75. *Daily Mail,* November 5, 1969, 1, 8. See also Jalloh, *African Entrepreneurship;* Bah, Harrell-Bond, Howard, and Skinner, *Community Leadership and the Transformation of Freetown (1801–1976);* Bah, *Fulbe Presence in Sierra Leone.*

76. Author's interview with Dr. Bah, Washington, DC, March 9, 1991. See also Jalloh, *African Entrepreneurship;* Harrell-Bond, Howard, and Skinner, *Community Leadership and the Transformation of Freetown (1801–1976);* Bah, *Fulbe Presence in Sierra Leone.*

77. Author's interview with Alhaji Seray-Wurie, Freetown, Sierra Leone, June 17, 1990. See also *Daily Mail,* July 22, 1981, 5.

78. Author's interview with Dr. Bah, Washington, DC, March 9, 1991. See also Bah, *Fulbe Presence in Sierra Leone*, "Sierra Leone–Guinea: Friction over Foulahs [Fula]," *West Africa*, December 20, 1982, 3259, 3261.

79. *Daily Mail*, November 20, 1975, 1; May 20, 1977, 1.

80. *Daily Mail*, July 9, 1973, 2.

81. *We Yone*, February 13, 1971, 3.

82. *Daily Mail*, October 17, 1973, 2.

83. *Daily Mail*, December 5, 1969, 10; *We Yone*, January 30, 1971, 2; *Daily Mail*, March 23, 1984, 12; June 12, 1984, 12.

84. *Sunday We Yone*, April 5, 1981, 7.

85. Alhaji Dr. Ahmadu Wurie died in 1977 after a long career. In 1974 he was awarded an honorary degree of Doctor of Civil Law by the University of Sierra Leone. In the same year he performed the hajj. Author's interview with Bai Sheka Wurie (relative of Alhaji Wurie), Lungi, Sierra Leone, September 28, 2008. See also *Daily Mail*, June 15, 1977, 1, 3; July 25, 1977, 1; *We Yone*, June 15, 1977, 16; Collier, *Sierra Leone*, 403.

86. *Daily Mail*, December 9, 1969, 2.

87. *Daily Mail*, December 12, 1969, 12; *Daily Mail*, December 8, 1969, 1; *We Yone*, 1971, 3.

88. *Daily Mail*, December 17, 1969, 7; *Sunday We Yone*, February 1, 1981, 12.

89. *Daily Mail*, November 3, 1982, 3. See also Tucker, *Mission Boy from Shebar*, 142.

90. *Daily Mail*, January 5, 1983, 5; *The Tablet*, March 11, 1978, 8; August 19, 1978, 6; May 7, 1980, 5.

91. *Daily Mail*, November 10, 1969, 2; July 14, 1981, 4; November 9, 1981, 5; *We Yone*, March 24, 1976, 11; February 7, 1979, 10; March 7, 1979, 11; *Sunday We Yone*, September 30, 1979, 15; October 7, 1979, 13; December 30, 15; *We Yone*, June 25, 1980, 12; August 20, 1980, 1, 12; October 22, 1980, 11; *Sunday We Yone*, April 12, 1981, 11; *We Yone*, May 6, 1981, 11; September 30, 1981, 13; December 21, 1984, 8; *The Tablet*, July 11, 1981, 1, 6.

92. *Unity*, July 23, 1968, 2; *Daily Mail*, July 23, 1968, 1. See also Jalloh, *African Entrepreneurship*; Bah, *Fulbe Presence in Sierra Leone*; Harrell-Bond, Howard, and Skinner, *Community Leadership and the Transformation of Freetown (1801–1976)*.

93. Harrell-Bond, Howard, and Skinner, *Community Leadership and the Transformation of Freetown (1801–1976)*, 273. See also MI/Q/34, MP 14–15, CP (69), 579, 12-11-1969.

94. *Daily Mail*, August 10, 1968, 8.

95. *Daily Mail*, August 14, 1968, 8; August 23, 1968, 8.

96. *Daily Mail*, August 29, 1968, 8.

97. *Daily Mail*, October 10, 1968, 12.

98. *Daily Mail*, October 11, 1968, 2.

99. *Daily Mail*, November 6, 1968, 8.

100. *Daily Mail*, November 10, 1969, 1.

101. *We Yone*, October 29, 1975, 8; October 20, 1976, 12; February 15, 1978, 1. See also Harrell-Bond, Howard, and Skinner, *Community Leadership and the*

Transformation of Freetown (1801–1976); Jalloh, *African Entrepreneurship*; Bah, *Fulbe Presence in Sierra Leone.*

102. *Daily Mail,* June 1, 1971, 8.

103. *Daily Mail,* November 11, 1971, 8; July 7, 1971, 8; *We Yone,* December 4, 1971, 2; *Daily Mail,* January 4, 1972, 1.

104. *Daily Mail,* July 7, 1971, 8; July 12, 1971, 1; October 20, 1976, 1. See also Straussberger, "Storming the Citadel"; Jalloh, *African Entrepreneurship*; Bah, *Fulbe Presence in Sierra Leone*; Harrell-Bond, Howard, and Skinner, *Community Leadership and the Transformation of Freetown (1801–1976).*

105. Author's interview with Alhaji Tejan-Jalloh, Freetown, Sierra Leone, June 21, 1990. See also *We Yone,* November, 15, 22, 1972; Adamolekun, *Sékou Touré's Guinea*; and Riviere, *Guinea*; Jalloh, *African Entrepreneurship*; Bah, *Fulbe Presence in Sierra Leone*; Harrell-Bond, Howard, and Skinner, *Community Leadership and the Transformation of Freetown (1801–1976).*

106. *Daily Mail,* August 6, 1971, 12. See also Harrell-Bond, Howard, and Skinner, *Community Leadership and the Transformation of Freetown (1801–1976).*

107. *Daily Mail,* August 11, 1975, 1, 4; *Daily Mail,* August 13, 1975, 1. See also Jalloh, *African Entrepreneurship*; Harrell-Bond, Howard, and Skinner, *Community Leadership and the Transformation of Freetown (1801–1976)*; Bah, *Fulbe Presence in Sierra Leone.*

108. *We Yone,* August 17, 1977, 1, 12.

109. *Daily Mail,* September 15, 1976, 8; Harrell-Bond, Howard, and Skinner, *Community Leadership and the Transformation of Freetown (1801–1976).*

110. *Daily Mail,* August 17, 1977, 2; *We Yone,* August 17, 1977, 1, 12.

111. T2/6/1, "Alhaji Momodu Bah to Permanent Secretary, Ministry of Interior, 5 September, 1975." See also *Sunday Flash,* April 18, 1976, 14; *Daily Mail,* November 3, 1977, 1, 8; *We Yone,* April 14, 1978; *Daily Mail,* March 4, 1978, 1; *Sunday We Yone,* July 8, 1973, 1; *We Yone,* November 20, 1974, 12; February 1, 1978, 7, 8; *We Yone,* March 8, 1978, 1; *Sunday We Yone,* February 26, 1978, 13, 15; March 5, 1978, 1, 2; May 4, 1980, 7; *We Yone,* January 28, 1981, 9; *The Tablet,* May 27, 1978, 7; June 24, 1978, 3; June 28, 1978, 5; March 28, 1979, 3; June 30, 1979, 8; *Sierra Leone Republican Constitution* (Freetown, Sierra Leone: Government Printer, 1971); Collier, *Sierra Leone,* 429.

112. *Sunday We Yone,* December 6, 1981, 1, 2; December 13, 1981, 3; *We Yone,* February 18, 1981, 12.

113. *Sunday We Yone,* January 17, 1982, 1.

114. *Sunday We Yone,* October 28, 1984, 8.

115. *West Africa,* October 5, 1968, 1161. See also Straussberger, "Storming the Citadel"; Jalloh, *African Entrepreneurship*; Bah, *Fulbe Presence in Sierra Leone*; Harrell-Bond, Howard, and Skinner, *Community Leadership and the Transformation of Freetown (1801–1976).*

116. Author's interview with E. T. Kamara. See also *Sunday We Yone,* March 17, 1974, 1, 12; *We Yone,* April 21, 1974, 1, 9; May 12, 1974, 1; *We Yone,* January 8, 1975, 8; June 4, 1975, 2; *We Yone,* September 17, 1975, 1; *We Yone,* March 16, 1975, 8; *Sunday We Yone,* May 4, 1975, 1; November 23, 1975, 12;

We Yone, January 21, 1976, 2; May 12, 1976, 6, 7; *Sunday We Yone,* August 15, 1976, 1; November 21, 1976, 1; *We Yone,* February 16, 1977, 12; *Sunday We Yone,* August 14, 1977, 1; *We Yone,* November 15, 1978, 2; May 21, 1980, 1; *Sunday We Yone,* 1981, 2; *We Yone,* February 4, 1981, 1; February 18, 1981, 2; August 19, 1981, 1; *Sunday We Yone,* June 26, 1983, 1; July 17, 1983, 2; *We Yone,* March 14, 1985, 1, 7; *The Tablet,* June 2, 1979, 2; October 24, 1979, 8; *Daily Mail,* September 12, 1985, 2; *The Tablet,* February 21, 1981, 1. See also Collier, *Sierra Leone,* 159, 174, 178, 214–15, 318, 465, 469, 470; Stevens, *What Life Has Taught Me,* 275, 346–53, 347; Jalloh, *African Entrepreneurship;* Bah, *Fulbe Presence in Sierra Leone;* Harrell-Bond, Howard, and Skinner, *Community Leadership and the Transformation of Freetown (1801–1976);* Reno, *Corruption and State Politics in Sierra Leone.*

117. *Daily Mail,* August 6, 1968, 8; *We Yone,* November 15, 1972, 3.

118. *Unity,* May 18, 1968, 8.

119. *Daily Mail,* October 28, 1969, 8.

120. *Daily Mail,* September 2, 1969, 1, 4.

121. *Daily Mail,* October 30, 1968, 1, 6.

122. *Daily Mail,* January 16, 1969, 3. See also Straussberger, "Storming the Citadel"; Jalloh, *African Entrepreneurship;* Bah, *Fulbe Presence in Sierra Leone;* Harrell-Bond, Howard, and Skinner, *Community Leadership and the Transformation of Freetown (1801–1976).*

123. *Daily Mail,* July 1, 1968, 2. See also Camara, *Political History of Guinea since World War Two,* 234; Bah, *Fulbe Presence in Sierra Leone;* Jalloh, *African Entrepreneurship;* Harrell-Bond, Howard, and Skinner, *Community Leadership and the Transformation of Freetown (1801–1976).*

124. *Daily Mail,* April 1, 1970, 1; April 9, 1970, 8.

125. *Daily Mail,* April 11, 1970, 8. See also Bah, *Fulbe Presence in Sierra Leone;* Jalloh, *African Entrepreneurship;* Harrell-Bond, Howard, and Skinner, *Community Leadership and the Transformation of Freetown (1801–1976).*

126. Author's interview with Alhaji Tejan-Jalloh, Freetown, Sierra Leone, June 21, 1990; *We Yone,* January 16, 1971, 5; January 23, 1971, 2, 7; March 20, 1971, 3; March 11, 1972, 5; November 22, 1972, 1; *Daily Mail,* November 23, 1978, 1; *We Yone,* November 21, 1973, 1; November 24, 1976, 1, 12. See also V. D. Du Bois, *The Rise of an Opposition to Sékou Touré.* Part 6: *The Activation of the Guinean Exiles: The Front de Liberation Nationale de Guinée* (FLAG). AUFS Reports, West African Series 9, no. 6 (New York: AUFS, July 1966); Collier, *Sierra Leone,* 76, 85, 118; Stevens, *What Life Has Taught Me,* 347.

127. MI/Q/42, 9-8-1971. See also Harrell-Bond, Howard, and Skinner, *Community Leadership and the Transformation of Freetown (1801–1976),* 277–78.

128. MI/Q/42, MP 4, 10-8-1971. See also Harrell-Bond, Howard, and Skinner, *Community Leadership and the Transformation of Freetown (1801–1976),* 278.

129. Author's interview with Alhaji Tejan-Jalloh, Freetown, Sierra Leone, June 21, 1990; author's interview with Dr. Easmon, Freetown, Sierra Leone, August 3, 1992; and author's interview with Dr. Bah, Washington, DC, March 9, 1991. See also *Daily Mail,* December 5, 1970, 1; December 7, 1970, 1; *West*

Africa, August 27, 1971; *Daily Mail*, August 11, 1971, 8; *We Yone*, July 27, 1975, 12; February 6, 1971, 1; February 13, 1971, 1, 3; March 27, 1971, 1, 3, 4; April 3, 1971, 1, 2, 6, 8; April 10, 1971, 1, 6, 7, 8; April 17, 1971, 1, 3, 6, 7, 8; June 5, 1971, 8; June 26, 1971, 1; July 3, 1971, 1; July 3, 1971, 12; July 10, 1971, 1; July 10, 1971, 12; August 14, 1971, 1, 2; September 15, 1971, 1; September 11, 1971, 1; October 30, 1971, 1, 12; December 18, 1971, 8; March 18, 1972, 1, 3; July 18, 1973, 2; Camara, *Political History of Guinea since World War Two*, 244; Stevens, *What Life Has Taught Me*, 346–53; *Africa Confidential*, March 17, 1972, 1, 2; Straussberger, "Storming the Citadel"; Bah, *Fulbe Presence in Sierra Leone*; Jalloh, *African Entrepreneurship*; Harrell-Bond, Howard, and Skinner, *Community Leadership and the Transformation of Freetown (1801–1976)*.

130. Author's interview with Alhaji Tejan-Jalloh, Freetown, Sierra Leone, June 21, 1990. See also MI/Q/42, MP 1, 28-4-1972; *Daily Mail*, May 20, 1972, 12; September 27, 1972, 2; Jalloh, *African Entrepreneurship*; Bah, *Fulbe Presence in Sierra Leone*; Harrell-Bond, Howard, and Skinner, *Community Leadership and the Transformation of Freetown (1801–1976)*, 278.

131. *We Yone*, January 23, 1974, 2; April 24, 1974, 5.

132. *We Yone*, November 14, 1973, 2; *Sunday We Yone*, September 30, 1973, 2.

133. *We Yone*, July 24, 1971, 1; July 31, 1971, 2, 11; August 7, 1971, 4, 5, 6, 7, 8; August 21, 1971, 3; August 28, 1971, 6; September 4, 1971, 8; September 11, 1971, 4; September 18, 1971, 5, 6; September 25, 1971, 3; October 16, 1971, 3; October 23, 1971, 5, 6; November 27, 1971, 3, 6, 7; December 4, 1971, 5, 6; December 11, 1971, 3; *Daily Mail*, July 10, 1976, 1, 4; *We Yone*, August 4, 1976, 1; November 29, 1978, 1. See also *L'Agression portugaise contre la Republique de Guinée*, Kaké, *Sékou Touré*; Du Bois, *Rise of an Opposition to Sékou Touré*; Collier, *Sierra Leone*, 111; Camara, *Political History of Guinea since World War Two*, 283; Straussberger, "Storming the Citadel."

134. *Daily Mail*, June 24, 1977, 1; Bah, *Fulbe Presence in Sierra Leone*.

135. Author's interview with E. T. Kamara. For a profile of E. T. Kamara, see *We Yone*, July 6, 1977, 4, 11; *Sunday We Yone*, September 4, 1977, 12; June 17, 1979, 1, 8, 9, 10, 11, 12, 17. See also Stevens, *What Life Has Taught Me*; Cartwright, *Politics in Sierra Leone*; Cox, *Civil-Military Relations*; Harrell-Bond, Howard, and Skinner, *Community Leadership and the Transformation of Freetown (1801–1976)*.

136. *We Yone*, February 18, 1976, 8.

137. *Daily Mail*, May 23, 1975, 1.

138. *Sunday We Yone*, July 27, 1975, 12.

139. *Daily Mail*, August 28, 1976, 1.

140. *Daily Mail*, August 2, 1977, 6.

141. *Daily Mail*, December 21, 1979, 5; April 11, 1983, 1, 12; *Sunday We Yone*, May 25, 1975, 2; May 18, 1980, 2, 5, 6.

142. Author's interview with Alhaji Tejan-Jalloh, Freetown, Sierra Leone, June 21, 1990. See also *Sunday We Yone*, March 5, 1978, 1; April 2, 1978, 6, 15; *The Tablet*, January 27, 1978, 2; February 25, 1978, 3; Camara, *Political History of Guinea since World War Two*, 231, 290.

143. *Sunday We Yone*, March 18, 1979, 1, 2, 3, 4; March 25, 1979, 1, 2, 7, 8, 9, 10, 12; April 1, 1979, 1; June 10, 1979, 7, 8; *The Tablet*, March 20, 1979, 1, 2, 6; March 23, 1979, 1, 3, 6; March 28, 1979, 3. See also Collier, *Sierra Leone*, 484–85.

144. *We Yone*, March 20, 1971, 1; September 4, 1971, 1; February 5, 1972, 6, 8; *Daily Mail*, January 28, 1980, 1; January 20, 1980, 1, 2; January 31, 1980, 1; February 1, 1980, 1, 2; May 30, 1981, 1, 8; June 24, 1983, 1, 8; September 7, 1983, 1, 8; *Sunday We Yone*, October 7, 1973, 1, 8; *We Yone*, July 17, 1974, 1; *Sunday We Yone*, October 6, 1974, 1, 2, 9, 11; *We Yone*, October 22, 1975, 9, 10; November 19, 1975, 2; *Sunday We Yone*, October 5, 1975, 1, 2, 3; October 19, 1975, 9, 11; December 14, 1975, 1, 16; *We Yone*, February 25, 1976, 2; April 7, 1976, 2; May 12, 1976, 2; September 22, 1976, 12; October 13, 1976, 1; *Sunday We Yone*, September 5, 1976, 2; October 3, 1976, 1; October 10, 1976, 1, 3, 9; *We Yone*, April 20, 1977, 3; July 6, 1977, 1, 2; July 20, 1977, 2; October 12, 1977, 1; October 19, 1977, 1, 2; *Sunday We Yone*, January 16, 1977, 2; July 17, 1977, 1; *We Yone*, June 28, 1978, 1; August 30, 1978, 2; September 13, 1978, 9; October 4, 1978, 1, 2, 7, 8, 9, 10; October 18, 1978, 1, 2; October 25, 1978, 8; November 29, 1978, 12; *Sunday We Yone*, October 8, 1978, 9; *We Yone*, October 3, 1979, 1, 3, 5; *Sunday We Yone*, July 6, 1980, 8; *The Tablet*, February 25, 1978, 3; August 9, 1978, 6. See also Collier, *Sierra Leone*, 216, 220, 262, 305, 306, 320–21, 325, 351, 355–56, 410, 461, 463, 473; *Rising Sun*, 208, 239–42, 410–11; Stevens, *What Life Has Taught Me*, 304, 378.

145. *Sunday We Yone*, March 13, 1977, 12.

146. *Daily Mail*, March 17, 1979, 1; March 19, 1979, 1, 8; March 20, 1979, 1, 4, 5, 8; March 21, 1979, 1, 4, 5, 8; March 22, 1979, 1, 8; March 23, 1979, 1, 8; March 30, 1979, 1, 8; *We Yone*, March 14, 1979, 1, 2; March 21, 1979, 1, 2, 6, 7, 12; March 28, 1979, 5.

147. *We Yone*, April 4, 1979, 1, 12.

148. *We Yone*, October 17, 1979, 1, 2; *Sunday We Yone*, October 21, 1979, 1, 2; *Sierra Leone: 12 Years of Economic Achievement and Political Consolidation under the APC and Dr. Siaka Stevens, 1968–1980* (Freetown, Sierra Leone: Office of the President, 1980), 526.

149. *We Yone*, October 22, 1980, 1; *The Tablet*, October 25, 1980, 1; *Daily Mail*, January 22, 1983, 1, 7, 8; January 24, 1983, 1, 7, 8; September 12, 1983, 1, 8; September 21, 1983, 1, 8; October 5, 1983, 1, 8; October 28, 1983, 2, 6; June 4, 1984, 1, 16; June 28, 1984, 1, 8; October 6, 1984, 1, 8, 9, 16; February 21, 1985, 1, 8; *We Yone*, December 19, 1979, 1, 2, 4, 12; *Sunday We Yone*, October 21, 1979, 1, 2, 3; December 23, 1979, 31; *We Yone*, January 30, 1980, 1, 12; March 26, 1980, 1, 12; December 17, 1980, 3; *Sunday We Yone*, February 3, 1980, 1, 2, 3; June 8, 1980, 1, 2, 7, 8, 9, 10; July 13, 1980, 16; August 17, 1980, 11, 12; August 31, 1980, 3, 5, 8; October 5, 1980, 2; October 26, 1980, 1, 2; January 4, 1981, 3; May 10, 1981, 3, 4; October 4, 1981, 1, 2; December 13, 1981, 2; *We Yone*, February 25, 1981, 3; May 6, 1981, 2; October 6, 1982, 1, 8; *Sunday We Yone*, October 24, 1982, 1; November 21, 1982, 2; July 10, 1983, 1; July 17, 1983, 1, 2; July 31, 1983, 2; *We Yone*, March 21, 1985, 2; March 28, 1985, 3, 6; *The Tablet*, January 30, 1980, 8; February 2, 1980, 2; February 27, 1980, 6; April 30, 1980, 5; June

4, 1980, 4; September 17, 1980, 6; October 4, 1980, 5. See also Collier, *Sierra Leone*, 544–45.

150. *Daily Mail*, October 17, 1979, 1, 2; October 18, 1979, 1, 2; October 20, 1979, 1, 8; October 22, 1979, 1, 2; October 23, 1979, 1; July 24, 1980, 1, 8; October 27, 1980, 1, 8; November 24, 1980, 1, 8; *Sunday We Yone*, February 10, 1980, 5.

151. *Sunday We Yone*, May 25, 1975, 1, 2; June 1, 1975, 2; June 8, 1975, 1, 12; *We Yone*, November 3, 1976, 1, 2; *Sunday We Yone*, November 7, 1976, 1, 2, 12; *We Yone*, April 20, 1977, 3; August 3, 1977, 12; *Sunday We Yone*, January 9, 1977, 1, 2, 12; January 16, 1977, 2; June 5, 1977, 3, 8; September 11, 1977, 9, 10; November 13, 1977, 11; April 23, 1978, 1, 2; *We Yone*, May 30, 1979, 1, 4, 16; *Sunday We Yone*, April 1, 1979, 7; November 18, 1979, 1, 16; *We Yone*, May 28, 1980, 1, 2; *Sunday We Yone*, June 8, 1980, 1, 2, 7, 8, 9, 10; July 20, 1980, 7, 8; July 27, 1980, 15, 16; *We Yone*, March 11, 1981, 1; May 20, 1981, 1, 5, 8, 12; May 27, 1981, 1, 2, 5, 9, 10, 11; June 3, 1981, 3, 4, 5, 10; January 27, 1982, 11; June 2, 1982, 1, 2; *Sunday We Yone*, May 30, 1982, 1, 8; *We Yone*, July 20, 1983, 7; August 18, 1983, 12; November 22, 1984, 1, 8; November 28, 1984, 1, 8; *Sunday We Yone*, November 18, 1984, 1; February 17, 1985, 1, 3, 6, 8; *The Tablet*, January 17, 1979, 1; March 23, 1979, 1; June 4, 1980, 4; May 2, 1981, 1, 6; May 16, 1981, 1, 6; May 27, 1981, 1, 6; May 30, 1981, 1, 3, 8; June 6, 1981, 4. See also *Rising Sun*, 208, 236–39, 241, 250, 412–13; Stevens, *What Life Has Taught Me*, 378–79.

152. *Daily Mail*, May 30, 1983, 1, 8; June 1, 1983, 1, 8; *We Yone*, October 10, 1973, 2; June 4, 1975, 2; June 11, 1975, 2, 8.

153. *Daily Mail*, January 24, 1985, 1, 3, 12; January 19, 1985, 3; January 26, 1985, 1, 3; July 20, 1985, 6; *We Yone*, January 16, 1985, 8; *Sunday We Yone*, May 24, 1981, 1, 3, 4, 7, 10; May 31, 1981, 1, 2, 3, 4, 7, 8, 9; *Daily Mail*, November 14, 1985, 3.

154. In 1978 an APC government built a bridge in Kambia linking Sierra Leone and Guinea, which greatly facilitated trade. See Collier, *Sierra Leone*, 425–26.

155. *We Yone*, June 28, 1972, 5; May 23, 1979, 12; *Sunday We Yone*, April 15, 1979, 1, 2; April 22, 1979, 1; April 29, 1979, 1; *Sunday We Yone*, May 6, 1979, 4; May 13, 1979, 12; Collier, *Sierra Leone*, 491, 493, 519, 524.

156. *We Yone*, January 23, 1974, 1, 8; *Sunday We Yone*, April 21, 1974, 1, 9; *Sunday We Yone*, July 13, 1975, 10; July 27, 1975, 11; *We Yone*, July 6, 1977, 10; March 8, 1978, 1, 2, 10, 12; *Sunday We Yone*, March 5, 1978, 11; March 2, 1980, 15; April 6, 1980, 15; April 20, 1980, 19, 20; May 3, 1981, 16; *We Yone*, March 11, 1981, 11; March 18, 1981, 14, 16; May 20, 1981, 11, 12; July 8, 1981, 15; July 21, 1982, 7; December 21, 1984, 8; *Sunday We Yone*, September 16, 1984, 8; September 23, 1984, 7; *The Tablet*, February 25, 1978, 3.

157. *We Yone*, May 22, 1974, 1.

158. *Sunday We Yone*, January 21, 1973, 6; *We Yone*, October 3, 1973, 1; *Sunday We Yone*, November 25, 1973, 1, 12.

159. *We Yone*, January 9, 1974, 8.

160. *Daily Mail*, September 1, 1978, 2; November 30, 1978, 1, 8; December 1, 1978, 1, 8; December 23, 1978, 32; May 4, 1979, 1; May 7, 1979, 1, 8; May

16, 1979, 8; December 31, 1980, 6; October 5, 1981, 1, 8; December 1, 1981, 2; December 30, 1981, 1, 2; August 18, 1982, 1; *Sunday We Yone*, September 30, 1973, 1, 9.

161. *Daily Mail*, September 14, 1977, 5; *Sunday We Yone*, January 5, 1975, 3, 5; December 6, 1981, 1, 2. See Jalloh, *African Entrepreneurship*, 31–150.

162. Author's interview with Alhaji Sanu Barrie, Freetown, Sierra Leone, August 4, 1990. See also *Daily Mail*, May 27, 1972, 12; *The Tablet*, October 18, 1980, 1, 6; Harris, *Sierra Leone: A Political History*.

163. *The Tablet*, February 5, 1978, 1, 2, 3; May 10, 1978, 3, 8; June 15, 1979, 4; June 28, 1980, 3; December 17, 1980, 2; March 7, 1981, 1, 6. See also Collier, *Sierra Leone*, 377; *Rising Sun*, 133; Daramy, *Constitutional Developments in the Post-Colonial State of Sierra Leone*; Samuel Hinton, *University Student Protests and Political Change in Sierra Leone* (New York: The Edwin Mellen Press, 2002); Daniel J. Paracka Jr., *The Athens of West Africa: A History of International Education at Fourah Bay College, Freetown, Sierra Leone* (New York: Routledge, 2003); Harris, *Sierra Leone: A Political History*; Foray, *Road to the One-Party State*; Dumbuya, *Reinventing the Colonial State*.

164. *Daily Mail*, January 27, 1972, 1; *Sunday We Yone*, May 25, 1980, 16; *The Tablet*, January 26, 1980, 1, 7.

165. *We Yone*, April 8, 1972, 5; *Rising Sun*, 122.

166. Author's interview with E. T. Kamara. See also *Daily Mail*, November 3, 1969, 1; *Daily Mail*, November 12, 1969, 1; November 13, 1969, 1; January 30, 1969, 8; March 29, 1969, 1; June 13, 1970, 1; August 2, 1971, 1; January 14, 1972, 8; February 19, 1972, 1; *Washington Post*, July 14, 1980, A21; *Daily Mail*, February 6, 1981, 1, 8; *Sunday We Yone*, July 25, 1982, 8; June 13, 1982, 5, 10; July 11, 1982, 1, 2; February 7, 1983, 315; March 7, 1983, 618–19; July 11, 1983, 1600; February 6, 1984, 262–62; June 27, 1983, 1504–505; July 9, 1984, 1398; February 18, 1985, 309; *Sunday We Yone*, October 17, 1982, 1, 8; November 21, 1982, 1, 2; *We Yone*, July 13, 1983, 2; September 15, 1982, 1, 2; *Sunday We Yone*, June 19, 1983, 8; July 10, 1983, 3, 4, 5, 7; July 31, 1983, 8; *We Yone*, July 18, 1984, 3, 4, 5, 7; August 22, 1984, 1; August 29, 1984, 1, 2; August 29, 1984, 1, 2; September 26, 1984, 3; December 6, 1984, 3; *Sunday We Yone*, September 16, 1984, 1, 8; September 23, 1984, 1, 3, 4; September 30, 1984, 1, 8; October 7, 1984, 8; *We Yone*, March 8, 1985, 3, 4; *Sunday We Yone*, March 17, 1985, 2; *The Tablet*, January 8, 1979, 8; August 1, 1979, 8; August 4, 1979, 1, 7, 8; August 8, 1979, 1; August 25, 1979, 1, 8; October 13, 1979, 6; May 7, 1980, 5; June 18, 1980, 8; October 1, 1980, 1, 5; October 18, 1980, 5; November 22, 1980, 3, 6; April 4, 1981, 3; June 27, 1981, 2; August 5, 1981, 8; *The Times*, June 2, 1983, 14; *New York Times*, June 21, 1984, A2; *Sierra Leone, 1968–1980*, 319, 423, 462; Stevens, *What Life Has Taught Me*, 287.

167. *We Yone*, November 5, 1975, 1, 3; November 12, 1975, 3, 4; *Sunday We Yone*, November 9, 1975, 5; December 7, 1975, 1.

168. *We Yone*, November 12, 1975, 1.

169. *The Tablet*, August 5, 1978, 8.

170. *Daily Mail,* February 19, 1970, 5; May 26, 1972, 1, 7; April 7, 1973, 1, 4; *Sunday We Yone,* January 27, 1985, 8; *The Tablet,* May 11, 1979, 1; May 15, 1979, 1, 3; June 3, 1979, 3; March 5, 1980, 1, 5; March 12, 1980, 1, 3; March 26, 1980, 2; March 29, 1980, 1, 6; May 17, 1980, 3, 6; October 25, 1980, 5; February 14, 1981, 1, 6; June 13, 1981, 1, 6; July 4, 1981, 3, 6.

171. *We Yone,* July 6, 1983, 8; July 13, 1983, 3, 6; August 3, 1983, 1; August 31, 1983, 8; *Sunday We Yone,* July 10, 1983, 1, 8; *The Tablet,* July 22, 1978, 1, 4; June 20, 1979, 1, 7; June 12, 1979, 1, 3; August 4, 1979, 1, 7, 8; August 8, 1979, 2, 8; August 11, 1979, 3, 8; August 15, 1979, 2; August 18, 1979, 2; August 31, 1979, 7; September 4, 1979, 1, 8; October 3, 1979, 3; October 6, 1979, 1, 2, 8; October 10, 1979, 2, 8; December 8, 1979, 1, 4; May 17, 1980, 1; May 17, 1980, 8; July 26, 1980, 3; August 13, 1980, 8; *Daily Mail,* September 18, 1985, 5, 8; *Sunday We Yone,* September 15, 1985, 1, 5.

172. *The Tablet,* June 12, 1979, 1, 3; August 4, 1979, 1, 7, 8; August 15, 1979, 2; August 18, 1979, 1, 3; August 31, 1979, 7; September 4, 1979, 2; *The Tablet,* May 17, 1980, 1; June 4, 1980, 4; June 24, 1981, 1, 6.

173. *The Tablet,* January 5, 1980, 3, 4.

174. Ibid.

175. *Sunday We Yone,* June 13, 1982, 5, 10; June 6, 1982, 3, 4; May 30, 1982, 3, 7; *We Yone,* September 15, 1983, 3, 6; *Sunday We Yone,* September 11, 1983, 2; September 18, 1983, 3, 6; *We Yone,* August 22, 1984, 1, 8; August 29, 1984, 3, 4; December 13, 1984, 1, 2, 3, 6, 7; December 21, 1984, 3, 4, 7; *Sunday We Yone,* September 9, 1984, 1, 8; *We Yone,* January 16, 1985, 3, 4; February 22, 1985, 1, 3, 8; February 27, 1985, 3, 6, 7; March 6, 1985, 3, 4; March 28, 1985, 7, 8; *Sunday We Yone,* February 3, 1985, 3, 4; *The Tablet,* May 19, 1979, 1, 8; August 25, 1979, 1, 8; October 13, 1979, 6; *The Tablet,* October 20, 1979, 4; December 5, 1979, 3; March 19, 1980, 1, 6; March 26, 1980, 2; November 8, 1980, 2; November 19, 1980, 1, 6; November 22, 1980, 3, 6; December 6, 1980, 5; December 13, 1980, 1, 6; *Sunday We Yone,* August 25, 1985, 3, 4; *The Tablet,* August 5, 1981, 8; August 8, 1981, 8.

176. *The Tablet,* June 1979, 1; June 9, 1979, 1; June 30, 1979, 1, 8; July 11, 1979, 2; January 5, 1980, 8; January 9, 1980, 4; March 5, 1980, 1, 5; March 8, 1980, 1, 2, 5; April 2, 1980, 1, 6; April 9, 1980, 1, 6; May 7, 1980, 7; May 14, 1980, 6; May 21, 1980, 5; August 2, 1980, 3, 8; August 9, 1980, 4, 6; November 5, 1980, 3, 6; November 26, 1980, 5; February 14, 1981, 3; March 25, 1981, 3; January 31, 1981, 15, 16; June 24, 1981, 1, 3. See also Bangura, *Sierra Leone and the Legacy of Failed Leaderships,* 53, 68.

177. *The Tablet,* May 10, 1978, 1, 3; July 8, 1978, 1, 8; July 12, 1978, 1; July 19, 1978, 1, 2; July 22, 1978, 6, 7; July 27, 1978, 2, 3; September 23, 1978, 3; January 6, 1979, 8; January 25, 1979, 2, 3; January 31, 1979, 1; February 9, 1979, 1, 2, 3; February 14, 1979, 1, 8; February 24, 1979, 5; February 28, 1979, 1; March 7, 1979, 2; March 28, 1979, 3; May 26, 1979, 1; June 15, 1979, 3; June 2, 1979, 1, 5; June 9, 1979, 1, 3; July 7, 1979, 1; August 4, 1979, 1, 7; August 11, 1979, 3, 8; August 15, 1979, 2; September 4, 1979, 2; September 29, 1979, 1, 3; October

6, 1979, 5, 8; October 24, 1979, 1, 4; January 5, 1980, 3; May 14, 1980, 6; May 28, 1980, 1, 3; June 4, 1980, 1, 3; July 2, 1980, 2; July 5, 1980, 7; July 9, 1980, 4; July 12, 1980, 8; August 9, 1980, 3, 8; August 23, 1980, 3; August 27, 1980, 2, 6; August 30, 1980, 2; September 3, 1980, 1, 8; September 27, 1980, 2, 5; October 18, 1980, 1, 3; November 22, 1980, 2; February 14, 1981, 5; April 15, 1981, 1, 6; June 13, 1981, 1, 6; June 13, 1981, 3; June 17, 1981, 1, 3, 6; June 24, 1981, 3, 6; August 5, 1981, 3, 8; August 8, 1981, 7. See also Kallon, *Political Economy of Corruption in Sierra Leone*; and Dumbuya, *Reinventing the Colonial State*.

178. *Unity*, May 18, 1968, 3, 7; *The Tablet*, June 28, 1980, 9; August 2, 1980, 3, 8; September 13, 1980, 1, 4; October 15, 1980, 1, 6; October 18, 1980, 1, 6; October 29, 1980, 1, 3, 6; December 6, 1980, 5; July 15, 1981, 1; August 8, 1981, 6; August 29, 1981, 7.

179. *The Tablet*, May 11, 1979, 3; November 14, 1979, 2; January 5, 1980, 3, 4; June 13, 1981, 2; July 11, 1981, 1, 6.

180. *Unity*, May 31, 1968, 3; *We Yone*, February 6, 1971, 2, 4, 5, 7; February 13, 1971, 6; February 27, 1971, 3, 8; March 13, 1971, 3; July 10, 1971, 1; November 6, 1971, 1, 8; November 27, 1971, 1, 8; December 24, 1971, 8; February 12, 1972, 2; *Daily Mail*, August 17, 1979, 1; August 23, 1979, 1, 2; September 20, 1979, 1; July 3, 1981, 1, 8; July 15, 1981, 1; September 17, 1981, 1, 8; December 29, 1981, 4, 8; May 28, 1982, 1, 4; July 26, 1982, 1, 2; October 18, 1982, 1, 7; January 14, 1983, 1, 4; January 19, 1983, 1, 7; February 4, 1983, 1, 4; February 7, 1983, 1, 7; February 14, 1983, 1, 4; May 16, 1983, 3, 5; May 23, 1983, 3; September 12, 1984, 1, 8; September 15, 1984, 1, 12; September 25, 1984, 1, 8; October 10, 1984, 1, 8; November 17, 1984, 9; November 24, 1984, 1, 8; December 7, 1984, 1, 12; February 7, 1985, 1, 8; March 9, 1985, 1, 12; *We Yone*, February 19, 1972, 1; February 26, 1972, 3; March 4, 1972, 1; May 27, 1972, 1, 2, 8; July 12, 1972, 1; July 9, 1972, 1, 7; November 8, 1972, 1, 6; November 15, 1972, 1; November 29, 1972, 1, 4; March 28, 1973, 1, 8; April 11, 1973, 3, 6; October 10, 1973, 1, 6; December 5, 1973, 1; *Sunday We Yone*, February 4, 1973, 8; March 18, 1973, 3, 5; April 8, 1973, 1, 3, 6; May 27, 1973, 4; July 1, 1973, 3; September 30, 1973, 3, 9; December 9, 1973, 1, 4, 8; *We Yone*, January 3, 1974, 2; February 13, 1974, 1, 3, 5, 8; June 19, 1974, 8; June 26, 1974, 3, 8; July 10, 1974, 5; September 11, 1974, 8; September 18, 1974, 2; *Sunday We Yone*, February 10, 1974, 1, 2, 12; February 17, 1974, 1, 2, 8; March 17, 1974, 1, 2; March 24, 1974, 1, 2; August 24, 1974, 28; *We Yone*, February 5, 1975, 2, 5, 6; February 12, 1975, 2; February 19, 1975, 2; May 21, 1975, 1; August 6, 1975, 2; August 13, 1975, 2; *Sunday We Yone*, February 2, 1975, 1, 12; February 9, 1975, 4, 6, 7, 10; February 16, 1975, 1; July 6, 1975, 1, 7, 8, 9, 13, 16; July 13, 1975, 6, 7, 10; October 26, 1975, 2; *We Yone*, February 11, 1976, 2; March 3, 1976, 6, 7; April 14, 1976, 5; May 12, 1976, 1; May 26, 1976, 3; June 9, 1976, 1, 12; September 1, 1976, 2; October 13, 1976, 2; October 20, 1976, 2; July 13, 1977, 3; July 27, 1977, 4; *Sunday We Yone*, January 30, 1977, 2; July 10, 1977, 1, 2; July 31, 1977, 3, 9; October 30, 1977, 1; *We Yone*, June 21, 1978, 1, 12; July 5, 1978, 2; July 12, 1978, 3, 11; November 8, 1978, 2; *Sunday We Yone*, January 15, 1978, 1; January 29, 1978, 1, 2; *We Yone*, March 7, 1979, 1, 2; May 2, 1979, 1, 3; May 30, 1979, 1; July 11, 1979, 8, 9, 10;

July 18, 1979, 6, 8, 11; July 25, 1979, 2; August 1, 1979, 1, 12; August 8, 1979, 12; August 15, 1979, 1; October 3, 1979, 3; October 10, 1979, 1; *Sunday We Yone,* January 7, 1979, 1, 2; January 28, 1979, 3, 15, 16; February 4, 1979, 1, 16; May 6, 1979, 3, 10; June 3, 1979, 1, 16; June 10, 1979, 1, 16; July 28, 1979, 1; August 12, 1979, 16; September 9, 1979, 1, 2; September 16, 1979, 1, 16; September 30, 1979, 3; *We Yone,* February 27, 1980, 16; March 5, 1980, 11, 13; March 12, 1980, 1, 2; March 19, 1980, 1, 3; April 16, 1980, 12; May 14, 1980, 16; May 28, 1980, 3, 11, 12; June 25, 1980, 1, 2, 12; July 16, 1980, 1, 3, 12; October 8, 1980, 3; December 10, 1980, 3; *Sunday We Yone,* January 6, 1980, 1, 2; April 13, 1980, 1; April 27, 1980, 5; May 11, 1980, 1; June 1, 1980, 1, 16; May 18, 1980, 16; May 25, 1980, 2, 3, 4; May 25, 1980, 16; June 8, 1980, 1, 2, 3, 7, 8, 9, 10; November 30, 1980, 1, 2: November 30, 1980, 12; February 8, 1981, 1, 11; April 5, 1981, 16; July 5, 1981, 1, 2; July 12, 1981, 16; July 12, 1981, 16; August 2, 1981, 16; September 20, 1981, 12; *We Yone,* September 2, 1981, 1; September 23, 1981, 1, 2; October 28, 1981, 6, 7, 8; June 2, 1982, 3, 4; July 7, 1982, 8; January 17, 1982, 12; *The Tablet,* January 12, 1979, 6; January 25, 1979, 2, 3; February 21, 1979, 2, 8; March 23, 1979, 5; July 11, 1979, 3; May 21, 1980, 3, 4; November 12, 1980, 2, 5; November 15, 1980, 4; January 31, 1981, 3, 5, 6; April 29, 1981, 1, 6; June 24, 1981, 3, 6; July 1, 1981, 1, 6; July 4, 1981, 3, 6; July 11, 1981, 2, 4, 5.

181. *We Yone,* February 4, 1976, 3, 11; February 18, 1976, 4, 5, 6; *Sunday We Yone,* January 30, 1977, 7, 15; February 6, 1977, 6, 7, 8, 10; *We Yone,* January 31, 1979, 5, 6, 7, 8, 9; *Sunday We Yone,* February 4, 1979, 8, 9, 10, 13; July 1, 1979, 1, 2, 3, 8, 9, 10, 12; July 8, 1979, 7, 8, 9, 10; July 15, 1979, 7, 8, 9; *We Yone,* March 26, 1980, 5; *Sunday We Yone,* March 2, 1980, 7, 10; March 9, 1980, 4, 6; March 23, 1980, 5, 6; June 15, 1980, 1, 2, 3, 7, 8, 9, 10, 13, 15; July 6, 1980, 13, 14, 16; February 1, 1981, 5, 6, 7, 10; June 28, 1981, 1, 3, 4, 7, 8, 9, 16; July 5, 1981, 8, 9, 14; *We Yone,* February 4, 1981, 3, 8, 9, 10, 13; July 1, 1981, 6, 7, 8; July 8, 1981, 8, 10; July 29, 1981, 2; June 30, 1982, 1, 2; July 7, 1982, 3, 4; July 16, 1982, 5, 8; November 3, 1982, 3, 5, 6; November 11, 1982, 3, 4, 5, 6; November 25, 1982, 12; *Sunday We Yone,* January 31, 1982, 1, 2, 3; May 30, 1982, 3, 7; July 4, 1982, 2, 3, 4, 5; July 11, 1982, 2, 5, 6, 7, 8; October 31, 1982, 1, 2, 3, 5; November 7, 1982, 1, 2, 3, 4, 5; November 14, 1982, 5, 6, 7, 8, 10; *We Yone,* June 20, 1983, 1, 8; July 6, 1983, 3, 6; July 13, 1983, 3, 6, 7; *Sunday We Yone,* June 19, 1983, 2, 7; July 3, 1983, 1, 2, 3, 4, 7; July 10, 1983, 3, 4, 5, 6, 7; July 17, 1983, 3, 7; *We Yone,* July 18, 1984, 3, 4, 5, 7; August 1, 1984, 4, 6; August 22, 1984, 2; August 29, 1984, 3, 4; September 5, 1984, 3; July 15, 1984, 1, 2; *Sunday We Yone,* August 5, 1984, 4, 6; September 23, 1984, 3, 4; *Sunday We Yone,* January 27, 1985, 1, 3, 6; February 3, 1985, 3, 4; *The Tablet,* June 24, 1978, 2, 3; July 5, 1978, 2, 3; July 8, 1978, 2, 3, 4, 8; July 12, 1978, 3; July 15, 1978, 2, 3; *Daily Mail,* January 30, 1984, 1, 4, 6, 7, 8, 12; February 3, 1984, 6, 7; October 20, 1984, 1; November 22, 1984, 1, 12; January 30, 1985, 1, 2, 8; May 4, 1979, 1, 3, 7; May 11, 1979, 5; May 15, 1979, 3, 5, 6; June 30, 1979, 1, 8; May 19, 1979, 1, 8; *The Tablet,* May 19, 1979, 5, 6; June 26, 1979, 5; July 4, 1979, 3; July 11, 1979, 2; August 1, 1979, 2, 3; December 5, 1979, 3; March 12, 1980, 4, 5; March 19, 1980, 3; June 18, 1980, 1; June 21, 1980, 7; July 9, 1980, 3, 6; July 12, 1980, 1, 6, 8; August 23, 1980, 3; *We Yone,*

264 *Notes to p. 138*

August 14, 1985, 3, 4; August 18, 1985, 3, 4; *Sunday We Yone,* September 1, 1985, 5. See also Sama Banya (former APC minister of finance in the Stevens government), *Looking Back: My Life and Times* (Freetown: Sierra Leone Writers Series, 2015), 415–30; Collier, *Sierra Leone,* 46, 68, 104–11, 145–53, 200–210, 244–55, 257, 258–60, 289–300, 345–49, 397–401, 445–52, 509–18, 549–50; *The Rising Sun,* 127, 181–83, 211, 213, 219, 222, 225, 249–50, 466–67; Stevens, *What Life Has Taught Me,* 7; Allen, "Sierra Leone"; Dumbuya, *Reinventing the Colonial State.*

182. *We Yone,* September 6, 1972, 5; September 20, 1972, 1; October 18, 1972, 3; *Sunday We Yone,* May 5, 1974, 12; June 16, 1974, 3, 9; June 23, 1974, 1, 3, 6, 7, 8; June 30, 1974, 1, 2, 3, 11; July 7, 1974, 3, 11; July 14, 1974, 12; July 28, 1974, 1, 4; July 28, 1974, 1, 4; August 18, 1974, 1, 2, 5; December 15, 1974, 1, 12; *We Yone,* July 2, 1975, 3, 4, 5, 6, 7; July 9, 1975, 4, 5, 6, 8; July 16, 1975, 4, 5, 6; September 3, 1975, 2; May 26, 1976, 1; *Sunday We Yone,* February 20, 1977, 2.

183. *We Yone,* March 6, 1975, 1, 3, 4; October 22, 1980, 1, 2, 3; November 26, 1980, 1, 2. See also *We Yone,* March 12, 1975, 2; March 26, 1975, 2, 3, 7; April 2, 1975, 7; May 7, 1975, 2; *Sunday We Yone,* March 9, 1975, 2, 8; March 23, 1975, 2, 9; March 30, 1975, 3, 7; April 20, 1975, 2 June 29, 1975, 1, 2, 7, 8, 9, 10; July 6, 1975, 3, 6; August 17, 1975, 1; *We Yone,* June 16, 1976, 6, 7, 8; June 30, 1976, 1, 2, 7, 8, 9, 10, 16; July 7, 1976, 3, 5, 6, 7; *We Yone,* July 14, 1976, 3; November 3, 1976, 9, 10; *Sunday We Yone,* September 5, 1976, 3; September 12, 1976, 2, 8; October 3, 1976, 1; October 17, 1976, 8; November 7, 1976, 5; *We Yone,* January 5, 1977, 1; April 20, 1977, 3; June 15, 1977, 7, 10; June 29, 1977, 1, 2, 6, 7, 10; July 6, 1977, 6, 7, 8, 9, 12; *Sunday We Yone,* January 30, 1977, 3, 4, 8, 9; July 3, 1977, 1, 5, 11, 16; October 6, 1977, 1, 2; *We Yone,* February 8, 1978, 3; July 5, 1978, 2, 8, 9, 10, 12; October 11, 1978, 2; November 8, 1978, 1, 12; November 22, 1978, 1, 2; June 29, 1983, 3; *Sunday We Yone,* June 26, 1983, 3, 7; July 10, 1983, 1, 2; July 31, 1983, 1, 8; *We Yone,* August 22, 1984, 1, 3, 4, 8; *Sunday We Yone,* August 12, 1984, 3, 6; *We Yone,* January 16, 1985, 1; February 15, 1985, 3, 4; March 28, 1985, 7, 8; *Sunday We Yone,* February 3, 1985, 1, 2; March 31, 1985, 2; *The Tablet,* November 25, 1978, 2, 3; February 24, 1979, 6; March 28, 1979, 3; May 19, 1979, 4; August 6, 1980, 1, 3; November 1, 1980, 5; November 5, 1980, 3, 6; November 19, 1980, 4; November 26, 1980, 5; *Sunday We Yone,* September 8, 1985, 1, 9; *Daily Mail,* September 18, 1985, 3; October 30, 1985, 2; *The Tablet,* May 13, 1981, 5; May 16, 1981, 5.

184. *We Yone,* March 14, 1979, 1. For the APC government's tough stance on profiteering, see September 19, 1979, 1, 2.

185. *Sunday We Yone,* February 5, 1978, 12. See also July 2, 1978, 1, 2, 8, 9, 12, 13; July 9, 1978, 3, 8, 9, 10, 14; July 16, 1978, 5, 6; October 8, 1978, 20; November 5, 1978, 1, 2; November 12, 1978, 1, 2; November 26, 1978, 5; December 31, 1978, 1; *We Yone,* January 10, 1979, 1, 2; April 25, 1979, 12; May 2, 1979, 1, 2, 3, 12; June 13, 1979, 16; July 11, 1979, 16; *Sunday We Yone,* April 15, 1979, 2; *We Yone,* March 5, 1980, 1, 3, 16; July 30, 1980, 3; December 10, 1980, 7, 11; December 17, 1980, 7; *Sunday We Yone,* March 2, 1980, 1, 2; March 9, 1980, 1, 2, 7; June 15, 1980, 1, 2, 3, 7, 8, 9, 10, 13, 15; July 6, 1980, 13, 14, 16; August 24, 1980, 36; September 14, 1980, 3; October 26, 1980, 3, 4; November 2, 1980, 1,

12; November 30, 1980, 3; December 7, 1980, 3, 15, 16; December 21, 1980, 2; February 1, 1981, 1, 2, 3; June 7, 1981, 1, 3, 45, 6; June 28, 1981, 1, 3, 4, 7, 8, 9, 16; September 20, 1981, 1; October 4, 1981, 3, 4; November 29, 1981, 3, 4; *We Yone,* January 28, 1981, 1; February 4, 1981, 1, 2; June 24, 1981, 1, 2; September 23, 1981, 1, 2, 3, 4; September 30, 1981, 1.

186. *Daily Mail,* December 9, 1968, 1, 2.

187. *Daily Mail,* April 27, 1970, 32.

188. *Daily Mail,* December 30, 1968, 1.

189. *Daily Mail,* September 6, 1969, 3; *Sunday We Yone,* April 14, 1974, 6; May 4, 1980, 3.

190. *Daily Mail,* December 15, 1969, 4, 5.

191. *Daily Mail,* December 13, 1975, 1, 6.

192. *Daily Mail,* February 9, 1983, 3; *Sunday We Yone,* September 28, 1980, 3, 4; *The Tablet,* March 22, 1980, 2, 6.

193. *Daily Mail,* June 24, 1983, 3; October 17, 1983, 12; June 9, 1984, 3; June 12, 1984, 3; *Daily Mail,* June 15, 1984, 1, 12; April 25, 1985, 2; *Sunday We Yone,* April 14, 1974, 2; *We Yone,* July 21, 1976, 2; *Sunday We Yone,* October 17, 1976, 2; *We Yone,* January 18, 1978, 6, 7; *Sunday We Yone,* September 16, 1979, 16; June 14, 1981, 2; *We Yone,* May 13, 1981, 6, 7; June 10, 1981, 9; October 28, 1981, 12; January 27, 1982, 12; *The Tablet,* November 5, 1980, 3, 6.

194. *Daily Mail,* February 15, 1971, 8; December 17, 1969, 8. For more information on Fula traders, see *Daily Mail,* August 6, 1968, 8; September 9, 1968, 8; and October 3, 1968, 12.

195. *Sunday We Yone,* June 3, 1973, 8.

196. *We Yone,* April 10, 1974, 1, 2; *Sunday We Yone,* June 23, 1974, 5, 8; June 30, 1974, 6; *We Yone,* September 19, 1979, 3.

197. *Daily Mail,* November 24, 1969, 8; *Sunday We Yone,* November 2, 1975, 1, 12.

198. *Daily Mail,* October 27, 1969, 12.

199. *Daily Mail,* November 7, 1969, 1, 12.

200. Ibid.

201. *Daily Mail,* November 11, 1969, 1, 8. See also *Sunday We Yone,* January 7, 1979, 3.

202. *Daily Mail,* November 11, 1969, 2.

203. *Daily Mail,* January 12, 1970, 3.

204. *Daily Mail,* March 14, 1970, 8; March 16, 1970, 1.

205. *Daily Mail,* February 18, 1970, 3.

206. *Daily Mail,* March 13, 1970, 1.

207. *Daily Mail,* April 7, 1970, 1.

208. *Daily Mail,* April 11, 1970, 8.

209. *Daily Mail,* April 21, 1970, 1.

210. *Daily Mail,* April 24, 1970, 8.

211. *Daily Mail,* May 22, 1970, 8.

212. *Daily Mail,* June 1, 1970, 1, 8.

213. *Daily Mail,* August 15, 1970, 2.

214. *Daily Mail,* April 9, 1975, 3; October 21, 1975, 3; *We Yone,* April 9, 1975, 2.

215. *Daily Mail,* February 9, 1978, 8.

216. *Daily Mail,* December 11, 1978, 2; *The Tablet,* February 20, 1980, 6; February 9, 1980, 3; August 30, 1980, 8; February 18, 1981, 3.

217. *Daily Mail,* October 9, 1979, 1, 2.

218. *We Yone,* September 25, 1971, 3, 7; *Daily Mail,* July 5, 1978, 1; July 6, 1978, 1; July 8, 1978, 1, 8; September 23, 1978, 1, 8; September 27, 1978, 1; September 28, 1978, 2; October 6, 1978, 1, 8; October 7, 1978, 1, 8; October 18, 1978, 8; October 24, 1978, 2: February 14, 1979, 1, 8; December 19, 1980, 1, 8; May 11, 1983, 5; June 24, 1983, 1, 8; June 18, 1984, 3, 12; June 25, 1984, 2; February 2, 1985, 1, 8; February 7, 1985, 2; *Sunday We Yone,* February 11, 1973, 1, 8; June 3, 1973, 1; December 30, 1973, 2; *We Yone,* November 27, 3; *Sunday We Yone,* March 3, 1974, 5; March 31, 1974, 12; April 7, 1974, 1; *Sunday We Yone,* December 1, 1974, 3, 6, 7, 10; *We Yone,* September 22, 1976, 1, 12; September 28, 1977, 1, 2, 12; September 4, 1977, 9; *We Yone,* June 28, 1978, 3; July 5, 1978, 3, 4; September 20, 1978, 2; September 27, 1978, 1, 2; *Sunday We Yone,* August 13, 1978, 7, 10; *We Yone,* February 14, 1979, 1; February 21, 1979, 6, 7, 8, 9; September 19, 1979, 1; *Sunday We Yone,* February 11, 1979, 7, 10; May 20, 1979, 12; *We Yone,* May 14, 1980, 3, 13; *Sunday We Yone,* February 24, 1980, 7; May 31, 1980, 5, 6; December 7, 1980, 3; October 4, 1981, 3, 4; *We Yone,* June 10, 1981, 6, 7, 10; July 13, 1983, 1, 8; July 20, 1983, 2; August 8, 1984, 4; September 5, 1984, 4.

219. *Daily Mail,* January 30, 1985, 1; *Sunday We Yone,* February 3, 1985, 2; *The New Citizen,* January 26, 1991, 7, 9.

220. *Daily Mail,* March 13, 1986, 3.

221. *Daily Mail,* September 8, 1984, 5; *Sunday We Yone,* May 10, 1981, 1, 16.

222. Alhaji Kuda Mansaray died at age seventy in July 1977. See *Daily Mail,* July 24, 1984, 9; *We Yone,* September 10, 1975, 1, 8; *Sunday We Yone,* August 31, 1975, 1, 12; July 24, 1977, 12.

223. Author's interview with Alhaji Tejan-Jalloh, Freetown, Sierra Leone, June 21, 1990; and author's interview with Dr. Bah, Washington, DC, March 9, 1991. See also Jalloh, "Alhaji Momodu Allie"; *Daily Mail,* August 5, 1968, 8; September 20, 1976, 1; October 18, 1976, 1; Bah, *Fulbe Presence in Sierra Leone.*

224. Author's interview with Dr. Sarif Easmon, Freetown, Sierra Leone, August 3, 1992.

225. Author's interview with Alhaji Baba Allie, Freetown, Sierra Leone, June 20, 1990. See also *Daily Mail,* February 23, 1970, 4.

226. Author's interview with Mohamed Cham, Freetown, Sierra Leone, June 10, 1990. See also *Unity,* August 13, 1966, 3.

227. Author's interview with Almamy Agibu Jalloh, Freetown, Sierra Leone, June 29, 1990. See also *Daily Mail,* September 29, 1977, 5.

228. Author's interview with Alhaji Mohamed Malal Jalloh (author's father), Freetown, Sierra Leone, June 3, 1990. See also *Daily Mail,* November 15, 1968, 2; We Yone, October 1971, 16, 23.

229. Author's interview with Alhaji Sanu Barrie, Freetown, Sierra Leone, August 4, 1990. See also *Sunday We Yone,* September 12, 1976, 2; Allen, "Sierra Leone."

230. *We Yone,* June 30, 1976, 15; *Sunday We Yone,* November 15, 1981, 1, 15.

231. Author's interview with Amadu Barrie (son of Alhaji Bailor Barrie), Silver Spring, Maryland, December 30, 1991. See also *Sunday We Yone,* May 3, 1981, 8, 9, 10.

232. *Daily Mail,* December 8, 1979, 3; December 21, 1981, 2; March 17, 1984, 7; *We Yone,* June 2, 1976, 12; June 1, 1977, 4; *The Tablet,* May 7, 1980, 4.

233. For more information on Jamil, see "Business Profile: Jamil Said Mohammed," *South: The Third World Magazine,* December 1982, 64; "The Jamil Factor," *West Africa,* March 11, 1985, 452; Reno, *Corruption and State Politics in Sierra Leone,* David Fasholé Luke, "Continuity in Sierra Leone: from Stevens to Momoh," *Third World Quarterly* 10 (1988): 67–78; David Fasholé Luke and Stephen P. Riley, "The Politics of Economic Decline in Sierra Leone," *Journal of Modern African Studies* 27 (1989): 133–41; Harris, *Sierra Leone: A Political History.*

234. Author's interview with Alhaji Seray-Wurie (former accountant of Alhaji Bailor Barrie), Freetown, Sierra Leone, June 17, 1990; and author's interview with Alhaji Sanu Barrie, Freetown, Sierra Leone, August 4, 1990. See also Jalloh, *African Entrepreneurship,* Reno, *Corruption and State Politics in Sierra Leone,* Luke, "Continuity in Sierra Leone"; Luke and Riley, "The Politics of Economic Decline in Sierra Leone."

235. *Daily Mail,* July 14, 1967, 8; November 11, 1983, 6.

236. *We Yone,* August 24, 1983, 1, 2; September 5, 1984, 1, 2; *Sunday We Yone,* September 9, 1984, 2; February 17, 1985, 2; *The Tablet,* May 27, 1978, 1, 6, 7; June 3, 1978, 8; August 11, 1979, 4, 5, 7; September 20, 1980, 1, 6; September 27, 1980, 5, 6; October 8, 1980, 1, 6; June 10, 1981, 1.

237. *West Africa,* "Sierra Leone–Guinea: Friction over Foulahs [Fula]," December 20, 1982, 3259, 3261.

238. Ibid.

239. *Daily Mail,* December 15, 1982, 1, 2, 7.

240. *Daily Mail,* January 25, 1982, 1, 7; January 30, 1982, 1, 11.

241. Almamy Agibu Jalloh died in 1995 and was buried at Kissy Road Cemetery in Freetown.

242. *We Yone,* May 14, 1980, 3, 13; *Sunday We Yone,* May 11, 1980, 16.

243. *Sunday We Yone,* January 31, 1982, 1, 12.

244. Author's interview with Almamy Agibu Jalloh, Freetown, Sierra Leone, June 29, 1990. See also *Daily Mail,* November 28, 1983, 2; December 2, 1983, 7; May 19, 1984, 2; May 23, 1984, 2; November 22, 1984, 2; *The Tablet,* June 10, 1978, 7; August 30, 1978, 2, 3; January 25, 1979, 6; February 14, 1979, 3, 7; February 21, 1979, 4, 7; February 28, 1979, 3.

245. *Daily Mail,* July 17, 1980, 2; *We Yone,* September 3, 1980, 4; *Sunday We Yone,* January 13, 1980, 16; October 11, 1981, 5, 10; January 27, 1985, 4. See also Dumbuya, *Reinventing the Colonial State.*

246. *The Tablet,* October 18, 1980, 1, 3.

247. *Daily Mail,* January 25, 1969, 1; January 29, 1969, 1, 6.

248. *Daily Mail,* January 9, 1969, 4; January 29, 1969, 1, 2; September 15, 1969, 8.

249. M. A. Jalloh, "Devaluation: A Rich Man's Cure," *We Yone,* April 11, 1979, 5, 8; See also *We Yone,* January 24, 1979, 3, 11; *Sunday We Yone,* February 4, 1979, 1, 2; February 11, 1979, 1, 3; November 29, 1978, 5, 8; December 3, 1978, 5, 12; December 10, 1978, 5, 6; *We Yone,* October 6, 1982, 3, 4; November 22, 1984, 1; February 22, 1985, 1, 8; February 27, 1985, 3, 6, 7; March 6, 1985, 1, 2; *The Tablet,* December 13, 1978, 6, 7; February 4, 1979, 1, 2, 8; September 27, 1980, 1, 3; May 2, 1981, 3; June 13, 1981, 1; July 11, 1981, 1, 6; August 5, 1981, 2, 4; Collier, *Sierra Leone,* 463; Stevens, *What Life Has Taught Me,* 68; Abdul K. Koroma, *Sierra Leone: The Agony of a Nation* (Freetown, Sierra Leone: Andromeda, 1996), 27–31; Luke, "Continuity in Sierra Leone"; Deveneaux, *Power Politics in Sierra Leone;* Luke and Riley, "Politics of Economic Decline in Sierra Leone"; A Zack-Williams and Stephen Riley, "Sierra Leone: The Coup and Its Consequences," *Review of African Political Economy* 56 (1993): 91–98; Alfred B. Zack-Williams, "Sierra Leone: The Political Economy of Civil War, 1991–98," *Third World Quarterly* 20 (1999); 143–62; Reno, *Corruption and State Politics in Sierra Leone;* Zack-Williams, "Sierra Leone: Crisis and Despair"; Allen, "Sierra Leone"; Harris, *Sierra Leone: A Political History;* Dumbuya, *Reinventing the Colonial State.*

250. *We Yone,* November 30, 1977, 1, 2; October 11, 1978, 1; *Sunday We Yone,* October 8, 1978, 2; *We Yone,* January 10, 1979, 1, 12; *West Africa,* February 12, 1979, 243; *We Yone,* June 27, 1979, 1, 12; July 4, 1979, 1, 2; *Sunday We Yone,* September 2, 1979, 1, 2; December 23, 1979, 1, 2; *We Yone,* January 30, 1980, 1, 2: February 13, 1980, 1, 2, 3; February 27, 1980, 1, 16; March 5, 1980, 1; March 12, 1980, 2, 3, 11; March 26, 1980, 2; April 2, 1980, 1; April 9, 1980, 1, 3; April 16, 1980, 2; April 23, 1980, 1; May 7, 1980, 1; May 14, 1980, 1; May 21, 1980, 1, 12; May 28, 1980, 1, 2; June 4, 1980, 1, 3, 4; June 11, 1980, 1, 2, 7, 8, 9, 10; June 25, 1980, 1, 2, 3, 4, 5, 6, 7; July 2, 1980, 1, 2, 3, 5, 6, 7, 8, 9, 10, 11, 12, 13, 14, 15, 16; July 9, 1980, 1, 2, 3, 5, 8, 10, 12; July 16, 1980, 1, 2; July 30, 1980, 5, 8; August 13, 1980, 1; September 3, 1980, 3, 8; October 1, 1980, 3, 4; October 8, 1980, 2, 6, 7, 8; October 29, 1980,, 1; December 10, 1980, 1, 2; December 25, 1980, 1, 2; *Sunday We Yone,* January 6, 1980, 1, 12; January 20, 1980, 1, 2; January 20, 1980, 3, 4; January 27, 1980, 1, 2, 3; February 10, 1980, 1; February 10, 1980, 7; February 17, 1980, 1, 2; February 24, 1980, 1, 16; March 2, 1980, 1, 2; March 9, 1980, 1, 2, 16; March 23, 1980, 1, 2, 3; March 30, 1980, 3, 5, 6; April 6, 1980, 1, 2, 3; April 13, 1980, 1, 2; April 20, 1980, 1, 2, 3, 4, 8; April 27, 1980, 1; May 4, 1980, 1, 7, 16; May 4, 1980, 7; May 11, 1980, 1, 2; June 1, 1980, 1, 7, 10; May 18, 1980, 1, 2; June 8, 1980, 1, 2, 7, 8, 9, 10, 16; June 15, 1980, 1; July 6, 1980, 1, 2, 3 7, 8, 9, 10, 11, 12, 20; July 13, 1980, 2, 3, 4, 5, 12; July 20, 1980, 1, 3, 4, 9, 12; July 27, 1980, 3, 17; August 3, 1980, 2, 3, 5, 6; August 10, 1980, 1; August 17, 1980, 1; September 7, 1980, 1, 3; September 14, 1980, 1, 12; September 21, 1980, 1; September 28, 1980, 1, 2, 4; October 5, 1980, 5, 6, 7, 8; October 19, 1980, 1, 3, 16; November 16, 1980, 1; November 23, 1980, 1; November 30, 1980, 1, 2; November 30, 1980, 1, 2; January 11, 1981, 1, 2; January 18, 1981, 1, 2; March

8, 1981, 1, 2; March 22, 1981, 1, 2; April 5, 1981, 1, 2; April 12, 1981, 1, 3, 10; May 24, 1981, 1; May 31, 1981, 1, 3, 4; June 7, 1981, 1, 2, 5, 6; June 14, 1981, 1, 3, 4, 5, 6, 11, 16; June 28, 1981, 1, 2; July 12, 1981, 5, 6, 12; July 26, 1981, 7, 8; *We Yone*, March 11, 1981, 1, 2; March 18, 1981, 1; March 25, 1981, 1, 2; April 1, 1981, 1; April 8, 1981, 1, 12; April 23, 1981, 1, 16; April 29, 1981, 1, 12; May 6, 1981, 1, 12; May 20, 1981, 1, 2, 3; June 3, 1981, 1; June 17, 1981, 3, 4; June 24, 1981, 1, 2; July 1, 1981, 1, 2; July 15, 1981, 5, 6; July 29, 1981, 5, 9; *The Tablet*, February 4, 1979, 1, 2; January 12, 1979, 4, 6; March 28, 1979, 3; December 21, 1979, 5; January 16, 1980, 2; January 16, 1980, 5; January 19, 1980, 3, 4; January 30, 1980, 1, 6, 8; January 9, 1980, 3, 6; March 8, 1980, 5; March 22, 1980, 2, 3, 6; March 29, 1980, 4; April 2, 1980, 5; April 5, 1980, 5; April 9, 1980, 2, 4; April 30, 1980, 8; May 10, 1980, 3, 4, 6, 7; May 21, 1980, 1, 7; May 21, 1980, 5, 6, 7; May 24, 1980, 5; June 4, 1980, 14, 8; June 18, 1980, 1, 3, 4, 7, 8; June 21, 1980, 1, 3, 6, 8; June 28, 1980, 1, 8; July 2, 1980, 1, 3, 5, 6, 7, 8; July 5, 1980, 1, 3, 6, 8; July 9, 1980, 1, 3, 7; July 30, 1980, 3; August 6, 1980, 1, 8; August 9, 1980, 1, 3; September 27, 1980, 1, 6; December 10, 1980, 1, 6; March 25, 1981, 1; April 15, 1981, 6; June 3, 1981, 1, 6; June 10, 1981, 3, 6; June 13, 1981, 3. See also Collier, *Sierra Leone*, 542, 550, 552; *Rising Sun*, 210, 230–36, 250–51, 463–64; Stevens, *What Life Has Taught Me*, 379–80, 382; Luke, "Continuity in Sierra Leone"; Bangura, *Sierra Leone and the Legacy of Failed Leaderships*, 53; Luke and Riley, "Politics of Economic Decline in Sierra Leone"; Reno, *Corruption and State Politics in Sierra Leone*; Zack-Williams and Riley, "Sierra Leone"; Zack-Williams, "Sierra Leone: Political Economy of Civil War"; Allen, "Sierra Leone"; Zack-Williams, "Sierra Leone: Crisis and Despair"; Harris, *Sierra Leone: A Political History*; Dumbuya, *Reinventing the Colonial State*.

251. *Sunday We Yone*, November 11, 1979, 1, 2; *The Tablet*, November 19, 1980, 3; November 22, 1980, 3, 6.

252. *Daily Mail*, January 28, 1969, 2, 6; January 17, 1980, 1, 2; March 15, 1980, 1; April 24, 1980, 1, 2; June 30, 1980, 1, 8; July 1, 1980, 1, 28; July 2, 1980, 1, 8; July 3, 1980, 1; July 7, 1980, 1, 2; October 17, 1981, 1, 8; October 25, 1982, 1, 7; February 18, 1983, 1, 11; February 28, 1983, 1; *We Yone*, September 26, 1979, 3, 11; November 21, 1979, 3; *The Tablet*, February 14, 1979, 1, 8; April 9, 1980, 6; June 18, 1980, 6, 8.

253. Author's interview with Alhaji Sanu Barrie, Freetown, Sierra Leone, August 4, 1990. See also *The Tablet*, May 7, 1980, 4; February 18, 1981, 1, 8; Koroma, *Agony of a Nation*, 27–31; Reno, *Corruption and State Politics in Sierra Leone*, 141–42; Allen, "Sierra Leone"; Harris, *Sierra Leone: A Political History*.

254. *Daily Mail*, February 23, 1981, 1, 8; February 25, 1981, 1, 8; March 2, 1981, 1, 8; March 25, 1981, 1, 8; July 6, 1981, 1, 8; July 7, 1981, 1, 8; July 8, 1981, 1, 8; July 9, 1981, 1, 8; July 13, 1981, 1, 8; July 15, 1981, 1, 8; March 30, 1983, 1, 7; May 6, 1983, 1, 8; May 9, 1983, 7; June 17, 1983, 3; October 20, 1984, 1, 16; *Sunday We Yone*, February 8, 1981, 1, 2, 3; February 15, 1981, 1, 3, 4, 10; February 22, 1981, 1, 3; March 1, 1981, 1, 3, 15, 16; March 8, 1981, 3; April 12, 1981, 1; May 17, 1981, 1, 4; August 16, 1981, 1, 2; October 18, 1981, 1, 2; *We Yone*, January 1, 1981, 1, 2; February 11, 1981, 1, 3; February 18, 1981, 1, 3; February

25, 1981, 1, 3, 9; March 11, 1981, 5; March 18, 1981, 1, 3, 4; March 25, 1981, 1, 2; May 13, 1981, 1, 2; May 27, 1981, 1; July 15, 1981, 1; November 18, 1981, 1, 2, 3, 4; November 25, 1981, 1, 12; December 2, 1981, 1, 2; December 23, 1981, 1, 5, 6; June 2, 1982, 1, 2; July 16, 1982, 1, 3, 4, 12; August 11, 1982, 3, 4; *Sunday We Yone*, January 24, 1982, 1; May 30, 1982, 1, 2; June 6, 1982, 1; June 13, 1982, 1, 2, 3, 4; June 20, 1982, 1; July 31, 1983, 1; August 12, 1984, 8; *The Tablet*, February 18, 1981, 1, 6; February 21, 1981, 1, 3, 5, 6; February 25, 1981, 1, 3, 4, 6; May 13, 1981, 1, 3; May 16, 1981, 1, 6; May 20, 1981, 1, 6; June 6, 1981, 3; *The Tablet*, July 1, 1981, 1, 6. See also Kallon, *Political Economy of Corruption in Sierra Leone*; Kpundeh, *Politics and Corruption in Africa*; Gerald H. Smith, "The Dichotomy of Politics and Corruption in a Neopatrimonial State: Evidence from Sierra Leone, 1968–1993," *Issue: A Journal of Opinion* 25 (1997): 58–62; Sahr John Kpundeh, "Limiting Administrative Corruption in Sierra Leone," *Journal of Modern African Studies* 32 (1994): 139–57; Kpundeh, *Politics and Corruption in Africa*; Dumbuya, *Reinventing the Colonial State*.

255. *Sunday We Yone*, October 18, 1981, 1, 2; November 29, 1981, 16; December 13, 1981, 1, 12; *We Yone*, May 27, 1981, 2; June 3, 1981, 2; August 5, 1981, 1; August 19, 1981, 6, 7; December 2, 1981, 1, 2; December 16, 1981, 1, 2; December 23, 1981, 5, 6; January 1, 1982, 16; January 6, 1982, 3, 9; January 13, 1982, 1; January 20, 1982, 8, 9; April 16, 1982, 2, 3, 4; July 14, 1982, 2; August 11, 1982, 1, 2, 3, 4; August 18, 1982, 1, 2; August 24, 1982, 2; September 1, 1982, 1, 2, 8; September 8, 1982, 1, 5, 6, 8; September 15, 1982, 1, 2, 3, 4; September 29, 1982, 1, 2; October 6, 1982, 8; October 13, 1982, 1, 7; October 28, 1982, 8; November 25, 1982, 3, 4, 12; *Sunday We Yone*, July 11, 1982, 1, 12; August 29, 1982, 2; September 5, 1982, 1, 2; September 12, 1982, 1, 2; September 26, 1982, 1, 8; October 3, 1982, 1, 2; October 10, 1982, 1; October 17, 1982, 1, 2, 8; October 24, 1982, 2; November 14, 1982, 2, 8; November 21, 1982, 5, 6; *We Yone*, August 15, 1984, 1, 2; October 24, 1984, 1, 2, 3, 6, 8; *We Yone*, November 22, 1984, 5, 6; December 6, 1984, 1; *Sunday We Yone*, October 28, 1984, 1, 8; November 18, 1984, 5, 6; *We Yone*, March 21, 1985, 3, 6; *Sunday We Yone*, May 26, 1985, 8. See also Kallon, *Political Economy of Corruption in Sierra Leone*; Kpundeh, *Politics and Corruption in Africa*; Smith, "Dichotomy of Politics and Corruption in a Neopatrimonial State"; Kpundeh, "Limiting Administrative Corruption in Sierra Leone"; Dumbuya, *Reinventing the Colonial State*.

256. *Daily Mail*, August 31, 1981, 1, 12; Reuters, New York, August 15, 1981; *Daily Mail*, September 9, 1981, 1, 2; September 10, 1981, 1, 8; September 12, 1981, 1, 8; *Sunday We Yone*, August 16, 1981, 1, 2, 7, 10; August 30, 1981, 1, 2, 3, 4, 15; September 6, 1981, 1, 2, 3, 4, 6, 7, 10; September 13, 1981, 1, 2, 3, 4; *We Yone*, August 19, 1981, 1, 2, 3, 4; *The Tablet*, August 8, 1981, 1, 8; August 29, 1981, 1, 3, 8. See also Bangura, *Sierra Leone and the Legacy of Failed Leaderships*, 57.

257. *Daily Mail*, September 21, 1981, 1, 8; September 26, 1981, 1, 8. See also Reuters, August 19, 1981; *Daily Mail*, October 5, 1981, 1; *Sunday We Yone*, September 20, 1981, 1, 16; September 27, 1981, 1, 2; October 4, 1981, 1, 3, 4; *We Yone*, September 2, 1981, 1, 3, 4, 12; September 9, 1981, 1, 2; September 30, 1981, 3, 4. See also Dumbuya, *Reinventing the Colonial State*.

258. *Sunday We Yone,* October 18, 1981, 16; November 1, 1981, 1; November 8, 1981, 2; November 15, 1981, 1, 2, 11, 12; November 22, 1981, 1, 2; November 22, 1981, 2; November 29, 1981, 7, 10; *We Yone,* November 11, 1981, 6, 7; November 18, 1981, 1, 11, 12; November 25, 1981, 9, 10; January 6, 1982, 3, 9; September 29, 1982, 1; October 20, 1982, 1, 2, 3, 4; *Sunday We Yone,* September 26, 1982, 1, 8; October 3, 1982, 8.

259. *Daily Mail,* October 28, 1983, 1, 16.

260. *Daily Mail,* August 18, 1984, 1, 12.

261. *Daily Mail,* September 22, 1984, 1, 12.

262. *Daily Mail,* June 17, 1985, 1, 2, 24; June 24, 1985, 1, 8; July 6, 1985, 3.

263. See Luke, "Continuity in Sierra Leone"; Koroma, *Agony of a Nation*; Luke and Riley, "Politics of Economic Decline in Sierra Leone"; Zack-Williams and Riley, "Sierra Leone"; Zack-Williams, "Sierra Leone: The Political Economy of Civil War"; Zack-Williams, "Sierra Leone: Crisis and Despair."

264. *We Yone,* May 1, 1971, 9, 10; May 8, 1971, 4; September 11, 1971, 1, 7; September 18, 1971, 8; September 25, 1971, 8. See also Conteh, *Management of Sierra Leone's Electoral Process.*

265. *Daily Mail,* April 24, 1969, 4; *We Yone,* April 15, 1972, 1, 8; June 28, 1972, 8; September 6, 1972, 3; 4; January 31, 1973, 3, 6, 8; *Sunday We Yone,* January 28, 1973, 1, 3, 10; February 25, 1973, 1; April 1, 1973, 1; May 6, 1973, 1, 5. See also Stevens, *What Life Has Taught Me,* 280; Harrell-Bond, Howard, and Skinner, *Community Leadership and the Transformation of Freetown (1801–1976).*

266. *Daily Mail,* March 24, 1970, 1; March 25, 1970, 1, 6. See also Forna, *Devil That Danced on the Water,* 174; Harrell-Bond, Howard, and Skinner, *Community Leadership and the Transformation of Freetown (1801–1976).*

267. *Daily Mail,* September 22, 1970, 1, 8; October 10, 1970, 1; January 26, 1971, 1; *We Yone,* January 23, 1971, 1, 8; May 8, 1971, 8; March 4, 1972, 1, 8; April 8, 1972, 1, 8; May 13, 1972, 2; May 27, 1972, 1; August 2, 1972, 1; January 31, 1973, 8; *Sunday We Yone,* February 18, 1973, 8; December 7, 1980, 20. See also *Rising Sun,* 107, 113, 132, 143, 170–71; Stevens, *What Life Has Taught Me,* 317–18, 322–31, 335–36; Turay and Abraham, *Sierra Leone Army;* Cox, *Civil-Military Relations in Sierra Leone;* Deveneaux, *Power Politics in Sierra Leone;* Forna, *Devil That Danced on the Water,* 187; Bangura, *Sierra Leone and the Legacy of Failed Leaderships,* 50; Harris, *Sierra Leone: A Political History;* Foray, *Road to the One-Party State;* Reno, *Corruption and State Politics in Sierra Leone;* Harell-Bond, Howard, and Skinner, *Community Leadership and the Transformation of Freetown (1801–1976).*

268. See Stevens's speech as president of the new Republic of Sierra Leone at the State Opening of Parliament—*We Yone,* June 19, 1971, 3, 6, 7. See also *Daily Mail,* April 22, 1971, 1, 2; *We Yone,* January 16, 1971, 3, 6, 8; January 23, 1971, 2, 7; 1971, 2, 4; April 3, 1971, 7; *Daily Mail,* April 20, 1971, 1, 8; (afternoon special edition), April 20, 1971, 1, 2, 3, 4; April 22, 1971, 1, 3, 4, 5, 8; April 27, 1971, 1, 8; April 23, 1971, 1, 2; April 26, 1971, 1; *We Yone,* April 10, 1971, 6, 7; April 17, 1971, 1; April 22, 1971, 1, 2, 3, 4; April 24, 1971, 1, 5, 7, 8; May 1, 1971, 4, 5, 9; May 8, 1971, 1, 2, 7, 8; May 15, 1971, 1, 4, 9; May 22, 1971, 3, 6, 8;

June 5, 1971, 1, 2, 4, 6; June 12, 1971, 1, 4, 8; June 26, 1971, 2; July 3, 1971, 10; July 10, 1971, 3; July 17, 1971, 3; July 31, 1971, 3, 10, 11; August 7, 1971, 1, 3, 5; August 21, 1971, 3; February 12, 1972, 5; April 15, 1972, 3; April 22, 1972, 1, 2, 5, 8; July 26, 1972, 3, 6; *Sunday We Yone*, April 22, 1973, 3, 4, 5; August 26, 1973, 3; *We Yone*, April 19, 1974, 1, 2, 3, 5, 9, 10, 15, 16, 23; *Sunday We Yone*, April 14, 1974, 1, 12; April 21, 1974, 2, 3, 7; *We Yone*, August 23, 1975, 2; *Sunday We Yone*, April 13, 1975, 1, 16; April 20, 1975, 1, 3, 4, 5, 6, 7, 12, 13, 24; *We Yone*, April 21, 1976, 2, 12; April 20, 1977, 1, 2, 3, 4, 5, 24; April 19, 1978, 3, 4, 5, 6, 7, 8; April 19, 1979, 1, 3, 4, 5, 6; April 16, 1980, 1; *Sunday We Yone*, April 20, 1980, 1, 2, 3, 4, 5, 6, 7, 8; April 19, 1981, 1, 2, 4, 5, 6, 10, 39; April 12, 1981, 2; *We Yone*, April 23, 1981, 2, 3, 7, 16; April 29, 1981, 3, 4, 8; April 21, 1982, 1, 8; *Sunday We Yone*, April 18, 1982, 1, 2; *We Yone*, April 19, 1985, 1, 3, 12; *The Tablet*, April 23, 1978, 1, 6, 8; April 18, 1981, 1, 8; *Sierra Leone, 1968–1980*, 48, 58, 67, 81–87, 93–103, 178, 230, 277, 325–26, 377, 432, 489–90; Stevens, *What Life Has Taught Me*, 240, 316, 323–24, 336–37, 353–58, 364–82; *Rising Sun*, 106, 118, 132, 367; Thompson, *Constitutional History and Law of Sierra Leone*, 107–44; Dumbuya, *Reinventing the Colonial State*; Harrell-Bond, Howard, and Skinner, *Community Leadership and the Transformation of Freetown (1801–1976)*.

269. Stevens, *What Life Has Taught Me*, 356; Filomina Chioma Steady, *Women and Collective Action in Africa* (New York: Palgrave MacMillan, 2006), 119–28.

270. Stevens, *What Life Has Taught Me*, 238.

271. *Daily Mail*, January 20, 1969, 1. See also Daramy, *Constitutional Developments in the Post-Colonial State of Sierra Leone*; Foray, *Road to the One-Party State*.

272. Author's interview with Alhaji Tejan-Jalloh, Freetown, Sierra Leone, June 21, 1990. See also MI/Q/34, MP 24, 12-11-1969; MI/Q/34, MP, 16; MI/Q/34, MP 17; MI/Q/34, MP 17, 18, 19-11-1969; *Daily Mail*, May 26, 1970, 8.

273. *Daily Mail*, June 2, 1970, 2. See also author's interview with Alhaji Tejan-Jalloh, Freetown, Sierra Leone, June 21, 1990; MI/Q/34, MP 17; Jalloh, *African Entrepreneurship*; Bah, *Fulbe Presence in Sierra Leone*; Harrell-Bond, Howard, and Skinner, *Community Leadership and the Transformation of Freetown (1801–1976)*, 274–78.

274. Author's interview with Alhaji Tejan-Jalloh, Freetown, Sierra Leone, June 21, 1990. See also MI/Q/34, MP 19, 25-11-1969; MI/Q/34, MP, CP (70) 171, 24-3-1970; *Daily Mail*, June 13, 1970, 8. See also Bah, *Fulbe Presence in Sierra Leone*; Jalloh, *African Entrepreneurship*; Harrell-Bond, Howard, and Skinner, *Community Leadership and the Transformation of Freetown (1801–1976)*.

275. Author's interview with Alhaji Tejan-Jalloh, Freetown, Sierra Leone, June 21, 1990. See also MI/Q/34, MP 25, 25-3-1970; MI/Q/34, MP 26, 19-5-1970; MI/Q/34, MP 27, 23-4-1970; MI/Q/34, MP 27, 23-4-1970; *Daily Mail*, June 22, 1970, 8; June 29, 1970, 1. See also Jalloh, *African Entrepreneurship*; Bah, *Fulbe Presence in Sierra Leone*; Harrell-Bond, Howard, and Skinner, *Community Leadership and the Transformation of Freetown (1801–1976)*.

276. Author's interview with Alhaji Tejan-Jalloh, Freetown, Sierra Leone, June 21, 1990. See also MI/Q/34, MP 30, 8-6-1970; MI/Q/34, MP 32,

13-6-1970; T2/5/3, MP 181, 16-10-1970; *Daily Mail,* June 25, 1970, 8. See also Harrell-Bond, Howard, and Skinner, *Community Leadership and the Transformation of Freetown (1801–1976).*

277. *Daily Mail,* September 23, 1970, 8; Harrell-Bond, Howard, and Skinner, *Community Leadership and the Transformation of Freetown (1801–1976).*

278. *Daily Mail,* September 26, 1970, 1; Harrell-Bond, Howard, and Skinner, *Community Leadership and the Transformation of Freetown (1801–1976).*

279. Author's interview with Alhaji Tejan-Jalloh, Freetown, Sierra Leone, June 21, 1990. See also T2/5/3, MP 181, 16-10-1970; MI/Q/34, MP 32, 13-6-1970; *Daily Mail,* October 2, 1970, 8; October 10, 1970, 8. See also Jalloh, *African Entrepreneurship;* Bah, *Fulbe Presence in Sierra Leone;* Harrell-Bond, Howard, and Skinner, *Community Leadership and the Transformation of Freetown (1801–1976).*

280. *We Yone,* January 10, 1973, 1; January 17, 1973, 3; January 31, 1973, 5, 6; February 7, 1973, 5; March 14, 1973, 1; March 21, 1973, 1; April 4, 1973, 1; April 11, 1973, 5; April 25, 1973, 1, 2, 3, 4; May 2, 1973, 1, 3, 5, 8; May 9, 1973, 1, 2, 6, 8; May 17, 1973, 1, 2, 4; May 23, 1973, 1, 8; June 13, 1973, 6; August 8, 1973, 2, 3; *Sunday We Yone,* January 7, 1973, 3; February 4, 1973, 1, 7, 8; *Sunday We Yone,* February 11, 1973, 1, 3, 4, 7, 8; February 18, 1973, 1, 3, 8; February 25, 1973, 1, 4, 5, 6, 8; March 4, 1973, 1, 3, 4, 8; March 11, 1973, 1, 4; March 25, 1973, 1, 4, 8; April 8, 1973, 1, 8; April 15, 1973, 1, 8; April 22, 1973, 1, 3, 4, 8; April 29, 1973, 1, 4, 8; May 6, 1973, 1, 3, 5, 6; May 13, 1973, 1, 8; *We Yone,* April 6, 1977, 2; *The Tablet,* September 17, 1978, 6.

281. *Sunday We Yone,* May 20, 1973, 1, 4, 8; *We Yone,* October 29, 1975, 2; *Sunday We Yone,* September 28, 1975, 2s. See also Conteh, *Management of Sierra Leone's Electoral Process;* Collier, *Sierra Leone,* 179, 180–81, 182–83, 186; *Rising Sun,* 122–28, 144, 152, 368–409; Reno, *Corruption and State Politics in Sierra Leone,* 98–99; Turay and Abraham, *Sierra Leone Army;* Bangura, *Sierra Leone and the Legacy of Failed Leaderships,* 46; Hayward and Kandeh, "Perspectives on Twenty-Five Years of Elections in Sierra Leone"; Harris, *Sierra Leone: A Political History;* Foray, *Road to the One-Party State;* Reno, *Corruption and State Politics in Sierra Leone;* Harrell-Bond, Howard, and Skinner, *Community Leadership and the Transformation of Freetown (1801–1976).*

282. *We Yone,* April 11, 1973, 1; *Sunday We Yone,* January 28, 1973, 5, 6. See also Jalloh, *African Entrepreneurship;* Daramy, *Constitutional Developments in the Post-Colonial State of Sierra Leone;* Harrell-Bond, Howard, and Skinner, *Community Leadership and the Transformation of Freetown (1801–1976).*

283. *We Yone,* February 16, 1977, 1, 12; February 23, 1977, 6, 7; March 12, 1977, 1, 5, 8; April 6, 1977, 1, 2, 5, 10, 12; April 13, 1977, 12; April 20, 1977, 1, 3, 23; April 27, 1977, 1, 3, 5, 8; May 4, 1977, 1, 2, 3, 4, 11, 12; May 11, 1977, 1, 2, 3, 8; May 18, 1977, 1, 2, 3, 5; May 25, 1977, 2; September 14, 1977, 1; September 21, 1977, 1, 2; September 28, 1977, 3; March 13, 1977, 1, 12; April 10, 1977, 1; *Sunday We Yone,* April 17, 1977, 1, 2, 3, 4, 5, 10, 12; April 24, 1977, 1, 2, 12; May 1, 1977, 1, 2; May 8, 1977, 1, 2, 3, 6, 7, 9, 12; May 22, 1977, 1, 5, 8, 11; July 17, 1977, 1, 16; September 11, 1977, 1; September 18, 1977, 1; September 25, 1977, 1, 2; October 2, 1977, 1, 12; May 21, 1978, 1, 2; *The Tablet,* May 26, 1979,

6; June 15, 1979, 6; June 20, 1979, 1, 5, 6; June 2, 1979, 1, 8; June 12, 1979, 1, 6; June 26, 1979, 1, 8; May 28, 1980, 6; June 28, 1980, 3; March 7, 1981, 1, 6; March 25, 1981, 5; April 15, 1981, 2, 3. See also Conteh, *Management of Sierra Leone's Electoral Process*; Collier, *Sierra Leone*, 360, 375–76, 378; *Rising Sun*, 141, 414–30; Bangura, *Sierra Leone and the Legacy of Failed Leaderships*, 54–57, 73, 74; Hayward and Kandeh, "Perspectives on Twenty-Five Years of Elections in Sierra Leone"; Hinton, *University Student Protests and Political Change in Sierra Leone*; Paracka, *Athens of West Africa*; Harris, *Sierra Leone: A Political History*; Dumbuya, *Reinventing the Colonial State*; Foray, *Road to the One-Party State*; Deveneaux, *Power Politics in Sierra Leone*; Reno, *Corruption and State Politics in Sierra Leone*.

284. *The Tablet*, April 25, 1981, 1, 6.

285. *We Yone*, November 15, 1978, 12; *The Tablet*, October 15, 1980, 1, 6; April 18, 1981, 1.

286. Paramount Chief Alhaji Dr. Alimamy Jaia Kaikai died in 1982 at the age of over one hundred years. He was one of the oldest reigning paramount chiefs of Pujehun District and had served in government since independence and acted as vice president on a number of occasions. He was dropped from the cabinet in 1980. See also *We Yone*, May 29, 1971, 3; *Daily Mail*, November 1, 1982, 1, 2; November 5, 1982, 1, 4; *Sunday We Yone*, April 17, 1977, 1, 2, 3, 4, 5, 10; May 8, 1977, 2; May 15, 1977, 1, 2; *We Yone*, February 27, 1980, 1, 16; October 28, 1982, 1; *The Tablet*, October 6, 1978, 1, 8; February 27, 1980, 1, 6; Collier, *Sierra Leone*, 211.

287. *Daily Mail*, September 16, 1978, 1, 8.

288. *Daily Mail*, June 28, 1978, 1, 8; *We Yone*, August 17, 1977, 12; *Sunday We Yone*, May 22, 1977, 1; *We Yone*, August 16, 1978, 2; *The Tablet*, February 14, 1981, 1, 6.

289. *Daily Mail*, May 5, 1977, 2, 5; May 7, 1977, 1, 4; May 9, 1977, 1; May 14, 1977, 1, 3; May 20, 1977, 1; July 19, 1977, 1; September 17, 1977, 1, 8; October 1, 1977, 1, 8; October 19, 1977, 2; *Sunday We Yone*, May 15, 1977, 1, 3, 12; September 18, 1977, 2; *The Tablet*, December 12, 1980, 1.

290. Author's interview with Bai Sheka Wurie, Lungi, Sierra Leone, September 28, 2008; author's interview with Alhaji Tejan-Jalloh, Freetown, Sierra Leone, June 21, 1990; and author's interview with Alhaji Seray-Wurie, Freetown, Sierra Leone, June 17, 1990. See also *The Tablet*, November 8, 1980, 1, 2; Daramy, *Constitutional Developments in the Post-Colonial State of Sierra Leone*.

291. Author's interview with Alhaji Tejan-Jalloh, Freetown, Sierra Leone, June 21, 1990; author's interview with Bai Sheka Wurie, Lungi, Sierra Leone, September 28, 2008; and author's interview with Alhaji Seray-Wurie, Freetown, Sierra Leone, October 27, 2008. See also *We Yone*, January 30, 1971, 2; *Sunday We Yone*, November 2, 1975, 6, 7, 8; June 1, 1975, 8; *We Yone*, July 7, 1976, 1; *Daily Mail*, June 2, 1978, 1, 8; August 8, 1978, 1, 8; January 20, 1979, 1; July 17, 1980, 1, 8; *We Yone*, May 28, 1975, 11; *Sunday We Yone*, May 25, 1975, 11; November 23, 1975, 9; *We Yone*, March 24, 1976, 11; August 9, 1978, 12; November 22, 1978, 1; *Sunday We Yone*, February 5, 1978, 11; February 12, 1978, 13; April 16, 1978, 1; *We Yone*, August 20, 1980, 1, 12; *Sunday We Yone*, August 24, 1980, 36;

November 9, 1980, 1, 2; *The Tablet*, October 8, 1980, 4; November 8, 1980, 1, 2; *Daily Mail*, March 23, 1984, 12; June 12, 1984, 12.

292. *We Yone*, June 1, 1977, 1, 2, 12; June 8, 1977, 1, 12; June 29, 1977, 5, 8; July 13, 1977, 4; July 20, 1977, 3, 9; July 27, 1977, 3, 10; August 3, 1977, 5, 9; October 5, 1977, 5, 8; October 19, 1977, 5, 8; *Sunday We Yone*, May 29, 1977, 1, 2, 12; June 5, 1977, 2; June 19, 1977, 5, 6; July 3, 1977, 7, 10; July 10, 1977, 16; July 13, 1977, 3; July 24, 1977, 3, 10; October 16, 1977, 5, 6; October 23, 1977, 7, 12; November 20, 1977, 2; December 11, 1, 16; *We Yone*, May 17, 1978, 1, 2; May 24, 1978, 1, 2, 3, 10; May 31, 1978, 1, 2, 7, 8, 9, 10, 12; June 7, 1978, 1, 2, 3, 5, 8, 10; *Sunday We Yone*, February 19, 1978, 1; May 21, 1978, 1; May 28, 1978, 1, 2, 7, 8, 9, 10; June 4, 1978, 1, 2, 3; August 5, 1979, 4, 13; August 12, 1979, 4.

293. *Daily Mail*, July 19, 1977, 1, 4.

294. *Daily Mail*, June 12, 1978, 2.

295. *Daily Mail*, May 30, 1977, 1, 4, 5.

296. *We Yone*, June 14, 1978, 1, 2, 3, 6, 7, 8; *Daily Mail*, June 14, 1978, 1; June 15, 1978, 1, 8; June 17, 1978, 1, 3, 4, 8; *We Yone*, June 21, 1978, 1, 2, 3, 6, 7, 8; March 11, 1972, 6; May 13, 1972, 2, 3, 8; April 23, 1975, 2; August 6, 1975, 3; August 20, 1975, 1, 2; September 17, 1975, 1, 8; December 3, 1975, 2; December 10, 1975, 7, 8, 9; *Sunday We Yone*, August 3, 1975, 1, 2, 3, 5, 6, 7, 8, 12; August 10, 1975, 1, 2, 3, 4; September 7, 1975, 8, 12; September 14, 1975, 12; September 21, 1975, 2; September 28, 1975, 1, 12; *We Yone*, June 28, 1978, 1; December 6, 1978, 1, 2, 12; *Sunday We Yone*, 1978, 1, 2, 3, 4, 7; June 18, 1978, 1, 2, 3, 4, 7, 8, 9, 11, 12, 16; June 25, 1978, 5; July 2, 1978, 7, 10; July 16, 1978, 1, 2; *The Tablet*, February 25, 1978, 1, 8; March 11, 1978, 8; May 22, 1978, 2, 3, 8; May 27, 1978, 1, 2, 3, 4; June 3, 1978, 2, 3, 6, 7; June 3, 1978, 2, 3, 6, 7; June 10, 1978, 1, 2, 3, 4; June 18, 1978, 1, 2, 3; June 21, 1978, 1, 3, 6; June 24, 1978, 1, 4; June 28, 1978, 2, 3; July 12, 1978, 2, 5; July 27, 1978, 2, 3; August 5, 1978, 1, 2; August 9, 1978, 1, 3; August 12, 1978, 1, 6; August 19, 1978, 1, 3, 6; August 24, 1978, 2, 3; October 6, 1978, 1; October 11, 1978, 1, 2, 3, 4; October 27, 1978, 2; November 1, 1978, 1, 6; November 25, 1978, 1, 8; April 14, 1979, 2, 3; May 22, 1979, 1; June 15, 1979, 3; June 12, 1979, 1, 3; June 26, 1979, 1, 6; June 30, 1979, 7; September 18, 1979, 1, 3; August 20, 1980, 3; April 29, 1981, 1; May 6, 1981, 1, 6; August 5, 1981, 1. See also Collier, *Sierra Leone*, 278–79, 434; *Rising Sun*, 119, 126, 139, 142–46, 245–67, 465–66; Stevens, *What Life Has Taught Me*, 239, 370, 382, 407; Thompson, *Constitutional History and Law of Sierra Leone*, 145–82; Bangura, *Sierra Leone and the Legacy of Failed Leaderships*, 56; Daramy, *Constitutional Developments in the Post-Colonial State of Sierra Leone*; Deveneaux, *Power Politics in Sierra Leone*; Harris, *Sierra Leone: A Political History*; Dumbuya, *Reinventing the Colonial State*.

297. Stevens, *What Life Has Taught Me*, 239. For Stevens's opposition to the proposed one-party system during the Albert Margai administration, see *Unity*, January 29, 1966, 3; Stevens, *What Life Has Taught Me*, 238–40; Foray, *The Road to the One-Party State*.

298. *Daily Mail*, February 17, 1978, 1, 8; May 17, 1978, 1.

299. *Daily Mail*, May 23, 1978, 1, 8. See also May 25, 1978, 1, 8.

300. *Daily Mail,* May 24, 1978, 1, 8.

301. *Daily Mail,* May 30, 1978, 1.

302. Under the one-party constitution there were two vice presidents: Vice President I and II. The former vice president, S. I. Koroma, was now Vice President I. See *The Tablet,* January 4, 1979, 8.

303. *Daily Mail,* June 23, 1978, 1, 8; *The Tablet,* October 11, 1978, 1, 6; June 30, 1979, 1, 8; March 22, 1980, 1, 6.

304. *Sunday We Yone,* January 20, 1980, 2; *The Tablet,* January 19, 1980, 1; *Sunday We Yone,* February 3, 1980, 16; *The Tablet,* January 23, 1980, 1, 8; January 26, 1980, 8; February 2, 1980, 1, 2.

305. *The Tablet,* February 18, 1981, 1, 4; March 7, 1981, 1, 6; March 25, 1981, 1, 5; January 28, 1981, 3, 6; April 4, 1981, 1, 4; April 11, 1981, 1, 6; April 15, 1981, 2, 3; April 25, 1981, 1, 3, 6; April 29, 1981, 1; April 29, 1981, 1; May 2, 1981, 1; *We Yone,* May 6, 1981, 3, 4; *The Tablet,* May 6, 1981, 1, 6; May 16, 1981, 3, 4, 6; May 20, 1981, 1, 3; May 30, 1981, 7; June 6, 1981, 1, 5; June 6, 1981, 3; July 4, 1981, 1, 6; July 11, 1981, 1, 6; August 5, 1981, 2. See also Conteh, *Management of Sierra Leone's Electoral Process;* Daramy, *Constitutional Developments in the Post-Colonial State of Sierra Leone;* Hayward and Kandeh, "Perspectives on Twenty-Five Years of Elections in Sierra Leone"; Reno, *Corruption and State Politics in Sierra Leone.*

306. Dr. Sama Banya, *Looking Back: My Life and Times* (Freetown: Sierra Leone Writers Series, 2015), 433. See also *We Yone,* April 21, 1982, 1, 8; May 13, 1982, 3, 6; *Sunday We Yone,* April 18, 1982, 1, 2; April 25, 1982, 1, 2; *The Tablet,* July 26, 1980, 1, 8.

307. *We Yone,* October 28, 1981, 4.

308. *Daily Mail,* April 8, 1982, 1; April 19, 1982, 3; April 28, 1982, 1, 3, 4; *Sunday We Yone,* February 22, 1981, 1; April 5, 1981, 2; June 7, 1981, 1, 2; September 27, 1981, 1, 2; October 18, 1981, 1, 2, 3, 4, 7; November 22, 1981, 1, 16; *We Yone,* March 11, 1981, 12; March 18, 1981, 7, 11; March 25, 1981, 5, 8; April 1, 1981, 3; May 6, 1981, 3, 4; December 2, 1981, 12; January 27, 1982, 1, 12; January 20, 1982, 3; January 20, 1982, 10; April 16, 1982, 1, 2, 3; April 21, 1982, 2, 3, 4, 7; April 28, 1982, 1, 2, 3; *We Yone,* June 2, 1982, 1, 2; *Sunday We Yone,* May 2, 1982, 1, 2; May 9, 1982, 1, 2, 3, 10; May 16, 1982, 1, 2, 3, 4, 5, 6, 7; May 30, 1982, 1, 2. See also *Rising Sun,* 212, 213, 218, 476–78; Stevens, *What Life Has Taught Me,* 11.

309. *Daily Mail,* June 9, 1982, 1, 2; June 11, 1982, 1, 7; June 25, 1982, 1, 8; June 28, 1982, 1, 7; *Sunday We Yone,* June 13, 1982, 1, 2; June 27, 1982, 1, 2, 12.

310. *We Yone,* August 22, 1984, 2. See also Eddie M. Turay, *The Prophecies of a Father* (self-pub., AuthorHouse, 2013), 74–75; and Bangura, *Sierra Leone and the Legacy of Failed Leaderships,* 73–74, 77.

311. *Daily Mail,* January 9, 1980, 1, 2; January 14, 1981, 7; *Sunday We Yone,* December 16, 1979, 2, 3, 5, 8; *We Yone,* January 9, 1980, 1, 2; February 27, 1980, 1, 3, 16; August 6, 1980, 1; August 27, 1980, 12; September 3, 1980, 1, 11; October 15, 1980, 11; November 5, 1980, 16; November 12, 1980, 12; November 26, 1980, 11; *Sunday We Yone,* May 11, 1980, 15; May 11, 1980, 16; August 17, 1980,

2; November 9, 1980, 11; January 11, 1981, 1, 11, 12; *We Yone*, May 6, 1981, 11; May 13, 1981, 11; July 8, 1981, 16; July 15, 1981, 15; November 18, 1981, 12; *The Tablet*, March 25, 1978, 8; October 21, 1978, 6; January 6, 1979, 1; June 26, 1979, 1, 6; November 17, 1979, 3; November 28, 1979, 1, 8; December 21, 1979, 3, 4; January 5, 1980, 1; January 9, 1980, 1, 3, 8; January 12, 1980, 3, 4, 7; *The Tablet*, January 16, 1980, 3; January 26, 1980, 6, 8; February 6, 1980, 6; February 20, 1980, 1, 6; August 6, 1980, 4; November 8, 1980, 1, 2; January 24, 1981, 1; March 25, 1981, 3; July 11, 1981, 1, 6. See also Bangura, *Sierra Leone and the Legacy of Failed Leaderships*, 54–57, 73–74.

312. *Daily Mail*, August 14, 1972, 2; August 16, 1977, 1, 8; May 30, 1977, 5; December 29, 1977, 1; May 15, 1979, 8; April 8, 1982, 3; August 31, 1983, 3; *We Yone*, November 26, 1975, 1, 12; *Sunday We Yone*, November 9, 1975, 6; December 7, 1975, 1, 12; December 14, 1975, 1; May 10, 1981, 1, 16.

313. *Daily Mail*, August 31, 1983, 3; September 16, 1983, 5.

314. *Daily Mail*, June 1, 1972, 8.

315. *Daily Mail*, June 28, 1982, 1, 7. Following his electoral defeat in 1982, Alhaji Dr. Abdulai B. Timbo was later appointed chief justice of Sierra Leone and elected as Fula chief or Alimamy for the Western Area. Interview with Alhaji Dr. Timbo, Freetown, Sierra Leone, October 30, 2008. See also *Sierra Express Media*, March 2, 2010, 1–7; *APC Times*, March 3, 2010, 1–2.

316. *Daily Mail*, August 13, 1982, 4, 7; February 10, 1984, 4.

317. *Daily Mail*, November 17, 1984, 3.

318. *Daily Mail*, February 14, 1978, 1, 8.

319. *Daily Mail*, September 3, 1963, 7; Turay, *Prophecies of a Father*, 86–87.

320. *Daily Mail*, December 5, 1972, 1; *The Tablet*, July 15, 1978, 8.

321. Author's interview with Almamy Agibu Jalloh, Freetown, Sierra Leone, June 29, 1990. See also Jalloh, *African Entrepreneurship*; Bah, *Fulbe Presence in Sierra Leone*.

322. *Daily Mail*, June 28, 1982, 1, 7; June 30, 1982, 1, 7; *Sunday We Yone*, June 27, 1982, 1, 2; *We Yone*, January 16, 1985, 1, 2; *Sunday We Yone*, February 3, 1985, 1, 2; *The Tablet*, June 5, 1980, 7.

323. Banya, *Looking Back: My Life and Times*, 430–33.

324. Author's interview with Alhaji Ambassador Amadu M. B. Jalloh, Arlington, Texas, March 1, 2009. See also *The Tablet*, June 2, 1979, 1, 8.

325. Author's interview with Hon. Eng. Alpha B. Barrie, Arlington, Texas, November 7, 2010.

326. Author's interview with Alhaji Sanu Barrie, Freetown, Sierra Leone, August 4, 1990; author's interview with Alhaji Amadu M. B. Jalloh, Arlington, Texas March 1, 2009.

327. *Daily Mail*, September 8, 1982, 1, 2; *We Yone*, May 13, 1982, 1, 2, 3, 8; June 30, 1982, 1, 12.

328. *Sunday We Yone*, June 24, 1979, 9.

329. *Daily Mail*, February 14, 1983, 1, 2. President Stevens relieved Alhaji Chernor Maju of his ministerial duties in August 1984, as reported in the *Daily Mail*, August 18, 1984, 1, 12.

330. *We Yone*, August 29, 1984, 1.

331. *Daily Mail*, May 3, 1982, 1, 3, 4; May 7, 1982, 1, 5; May 7, 1982, 1, 3, 4; May 12, 1982, 1; June 30, 1982, 1, 7; November 19, 1982, 8; June 13, 1983, 1, 8; June 23, 1984, 3; *We Yone*, February 13, 1971, 3; May 26, 1982, 1, 2.

332. *We Yone*, June 26, 1974, 1; May 21, 1975, 1; May 12, 1976, 2; *The Tablet*, December 12, 1979, 1.

333. In 1982 the president of the SLMC was Alhaji M. S. Mustapha, MP for Bo North Constituency. See *Sunday We Yone*, September 26, 1982, 2, 8.

334. *Daily Mail*, May 18, 1979, 2.

335. *We Yone*, January 8, 1972, 1.

336. *Daily Mail*, August 10, 1983, 2; June 30, 1984, 6; *We Yone*, October 16, 1974, 2; *Sunday We Yone*, June 1, 1975, 8.

337. *Daily Mail*, April 26, 1979, 8.

338. *We Yone*, October 11, 1972, 4; *Daily Mail*, July 28, 1976, 1; March 17, 1977, 1; May 20, 1977, 1; November 19, 1981, 2; July 14, 1982, 2; *Sunday We Yone*, October 21, 1973, 8; June 30, 1974, 2; *We Yone*, April 28, 1982, 2. See also Collier, *Sierra Leone*, 32, 53, 54, 76, 89, 112, 118, 155, 170, 186, 217, 358, 376, 406, 416, 472, 479, 522.

339. *We Yone*, May 15, 1971, 3, 9; April 22, 1972, 1; *Daily Mail*, July 27, 1972; *We Yone*, November 8, 1972, 1, 6; April 2, 1975, 6, 7; *Sunday We Yone*, July 26, 1981, 2; August 2, 1981, 1, 3. See also Jalloh and Skinner, *Islam and Trade in Sierra Leone*.

340. *Daily Mail*, May 2, 1972, 1; May 13, 1972, 1, 2; November 27, 1972, 1; August 30, 1976, 1; *Sunday We Yone*, September 23, 1973, 1, 8; *We Yone*, October 3, 1973, 2; February 13, 1974, 2, June 30, 1976, 1; *Sunday We Yone*, August 29, 1976, 1.

341. *Unity*, May 4, 1968, 2.

342. *Daily Mail*, May 21, 1970, 8; *Sunday We Yone*, December 25, 1977, 1, 40; May 24, 1981, 13, 14; *The Tablet*, May 3, 1978, 1; May 10, 1978, 5, 6; May 22, 1978, 5; May 27, 1978, 5; June 3, 1978, 5; August 8, 1979, 1, 6; January 23, 1980, 1, 8; January 26, 1980, 8.

343. *Daily Mail*, December 23, 1968, 1, 4, 8.

344. *Daily Mail*, May 30, 1969, 1, 9.

345. *Sunday We Yone*, December 1, 1974, 1.

346. *Daily Mail*, April 26, 1971, 1; *We Yone*, May 17, 1973, 1, 4; May 23, 1973, 1; August 15, 1973, 1, 2, 6; June 11, 1975, 2; July 9, 1975, 1, 8; July 16, 1975, 2, 3; August 6, 1975, 1; *Sunday We Yone*, July 13, 1975, 1, 12; *The Tablet*, March 25, 1978, 8; January 24, 1981, 3. See also *Sierra Leone, 1968–1980*, 88; *Rising Sun*, 156–57, 163, 167.

347. *Daily Mail*, May 8, 1971, 8.

348. Author's interview with Alhaji Maju, Freetown, Sierra Leone, November 14, 1991. See also *Daily Mail*, April 22, 1971, 2; May 12, 1982, 1, 2.

349. *Daily Mail*, February 22, 1971, 8; January 10, 1972, 1. See also *Sunday We Yone*, May 6, 1979, 6.

350. *Daily Mail*, January 18, 1971, 4.

351. *Daily Mail*, February 8, 1969, 12.

352. *Daily Mail*, February 26, 1970, 6; March 2, 1970, 4.

353. *Daily Mail*, February 12, 1971, 4.

354. *We Yone*, February 12, 1972, 1, 8; February 19, 1972, 2; *Daily Mail*, February 24, 1972, 1, 4; February 11, 1972, 1, 8; *We Yone*, February 26, 1972, 2; September 20, 1972, 3; October 10, 1973, 1.

355. *Daily Mail*, July 18, 1972, 1, 4; *We Yone*, October 17, 1973, 1.

356. *Daily Mail*, October 31, 1972, 1, 4; *We Yone*, August 29, 1973, 1.

357. *Daily Mail*, April 22, 1972, 1, 2, 3.

358. *Daily Mail*, January 27, 1973, 1, 2; *Sunday We Yone*, January 28, 1973, 10.

359. *Sunday We Yone*, January 13, 1974, 1, 2, 9.

360. *Sunday We Yone*, December 1, 1974, 1, 11.

361. *Daily Mail*, September 1, 1970, 2.

362. *Daily Mail*, November 13, 1975, 4.

363. *Sunday We Yone*, December 29, 1974, 8; *Daily Mail*, November 21, 1975, 4; *We Yone*, January 1, 1975, 8; November 19, 1975, 2; *Sunday We Yone*, January 12, 1975, 3; January 19, 1975, 8; November 23, 1975, 12; December 21, 1975, 1.

364. *We Yone*, June 11, 1975, 1; *Sunday We Yone*, October 9, 1977, 1, 2.

365. *Daily Mail*, June 1, 1978, 2.

366. *Daily Mail*, June 5, 1978, 2; June 6, 1978, 4, 5; June 7, 1978, 4, 6.

367. *Daily Mail*, June 7, 1978, 8.

368. *Daily Mail*, June 10, 1978, 1, 8; June 13, 1978, 1.

369. *Daily Mail*, July 5, 1984, 1, 8; August 18, 1984, 5; *Sunday We Yone*, May 11, 1980, 16; September 20, 1981, 2; September 27, 1981, 1, 3, 4; *We Yone*, February 18, 1981, 2; July 22, 1981, 1; November 18, 1981, 12; January 13, 1982, 6; September 8, 1982, 1; *The Tablet*, February 27, 1980, 1, 6; November 26, 1980, 2.

370. *Daily Mail*, July 20, 1985, 1, 16; August 3, 1985, 1, 7; August 24, 1985, 1, 5; November 30, 1985, 1, 9; *We Yone*, January 28, 1976, 1, 3, 4; February 18, 1976, 1, 8; February 25, 1976, 1; March 3, 1976, 1, 8; March 10, 1976, 2; *Sunday We Yone*, September 21, 1980, 6, 7, 8; *We Yone*, March 21, 1985, 1, 8; January 27, 1985, 1, 2, 3, 8; May 19, 1985, 1, 8; *The Tablet*, January 17, 1979, 1; February 2, 1980, 1, 6; August 9, 1980, 1, 3; *Sunday We Yone*, April 28, 1985, 1; September 29, 1985, 1, 8; *Daily Mail*, September 12, 1985, 3, 16; October 30, 1985, 1, 8; November 14, 1985, 1, 2, 12; November 30, 1985, 2; November 30, 1985, 4; *West Africa*, August 12, 1985, 1632; August 19, 1985, 1684, 1722; October 7, 1985, 2071; October 14, 1985, 2177; December 9, 1985, 2612. See also *Rising Sun*, 216, 243–44; Stevens, *What Life Has Taught Me*, 414–15; Luke, "Continuity in Sierra Leone"; Bangura, *Sierra Leone and the Legacy of Failed Leaderships*, 58, 61–68; Luke and Riley, "Politics of Economic Decline"; Harris, *Sierra Leone: A Political History*; Dumbuya, *Reinventing the Colonial State*; Frank J. Coppa, ed., *Encyclopedia of Modern Dictators* (New York: Peter Lang, 2006).

371. Author's interview with Alhaji Tejan-Jalloh, Freetown, Sierra Leone, June 21, 1990. See also *Daily Mail*, March 27, 1984, 1, 8; April 16, 1984, 1, 8; *West Africa*, April 2, 1984; *We Yone*, August 22, 1984, 1; Lewin, *Ahmed Sékou Touré*

(1922–1984); Camara, *Political History of Guinea since World War Two*, 236, 242–43, 261–89; Straussberger, "Storming the Citadel."

372. *Daily Mail*, March 14, 1985, 1, 12; March 16, 1985, 1, 5, 12; *We Yone*, March 14, 1985, 1, 7; *Sunday We Yone*, February 3, 1985, 1, 2.

Chapter Four

1. President Momoh died in August 2003. Author's interview with E. T. Kamara, Dallas, Texas, November 13, 2011; *Sunday We Yone*, March 8, 1981, 3. See also Fyle, *Historical Dictionary of Sierra Leone*.

2. *We Yone*, August 24, 1972, 16; August 24, 1973, 16. See also Stevens, *What Life Has Taught Me*, 337–42, 345, 349, 358–59; *Rising Sun*, 109–12; *Sierra Leone, 1968–1980*, 84; Turay and Abraham, *Sierra Leone Army*; Cox, *Civil-Military Relations in Sierra Leone*.

3. Turay and Abraham, *Sierra Leone Army*, 161.

4. Ibid.

5. Author's interview with E. T. Kamara, Dallas, Texas, November 13, 2011. See also *Sunday We Yone*, March 16, 1975, 8; May 15, 1977, 1; *We Yone*, May 25, 1977, 1, 2; June 21, 1978, 2; July 5, 1978, 2; August 16, 1978, 2; *Sunday We Yone*, September 9, 1979, 1; January 11, 1981, 12; *Sierra Leone, 1968–1980*, 530; *West Africa*, November 21, 1983, 2708; *Daily Mail*, November 30, 1985, 5; January 26, 1987, 6; January 26, 1988, 3, 4, 10; January 26, 1990, 3, 4; Stevens, *What Life Has Taught Me*; Koroma, *Agony of a Nation*, 46–56; Turay and Abraham, *Sierra Leone Army*; Harris, *Sierra Leone: A Political History*; Dumbuya, *Reinventing the Colonial State*.

6. Author's interview with Alhaji Chernor Sie, Freetown, Sierra Leone, October 31, 2010. See also *Sunday We Yone*, August 31, 1975, 5, 8; *We Yone*, June 2, 1976, 10; *Sunday We Yone*, February 5, 1978, 11; *The Tablet*, December 2, 1978, 4; *We Yone*, February 4, 1981, 14; August 3, 1983, 7; August 14, 1985, 6; November 22, 1978, 1; *Sunday We Yone*, February 5, 1978, 11; February 12, 1978, 13; April 16, 1978, 1; *Daily Mail*, December 17, 1969, 7; *Sunday We Yone*, February 1, 1981, 12; *Daily Mail*, November 10, 1969, 2; July 14, 1981, 4; November 9, 1981, 5; *We Yone*, March 24, 1976, 11; October 22, 1980, 11; December 21, 1984, 8; *The Tablet*, June 17, 1981, 2; June 27, 1981, 1, 8; July 4, 1981, 2, 6; *Daily Mail*, September 18, 1989, 5; July 23, 1990, 7; Turay and Abraham, *Sierra Leone Army*.

7. *Daily Mail*, November 14, 1985, 1, 11; November 30, 1985, 1, 9, 10.

8. *We Yone*, August 14, 1985, 1, 2, 6; August 21, 1985, 1, 6; *Sunday We Yone*, August 25, 1985, 1, 2; September 1, 1985, 1, 2, 3, 4; September 8, 1985, 2; September 15, 1985, 1, 2, 5; September 29, 1985, 1, 2, 3, 6, 7; October 6, 1985, 1, 2, 3, 4, 7; *Daily Mail*, September 12, 1985, 1, 2, 17; September 26, 1985, 1, 2, 8; September 18, 1985, 1, 5, 8; October 8, 1985, 1, 3, 5, 7, 12; October 19, 1985, 1; October 30, 1985, 1, 8; November 9, 1985, 1, 2; November 20, 1985, 1, 2, 12; November 30, 1985, 4; *Sunday We Yone*, April 28, 1985, 1.

9. *Sunday We Yone*, September 15, 1985, 2; *Daily Mail*, September 12, 1985, 1, 11.

10. *Address by His Excellency the President Major-General Dr. Joseph Saidu Momoh Delivered on the Occasion of His Inauguration, Freetown, 26 January 1986* (Freetown: Sierra Leone Government, 1986). See also *We Yone*, August 14, 1985, 1, 2, 6; August 21, 1985, 1, 6; *West Africa*, April 19, 1985, 1722; August 12, 1985, 1635; September 9, 1985, 1847; September 23, 1985, 1948; October 7, 1985, 2073–74; October 14, 1985, 2142–43; October 17, 1985, 2071; February 3, 1986, 229; September 15, 1986, 1914; December 1, 1986, 2495, 2497; *New York Times*, November 29, 1985, A5; *We Yone*, January 22, 1986, 1–7; *Daily Mail*, January 27, 1986, 1, 3, 9, 44; January 22, 1986, 1, 8; *We Yone*, January 30, 1986, 1, 3, 4, 6, 7, 8; *Sunday We Yone*, February 2, 1986, 1, 3, 4, 6, 7; *Daily Mail*, February 6, 1986, 2; *We Yone*, February 6, 1986, 3, 4; May 29, 1986, 3; June 5, 1986, 3, 4; June 18, 1986, 2; June 13, 1986, 5, 6; *Daily Mail*, October 17, 1986, 12; November 28, 1986, 1; *Sunday We Yone*, December 7, 1986, 3, 9, 10; *We Yone*, December 12, 1986, 4, 6; May 23, 1987, 3, 4, 7; December 18, 1987, 3, 7; *Daily Mail*, January 8, 1988, 3, 5; January 26, 1988, 1, 20; December 3, 1988, 3, 6, 25, 26; *We Yone*, September 2, 1989, 3; *The National*, July 26–30, 1990, 2; *Daily Mail*, January 26, 1991, 3, 5; *The Vision*, August 20–27, 1992, 1, 2; *Africa Report*, "Momoh's New Order," July–August, 1986; Bangura, *Sierra Leone and the Legacy of Failed Leadership*, 67–68; Banya, *Looking Back: My Life and Times*, 467–68; Koroma, *The Agony of a Nation*, 57–60; Hayward and Kandeh, "Perspectives on Twenty-Five Years of Elections in Sierra Leone"; Luke, "Continuity in Sierra Leone"; Luke and Riley, "Politics of Economic Decline in Sierra Leone"; Alie, *Sierra Leone since Independence*, 114–38; Conteh-Morgan and Dixon-Fyle, *Sierra Leone at the End of the Twentieth Century*, 121–26; Zack-Williams and Riley, "Sierra Leone"; Zack-Williams, "Sierra Leone: The Political Economy of Civil War"; Zack-Williams, "Sierra Leone: Crisis and Despair"; Harris, *Sierra Leone: A Political History*; Dumbuya, *Reinventing the Colonial State*; Reno, *Corruption and State Politics in Sierra Leone*.

11. Author's interview with Alhaji Sanu Barrie, Freetown, Sierra Leone, August 4, 1990. See also *Daily Mail*, September 26, 1985, 2; *New Shaft*, July 2–8, 1990, 1, 5; *The Vision*, September 11–18, 1991, 1, 5; *The New Citizen*, September 16, 1991, 5, 7.

12. *Daily Mail*, December 22, 1987, 1.

13. *West Africa*, September 8, 1986, 1897; *We Yone*, February 14, 1987, 1, 3, 4, 8; October 10, 1987, 5, 6; October 24, 1987, 1, 2; January 18, 1989, 1, 2; March 31, 1989, 1, 2; August 26, 1989, 1; September 16, 1989, 1, 12. See also Reno, *Corruption and State Politics in Sierra Leone*; Dumbuya, *Reinventing the Colonial State*.

14. Author's interview with Alhaji Sanu Barrie, Freetown, Sierra Leone, August 4, 1990. See also *We Yone*, March 6, 1986, 4, 6; November 12, 1986, 3, 4.

15. *We Yone*, May 20, 1989, 1, 7.

16. *We Yone*, January 6, 1990, 1, 8; January 13, 1990, 1, 6.

17. *We Yone*, May 29, 1986, 2.

18. *We Yone*, December 12, 1986, 1.

19. Author's interview with Alhaji Sidique, Freetown, Sierra Leone, October 27, 2008. See also *Daily Mail*, December 24, 1986, 6; October 27, 1988, 2, 3; *Sunday We Yone*, August 9, 1987, 8.

20. *Daily Mail*, March 13, 1986, 3; September 1, 1988, 2.

21. Author's interview with Alhaji Seray-Wurie, Freetown, Sierra Leone, June 17, 1990. See also *We Yone*, March 6, 1986, 2; *Sunday We Yone*, September 14, 1986, 2; Bah, *Fulbe Presence in Sierra Leone*.

22. *We Yone*, January 16, 1987, 8.

23. Author's interview with Alhaji Seray-Wurie, Freetown, Sierra Leone, June 17, 1990. See also *We Yone*, September 14, 1986, 2; January 16, 1987, 8.

24. Author's interview with Ijatu Barrie (daughter of Alhaji Bailor Barrie), Silver Spring, Maryland, December 21, 1991. See also *Daily Mail*, April 15, 1989, 1, 8; *We Yone*, April 19, 1989, 1, 8.

25. *We Yone*, May 2, 1986, 5.

26. Author's interview with Alhaji Sidique, Freetown, Sierra Leone, October 27, 2008. Personal correspondence of Alim Jallo-Jamboria (interim president of the Sierra Leone Fullah Progressive Union) to The Hon. Inspector-General of Police, Sierra Leone Police, December 19, 1989; a copy is with the author. Personal correspondence of Hon. Alhaji M. L. Sidique (minister of labour) to Mr. Alim jallo-Jamboria, January 17, 1990; a copy of the letter is with the author. "The Constitution of the Fullah [Fula] Progressive Union: 'Fottal–Eh-Pottal,'" January 1990; a copy is with the author.

27. Author's interview with Alhaji Sanu Barrie, Freetown, Sierra Leone, August 4, 1990. See also *New Citizen*, January 27, 1990, 8; Bah, *Fulbe Presence in Sierra Leone*.

28. Author's interview with Mrs. Fatmata Binta Stevens (née Jalloh), Freetown, Sierra Leone, February 14, 2009.

29. *We Yone*, June 18, 1986, 1, 5; *Daily Mail*, June 21, 1986, 1, 2; *We Yone*, October 30, 1987, 8.

30. *We Yone*, July 29, 1987, 8.

31. *Daily Mail*, November 28, 1986, 1, 2.

32. *The New Citizen*, August 1, 1987, 8; *We Yone*, November 28, 1987, 8.

33. *We Yone*, October 23, 1986, 2; December 23, 1986, 8; *Daily Mail*, July 14, 1989, 1, 8; *We Yone*, July 15, 1989, 1, 8; *Daily Mail*, July 18, 1989, 1, 8; August 3, 1989, 5; August 3, 1989, 1, 5, 10; *We Yone*, August 19, 1989, 3, 4; *Daily Mail*, October 16, 1989, 3; December 21, 1989, 2; December 21, 1989, 2.

34. *We Yone*, November 27, 1986, 2; *Daily Mail*, March 1, 1990, 1, 10; March 7, 1990, 2. See also Koroma, *Agony of a Nation*, 250.

35. *Daily Mail*, October 16, 1989, 3.

36. Author's interview with Alhaji Sanu Barrie, Freetown, Sierra Leone, August 4, 1990. See also *The New Citizen*, January 26, 1991, 7, 9.

37. Author's interview with Alhaji Sidique, Freetown, Sierra Leone, October 27, 2008. See also *Daily Mail*, January 26, 1990, 2.

38. *Daily Mail,* December 12, 1985, 5; December 16, 1985, 1, 3; December 23, 1985, 1, 24.

39. *Daily Mail,* May 28, 1986, 1.

40. Koroma, *Agony of a Nation,* 74–75.

41. *Daily Mail,* September 23, 1988, 3; April 18, 1990, 2; Bah, *Fulbe Presence in Sierra Leone,* 71–106.

42. Author's interview with Alhaji Sanu Barrie, Freetown, Sierra Leone, August 4, 1990. See also *Daily Mail,* January 15, 1987, 3, 7; *Daily Mail,* January 26, 1987, 5; May 29, 1987, 1, 20; *Sunday We Yone,* June 7, 1987, 3; *Daily Mail,* August 29, 1987, 1, 12; October 1, 1988, 3, 7; October 5, 1988, 5, 7; August 30, 1989, 1, 12; *We Yone,* July 7, 1990, 8, 11; *Daily Mail,* August 27, 1990, 1, 12; January 16, 1991, 1, 12; *We Yone,* February 23, 1991, 2, 8; *Weekend Spark,* July 26, 1991, 2; *We Yone,* April 10, 1992, 8.

43. *We Yone,* February 8, 1992, 1, 3, 6; Eddie M. Turay, *The Prophecies of a Father* (self-pub., AuthorHouse, 2013).

44. *Sunday We Yone,* July 12, 1987, 1, 8; July 19, 1987, 3, 6. See also interview with Alhaji Sanu Barrie; *Daily Mail,* January 29, 1991, 1, 12; January 9, 1986, 3; February 14, 1987, 5; *Sunday We Yone,* February 22, 1987, 5, 6; *Daily Mail,* April 21, 1989, 2. See also Dumbuya, *Reinventing the Colonial State.*

45. *Daily Mail,* January 15, 1986, 3; March 13, 1986, 1, 10; February 14, 1987, 1, 2, 5, 8.

46. *Daily Mail,* November 30, 1986, 7.

47. *Daily Mail,* December 12, 1985, 1, 8. See also January 9, 1986, 2.

48. *Daily Mail,* September 24, 1986, 5.

49. *Daily Mail,* November 28, 1986, 5.

50. *Daily Mail,* May 29, 1987, 20.

51. *Daily Mail,* November 24, 1987, 2.

52. Author's interview with Alhaji Baba Allie, Freetown, Sierra Leone, June 20, 1990.

53. Author's interview with Almamy Agibu Jalloh, Freetown, Sierra Leone, June 29, 1990.

54. Author's interview with Almamy Agibu Jalloh, Freetown, June 29, 1990; *Daily Mail,* January 1, 1986, 5; February 6, 1986, 1, 8; April 11, 1986, 1, 8; April 19, 1986, 3; June 14, 1986, 1, 2; July 2, 1986, 1, 5, 8, 9, 15, 16; August 15, 1986, 12; September 27, 1986, 1, 8, 20; December 24, 1986, 3, 8; Jalloh, *African Entrepreneurship.*

55. *Daily Mail,* December 23, 1985, 16.

56. Author's interview with Almamy Agibu Jalloh, Freetown, Sierra Leone, June 29, 1990. See also Jalloh, *African Entrepreneurship,* 113–50; Alhaji M. L. Sidique, "Tribute to the Late Alimami Agibu Jalloh," *Uni-Week,* September 21, 1995, 6; *Daily Mail,* October 7, 1978, 3.

57. *Daily Mail,* January 1, 1986, 3. See also January 9, 1986, 2.

58. *Daily Mail,* January 22, 1986, 1, 8.

59. Author's interview with Almamy Agibu Jalloh, Freetown, Sierra Leone, June 29, 1990.

60. Author's interview with Alhaji Sanu Barrie, Freetown, Sierra Leone, August 4, 1990. See also *Daily Mail,* February 14, 1987, 1, 2, 5, 8; February 21, 1987, 1, 2, 8; March 5, 1987, 1, 2, 8; March 18, 1987, 1, 8; April 27, 1987, 2, 7; June 6, 1987, 1, 8; June 16, 1987, 1, 2, 8; June 23, 1987, 1, 8; July, 1987, 1, 2, 12; July 8, 1987, 1, 3, 8; July 23, 1987, 1, 2; August 18, 1987, 1, 2, 5, 13; August 29, 1987, 1, 12; November 24, 1987, 1, 4, 5, 8; November 26, 1987, 1, 4, 5, 8; November 28, 1, 2, 5; December 12, 1987, 1, 8.

61. Author's interview with Alhaji Sanu Barrie, Freetown, Sierra Leone, August 4, 1990 See also *Daily Mail,* April 12, 1989, 1, 8; *We Yone,* April 19, 1989, 1, 8; *Awareness Times Newspaper,* April 19, 2011.

62. Author's interview with Alhaji Sanu Barrie, Freetown, Sierra Leone, August 4, 1990.

63. Author's interview with E. T. Kamara, Dallas, Texas, November 13, 2011. See also *Daily Mail,* June 14, 1987, 1, 2; November 30, 1985, 3; December 12, 1985, 1, 2; *Sunday We Yone,* March 16, 1986, 1, 2; *Daily Mail,* January 1, 1986, 5; February 6, 1986, 1; March 21, 1986, 1, 10; April 11, 1986, 1, 8; *Sunday We Yone,* April 13, 1986, 3, 4; *We Yone,* April 18, 1987, 3; *Daily Mail,* April 19, 1986, 3; *We Yone,* April 23, 1986, 3, 6; June 5, 1986, 3, 4; *Daily Mail,* June 14, 1986, 1; *Sunday We Yone,* June 29, 1986, 1, 2, 5, 6; *Daily Mail,* July 2, 1986, 1, 5, 16; *We Yone,* August 15, 1986, 3, 4, 5; *Daily Mail,* August 15, 1986, 1, 2; *Sunday We Yone,* September 7, 1986, 3, 6; *Daily Mail,* September 27, 1986, 1, 8, 20; October 17, 1986, 12; *We Yone,* November 27, 1986, 1; *Daily Mail,* November 28, 1986, 1, 2; *We Yone,* December 1, 1986, 1–8; *Daily Mail,* December 24, 1986, 1, 26; January 26, 1987, 1; February 14, 1987, 1, 2, 5, 8; February 21, 1987, 1, 8; March 5, 1987, 1, 8; *We Yone,* March 24, 1987, 3, 4; *Daily Mail,* April 27, 1987, 2, 7; June 6, 1987, 1, 8; *Sunday We Yone,* June 14, 1987, 5, 6; *We Yone,* June 24, 1987, 3, 6, 7; *Sunday We Yone,* June 28, 1987, 3, 4; *We Yone,* July 2, 1987, 3, 4; *Daily Mail,* July 8, 1987, 1, 8; August 18, 1987, 1, 2, 13; August 29, 1987, 1, 12; *We Yone,* October 30, 1987, 3, 4; *Daily Mail,* November 28, 1987, 1, 2, 3, 4, 5, 6, 28; October 27, 1988, 1, 8; December 3, 1988, 1, 2, 28; January 7, 1989, 1, 3, 16; *We Yone,* January 26, 1989, 1, 2, 3, 4, 8; *Daily Mail,* January 28, 1989, 1, 2; *We Yone,* February 11, 1989, 1–6; *Daily Mail,* March 6, 1989, 1, 3, 7, 8; *We Yone,* January 18, 1989, 1, 2; April 26, 1989, 3, 4; May 5, 1989, 3; *Daily Mail,* June 8, 1989, 4, 5; *We Yone,* June 10, 1989, 3, 4, 6; *Daily Mail,* June 13, 1989, 1, 4, 5, 8; June 17, 1989, 4, 5; June 23, 1989, 1, 2, 14; *We Yone,* June 24, 1989, 5, 6; *Daily Mail,* July 1, 1989, 1, 8; July 7, 1989, 1, 4, 8; October 16, 1989, 1, 8; October 21, 1989, 1, 8; October 25, 1989, 5, 7; October 31, 1989, 1, 3, 7, 8; *We Yone,* November 4, 1989, 1, 8; *Daily Mail,* November 6, 1989, 1, 8; *We Yone,* November 11, 1989, 3; *Daily Mail,* December 1, 1989, 1, 2, 3, 28; *We Yone,* December 22, 1989, 3, 10; *Daily Mail,* January 4, 1990, 1, 12; January 9, 1990, 1, 4; January 17, 1990, 1, 6; January 26, 1990, 1, 20; February 16, 1990, 3, 7; March 1, 1990, 3, 7; March 7, 1990, 3, 7; March 10, 1990, 1, 3, 4, 8; *We Yone,* March 10, 1990, 3, 4, 9; *Daily Mail,* March 24, 1990, 1, 12; *We Yone,* April 18, 1990, 1–6; *We Yone,* April 27, 1990, 1, 2, 13, 14; *Daily Mail,* April 27, 1990, 1, 9, 23; *We Yone,* June 9, 1990, 3, 4; June 16, 1990, 5, 6, 8; *Daily Mail,* July 23, 1990, 2; *We Yone,* June 23, 1990, 5, 7, 8; June 30, 1990,

5, 7; *Daily Mail,* August 30, 1990, 5; September 18, 1990, 9; September 22, 1990,
1, 12; September 29, 1990, 9; October 20, 1990, 1, 12; November 12, 1990, 1,
12; November 28, 1990, 1, 2, 3, 5, 7, 15, 16; *We Yone,* December 1, 1990, 3, 4, 20;
Daily Mail, January 8, 1991, 1, 12; *We Yone,* May 31, 1991, 2, 3, 4, 7; *Daily Mail,*
June 21, 1991, 1, 12; August 23, 1991, 5, 6, 7, 8, 9; *We Yone,* October 9, 1991, 3, 4,
7; *Daily Mail,* December 14, 1991, 3. See also Luke, "Continuity in Sierra Leone";
Bangura, *Sierra Leone and the Legacy of Failed Leadership,* 69; Koroma, *Agony of a
Nation,* 57–87; Luke and Riley, "Politics of Economic Decline in Sierra Leone";
Reno, *Corruption and State Politics in Sierra Leone;* Zack-Williams and Riley, "Sierra
Leone"; Zack-Williams, "Sierra Leone: Crisis and Despair"; Alie, *Sierra Leone since
Independence,* 118–29; Conteh-Morgan and Dixon-Fyle, *Sierra Leone at the End of the
Twentieth Century,* 121–26; Harris, *Sierra Leone: A Political History.*

64. *Broadcast by His Excellency the President Major-General Dr. J. S. Momoh on the
Occasion of the Twenty-Sixth Anniversary of the Republic of Sierra Leone Independence*
(Freetown: Sierra Leone Government, 1987).

65. *Sunday We Yone,* June 4, 1987, 1, 3, 4, 8; June 21, 1987, 3, 4. See also,
Zack-Williams, "Sierra Leone: Crisis and Despair"; Luke, "Continuity in Sierra
Leone"; Luke and Riley, "Politics of Economic Decline."

66. *We Yone,* June 24, 1989, 1, 8. See also Luke and Riley, "Politics of Economic Decline in Sierra Leone"; Zack-Williams, "Sierra Leone: Crisis and
Despair"; Luke, "Continuity in Sierra Leone."

67. *Daily Mail,* June 16, 1987, 1, 2; *Sunday We Yone,* June 21, 1987, 1, 8; *We
Yone,* June 24, 1987, 2, 4, 7. See also *We Yone,* February 19, 1986, 3; *West Africa,*
March 31, 1986, 656; *Sunday We Yone,* April 13, 1986, 1, 2, 3, 4; *We Yone,* April
27, 1986, 1; June 13, 1986, 1, 8; *Sunday We Yone,* December 7, 1986, 3, 4; *Daily
Mail,* July 1, 1987, 3; March 21, 1986, 1, 10; April 3, 1986, 1, 3, 8; June 26, 1986,
3; *Sunday We Yone,* June 29, 1986, 1, 2; *Daily Mail,* July 2, 1986, 1, 5, 16; August
15, 1986, 1, 2; September 27, 1986, 1, 20; November 28, 1986, 1, 2; January 26,
1987, 5; February 14, 1987, 5; June 6, 1987, 1, 8; June 16, 1987, 1, 8; *Daily Mail,*
June 23, 1987, 1, 8; *Daily Mail,* July 1, 1987, 8; *Daily Mail,* October 28, 1987, 8;
Sunday We Yone, July 24, 1988, 5, 6, 7; *Daily Mail,* October 8, 1988, 1, 8; October
17, 1988, 3, 5; *We Yone,* June 24, 1989, 5, 6; July 1, 1989, 3, 6; *Daily Mail,* August
30, 1989, 1, 12; October 3, 1989, 1, 4. See also Koroma, *Agony of a Nation,* 131–
33; Luke, "Continuity in Sierra Leone"; Reno, *Corruption and State Politics in
Sierra Leone;* Alie, *Sierra Leone since Independence,* 128–29; Conteh-Morgan and
Dixon-Fyle, *Sierra Leone at the End of the Twentieth Century,* 121–26; Dumbuya,
Reinventing the Colonial State.

68. *We Yone,* November 19, 1986, 1, 2, 3, 4. See also, *West Africa,* March 31,
1986, 656; August 25, 1986, 1791; August 18, 1986, 1718; September 22, 1986,
2001; December 8, 1986, 2554; Luke, "Continuity in Sierra Leone"; Luke and
Riley, "Politics of Economic Decline in Sierra Leone"; Zack-Williams and Riley,
"Sierra Leone"; Dumbuya, *Reinventing the Colonial State.*

69. *Daily Mail,* November 5, 1988, 1, 8; December 3, 1988, 26; January 20,
1989, 1, 8. See also Koroma, *Agony of a Nation,* 73–77; Zack-Williams, "Sierra
Leone: Crisis and Despair"; Reno, *Corruption and State Politics in Sierra Leone.*

70. *Daily Mail*, April 27, 1989, 1, 2, 24; *The New Citizen*, November 18, 1989, 1, 2.

71. *We Yone*, February 13, 1986, 4; January 9, 1987, 1, 2; October 10, 1987, 8.

72. *We Yone*, December 16, 1989, 1, 2, 7, 8. See also *West Africa*, January 9–15, 1989, 10; February 20–26, 1989, 259; March 27–April 2, 1989, 474; *Daily Mail*, December 21, 1989, 1, 8; *We Yone*, January 13, 1990, 5, 6; *The New Citizen*, December 9, 1989, 1, 5, 8. See also Luke, "Continuity in Sierra Leone"; Luke and Riley, "Politics of Economic Decline in Sierra Leone"; Zack-Williams and Riley, "Sierra Leone"; Reno, *Corruption and State Politics in Sierra Leone*; Dumbuya, *Reinventing the Colonial State*.

73. *West Africa*, January 8–14, 1990, 24; *We Yone*, January 13, 1990, 1, 6; January 26, 1990, 5, 7; March 17, 1990, 5, 6; March 31, 1990, 3, 4, 10; *Daily Mail*, November 28, 1990, 1, 16; August 12, 1991, 1, 10; December 14, 1991, 1, 8; February 28, 1992, 1, 3, 8; *We Yone*, February 3, 1990, 3, 6; January 12, 1991, 2; March 18, 1991, 5, 6; *We Yone*, December 11, 1991, 1, 6; December 20, 1991, 3, 5, 6. See also Dumbuya, *Reinventing the Colonial State*.

74. *Daily Mail*, May 17, 1990, 1, 8; *We Yone*, April 7, 1990, 3, 4; May 12, 1990, 8; August 18, 1990, 1, 8; December 15, 1990, 3, 4; December 29, 1990, 5, 6. See also Luke, "Continuity in Sierra Leone"; Luke and Riley, "Politics of Economic Decline in Sierra Leone"; Zack-Williams and Riley, "Sierra Leone"; Zack-Williams, "Sierra Leone: Crisis and Despair"; Reno, *Corruption and State Politics in Sierra Leone*.

75. *Sunday We Yone*, July 6, 1985, 1; *Daily Mail*, September 26, 1985, 2; November 14, 1985, 6; December 12, 1985, 1, 2; *We Yone*, February 27, 1986, 1, 8; March 6, 1986, 4; *Daily Mail*, April 8, 1986, 1, 8; April 11, 1986, 1, 8; *We Yone*, May 5, 1986, 3, 8; *Daily Mail*, May 28, 1986, 1; August 15, 1986, 1, 2, 11; August 27, 1986, 1, 2, 8; August 29, 1987, 8; October 17, 1986, 2; *We Yone*, November 12, 1986, 1, 8; *Sunday We Yone*, December 7, 1986, 1, 11; *We Yone*, December 12, 1986, 8; December 17, 1986, 2; December 23, 1986, 2; *Daily Mail*, January 15, 1987, 3, 7; January 26, 1987, 5; June 6, 1987, 1, 8; August 29, 1987, 1, 12; *We Yone*, September 12, 1987, 8; September 25, 1987, 8; October 10, 1987, 8; November 21, 1987, 1, 2; *Daily Mail*, December 16, 1987, 1, 8; *Sunday We Yone*, February 7, 1988, 1; *Daily Mail*, April 8, 1988, 2; October 1, 1988, 3, 7; October 5, 1988, 5, 7; *We Yone*, January 18, 1989, 1, 4, 6; *Daily Mail*, March 6, 1989, 1, 2; March 10, 1989, 1; *We Yone*, March 31, 1989, 1; *Daily Mail*, April 7, 1989, 1, 8; *We Yone*, May 13, 1989, 1–4; May 20, 1989, 1, 7; July 8, 1989, 3, 4, 6; *Daily Mail*, July 14, 1989, 3; *We Yone*, August 12, 1989, 1; *Daily Mail*, August 30, 1989, 1, 12; *We Yone*, January 6, 1990, 1; April 7, 1990, 1, 2; June 2, 1990, 3, 4; *Daily Mail*, August 27, 1990, 1, 12; *We Yone*, October 27, 1990, 1, 7; *Daily Mail*, November 12, 1990, 1, 12; January 16, 1991, 12; June 7, 1991, 3; December 14, 1991, 2; February 10, 1992, 1, 2. See also Conteh-Morgan and Dixon-Fyle, *Sierra Leone at the End of the Twentieth Century*, 121–26; Koroma, *The Agony of a Nation*, 71–77; Zack-Williams, "Sierra Leone: Crisis and Despair"; Dumbuya, *Reinventing the Colonial State*.

76. *Daily Mail*, December 16, 1985, 1, 6; *We Yone*, January 30, 1986, 1; February 13, 1986, 7; April 1, 1986, 2, 8; *Daily Mail*, April 19, 1986, 5; We Yone, August

1, 1986, 2, 8; *Sunday We Yone*, December 7, 1986, 1, 11; *Daily Mail*, March 18, 1987, 1, 8; April 21, 1989, 2; *We Yone*, June 24, 1989, 1, 2; July 22, 1989, 2, 8; July 29, 1989, 8; *Daily Mail*, February 17, 1992, 1, 8; *We Yone*, January 13, 1990, 1, 6; Dumbuya, *Reinventing the Colonial State.*

77. *Daily Mail*, December 16, 1985, 1, 6; January 9, 1986, 1, 10; January 1, 1986, 1, 5; *We Yone*, February 13, 1986, 2; *Sunday We Yone*, June 29, 1986, 1, 2, 3, 4; July 13, 1986, 3, 5; *We Yone*, July 17, 1986, 1, 3; *Daily Mail*, July 2, 1986, 1, 2; *We Yone*, August 1, 1986, 1, 8; *Daily Mail*, August 6, 1986, 1, 3, 13; August 15, 1986, 1, 2; August 16, 1986, 1, 8; August 27, 1986, 1, 5, 8; *Sunday We Yone*, August 31, 1986, 4, 9; *We Yone*, September 19, 1986, 1; *Daily Mail*, October 17, 1986, 1, 12; *Sunday We Yone*, December 7, 1986, 2; *We Yone*, December 17, 1986, 5, 6; January 9, 1987, 8; *Daily Mail*, February 14, 1987, 1, 2, 5, 8; February 26, 1987, 1, 8; March 5, 1987, 1, 2, 8; May 8, 1987, 1, 2; May 29, 1987, 1, 20; June 23, 1987, 1, 8; *We Yone*, June 24, 1987, 1; *Sunday We Yone*, June 28, 1987, 7; *We Yone*, July 9, 1987, 3, 4; *Daily Mail*, August 18, 1987, 1, 14; November 26, 1987, 1, 8; December 16, 1987, 2; December 22, 1987, 1; June 1, 1989, 1, 10; *We Yone*, June 10, 1989, 3, 4, 6; June 17, 1989, 3, 4; *Daily Mail*, July 4, 1989, 1, 8; July 18, 1989, 5; *Weekend Spark*, August 11, 1989, 1, 4; *The New Citizen*, January 13, 1990, 1, 8; *We Yone*, April 27, 1990, 1; May 5, 1990, 3, 4; *Daily Mail*, May 7, 1990, 1, 12; *We Yone*, May 12, 1990, 3, 4; *Daily Mail*, September 11, 1990, 9; *We Yone*, September 22, 1990, 3, 6; *Daily Mail*, January 16, 1991, 1, 9; May 30, 1991, 3, 9; November 8, 1991, 1, 8; November 14, 1991, 1, 8. See also Conteh-Morgan and Dixon-Fyle, *Sierra Leone at the End of the Twentieth Century*, 121–26; Koroma, *Agony of a Nation*, 71–73; Dumbuya, *Reinventing the Colonial State.*

78. *Daily Mail*, January 22, 1986, 1, 8; *We Yone*, January 16, 1987, 1; January 23, 1987, 5; *Daily Mail*, February 21, 1987, 3, 7; *We Yone*, April 18, 1987, 3; *Daily Mail*, September 22, 1989, 1, 8, 2; March 24, 1990, 2. See also Zack-Williams, "Sierra Leone: Crisis and Despair"; Conteh-Morgan and Dixon-Fyle, *Sierra Leone at the End of the Twentieth Century*, 121–26; Dumbuya, *Reinventing the Colonial State.*

79. *Daily Mail*, January 15, 1986, 3; Conteh-Morgan and Dixon-Fyle, *Sierra Leone at the End of the Twentieth Century*, 121–26; Dumbuya, *Reinventing the Colonial State.*

80. *Sunday We Yone*, July 13, 1986, 2; *Daily Mail*, January 15, 1986, 3; January 1, 1986, 1, 5; February 11, 1986, 3; *Sunday We Yone*, August 31, 1986, 3, 6; *We Yone*, November 5, 1986, 8; January 16, 1987, 1, 8; January 31, 1987, 8; March 24, 1987, 8; *The New Citizen*, August 8, 1987, 1, 3; *West Africa*, August 10, 1987, 1524; *The New Citizen*, August 15, 1987, 1, 2; August 22, 1987, 1, 7; September 26, 1987, 1, 2, 5; *Daily Mail*, December 12, 1987, 1, 3, 8; *We Yone*, December 23, 1987, 1; *Daily Mail*, December 24, 1987, 1, 12; *We Yone*, December 31, 1986, 3; *Daily Mail*, January 8, 1988, 1, 5; January 18, 1988, 1, 8; January 30, 1988, 1, 8; February 19, 1988, 1, 2, 8; April 8, 1988, 1, 4; *Sunday We Yone*, April 14, 1988, 2; *Daily Mail*, April 21, 1988, 1, 8; July 21, 1988, 2; *Sunday We Yone*, July 24, 1988, 1, 2; July 31, 1988, 8; *Daily Mail*, August 6, 1988, 3, 8; *We Yone*, August 14, 1988, 2; August 19, 1989, 1, 2; *Daily Mail*, August 25, 1988, 1, 8; September 1, 1988,

1, 3, 8; September 21, 1988, 1; September 28, 1988, 1, 8; October 1, 1988, 1, 2, 8; October 27, 1988, 1, 8; November 28, 1988, 12; March 10, 1989, 1, 8; *We Yone,* July 8, 1989, 8; August 12, 1989, 1, 8; September 2, 1989, 1, 12; November 25, 1989, 8; December 9, 1989, 1; December 22, 1989, 12; April 7, 1990, 1, 8; April 18, 1990, 1, 12; August 26, 1989, 8; March 31, 1990, 2; *Daily Mail,* May 17, 1990, 2; August 18, 1990, 3, 12; November 5, 1990, 1, 12; November 12, 1990, 3; *We Yone,* December 2, 1991, 1, 2, 4; December 8, 1990, 3, 7; March 8, 1991, 6; March 11, 1991, 1, 2; November 16, 1991; November 16, 1991, 6; *Daily Mail,* November 28, 1991, 1, 11, 12; *Weekend Spark,* December 6, 1991, 1, 2; *New Shaft,* December 10–16, 1991, 1, 2, 8; *We Yone,* December 11, 1991, 3, 4; December 20, 1991, 5, 6. See also Kpundeh, *Politics and Corruption in Africa;* Smith, "Dichotomy of Politics and Corruption in a Neopatrimonial State"; Conteh-Morgan and Dixon-Fyle, *Sierra Leone at the End of the Twentieth Century,* 121–26; Kpundeh, "Limiting Administrative Corruption in Sierra Leone"; Dumbuya, *Reinventing the Colonial State.*

81. *The New Citizen,* August 1, 1987, 1, 2; *Daily Mail,* September 8, 1987, 2; October 19, 1987, 10; October 28, 1987, 12; May 11, 1988, 5, 7; *West Africa,* May 30, 1988, 994; *Daily Mail,* July 6, 1988, 1, 8; July 21, 1988, 1, 2; July 31, 1988, 1, 2; September 13, 1988, 1, 8; October 27, 1988, 1, 8; *We Yone,* February 11, 1991, 2. See also Kpundeh, *Politics and Corruption in Africa;* Smith, "Dichotomy of Politics and Corruption in a Neopatrimonial State"; Kpundeh, "Limiting Administrative Corruption in Sierra Leone"; Dumbuya, *Reinventing the Colonial State.*

82. *Daily Mail,* May 28, 1988, 1, 10; *West Africa,* May 30, 1988, 994; *Daily Mail,* October 27, 1988, 1, 8; May 7, 1990, 1, 12; *We Yone,* December 23, 1987, 1, 11; *Sunday We Yone,* February 7, 1988, 1; February 14, 1988, 8; July 31, 1988, 1, 2, 8; *We Yone,* December 16, 1989, 3, 4; January 20, 1990, 2; April 14, 1990, 8; April 21, 1990, 3, 6. See also Kpundeh, *Politics and Corruption in Africa;* Smith, "Dichotomy of Politics and Corruption in a Neopatrimonial State"; Kpundeh, "Limiting Administrative Corruption in Sierra Leone"; Dumbuya, *Reinventing the Colonial State.*

83. *Sunday We Yone,* April 14, 1988, 3, 4, 7; September 18, 1988, 1, 7, 8; *We Yone,* October 6, 1990, 8. See also Kpundeh, *Politics and Corruption in Africa;* Smith, "Dichotomy of Politics and Corruption in a Neopatrimonial State"; Kpundeh, "Limiting Administrative Corruption in Sierra Leone"; Dumbuya, *Reinventing the Colonial State.*

84. *Daily Mail,* January 15, 1986, 8; *We Yone,* February 13, 1986, 2; February 20, 1986, 2, 7; March 4, 1986, 2; March 6, 1986, 1; *Daily Mail,* April 11, 1986, 1, 8; *Sunday We Yone,* April 13, 1986, 8; *We Yone,* May 2, 1986, 1; *Daily Mail,* August 15, 1986, 2, 11; *We Yone,* December 23, 1986, 1; January 23, 1987, 1, 3, 7; January 23, 1987, 8; January 31, 1987, 1, 8; *Daily Mail,* March 18, 1987, 8; September 3, 1987, 1, 2, 8; September 10, 1987, 1, 3, 10; September 21, 1987, 1, 12; *We Yone,* November 21, 1987, 1; *Daily Mail,* March 3, 1988, 2; April 14, 1988, 1, 8; May 6, 1988, 2; January 14, 1989, 1, 8; *We Yone,* January 18, 1989, 8; *The New Citizen,* March 25, 1989, 1, 12; *Daily Mail,* June 1, 1989, 2; *We Yone,* August 5, 1989, 1; *Daily Mail,* September 22, 1989, 1; *We Yone,* September 23, 1989, 3, 4; *Daily*

Mail, October 3, 1989, 1, 8; October 16, 1989, 1, 8; November 6, 1989, 5; *We Yone*, December 9, 1989, 1, 2; *Daily Mail*, December 12, 1989, 1, 2, 8; December 15, 1989, 1, 8; *We Yone*, December 22, 1989, 1, 12; January 13, 1990, 5, 6; January 13, 1990, 1, 8; January 26, 1990, 1; February 3, 1990, 1; *Daily Mail*, February 16, 1990, 8; *We Yone*, March 3, 1990, 1, 8; *Daily Mail*, March 10, 1990, 1, 8; *We Yone*, April 14, 1990, 8; April 21, 1990, 1; *Daily Mail*, September 22, 1990, 2. See also Koroma, *The Agony of a Nation*, 73–75; Dumbuya, *Reinventing the Colonial State*.

85. *Sunday We Yone*, July 6, 1985, 1, 8; *Daily Mail*, January 9, 1986, 1, 10; February 6, 1986, 1, 8; February 25, 1986, 1, 5; *We Yone*, March 6, 1986, 1, 8; *Daily Mail*, March 13, 1986, 1, 10; April 8, 1986, 1, 8; April 11, 1986, 3; *We Yone*, May 23, 1986, 1, 2, 3, 4, 6, 8; *Sunday We Yone*, June 29, 1986, 1, 2; July 27, 1986, 3, 4; *Daily Mail*, August 15, 1986, 5, 12; *We Yone*, August 15, 1986, 1, 2, 3; *Daily Mail*, August 16, 1986, 1, 8; *West Africa*, August 25, 1986, 1791; August 18, 1986, 1718; September 22, 1986, 2001; December 8, 1986, 2554; *Sunday We Yone*, September 14, 1986, 1, 2, 7; *Daily Mail*, September 27, 1986, 1, 8, 20; October 17, 1986, 3; December 24, 1986, 3, 8; *The New Citizen*, August 1, 1987, 1, 3; *Daily Mail*, February 21, 1987, 1, 2, 8; *We Yone*, July 29, 1987, 1, 8; *Daily Mail*, August 18, 1987, 1, 14; November 24, 1987, 3, 7; January 8, 1988, 1, 5; January 14, 1988, 1, 8; January 18, 1988, 3; January 30, 1988, 1, 8; August 11, 1988, 8; October 8, 1988, 1, 8; October 20, 1988, 1; December 16, 1988, 1, 8; *We Yone*, May 5, 1989, 1, 8; July 1, 1989, 1, 3, 4; *Daily Mail*, July 11, 1989, 1, 8; July 22, 1989, 2; August 3, 1989, 1, 2; *We Yone*, September 23, 1989, 5, 6; *Daily Mail*, October 3, 1989, 2; *Weekend Spark*, October 20, 1989, 1; *We Yone*, October 21, 1989, 1; October 28, 1989, 1, 8; November 4, 1989, 1, 3, 4, 6, 8; November 11, 1989, 1, 8; November 25, 1989, 1, 3, 10, 12; *We Yone*, January 6, 1990, 3, 6; January 13, 1990, 1, 8; *Daily Mail*, January 17, 1990, 6; *The New Citizen*, January 20, 1990, 1, 3; *We Yone*, January 26, 1990, 3, 4; *Daily Mail*, February 16, 1990, 1, 8; *The New Citizen*, February 17, 1990, 1, 2; *Daily Mail*, March 7, 1990, 1, 8; March 30, 1990, 1, 12; *We Yone*, June 30, 1990, 1, 12; July 17, 1990, 2; July 28, 1990, 1; *Daily Mail*, August 18, 1990, 3; *The New Citizen*, September 1, 1990, 1, 4; *We Yone*, September 3, 1990, 1; *Daily Mail*, September 5, 1990, 1, 11; *We Yone*, October 1, 1990, 1; *Weekend Spark*, November 16, 1990, 1, 4;, November 23, 1990, 1; *Daily Mail*, February 16, 1991, 2; *We Yone*, February 22, 1991, 1, 2; March 8, 1991, 5; *Daily Mail*, May 30, 1991, 9; *We Yone*, November 24, 1990, 3, 5, 6; *Daily Mail*, June 3, 1991, 2; *Progress*, July 27, 1991, 1; *Daily Mail*, July 29, 1991, 1, 3; *Daily Mail*, September 27, 1991, 1, 3, 8; *We Yone*, October 14, 1991, 1, 7; *Daily Mail*, February 28, 1992, 1, 3, 8. See also Zack-Williams, "Sierra Leone: Crisis and Despair"; Conteh-Morgan and Dixon-Fyle, *Sierra Leone at the End of the Twentieth Century*, 121–26; Dumbuya, *Reinventing the Colonial State*.

86. *Daily Mail*, January 9, 1986, 3; January 1, 1986, 1, 5; *Sunday We Yone*, August 31, 1986, 5; *We Yone*, July 22, 1989, 3, 4, 7; July 29, 1989, 3, 4; August 5, 1989, 3, 5, 6, 7; August 12, 1989, 1, 2, 3, 8; August 19, 1989, 3, 6; August 26, 1989, 1, 2, 4, 7. See also Conteh-Morgan and Dixon-Fyle, *Sierra Leone at the End of the Twentieth Century*, 121–26; Dumbuya, *Reinventing the Colonial State*.

87. *We Yone,* January 22, 1986, 6, 7; *Daily Mail,* May 28, 1986, 2; *We Yone,* June 5, 1986, 6; *Sunday We Yone,* December 7, 1986, 1; *Daily Mail,* January 15, 1987, 1, 10; *We Yone,* January 23, 1987, 1; *West Africa,* February 16, 1987, 300; *Sunday We Yone,* February 22, 1987, 1, 8; July 5, 1987, 1, 2; *Daily Mail,* July 23, 1987, 1, 2; *The New Citizen,* September 9, 1991, 1, 8; September 19, 1987, 1, 2; *We Yone,* September 19, 1987, 1, 3, 4, 8; *The New Citizen,* October 3, 1987, 1, 4; *We Yone,* April 14, 1988, 3, 4; *Daily Mail,* September 21, 1988, 4; *We Yone,* September 30, 1987, 8; *Daily Mail,* November 1, 1988, 1, 8; *We Yone,* January 18, 1989, 8; *Daily Mail,* January 20, 1989, 1, 8; January 25, 1989, 3; *We Yone,* January 26, 1989, 3, 4; *Daily Mail,* February 11, 1989, 1, 8; February 17, 1989, 1, 10; March 6, 1989, 1, 8; *We Yone,* March 31, 1990, 1; *Daily Mail,* July 1, 1989, 1, 8; *We Yone,* July 1, 1989, 1; *Daily Mail,* July 22, 1989, 1, 8; *Weekend Spark,* August 18, 1989, 1, 4; *Daily Mail,* October 3, 1989, 1, 8; *We Yone,* October 14, 1989, 1, 6; January 6, 1990, 4, 6; *Daily Mail,* February 8, 1990, 3; *We Yone,* February 24, 1990, 1, 8; May 5, 1990, 1, 8; May 12, 1990, 2, 7; *We Yone,* May 19, 1990, 3, 4; May 26, 1990, 3, 4; June 2, 1990, 1, 10; *Daily Mail,* June 5, 1990, 1, 8; *We Yone,* June 9, 1990, 1, 2; June 16, 1990, 3, 4, 10; June 23, 1990, 1, 2, 5, 7, 8; June 30, 1990, 1, 4, 5, 7; August 4, 1990, 1, 2; October 27, 1990, 2; *New Shaft,* September 17–23, 1991, 1, 6; *We Yone,* September 18, 1991, 2, 3, 4, 6; *Daily Mail,* October 10, 1991, 1, 10; *We Yone,* August 11, 1990, 1; November 3, 1990, 8; *The Chronicle,* February 26, 1991, 8; *We Yone,* March 11, 1991, 1, 8; *For Di People,* September 3, 1991, 1, 5; *We Yone,* October 14, 1991, 1, 8; *Daily Mail,* October 31, 1991, 1, 8; *Weekend Spark,* November 1, 1991, 1, 3; *Daily Mail,* January 31, 1992, 1, 2; *We Yone,* February 1, 1992, 1, 2; *Daily Mail,* February 17, 1992, 1, 7; *We Yone,* February 19, 1992, 1, 2; March 3, 1992, 3, 6, 7; March 21, 1992, 2, 3, 4, 5, 7. See also Conteh-Morgan and Dixon-Fyle, *Sierra Leone at the End of the Twentieth Century,* 121–26; Koroma, *Agony of a Nation,* 73–74; Dumbuya, *Reinventing the Colonial State.*

88. *We Yone,* March 25, 1989, 1, 8; *Daily Mail,* March 28, 1989, 1, 5, 12; April 21, 1989, 1, 3, 8; May 12, 1989, 1, 16; July 4, 1989, 1, 8; July 22, 1989, 2; *We Yone,* September 9, 1989, 1, 3; September 16, 1989, 3, 4; *Weekend Spark,* September 22, 1989, 1, 4; *Daily Mail,* December 12, 1989, 1, 2, 8; December 15, 1989, 1, 8; March 10, 1990, 1, 8; March 30, 1990, 3, 8, 9; May 7, 1990, 1, 12; May 12, 1990, 2; May 17, 1990, 1, 8; September 18, 1990, 9. See also Zack-Williams, "Sierra Leone: Crisis and Despair"; Conteh-Morgan and Dixon-Fyle, *Sierra Leone at the End of the Twentieth Century,* 121–26; Koroma, *Agony of a Nation,* 71–77; Dumbuya, *Reinventing the Colonial State.*

89. *We Yone,* November 27, 1986, 8; *Daily Mail,* May 16, 1991, 9; May 23, 1991, 7; *We Yone,* July 23, 1990, 2, 3, 4; *Daily Mail,* November 8, 1991, 3, 7. See also Zack-Williams, "Sierra Leone: Crisis and Despair"; Conteh-Morgan and Dixon-Fyle, *Sierra Leone at the End of the Twentieth Century,* 121–26; Dumbuya, *Reinventing the Colonial State.*

90. *Sunday We Yone,* July 6, 1985, 3, 4; *We Yone,* June 25, 1986, 1, 2; *Sunday We Yone,* June 29, 1986, 1, 2, 3, 4; July 13, 1986, 3, 4, 6; *We Yone,* July 17, 1986, 3, 4, 6; *Sunday We Yone,* July 27, 1986, 3, 4; August 31, 1986, 3; *We Yone,* November 27, 1986, 8; *Sunday We Yone,* February 22, 1987, 3, 4, 6; *We Yone,* February 14,

1987, 5, 6; *Daily Mail,* May 29, 1987, 1, 20; *Sunday We Yone,* June 21, 1987, 1, 8; *Daily Mail,* June 23, 1987, 1, 8; *We Yone,* June 24, 1987, 2, 4, 7; *Sunday We Yone,* June 28, 1987, 1, 2, 3, 4, 7, 8; *Daily Mail,* July 1, 1987, 1, 2, 12; *We Yone,* July 2, 1987, 1, 3, 4, 8; *Sunday We Yone,* July 5, 1987, 3, 7; *Daily Mail,* July 8, 1987, 1, 3; *We Yone,* July 9, 1987, 3, 4; *Sunday We Yone,* July 12, 1987, 3, 4, 6; *Daily Mail,* August 18, 1987, 5; *Sunday We Yone,* July 19, 1987, 2, 6; *Daily Mail,* August 29, 1987, 1, 12; *Sunday We Yone,* February 7, 1988, 3, 4; *We Yone,* June 24, 1989, 1, 4, 8; *Daily Mail,* June 25, 1988, 1, 8; June 30, 1988, 1, 3, 4, 8; July 6, 1988, 3, 4, 5; July 15, 1988, 1, 3, 5, 8; *Sunday We Yone,* July 24, 1988, 5, 6, 7; July 31, 1988, 5, 6, 7; August 14, 1988, 5, 6, 7; *We Yone,* June 17, 1989, 1, 2; *Daily Mail,* July 1, 1989, 1, 2, 8; *We Yone,* July 1989, 1, 8; *Daily Mail,* July 4, 1989, 1, 4, 5, 8; July 7, 1989, 1, 2, 4, 5; *We Yone,* July 8, 1989, 3, 4, 6; *Daily Mail,* July 11, 1989, 4, 5; July 14, 1989, 3, 4, 5; *We Yone,* July 15, 1989, 3, 6, 7; *Daily Mail,* July 18, 1989, 5; July 22, 1989, 3; *We Yone,* July 22, 1989, 1, 8; *Daily Mail,* July 27, 1989, 1, 8; December 1, 1989, 1, 28; *We Yone,* December 2, 1989, 1, 12; December 9, 1989, 3, 4; *Daily Mail,* December 12, 1989, 1, 8; *We Yone,* December 16, 1989, 3, 4; January 13, 1990, 1, 2, 7, 8; *Daily Mail,* January 17, 1990, 1, 6; *We Yone,* January 20, 1990, 1, 8; January 26, 1990, 5, 7; February 3, 1990, 3, 6, 7; February 24, 1990, 3, 4, 8; *Daily Mail,* March 1, 1990, 1, 4, 10; *We Yone,* March 3, 1990, 3, 4, 6; *Daily Mail,* March 7, 1990, 1, 8; June 8, 1990, 1; *We Yone,* June 23, 1990, 3, 4, 9; June 30, 1990, 1, 12; *Daily Mail,* July 2, 1990, 1, 2, 8; *Weekend Spark,* July 5, 1991, 1, 4; *Daily Mail,* July 5, 1991, 6, 7; *We Yone,* July 7, 1990, 3, 4, 5, 6, 8; *Daily Mail,* July 13, 1991, 6, 7, 9; *We Yone,* July 14, 1990, 1, 3, 5, 7, 12; July 23, 1990, 3, 4, 7, 8; July 28, 1990, 5, 6, 7; *Daily Mail,* July 29, 1991, 3, 4, 5; August 5, 1991, 4, 5; *We Yone,* September 18, 1991, 3, 6; December 11, 1991, 1, 6; *Daily Mail,* December 14, 1991, 1, 3, 8; *We Yone,* December 15, 1990, 1, 5, 7, 8; December 20, 1991, 3, 5, 6, 8. See also Koroma, *Agony of a Nation,* 71–73; Conteh-Morgan and Dixon-Fyle, *Sierra Leone at the End of the Twentieth Century,* 121–26; Dumbuya, *Reinventing the Colonial State.*

91. *We Yone,* February 13, 1986, 5, 6; February 19, 1986, 3, 6; February 27, 1986, 3, 6; December 12, 1986, 5, 6; December 17, 1986, 5, 6; December 23, 1987, 4, 9, 10.

92. *Sunday We Yone,* February 22, 1987, 1, 8; *Daily Mail,* August 29, 1989, 1, 12. See also *West Africa,* January 27, 1986, 217; February 10, 1986, 321; Reno, *Corruption and State Politics in Sierra Leone;* Dumbuya, *Reinventing the Colonial State.*

93. *We Yone,* November 21, 1987, 3, 4, 6, 7. See also *We Yone,* November 28, 1987, 1, 2, 8; *West Africa,* November 16, 1987, 2251; January 18, 1998, 104; December 5–11, 1988, 2309. See also Zack-Williams, "Sierra Leone: Crisis and Despair"; Reno, *Corruption and State Politics in Sierra Leone;* Dumbuya, *Reinventing the Colonial State.*

94. *We Yone,* December 22, 1989, 1, 12; *West Africa,* December 25–January 7, 1989, 2166; *We Yone,* January 6, 1990, 1; *The New Citizen,* January 13, 1990, 1, 2; *We Yone,* January 13, 1990, 1, 7; *Daily Mail,* January 17, 1990, 1, 12; January 8–14, 1990, 24. See also Zack-Williams, "Sierra Leone: Crisis and Despair";

Reno, *Corruption and State Politics in Sierra Leone*; Dumbuya, *Reinventing the Colonial State*.

95. *We Yone*, December 5, 1987, 1, 2, 8; December 5, 1987, 8; December 18, 1987, 1, 2, 8; December 23, 1987, 8; *Sunday We Yone*, February 7, 1988, 8; *West Africa*, August 14–20, 1989, 1327; February 5–11, 1990, 197; April 30–May 6, 1990, 740; *Weekend Spark*, September 29, 1989, 1, 4; *We Yone*, December 9, 1989, 1, 2, 3, 4; December 22, 1989, 1, 12; January 6, 1990, 1; *The New Citizen*, January 13, 1990, 1, 2; *We Yone*, January 13, 1990, 1, 7; *Daily Mail*, January 17, 1990, 1, 12; *The New Citizen*, January 20, 1990, 1; *We Yone*, January 20, 1990, 1, 8; *Daily Mail*, January 26, 1990, 19; *Weekend Spark*, January 26, 1990, 1; *We Yone*, January 26, 1990, 1, 12; *Daily Mail*, February 1, 1990, 1; *We Yone*, February 3, 1990, 1, 2; *Daily Mail*, February 8, 1990, 1, 8; *We Yone*, February 10, 1990, 1, 2, 3, 8; March 3, 1990, 1, 8; *Daily Mail*, February 16, 1990, 8; *We Yone*, February 17, 1990, 1, 5, 7, 8; February 24, 1990, 1, 8; March 10, 1990, 8; March 24, 1990, 1, 2, 9; *Daily Mail*, March 30, 1990, 1, 9, 12; *We Yone*, April 7, 1990, 1; *Daily Mail*, April 11, 1990, 1. See also Koroma, *Agony of a Nation*, 73–77; Reno, *Corruption and State Politics in Sierra Leone*, 162–66; Dumbuya, *Reinventing the Colonial State*.

96. *Sunday We Yone*, February 14, 1988, 1, 2, 3, 7, 8. See also Reno, *Corruption and State Politics in Sierra Leone*.

97. Author's interview with Alhaji Mohamed "Texaco" Bah, Freetown, Sierra Leone, May 26, 1990; *Daily Mail*, March 11, 1988, 8; November 24, 1987, 1, 4, 5, 8; November 26, 1987, 1, 4, 5, 8; November 28, 1987, 1, 2, 5, 6, 28; December 12, 1987, 1, 8; December 16, 1987, 1, 8; December 22, 1987, 8; January 8, 1988, 1, 3, 5; February 19, 1988, 1, 8; March 11, 1988, 1, 8; April 8, 1988, 3; April 14, 1988, 1, 2, 4, 8; April 21, 1988, 1, 8; May 28, 1988, 1, 10; June 9, 1988, 3; June 15, 1988, 1, 3. See also Bah, *Fulbe Presence in Sierra Leone*; Reno, *Corruption and State Politics in Sierra Leone*, 147–49; Koroma, *The Agony of a Nation*, 75.

98. *West Africa*, December 10–16, 1990, 2996. See also *West Africa*, February 5–11, 1990, 164; August 6–12, 1990, 2238.

99. January 13–19, 1992, 66–67.

100. *We Yone*, May 29, 1986, 1, 2, 3, 7, 8. See also *West Africa*, October 7, 1985, 2071; January 13, 1986, 104; and May 26, 1986, 1096. Additionally, see Conteh, *Management of Sierra Leone's Electoral Process*; Hayward and Kandeh, "Perspectives on Twenty-Five Years of Elections in Sierra Leone"; Reno, *Corruption and State Politics in Sierra Leone*; Dumbuya, *Reinventing the Colonial State*.

101. *We Yone*, February 6, 1986, 1, 2; April 23, 1986, 1, 2, 8; *West Africa*, May 12, 1986, 981–82, 1025; *We Yone*, May 23, 1986, 1, 2, 3, 4, 6, 8; May 29, 1986, 8; October 17, 1986, 8; October 23, 1986, 2. See also Hayward and Kandeh, "Perspectives on Twenty-Five Years of Elections in Sierra Leone"; Dumbuya, *Reinventing the Colonial State*.

102. See J. Sorie Conteh, "Elusive Ideals," *West Africa*, April 28–May 5, 1991; *Agony of a Nation*, 58–59, 112; *West Africa*, June 2, 1986, 1149; and Bangura, *Sierra Leone and the Legacy of Failed Leadership*, 70.

103. For more information on Dr. Jusu-Sheriff, see *Daily Mail*, March 17, 1990, 3; and *Awareness Times*, December 31, 2009.

104. *Daily Mail,* December 6, 1985, 1, 10; *We Yone,* January 30, 1986, 1, 8; *Daily Mail,* March 27, 1986, 1, 16; April 3, 1986, 1, 8; April 4, 1986, 1, 6, 7; April 8, 1986, 1, 3, 8; April 11, 1986, 1, 8; *Sunday We Yone,* April 13, 1986, 1, 2; *We Yone,* May 2, 1986, 1, 2, 3, 4; May 5, 1986, 1, 2, 3, 4; *Daily Mail,* May 8, 1986, 1, 3, 5, 8; May 28, 1986, 1, 7, 8, 20; *We Yone,* June 5, 1986, 1, 2, 5, 7, 8; *Daily Mail,* June 7, 1986, 1, 3, 4, 5, 12; June 14, 1986, 1, 14; *We Yone,* June 18, 1986, 1; *Sunday We Yone,* June 29, 1986, 3, 4; July 27, 1986, 1, 8; *Daily Mail,* August 6, 1986, 2; August 16, 1986, 1, 8; August 17, 1986, 1; *Sunday We Yone,* November 9, 1986, 5, 6; *We Yone,* January 31, 1987, 1; April 11, 1987, 8. See also Banya, *Looking Back: My Life and Times,* 469–74.

105. *We Yone,* April 23, 1986, 2; June 5, 1986, 1, 2, 5; *Daily Mail,* March 28, 1989, 6.

106. Author's interview with Almamy Agibu Jalloh, Freetown, Sierra Leone, June 29, 1990; author's interview with Alhaji Sidique, Freetown, Sierra Leone, October 27, 2008. See also *Daily Mail,* February 26, 1987, 3; *We Yone,* May 5, 1986, 1, 2, 3; May 5, 1986, 1, 2, 3, 4; October 27, 1990, 3, 6; Turay, *Prophecies of a Father,* 88–90.

107. Author's interview with Hon. Alpha B. Barrie, Arlington, Texas, November 7, 2010. See also *We Yone,* May 5, 1986, 1, 2, 3; *Daily Mail,* April 15, 1989, 1, 8.

108. Author's interview with Hon. Alpha B. Barrie, Arlington, Texas, November 7, 2010 and author's interview with Dr. Bah, Washington, DC, March 9, 1991. See also Bah, *Fulbe Presence in Sierra Leone.*

109. Author's interview with Alhaji Sidique, Freetown, Sierra Leone, October 27, 2008. See also *Daily Mail,* July 2, 1986, 2; *We Yone,* June 13, 1986, 1, 2, 3, 6, 8; *Daily Mail,* June 14, 1986, 1, 2; June 21, 1986, 5; June 26, 1986, 2; August 27, 1986, 2; February 26, 1987, 3; November 24, 1987, 2; September 23, 1988, 2; November 25, 1988, 1, 3, 4; February 26, 1991, 5; *The New Citizen,* September 9, 1, 8; December 23, 1991, 10; Koroma, *Agony of a Nation,* 57–59.

110. *Daily Mail,* November 30, 1985, 1, 2, 4; *The Tablet,* February 14, 1981, 1, 6.

111. Author's interview with Alhaji Sidique, Freetown, Sierra Leone, October 27, 2008 and author's interview with Alhaji Maju, Freetown, Sierra LeoneNovember 14, 1991. See also Koroma, *Agony of a Nation;* Dumbuya, *Reinventing the Colonial State;* and Kpundeh, *Politics and Corruption in Africa.*

112. Author's interview with Alhaji Seray-Wurie, Freetown, Sierra Leone, June 17, 1990. See also *We Yone,* September 30, 1989, 1; Jalloh, *African Entrepreneurship;* and Bah, *Fulbe Presence in Sierra Leone.*

113. Author's interview with Alhaji Tejan-Jalloh, Freetown, Sierra Leone, June 21, 1990. See also *Daily Mail,* June 19, 1990, 2.

114. Author's interview with Almamy Agibu Jalloh, Freetown, Sierra Leone, June 29, 1990. See also *Daily Mail,* June 12, 1990, 2; Jalloh, *African Entrepreneurship;* and Bah, *Fulbe Presence in Sierra Leone.*

115. Author's interview with Alhaji Tejan-Jalloh, Freetown, Sierra Leone, June 21, 1990. See also *Sunday We Yone,* September 18, 1988, 2; *Daily Mail,*

September 28, 1988, 2, 3; H. M. Joko Smart, *Sierra Leone Customary Law* (Freetown, Sierra Leone: Atlantic Printers, 1983); Harrell-Bond, Howard, and Skinner, *Community Leadership and the Transformation of Freetown (1801–1976)*.

116. Author's interview with Lamin Bah (son of Alhaji Sajalieu Bah), Arlington, Texas, May 20, 2017. See also the Ansarul Alumni Association website, www.ansarulalumni.org, accessed February 26, 2018.

117. *Daily Mail*, June 6, 1987; May 28, 1988, 5; May 12, 1989, 1, 3; October 21, 1989, 5; April 18, 1990, 1, 12; July 23, 1990, 5; March 21, 1991, 6; March 26, 1991, 6; April 10, 1991, 5; March 30, 1992, 2.

118. *Daily Mail*, August 15, 1986, 1, 12; June 6, 1987, 4; October 27, 1988, 3; March 20, 1989, 8; April 7, 1989, 2; July 4, 1989, 1, 8; July 4, 1989, 1.

119. *Daily Mail*, March 18, 1987, 5. See also *Daily Mail*, May 7, 1990, 2.

120. *Daily Mail*, May 29, 1987, 7.

121. *Daily Mail*, September 1, 1988, 1, 8.

122. *Daily Mail*, August 25, 1989, 1, 2.

123. *Daily Mail*, October 7, 1989, 2.

124. *Daily Mail*, February 25, 1991, 12.

125. *Daily Mail*, August 5, 1991, 1, 4. See also *Daily Mail*, June 14, 1991, 7.

126. For more information on the RUF, see Lansana Gberie, *A Dirty War in West Africa: The RUF and the Destruction of Sierra Leone* (Bloomington: Indiana University Press, 2005); Ibrahim Abdullah, ed., *Between Democracy and Terror: The Sierra Leone Civil War* (Dakar, Senegal: CODESRIA, 2004); Dumbuya, *Reinventing the Colonial State*; Paul Richards, *Fighting for the Rainforest: War, Resources and Youth in Sierra Leone* (London: James Curry, 1996); Ibrahim Abdullah, "Bush Path to Destruction: The Origin and Character of the Revolutionary United Front/Sierra Leone," *Journal of Modern African Studies* 36 (1998) 203–35; Zack-Williams and Riley, "Sierra Leone"; Zack-Williams, "Sierra Leone: The Political Economy of Civil War"; William Reno, *Warlord Politics and African States* (Boulder, CO: Lynne Reinner, 1998); A. B. Zack-Williams, "Sierra Leone: Crisis and Despair," *Review of African Political Economy* 49 (1990): 22–33; David Harris, *Civil War and Democracy in West Africa* (New York: I. B. Tauris, 2012); Harris, *Sierra Leone: A Political History*; Dumbuya, *Reinventing the Colonial State*; Koroma, *Agony of a Nation*; Reno, *Corruption and State Politics in Sierra Leone*; Lansana Gberie, "Liberia and Sierra Leone: Civil Wars, 1989–2004," in *Daily Lives of Civilians in Wartime Africa: From Slavery Days to Rwandan Genocide*, ed. John Laband (London: Greenwood, 2007; M. A. Mohamed Salih, *African Democracies and African Politics* (London: Pluto Press, 2001); A. B. Zack-Williams, "Sierra Leone: The Political Economy of Civil War, 1991–1998," *Third World Quarterly* 20 (1999): 143–62.

127. *Daily Mail*, April 23, 1991, 3. See also Dumbuya, *Reinventing the Colonial State*.

128. *Daily Mail*, January 26, 1991, 2. See also Zack-Williams and Riley, "Sierra Leone"; Dumbuya, *Reinventing the Colonial State*.

129. *West Africa*, May 11–17, 1992, 785.

130. *The New Citizen*, September 29, 1990, 1, 3; *Progress*, April 6, 1991, 1, 4; *Daily Mail*, April 12, 1991, 1–4; *The New Citizen*, April 27, 1991, 1, 8; *The Globe*,

April 6–9, 1991, 1, 7; *New Shaft,* April 29–May 5, 1991, 1, 2, 7; *Weekend Spark,* April 19, 1991, 1, 3, 4; *The Vision,* April 17–24, 1991, 1–6; *The New Citizen,* May 4, 1991, 1, 2, 3, 6; *The New Citizen,* May 11, 1991, 1, 3, 6; *The National,* May 9–13, 1991, 1, 2, 3, 8; *Weekend Spark,* May 24, 1991, 1, 4; *The Globe,* June 15–19, 1991, 1, 2, 3, 4, 6; *Weekend Spark,* August 16, 1991, 1, 2, 4; *The Vision,* September 11–18, 1991, 1, 3; *Weekend Spark,* October 18, 1991, 1, 4; *The Chronicle,* October 17–24, 1991, 4; *Weekend Spark,* November 29, 1991, 1, 4; *The New Citizen,* December 2, 1991, 1, 2, 8; *Weekend Spark,* December 6, 1991, 1; December 13, 1991, 1, 4; *The New Citizen,* December 23, 1991, 1, 6, 7, 10; January 6, 1992, 1, 2, 8, 9; *West Africa,* January 27–February 2, 1992, 146; February 10–16, 1992, 241; March 23–29, 1992, 494–97; *Daily Mail,* May 4, 1992, 1, 2, 4; May 11, 1992, 1–4; May 15, 1992, 1, 2, 3, 5, 7; May 21, 1992, 1–4; May 29, 1992, 1–2; *The New People,* May 3, 2010, 1; *The Patriotic Vanguard,* July 2, 2010, 1–7; *Awareness Times,* September 30, 2011, 1–3; *Concord Times,* January 30, 2014, 1–2; *Sierra Express Media,* February 12, 2014, 1–3; *The Patriotic Vanguard,* February 12, 2014, 1–6. See also Koroma, *Agony of a Nation,* 137–55, 176–77, 179–228, 244–46; Zack-Williams and Riley, "Sierra Leone"; Bangura, *Sierra Leone and the Legacy of Failed Leadership,* 71, 78–80; C. Magbaily Fyle, "The Military and Civil Society in Sierra Leone: The 1992 Military Coup d'Etat," *Africa Development* 18, no. 2 (1994): 127–46; Koroma, *Agony of a Nation,* 137–55; Zack-Williams, "Sierra Leone: The Political Economy of Civil War"; Kpundeh, "Limiting Administrative Corruption in Sierra Leone"; Alie, *Sierra Leone since Independence,* 129–41; Conteh-Morgan and Dixon-Fyle, *Sierra Leone at the End of the Twentieth Century,* 126–36; Turay, *Prophecies of a Father,* 112–18; Joseph A. Opala, "'Ecstatic Renovation': Street Art Celebrating Sierra Leone's 1992 Revolution," *African Affairs* 93 (1994): 195–218; Jimmy D. Kandeh, *Coups from Below: Armed Subalterns and State Power in West Africa* (New York: Palgrave MacMillan, 2004); Gberie, *Dirty War in West Africa;* Dumbuya, *Reinventing the Colonial State.*

131. *New Shaft,* May 5–10, 1992, 1, 2.

132. *Daily Mail,* May 4, 1992, 1, 2, 4. See also May 11, 1992, 1, 2, 3, 4; May 15, 1992, 1, 2, 3, 5, 7; May 21, 1992, 1, 2, 3, 4; May 29, 1992, 1, 2; *West Africa,* May 11–17, 1992, 785–89; October 4–10, 1993, 1778; *The Africa Report,* July-August, 1992. See also Koroma, *Agony of a Nation;* Zack-Williams, "Sierra Leone: Crisis and Despair"; Fyle, "The Military and Civil Society in Sierra Leone"; Dumbuya, *Reinventing the Colonial State;* Gberie, "Liberia and Sierra Leone: Civil Wars, 1989–2004"; Zack-Williams, "Sierra Leone: The Political Economy of Civil War, 1991–98."

Conclusion

1. Author's interview with Almamy Agibu Jalloh, Freetown, Sierra Leone, June 29, 1990; author's interview with Alhaji Tejan-Jalloh, Freetown, Sierra Leone, June 21, 1990; author's interview with Alhaji Sanu Barrie, Freetown,

Sierra Leone, August 4, 1990; and author's interview with Alhaji Seray-Wurie, Freetown, Sierra Leone, June 17, 1990. See also Jalloh, *African Entrepreneurship*.

2. Author's interview with Alhaji Tejan-Jalloh, Freetown, Sierra Leone, June 21, 1990. See also Jalloh, *African Entrepreneurship*.

3. Author's interview with Alhaji Sidique, Freetown, Sierra Leone, October 27, 2008.

4. Ibid.; Jalloh, *African Entrepreneurship*.

5. Author's interview with Almamy Agibu Jalloh, Freetown, Sierra Leone, June 29, 1990; Jalloh, *African Entrepreneurship*; Camara, *Political History of Guinea since World War Two*.

6. Author's interview with Dr. Timbo, Freetown, Sierra Leone, October 30, 2008 and author's interview with Ambassador Tejan-Jalloh, October 25, 2008; Jalloh, *African Entrepreneurship*.

7. Author's interview with Alhaji Tejan-Jalloh, Freetown, Sierra Leone, June 21, 1990 and author's interview with Almamy Agibu Jalloh, Freetown, Sierra Leone, June 29, 1990; Jalloh, *African Entrepreneurship*.

8. See Jalloh, *African Entrepreneurship*, 113–50; Jalloh, "The Fula and the Motor Transport Business in Freetown, Sierra Leone," *African Economic History* 26 (1998): 63–81; Jalloh, "Muslim Fula Merchants and the Motor Transport Business," 119–35.

9. See Jalloh, *African Entrepreneurship*, 151–87; Jalloh "The Fula and Islamic Education in Freetown," 51–68; Jalloh and Skinner, *Islam and Trade in Sierra Leone*.

10. See Jalloh, *African Entrepreneurship*, 151–87; Jalloh and Skinner, *Islam and Trade in Sierra Leone*; Steady, *Women and Leadership in West Africa*.

11. Author's interview with Alhaji Seray-Wurie, Freetown, Sierra Leone, June 17, 1990.

Bibliography

Primary Sources

1963 Population Census of Sierra Leone. 3 vols. Freetown, Sierra Leone: Government Printer, 1965.

Address by His Excellency the President Major-General Dr. Joseph Saidu Momoh Delivered on the Occasion of His Inauguration, Freetown, 26 January 1986. Freetown: Sierra Leone Government, 1986.

Aerial Survey of Livestock and Resources in Sierra Leone. London: Hunting Technical Services, 1979.

L'Aggression portugaise contre la Republique de Guinée. Conakry, Guinea: INRDG, 1971. *Agricultural Survey of 1967/8.* Freetown, Sierra Leone: Government Printer, 1968.

Amin, Samir. *Le Mali, La Guinée et le Ghana: Trois expériences africaines de développement.* Paris: PUF, 1965.

Amnesty International. *Guinée: Emprisonment, "disparitions," et assassinats politiques en Republique populaire et revolutionnaire de Guinée.* Paris: Francophones d'Amnesty International, 1982.

Background to Sierra Leone. Freetown, Sierra Leone: State House, 1980.

Blyden, Edward W. *Black Spokesman: Selected Published Writings of Edward Wilmot Blyden.* Edited by H. R. Lynch. London: Frank Cass, 1971.

———. *Christianity, Islam, and the Negro Race.* Baltimore: Black Classic Press, 1994.

Broadcast by His Excellency the President Major-General Dr. J. S. Momoh on the Occasion of the Twenty-Sixth Anniversary of the Republic of Sierra Leone Independence. Freetown, Sierra Leone: Government Printer, 1987.

Cox-George, N. A. *Report on African Participation in the Commerce of Sierra Leone.* Freetown, Sierra Leone: Government Printer, 1957.

Cox-George, N. A., and Working Party. *Report of the Working Party on Capital Availability and Sierra Leone Entrepreneurship.* Freetown: Bank of Sierra Leone, 1969.

Directory of Business and Industry for Western Area and Multiunit Firms. Freetown, Sierra Leone: Central Statistics Office, 1968.

Directory of Business and Industry for Western Area and Multiunit Firms. Freetown, Sierra Leone: Central Statistics Office, 1970.

Household Survey of the Western Province. Freetown, Sierra Leone: Central Statistics Office, 1967.

Karefa-Smart, John A. M. *Rainbow Happenings: A Memoir.* Self-published, Xlibris, 2010.

Koroma, Abdul K. *Sierra Leone: The Agony of a Nation.* Freetown, Sierra Leone: Andromeda Publications, 1996.

Laing, A. G. *Travels in the Timanee, Kooranko, and Soolima Countries.* London: John Murray, 1825.

Legislation of Sierra Leone, 1969. Freetown, Sierra Leone: Government Printer, 1969.

Mouser, Bruce L., ed. *Guinea Journals: Journeys into Guinea-Conakry during the Sierra Leone Phase, 1800–1821.* Washington, DC: University Press of America, 1979.

National Development Plan, 1974/5–1978/9. Freetown, Sierra Leone: Government Printing Department, 1974.

National Livestock Policy and Programme Workshop. Freetown, Sierra Leone: Ministry of Agriculture, Forestry, and Fisheries, 1991.

Nkrumah, Kwame. *I Speak of Freedom: A Statement of African Ideology.* New York: Fredrick A. Praeger, 1961.

Okoye, C. S. *An Analysis of the Sierra Leone 1974 Population Census Data.* Vol. 4. Freetown, Sierra Leone: Central Statistics Office, 1981.

Pratt, Solomon A. J. *An Autobiography: Jolliboy: "A Most Un-Ordinary African Boy" From Street Starch Hawker to United Nations Debate Champion.* Self-published, Lulu, 2010.

Rankin, F. H. *The White Man's Grace: A Visit to Sierra Leone in 1834.* London: Richard Bentley Press, 1836.

Register of Foreign Nationals. Freetown: Sierra Leone Police Immigration Department, n.d.

Register of Motor Vehicles. Freetown: Sierra Leone Police License Office, n.d.

Register of Property Titles. Freetown, Sierra Leone: Office of the Administrator-General, n.d.

Report of the Commission of Inquiry into the Price Structure of Motor Vehicles and their Spare Parts. Freetown, Sierra Leone: Government Printer, 1962.

Report of the Forster Commission of Inquiry on the Assets of Ex-Ministers and Ex-Deputy Ministers. Freetown, Sierra Leone: Government Printer, 1968.

The Rising Sun: A History of the All People's Congress Party of Sierra Leone. Freetown: APC Secretariat, 1982.

Sierra Leone: 12 Years of Economic Achievement and Political Consolidation under the APC and Dr. Siaka Stevens, 1968–1980. Freetown, Sierra Leone: Office of the President, 1980.

The Sierra Leone Business Directory, 1985–1986. Washington, DC: Sierra Leone Business Advisory Service, n.d.

Sierra Leone Directory of Commerce: Industry and Tourism. London: Ministry of Information and Broadcasting, 1985.

Sierra Leone Gazette. Freetown, Sierra Leone: Government Printer, 1965–92.

Sierra Leone Livestock Development Study. Vol. 1. London: Hunting Technical Services, 1979.

Sierra Leone Republican Constitution. Freetown, Sierra Leone: Government Printer, 1971.

Sierra Leone Trade Journal. Freetown, Sierra Leone: Ministry of Information and Broadcasting. Vol. 1 (1961); Vol. 5 (1965); Vol. 6 (1966).

Sierra Leone Year Book. Freetown: *Daily Mail,* 1961–66, 1968–69, 1970–73, 1978.

Sierra Leonean Heroes: Fifty Great Men and Women Who Helped to Build Our Nation. Freetown, Sierra Leone: Government Printer, 1988.

Sierra Leonean Heroes: Thirty Great Men and Women Who Helped to Build Our Nation. Freetown, Sierra Leone: Government Printer, 1988.

Stevens, Siaka Probyn. *What Life Has Taught Me.* London: Kensal Press, 1984.

The Ten-Year Plan of Economic and Social Development for Sierra Leone. Freetown, Sierra Leone: Government Printer, 1962.

Thomas, Armand C. *The Population of Sierra Leone.* Freetown, Sierra Leone: Demographic Research Training Unit, Fourah Bay College, 1983.

Touré, Ahmed Sékou. *L'Action politique du Parti démocratique de Guinée.* 18 vols. Conakry, Guinea: INRNG, 1958–72.

Transportation Consultants. *Transportation Survey of Sierra Leone.* Washington, DC: Transportation Consultants, 1963.

Tucker, Peter. *The Mission Boy from Shebar: An Autobiography.* Self-published, AuthorHouse, 2011.

Turay, Eddie M. Turay. *The Prophecies of a Father.* Self-published, AuthorHouse, 2013.

Watt, James. *Journal of James Watt: Expedition to Timbo, the Capital of the Fula Empire in 1794.* Edited by Bruce L. Mouser. Madison: African Studies Program, University of Wisconsin, Madison, 1994.

Winterbottom, Thomas. *An Account of the Native Africans in the Neighborhood of Sierra Leone.* Vol. 1. 2nd ed. London: Frank Cass, 1969.

Secondary Sources

Abdullah, Ibrahim. "Bush Path to Destruction: The Origin and Character of the Revolutionary United Front/Sierra Leone." *Journal of Modern African Studies* 36 (1998): 203–35.

Abun-Nasr, J. M. *The Tijaniyya: A Sufi Order in the Modern World.* London: Oxford University Press, 1965.

Adamolekun, Ladipo. *Sékou Touré's Guinea: An Experiment in Nation Building.* London: Methuen, 1976.

Adamu, Mahdi. *The Hausa Factor in West African History.* Zaria, Nigeria: Ahmadu Bello University Press, 1978.

Adamu, Mahdi, and A. H. M. Kirk-Greene, eds. *Pastoralists of the West African Savanna.* Manchester, UK: Manchester University Press, 1986.

Adi, Hakim, and Marika Sherwood. *Pan African History: Political Figures from Africa and the Diaspora since 1787.* New York: Routledge, 2003.

Alharazim, M. Saif'ud Deen. "The Origin and Progress of Islam in Sierra Leone." *Sierra Leone Studies* 21 (1939): 13–26.

Ali, M. M. *A Manual of Hadith.* London: Curzon Press, 1983.

Alie, Joe A. D. *Sierra Leone since Independence: History of a Postcolonial State*. Accra, Ghana: Africa Future Publishers, 2006.

Allen, Christopher. *A New History of Sierra Leone*. New York: St. Martin's Press, 1980.

———. "Sierra Leone Politics since Independence." *African Affairs* 67 (1968): 305–29.

Aluko, O. "The Expulsion of Illegal Aliens from Nigeria: A Study of Nigeria's Decision-Making." *African Affairs* 84 (1985): 539–60.

Amatori, Franco, and Geoffrey Jones, eds. *Business History around the World*. Cambridge: Cambridge University Press, 2003.

Aminu, Jibril. "Towards a Strategy for Education and Development in Africa." In *Islam in Africa*, edited by Nura Alkali, Adamu, Awwal Yadudu, Rashid Motem, and Haruna Salihi, 87–96. Ibadan, Nigeria: Spectrum Books, 1993.

Anderson, J. N. D. *Islamic Law in Africa*. London: Frank Cass, 1978.

Arcin, André. *Histoire de la Guinée française*. Paris: Challamel, 1910.

———. *La Guinée française: Races, religions, coutumes, production, et commerce*. Paris: Methuen, 1907.

Arhin, Kwame, *West African Traders in Ghana in the Nineteenth and Twentieth Centuries*. London: Longman, 1979.

———. Paul Hesp, and Laurens van der Laan, eds. *Marketing Boards in Tropical Africa*. London: Routledge and Kegan Paul, 1985.

Asiwaju, A. I., Michael Crowder, and P. Olisanwuche Esedebe, eds. *Tarikh: Pan-Africanism*. Vol. 6. No. 3. London: Longman, 1980.

Asiwaju, A. I., ed. *Partitioned Africans: Ethnic Relations across Africa's International Boundaries, 1884–1984*. New York: St. Martin's Press, 1985.

Assensoh, A. B. *African Political Leadership: Jomo Kenyatta, Kwame Nkrumah, and Julius K. Nyerere*. Malabar, FL: Krieger Publishing, 1998.

Awogbade, M. O. *Fulani Pastoralism: Jos Case Study*. Zaria: Ahmadu Bello University Press, 1983.

Azarya, Victor. *Aristocrats Facing Change: The Fulbe in Guinea, Nigeria, and Cameroon*. Chicago: University of Chicago Press, 1978.

Bah, M. Alpha. "Fulbe Migration and Settlement in Koindu among the Kissi of Sierra Leone." PhD diss., Howard University, 1983.

———. *Fulbe Presence in Sierra Leone: A Case History of Twentieth-Century Migration and Settlement among the Kissi of Koindu*. New York: Peter Lang, 1998.

Bangura, Abdul K. *Multilingualism and Diglossia in Sierra Leone*. Lawrenceville, VA: Brunswick, 1991.

Bangura, Joseph J. "The Temne in Freetown History: Rethinking the History of the Sierra Leone Colony, 1890–1961." PhD diss., Dalhousie University, 2006.

———. *The Temne of Sierra Leone: Africa Agency in the Making of a British Colony*. Cambridge University Press, 2017.

Bangura, Mohamed M. *Sierra Leone and the Legacy of Failed Leaderships: Essays from Asylum*. Laurel, MD: African Renaissance Books, 2003.

Banton, Michael. "The Origins of Tribal Administration in Freetown." *Sierra Leone Studies* 2 (1954): 109–19.

———. *West African City: A Study of Tribal Life in Freetown*. London: Oxford University Press, 1957.

Barry, Boubacar. *Bokar Biro: Le Dernier Grand Almami du Futa Djalon*. Paris: ABC, 1978.

Barrows, Walter. *Grassroots Politics in an African State: Integration and Development in Sierra Leone*. New York: Africana Publishing, 1976.

Barth, Fredrick, ed. *Ethnic Groups and Boundaries: The Social Organization of Culture Difference*. London: Allen, 1969.

Bascom, W. R. "The Esusu: A Credit Institution of the Yoruba." *Journal of the Royal Anthropological Institute* 82 (1952): 63–69.

Basedau, Matthias, Gero Erdmann, Andreas Mehler, eds. *Votes, Money and Violence: Political Parties and Elections in Sub-Saharan Africa*. Uppsala, Sweden: Nordic Africa Institute, 2007.

Beckley, Josie A. "The Northern Province: The Livestock in the Northern Province of Sierra Leone." BA thesis, Fourah Bay College, University of Sierra Leone, 1973.

Berman, Bruce J., and Colin Leys, eds. *African Capitalists in African Development*. Boulder, CO: Lynne Rienner, 1994.

Berzina, C. "Material on the Ethnohistory of Fulbe." *Sovetskaya ethnografia* (1971): 43–52.

Beveridge, A. A., and A. R. Oberscall. *African Businessmen and Development in Zambia*. Princeton, NJ: Princeton University Press, 1979.

Beydoun, Lina. "Lebanese Migration to Sierra Leone: Issues of Transnationalism, Gender, Citizenship, and the Construction of a Globalized identity." PhD diss., Wayne State University, 2005.

Birmingham, David. *Kwame Nkrumah: The Father of African Nationalism*. Athens: Ohio University Press, 1998.

Byrne, Joseph. "Sierra Leone: Trade and Communications." *Journal of the African Society* 29 (October 1929): 1–6.

Camara, Mohamed Saliou. *Political History of Guinea since World War Two*. New York: Peter Lang, 2014.

Carlton-Carew, Sekoyeo Hector. *A Mixed Bag of Memories: Reminiscences of Colonial and Postcolonial Life in Sierra Leone*. Salt Lake City, UT: Aardvark Global Publishing, 2007.

Cartwright, John R. *Political Leadership in Sierra Leone*. Toronto: University of Toronto Press, 1978.

———. *Politics in Sierra Leone, 1964–1967*. Toronto: University of Toronto Press, 1970.

Chandler, Jr., Alfred, Franco Amatori, and Takashi Hikino, eds. *Big Business and the Wealth of Nations*. New York: Cambridge University Press, 1999.

Clapham, Christopher. *Liberia and Sierra Leone: An Essay in Comparative Politics*. London: Cambridge University Press, 2008.

Clarke, J. I., ed. *Sierra Leone in Maps*. London: University of London Press, 1969.

Clarke, Peter B. *West Africa and Islam.* London: Edward Arnold, 1982.

Cohen, Abner. "Cultural Strategies in the Organization of Trading Diasporas." In *The Development of Indigenous Trade and Markets in West Africa,* edited by C. Meillassoux, 266–84. London: Oxford University Press, 1971.

———. *Custom and Politics in Urban Africa: A Study of Hausa Migrants in Yoruba Towns.* Berkeley: University of California Press, 1969.

———. *The Politics of Elite Culture: Explorations in the Dramaturgy of Power in a Modern African Society.* Berkeley: University of California Press, 1981.

———. "The Social Organization of Credit in a West African Cattle Market." *Africa* 35 (1965): 8–20.

Cole, Gibril R. *The Krio of West Africa: Islam, Culture, Creolization, and Colonialism in the Nineteenth Century.* Athens: Ohio University Press, 2013.

———. "Religious Plurality and Economic Sustainability: Muslim Merchants in the Colonial Economy of Nineteenth Century Freetown," *African Economic History* 36 (2008): 79–93.

Collier, Gershon. *Sierra Leone: Experiment in Democracy in an African Nation.* New York: New York University Press, 1970.

Conteh, Mohamed N'fah-Alie. *The Management of Sierra Leone's Electoral Process—An Introduction.* Saarbrücken, Germany: Lambert Academic Publishing, 2016.

———. *Paramount Chieftaincy in Sierra Leone: History and Electoral Process.* Saarbrücken, Germany: Lambert Academic Publishing, 2016.

Conteh-Morgan, Earl, and Mac Dixon-Fyle. *Sierra Leone at the End of the Twentieth Century: History, Politics, and Society.* New York: Peter Lang, 1999.

Conton, W. F. "The Educational System of Sierra Leone." *Journal of Education* 1 (1966): 3–7.

Coppa, Frank J., ed. *Encyclopedia of Modern Dictatorship: From Napoleon to the Present.* New York: Peter Lang, 2006.

Cox, S. T. *Civil-Military Relations in Sierra Leone: A Case Study of African Soldiers in Politics.* Cambridge, MA: Harvard University Press, 1976.

Cox-George, N. A. *Finance and Development in West Africa: The Sierra Leone Experience.* London: D. Dobson Books, 1961.

———. *Report on African Participation in the Commerce of Sierra Leone.* Freetown, Sierra Leone: Government Printer, 1957.

———. *Report of the Working Party on Capital Availability and Sierra Leone Entrepreneurship.* Freetown: Bank of Sierra Leone, 1969.

Cruise O'Brien, D. B. *The Mourides of Senegal: The Political and Economic Organization of an Islamic Brotherhood.* London: Clarendon Press, 1971.

Cruise O'Brien, D. B., and C. Coulon, eds. *Charisma and Brotherhood in African Islam.* London: Oxford University Press, 1988.

Curtin, Philip D. *Cross-Cultural Trade in World History.* Cambridge: Cambridge University Press, 1992.

Dalby, David. "The Military Takeover in Sierra Leone." *The World Today* 23 (1967): 354–60.

Dallby, T. D. P. "Language Distribution in Sierra Leone." *Sierra Leone Language Review* 1 (1962): 62–67.

Dalton, K. G. "A Fula Settlement in Mendeland." *Sierra Leone Geographical Association Bulletin* 6 (1962): 3–17.

Daramy, Shiekh Batu. *Constitutional Developments in the Post-Colonial State of Sierra Leone, 1961–1984*. New York: The Edwin Mellen Press, 1993.

Dawson, John. "Race and Inter-Group Relations in Sierra Leone: Part 2." *Race* 6 (1965): 217–31.

Denzer, Laray. "Women in Freetown Politics, 1914–61: A Preliminary Study." *Africa* 57 (1987): 439–56.

Derman, William. *Serfs, Peasants, and Socialists*. Berkeley: University of California Press, 1982.

Deveneaux, Gustav H. K. *Power Politics in Sierra Leone*. Ibadan, Nigeria: African Universities Press, 1982.

Dixon-Fyle, Mac, and Gibril Cole, eds. *New Perspectives on the Sierra Leone Krio*. New York: Peter Lang, 2006.

Dorjahn, Vernon R. "African Traders in Central Sierra Leone." In *Markets in Africa*, edited by Paul Bohannan and George Dalton, 61–88. Evanston, IL: Northwestern University Press, 1962.

Dorjahn, Vernon R., and Christopher Fyfe. "Landlord and Stranger: Change in Tenancy Relations in Sierra Leone." *Journal of African History* 3 (1962): 391–97.

Dorjahn, Vernon R., and Barry L Isaac, eds. *Essays on the Economic Anthropology of Liberia and Sierra Leone*. Philadelphia: Institute for Liberian Studies, 1979.

Dorman, Sara, Daniel Hammett, and Paul Nugent, eds. *Making Nations, Creating Strangers: States and Citizenship in Africa*. Boston: Brill, 2007.

Du Bois, V. D. *The Rise of an Opposition to Sékou Touré*. Part 6: *The Activation of the Guinean Exiles: The Front de Liberation Nationale de Guinée (FLAG)*. AUFS Reports, West African Series 9, no. 6. New York: AUFS, July 1966.

Dumbuya, Peter A. *Reinventing the Colonial State: Constitutionalism, One-Party Rule, and Civil War in Sierra Leone*. Self-published, iUniverse, 2008.

Dunn, John, ed. *West African States: Failure and Promise, A Study in Comparative Politics*. London: Cambridge University Press, 1979.

Eades, J. S. *Strangers and Traders: Yoruba Migrants, Markets, and the State in Northern Ghana*. Trenton, NJ: Africa World Press, 1994.

Esedebe, Olisanwuche. *Pan Africanism: The Idea and Movement 1776–1963*. 2nd ed. Washington, DC: Howard University Press, 1994.

Fisher, Humphrey J. "Elections and Coups in Sierra Leone, 1967." *Journal of Modern African Studies* 7 (1969): 611–36.

Foray, Cyril P. *Historical Dictionary of Sierra Leone*. London: Scarecrow Press, 1977.

———. "The Road to the One-Party State: The Sierra Leone Experience." Africanus Horton Memorial Lecture delivered at the Centre of African Studies, University of Edinburgh, November 9, 1988.

Forde, Enid, and Milton Harvey. "Graphical Analysis of Migration to Freetown." *Sierra Leone Geographical Journal* 13 (1969): 13–27.

Forna, Aminatta. *The Devil That Danced on the Water*. New York: Atlantic Monthly, 2002.

Forrest, Tom. *The Advance of African Capital: The Growth of Nigerian Private Enterprise*. Charlottesville: University Press of Virginia, 1994.

Fowler, D. A. L. "The Urban Informal Sector in Sierra Leone: Some Conceptual and Policy Issues." *Africana Research Bulletin* 6 (1976): 4–33.

Fyfe, Christopher. *A History of Sierra Leone*. London: Oxford University Press, 1962.

———. *Sierra Leone Inheritance*. Oxford: Oxford University Press, 1964.

Fyfe, Christopher, and J. S. Trimingham. "The Early Expansion of Islam in Sierra Leone." *Sierra Leone Bulletin of Religion* 2 (1960): 3–24.

Fyfe, Christopher, and E. Jones, eds. *Freetown: A Symposium*. Freetown: Sierra Leone University Press, 1968.

Fyle, C. Magbaily. "Fula Diaspora: The Sierra Leone Experience." In *History and Socio-Economic Development in Sierra Leone*, edited by C. Magbaily Fyle, 101–23. Freetown: SLADEA, 1988.

———. *Historical Dictionary of Sierra Leone*. Lanham, MD: Scarecrow Press, 2006.

———. *Development in Sierra Leone*, edited by C. Magbaily Fyle, 101–23. Freetown, Sierra Leone: SLADEA, 1988.

———. *The History of Sierra Leone: A Concise Introduction*. London: Evans Brothers, 1981.

———. "Indigenous Commerce and Entrepreneurship: The Sierra Leone Hinterland in the Nineteenth Century." In *History and Socio-Economic Development in Sierra Leone*, edited by C. Magbaily Fyle, 61–80. Freetown, Sierra Leone: SLADEA, 1988.

———. *A Nationalist History of Sierra Leone*. Freetown, Sierra Leone: np, 2011.

———. *The Solima Yalunka Kingdom*. Freetown, Sierra Leone: Nyakon Publishers, 1979.

———. ed. *The State and the Provision of Social Services in Sierra Leone since Independence*. Dakar, Senegal: CODESRIA, 1993.

Garlick, Peter C. *African Traders and Economic Development in Ghana*. London: Oxford University Press, 1971.

Gberie, Lansana. *A Dirty War in West Africa: The RUF and the Destruction of Sierra Leone*. Bloomington: Indiana University Press, 2005.

George, Thomas B. *Sierra Leone: Democracy and Reform*. Denver, CO: Outskirts Press, 2009.

Georgestone, Donald. *Focus on Sierra Leone*. Self-published, Xlibris, 2009.

Goerg, Odile. *Commerce et colonization en Guinée, 1850–1913*. Paris: Editions L'Harmattan, 1986.

Gomez, Michael A. *Pragmatism in the Age of Jihad*. Cambridge: Cambridge University Press, 1992.

Greenhalgh, Peter. *West African Diamonds, 1919–83: An Economic History*. Manchester: Manchester University Press, 1985.

Gusau, Sule A. "Prospects and Problems of Islamic Banking in Africa." In *Islam in Africa*, edited by Nura Alkali, Adamu, Awwal Yadudu, Rashid Motem, and Haruna Salihi, 354–63. Ibadan, Nigeria: Spectrum Books, 1993.

Harrell-Bond, Barbara E. *Modern Marriage in Sierra Leone: A Study of the Professional Group*. The Hague: Mouton, 1975.

———. "The Unofficial Urban Courts in Freetown: The Institutionalization of Tribal Headmen." American Universities Field Staff Reports. Hanover, NH: American Universities Field Staff, 1979.

Harrell-Bond, Barbara E., Allen M. Howard, and David E. Skinner. *Community Leadership and the Transformation of Freetown (1801–1976)*. The Hague: Mouton, 1978.

Harris, David. *Civil War and Democracy in West Africa*. New York: I. B. Tauris, 2012.

———. *Sierra Leone: A Political History*. Oxford: Oxford University Press, 2014.

Harvey, Milton. "Implications of Migration to Freetown: A Study of the Relationship between Migrants, Housing and Occupation." *Civilizations* 18 (1968): 247–67.

Hayward, Fred M., and Jimmy D. Kandeh. "Perspectives on Twenty-Five Years of Elections in Sierra Leone." In *Elections in Independent Africa*, edited by Fred M. Hayward, 25–59. Boulder, CO: Westview Press, 1987.

Hideaki, Miyajima, Takeo Kikkawa, and Takashi Hikino, eds. *Policies for Competitiveness: Comparing Business-Government Relationships in the "Golden Age of Capitalism."* New York: Oxford University Press, 1999.

Hill, Polly. *Studies in Rural Capitalism in West Africa*. Cambridge: Cambridge University Press, 1970.

Hinton, Samuel. *University Student Protests and Political Change in Sierra Leone*. New York: Edwin Mellen Press, 2002.

Hiskett, Mervyn. *The Development of Islam in West Africa*. London: Longman, 1984.

Hodgkin, Thomas. *African Political Parties*. Baltimore: Penguin Books, 1961.

Hopkins, A. G. "African Economic History: The First Twenty-Five Years." *Journal of African History* 30 (1989): 157–63.

———. "Big Business in African Studies." *Journal of African History* 28 (1987): 119–40.

———. *An Economic History of West Africa*. New York: Columbia University Press, 1973.

Hoselitz, B. F. "The Development of African Entrepreneurs." In *Economic Development in Africa*, edited by E. F. Jackson, 86–105. New York: Augustus M. Kelley, 1971.

Howard, Allen M. "Bigmen, Traders, and Chiefs: Power, Commerce, and Spatial Change in the Sierra Leone–Guinea Plain, 1865–1895." PhD diss., University of Wisconsin at Madison, 1972.

———. "The Relevance of Spatial Analysis for African Economic History: The Sierra Leone—Guinea System." *Journal of African History* 17 (1976): 365–88.

———. "The Role of Freetown in the Commercial Life of Sierra Leone." In *Freetown: A Symposium*, edited by Christopher Fyfe and Eldred Jones, 38–64. Freetown: Sierra Leone University Press, 1968.

Isaac, Barry L. "Business Failure in a Developing Town: Pendembu, Sierra Leone." *Human Organization* 30 (1971): 288–94.

———. "European, Lebanese, and African Traders in Pendembu, Sierra Leone: 1908–1968." *Human Organization* 33 (1974): 111–21.

———. "Traders in Pendumbu, Sierra Leone: A Case Study in Entrepreneurship." PhD diss., University of Oregon, 1969.

Jabati, S. A. *Agriculture in Sierra Leone*. New York: Vantage Press, 1978.

Jack, Daniel T. *Economic Survey of Sierra Leone*. Freetown, Sierra: Government Printer, 1958.

Jackson, Robert H., and Carl G. Rosberg. *Personal Rule in Black Africa: Prince, Autocrat, Prophet, Tyrant*. Berkeley: University of California Press, 1982.

Jal'lo, Mohammed Suleiman. "A Short Sketch of the Life and Work of the Late Alimamy Jamburia, Tribal Ruler of the Freetown Foulah's." *Sierra Leone Studies* 22 (1939): 40–44.

Jalloh, Alusine. *African Entrepreneurship: Muslim Fula Merchants in Sierra Leone*. Akron: Ohio University Press, 1999.

———. "African Muslim Business in Postcolonial West Africa." In *Black Business and Economic Power*, edited by Alusine Jalloh and Toyin Falola, 311–30. Rochester, NY: University of Rochester Press, 2002.

———. "Alhaji Momodu Allie: Muslim Fula Entrepreneur in Colonial Sierra Leone." In Alusine Jalloh and David E. Skinner, eds., *Islam and Trade in Sierra Leone*, 65–86. Trenton, NJ: Africa World Press, 1997.

———. "The Fula and Islamic Education in Freetown, Sierra Leone." *American Journal of Islamic Social Sciences* 14 (Winter 1997): 51–68.

———. "The Fula and the Motor Transport Business in Freetown, Sierra Leone." *African Economic History* 26 (1998) 63–81.

———. "The Fula Trading Diaspora in Colonial Sierra Leone." In *The African Diaspora*, edited by Alusine Jalloh and Stephen E. Maizlish, 22–38. College Station: Texas A&M University Press, 1996.

———. "Informal Credit and Politics in Sierra Leone." *African Economic History* 31 (2003): 91–110.

———. "In Search of Profits: Muslim Fula Merchants in Freetown, 1930–1978." PhD diss., Howard University, 1993.

———. "Muslim Fula Business Elites and Politics in Sierra Leone." *African Economic History* 35 (2007): 89–104.

———. "Muslim Fula Merchants and the Motor Transport Business in Freetown, 1961–1978." In Alusine Jalloh and David E. Skinner, eds., *Islam and Trade in Sierra Leone*, 119–36. Trenton, NJ: Africa World Press, 1997.

———. "Reconstructing Modern African Business History." In *Africanizing Knowledge: African Studies Across the Disciplines*, edited by Toyin Falola and Christian Jennings, 149–61. Piscataway, NJ: Transaction Publishers, 2002.

Jalloh, Alusine, and David E. Skinner, eds. *Islam and Trade in Sierra Leone.* Trenton, NJ: Africa World Press, 1997.

Jalloh, Alusine, and Stephen E. Maizlish, eds. *The African Diaspora.* College Station: Texas A & M University Press, 1996.

Jalloh, Alusine, and Toyin Falola, eds. *Black Business and Economic Power.* Rochester, NY: University of Rochester Press, 2002.

Jalloh, Assanatu. "Problems and Challenges of an Educated Fullah Woman." BA thesis, Fourah Bay College, University of Sierra Leone, 1986.

Jalloh, M. S. "The Life of Omar Jamboria." *Sierra Leone Studies* 12 (1919): 3–14.

Jalloh-Jamboria, Omar. "The Story of Jihad or Holy War of the Fulah." *Sierra Leone Studies* 3 (1919): 10–17.

Jarrett, H. R. "The Port and Town of Freetown." *Geography* 40 (1955): 108–18.

———. "Recent Port and Harbour Developments at Freetown." *Scottish Geographical Magazine* 71 (1955): 157–64.

———. "Rents, Roads, and Railways." *Sierra Leone Studies* (December 1955): 36–43.

———. "Some Aspects of the Urban Geography of Freetown, Sierra Leone." *Geographical Review* 46 (1956): 334–54.

Johanny, M. "Agricultural Change and Peasant Farmer Resistance: The Case of the Traditional Upland Rice Farmer in Sierra Leone." *Rural Africana* 10 (1981): 9–17.

Kaba, Lansiné. "From Colonialism to Autocracy: Guinea under Sékou Touré, 1957–1984." In *Decolonization and African Independence: The Transfer of Power, 1960–1980,* edited by P. Gifford and W. R. Louis, 225–44. New Haven, CT: Yale University Press, 1988.

Kaindaneh, Peter M. "State Provision of Transport and Communication Services in Sierra Leone." In *The State and the Provision of Social Services in Sierra Leone since Independence. 1961–1991,* edited by C. Magbaily Fyle, 20–43. Dakar, Senegal: CODESRIA, 1993.

Kaké, Ibrahima Baba. *Sékou Touré: Le hero et el tyran.* Paris: Jeune Afrique Livres, 1987.

Kallon, Kelfala M. "An Economic Analysis of Private Indigenous Entrepreneurship in Sierra Leone." PhD diss., University of Virginia, 1983.

———. *The Economics of Sierra Leonean Entrepreneurship.* Lanham, MD: University Press of America, 1990.

———. *The Political Economy of Corruption in Sierra Leone.* New York: The Edwin Mellen Press, 2004.

Kaloko, Franklyn. *The Future in the Past.* Self-published, iUniverse, 2005.

Kamara, E. T. *The True Story behind Blood Diamonds: A Political Historical Journey of a Lifetime.* Charleston, SC: CreateSpace, 2016.

Kandeh, Jimmy D., *Coups from Below: Armed Subalterns and State Power in West Africa.* New York; Palgrave MacMillan, 2004.

———. "Politicization of Ethnic Identities in Sierra Leone." *African Studies Review* 35 (1992): 81–99.

Kandeh, Jimmy D., Ricardo Rene Laremont, and Rachel Cremona. "Ethnicity and National Identity in Sierra Leone." In *Borders, Nationalism, and the African State*, edited by Ricardo René Larémont, 179–229. Boulder, CO: Lynne Reinner, 2005.

Kaniki, M. H. Y. "Attitudes and Reactions towards the Lebanese in Sierra Leone during the Colonial Period." *Canadian Journal of African Studies* 7 (1973): 97–113.

———. "Economic Change in Sierra Leone during the 1930s." *Transafrican Journal of History* 3 (1973): 72–95.

———. "The Economic and Social History of Sierra Leone, 1929–1939." PhD diss., University of Birmingham, 1972.

Karimu, M. J. J., and P. Richards. "Upland and Swamp Rice Farming Systems in Sierra Leone: The Social Context of Technological Change." *Africa* 51 (1981): 596–620.

Katzin, M. "The Role of the Small Entrepreneur." In *Economic Transition in Africa*, edited by M. J. Herskovits and M. Harwitz, 179–98. Evanston, IL: Northwestern University Press, 1964.

Kennedy, Paul. *African Capitalism*. Cambridge: Cambridge University Press, 1988.

Kennedy, Scott. *The Business of Lobbying in China*. Cambridge, MA: Harvard University Press, 2005.

Ketkar, S. L. "The Economics of Education in Sierra Leone." *Journal of Modern African Studies* 15 (1977): 310–15.

Kilby, P. *African Enterprise: The Nigerian Bread Industry*. Palo Alto, CA: Hoover Institution, 1965.

Kilson, Martin. *Political Change in a West African State: A Study of the Modernization Process in Sierra Leone*. Cambridge, MA: Harvard University Press, 1966.

Kirk-Greene, A. H. M. *The Cattle People of Nigeria*. London: Oxford University Press, 1959.

Knickel, K. W. *Farming Systems Development: Smallholder Swamp Rice Systems in Sierra Leone*. Hamburg, Germany: Verlag Weltarchiv, 1988.

Kpundeh, Sahr John. "Limiting Administrative Corruption in Sierra Leone." *Journal of Modern African Studies* 32 (1994): 139–57.

———. *Politics and Corruption in Africa: A Case Study of Sierra Leone*. Lanham, MD: University Press of America, 1995.

Krafona, Kwesi, ed. *Organisation of African Unity: Essays in Honour of Kwame Nkrumah*. London: Afroworld, 1988.

Kritzeck, James, and William H. Lewis, eds. *Islam in Africa*. New York: Van Nostrand, 1969.

Kuczynski, R. R. *Demographic Survey of the British Colonial Empire*. Vol. 1. London: Oxford University Press, 1948.

Kumpayi, R. A. A. "The Livestock Industry in Sierra Leone." BS thesis, Fourah Bay College, University of Sierra Leone, 1966.

Kuper, Hilda, ed. *Urbanization and Migration in West Africa*. London: Longman, 1965.

Laan, H. L. van der. *The Lebanese Traders in Sierra Leone.* The Hague: Mouton, 1975.

———. *The Sierra Leone Diamonds: An Economic Study Covering the Years 1952–1961.* London: Oxford University Press, 1965.

Laband, John. *Daily Lives of Civilians in Wartime Africa: From Slavery Days to Rwandan Genocide.* London: Greenwood, 2007.

Last, Murray, and Paul Richards, eds. *Sierra Leone 1787–1987: Two Centuries of Intellectual Life.* Manchester: Manchester University Press, 1987.

Leigh, Emmanuel S. E. *The Sierra Leone Financial System.* Freetown, Sierra Leone: Author House, 2004.

Leighton, Neil O. "The Lebanese in Sierra Leone." *Transition* 9 (1974): 23–29.

———. "Lebanese Emigration: Its Effect on the Political Economy of Sierra Leone." In *The Lebanese in the World: A Century of Emigration,* edited by Albert Hourani and Nadim Shehadi, 579–601. London: I. B. Tauris, 1992.

Levtzion, Nehemia, and Humphrey J. Fisher, eds. *Rural and Urban Islam in West Africa.* Boulder, CO: Lynne Rienner, 1987.

Lewin, André. *Ahmed Sékou Touré (1922–1984): Président de la Guinée.* Paris: L'Harmattan, 2009.

Lewis, I. M., ed. *Islam in Tropical Africa.* London: Oxford University Press, 1966.

Lewis, Roy. *Sierra Leone, A Modern Potrait.* London: Longman, 1954.

Lindberg, Staffan I. *Democracy and Elections in Africa.* Baltimore: The Johns Hopkins University Press, 2006.

Lovejoy, Paul E. *Caravans of Kola: The Hausa Kola Trade, 1700–1900.* Zaria, Nigeria: Ahmadu Bello University Press, 1980.

Lucan, Talabi A. *The Life and Times of Paramount Chief Madam Ella Koblo Gulama: An Eminent Sierra Leonean Woman of the 20th Century.* Freetown: Sierra Leone Association of Writers and Illustrators, 2003.

Luke, David Fashole. "Continuity in Sierra Leone: From Stevens to Momoh." *Third World Quarterly* 10 (1988): 67–78.

Luke, David Fashole, and Stephen P. Riley. "The Politics of Economic Decline in Sierra Leone." *Journal of Modern African Studies* 27 (1989): 133–41.

Lynch, Hollis R. *Edward Wilmot Blyden: Pan-Negro Patriot, 1832–1912.* London: Oxford University Press, 1967.

MacGaffey, Janet. *Entrepreneurs and Parasites: The Struggle for Indigenous Capitalism in Zaire.* New York: Cambridge University Press, 1987.

MacKenzie, W. J. M., and Kenneth Robinson, eds. *Five Elections in Africa.* Oxford: Oxford University Press, 1960.

Manby, Bronwen. *Struggles for Citizenship in Africa.* London: Zed Books, 2009.

Mannan, M. A. *Islamic Economics.* Lahore, Pakistan: Ashraf Publications, 1970.

Marty, P. "Etude sur L'Islam en Guineé." Translated by E. F. Sayers. *Sierra Leone Studies* 19 (1933): 3–35.

Merani, H. V., and H. L. van der Laan. "The Indian Traders in Sierra Leone." *African Affairs* 78 (1979): 240–50.

McKay, J. "Commercial Life in Freetown." In *Freetown: A Symposium*, edited by Christopher Fyfe and Eldred Jones, 65–76. Freetown: Sierra Leone University Press, 1968.

McGowan, Winston. "The Establishment of Long-Distance Trade between Sierra Leone and Its Hinterland, 1787–1821." *Journal of African History* 31 (1990): 25–41.

Meillassoux, Claude, ed. *The Development of Indigenous Trade and Markets in West Africa*. London: Oxford University Press, 1971.

Miyajima, Hideaki, Takeo Kikkawa, and Takashi Hikino, eds. *Policies for Competitiveness: Comparing Business-Government Relationships in the "Golden Age of Capitalism."* New York: Oxford University Press, 1999.

Nafziger, E. Wayne. *African Capitalism: A Case Study in Nigerian Entrepreneurship*. Stanford, CA: Hoover Institution Press, 1977.

Nkrumah, Kwame. *I Speak of Freedom: A Statement of African Ideology*. New York: Fredrick A. Praeger, 1961.

Nugent, P., and A. I. Asiwaju, eds. *African Boundaries: Barriers, Conduits, and Opportunites*. New York: Pinter, 1996.

Olu-Wright, R. J. "The Physical Growth of Freetown." In *Freetown: A Symposium*, edited by Christopher Fyfe and Eldred Jones, 24–37. Freetown: Sierra Leone University Press, 1968.

Paracka, Jr., Daniel J. *The Athens of West Africa: A History of International Education at Fourah Bay College, Freetown, Sierra Leone*. New York: Routledge, 2003.

Peil, Margaret. "The Expulsion of West African Aliens." *Journal of Modern African Studies* 9 (1971): 205–29.

Porter, Arthur T. *Creoledom: A Study of the Development of Freetown Society*. London: Oxford University Press, 1963.

Posner, Daniel N. *Institutions and Ethnic Politics in Africa*. Cambridge: Cambridge University Press, 2005.

Proudfoot, Leslie. "Mosque-Building and Tribal Separatism in Freetown." *Africa* 29 (1959): 405–15.

———. "Towards Muslim Solidarity in Freetown." *Africa* 31 (1961): 147–56.

Proudfoot, Leslie, and H. S. Wilson. "Muslim Attitudes to Education in Sierra Leone." *Muslim World* (1960): 86–96.

Reno, William. *Corruption and State Politics in Sierra Leone*. Cambridge: Cambridge University Press, 1995.

———. *Warlord Politics and African States*. Boulder, CO: Lynne Rienner, 1998.

Riddell, J. B. *The Spatial Dynamics of Modernization in Sierra Leone: Structure, Diffusion, and Response*. Evanston, IL: Northwestern University Press, 1970.

———. "Transport Network Evolution in the Post-Independence Period." *Sierra Leone Geographical Journal* 14 (1970): 20–30.

Riviere, Claude. *Guinea: The Mobilization of a People*. Ithaca, NY: Cornell University Press, 1977.

Roberts, George O. *The Anguish of Third World Independence: The Sierra Leone Experience*. Washington, DC: University Press of America, 1982.

Rodinson, M. *Islam and Capitalism*. Austin: University of Texas Press, 1978.

Rodney, Walter. *A History of the Upper Guinea Coast, 1545–1800.* Oxford: Clarendon Press, 1970.

———. "Jihad and Social Revolution in Futa Jallon." *Journal of the Historical Society of Nigeria* 4 (1968): 3–14.

Rosen, D. M. "Diamonds, Diggers, and Chiefs: The Politics of Fragmentation in a West African Society." PhD diss., University of Illinois, Urbana-Champaign, 1973.

Salih, M. A. Mohammed. *African Democracies and African Politics.* London: Pluto Press, 2001.

Sanneh, Lamin. "Christian-Muslim Encounter in Freetown in the Nineteenth Century and the Implications for Mission Today." *Bulletin of the Secretarial for Non-Christian Religions* (Rome) 12, nos. 1–2 (1977): 13–21.

———. *The Crown and the Turban: Muslims and West African Pluralism.* Boulder, CO: Westview Press, 1997.

———. "Modern Education among Freetown Muslims and the Christian Stimulus." In *Christianity in Independent Africa,* edited by Edward Fashole-Luke, Richard Gray, Adrian Hastings, and Godwin Tasie, 316–33. Bloomington: Indiana University Press, 1978.

———. *West African Christianity: The Religious Impact.* New York: Orbis Books, 1983.

Sawi, F. M. B. "The S.L.P.M.B.: 1949–67." Master's thesis, Birmingham University, 1972.

Sayers, E. F. "Foreword" to *Islam in Guinée,* edited by Paul Marty. *Sierra Leone Studies* 19 (1935): 47–48.

Saylor, R. G. *The Economic System of Sierra Leone.* Durham, NC: Duke University Press, 1967.

Schatz, Sayre P. *Nigerian Capitalism.* Berkeley: University of California Press, 1977.

Schmidt, Elizabeth. *Cold War and Decolonization in Guinea, 1946–1958.* Athens: Ohio University Press, 2007.

———. *Mobilizing the Masses: Gender, Ethnicity, and Class in the Nationalist Movement in Guinea, 1939–1958.* Portsmouth, NH: Heinemann, 2005.

Sengova, Joko. "The National Languages of Sierra Leone: A Decade of Policy Experimentation." In *Sierra Leone, 1787–1987,* edited by Murray Last and Paul Richards, 519–30. Manchester: University of Manchester Press, 1987.

Sesay, S. M. "Drivers in the Transport Industry: A Case Study of Road Transport in Sierra Leone." *Sierra Leone Studies* 19 (1966): 86–97.

———. "Factors Influencing the Pattern of Road Density in Sierra Leone." *Sierra Leone Geographical Journal* 12 (1968): 17–26.

———. "Transport in Relation to Social and Economic Development in Sierra Leone." PhD diss., University of Durham, 1967.

Sesay, Christian F., Jr. *The Odyssey of the All People's Congress: A History from Siaka Probyn Stevens to Ernest Bai Koroma.* Self-published, DiggyPod, 2016.

Shack, William A. "Open Systems and Closed Boundaries: The Ritual Process of Stranger Relations in New African States." In *Strangers in African Societies*, edited by William A. Shack and Elliot P. Skinner, 37–47. Berkeley: University of California Press, 1979.

Shyllon, Leslie E. T. *Two Centuries of Christianity in an African Province of Freedom: Sierra Leone, A Case Study of European Influence and Culture in Church Development.* Freetown, Sierra Leone: Print Sundries and Stationers, 2008.

Sibthorpe, A. B. C. *The History of Sierra Leone.* 4th. London: Frank Cass, 1970.

Skinner, David E. "The Arabic Letter Books as a Source for Sierra Leone History." *Africana Research Bulletin* (1973): 3–16.

———. "The Development of Islam in Sierra Leone during the Nineteenth Century." PhD diss., University of California, Berkeley, 1971.

———. "Islam and Education in the Colony and Hinterland of Sierra Leone, 1750–1914." *Canadian Journal of African Studies* 10 (1976): 499–520.

———. "Sierra Leone Relations with the Northern Rivers and the Influence of Islam in Sierra Leone." *International Journal of Sierra Leone Studies* 1 (1988): 64–90.

Skinner, David E., Barbara Harrell-Bond, and Allen Howard. "A Profile of Urban Leaders in Freetown, Sierra Leone 1905–1945." *Tarikh* 7 (1981): 11–19.

Skinner, Elliot P. "Strangers in West African Societies." *Africa* 33 (1963): 307–20.

Smart, H. M. Joko. *Sierra Leone Customary Family Law.* Freetown, Sierra Leone: Atlantic Printers, 1983.

Smith, Gerald H. "The Dichotomy of Politics and Corruption in a Neopatrimonial State: Evidence from Sierra Leone." *Issue: A Journal of Opinion* 25 (1997): 58–62.

Spenser, Dunstan S. C. "Rice Policy in Sierra Leone: Rice Production in Sierra Leone." In *Rice in West Africa: Policy and Economics*, edited by S. R. Pearson, J. D. Stryker, and C. P. Humphreys, 175–225. Stanford, CA: Stanford University Press, 1981.

Spring, Anita, and Barbara E. McDade, eds. *African Entrepreneurship: Theory and Reality.* Gainesville: University Press of Florida, 1998.

Steady, Filomina Chioma. *Female Power in Africa Politics: The National Congress of Sierra Leone.* Los Angeles: California Institute of Technology Munger African Library Notes, 1975.

———. *Women and Collective Action in Africa.* New York: Palgrave MacMillan, 2006.

———. *Women and Leadership in West Africa: Mothering the Nation and Humanizing the State.* New York: Palgrave, 2011.

———. "Women's Associations and Female Education in Sierra Leone." In *New Perspectives on the Sierra Leone Krio*, edited Mac Dixon-Fyle and Gibril Cole, 267–85. New York: Peter Lang, 2006.

Stevens, Siaka P. *What Life Has Taught Me.* Bourne End, Buckinghamshire, UK: Kensal Press, 1984.

Straussberger, John. "The 'Particular Situation' in the Futa Jallon: Ethnic Conflict, Political Community, and Belonging in Twentieth-Century Guinea." PhD diss., Columbia University, 2014.

———. "Storming the Citadel: Decolonization and Political Contestation in Guinea's Futa Jallon, 1945–61." *Journal of African History* 57 (2016): 231–49.

Summer, D. L. *Education in Sierra Leone.* Freetown: Sierra Leone University Press, 1963.

Tauxier, Louis. *Moeurs et histoire des Peuls.* Paris: Payot, 1937.

Taylor, A. T. Beresford. *Money and Banking in Sierra Leone.* Milan, Italy: Finafrica, Cassa di Risparmio delle Provincie Lombarde, 1980.

Tejan-Jalloh, Umu Kultumie. *Telling It As It Was: The Career of a Sierra Leonean Woman in Public Service: A Memoir.* Freetown: Sierra Leone Writers Series, 2016.

Tejan-Jalloh, C. M. "Why This Campaign of Hate against Foulahs?" *Unity*, March 21, 1969, 2, 6.

Thompson, Bankole. *The Constitutional History and Law of Sierra Leone (1961–1995).* New York: University Press of America, 1997.

Tolliday, Steven W., ed. *Government and Business.* Brookfield, VT: Ashgate, 1992.

Tonah, Steve. *The Fulani in Ghana: Migration History, Integration and Resistance.* Accra: University of Ghana, 2005.

Touchberry, R. W. *A Study of the N'dama Cattle at the Musaia Animal Husbandry Station in Sierra Leone.* Urbana: University of Illinois Agricultural Experimental Station, 1967.

Touré, Ahmed Sékou. *L'Action politique du Parti démocratique de Guinée.* 18 vols. Conakry, Guinea: INRNG, 1958–72.

Trimingham, J. S. *A History of Islam in West Africa.* Oxford: Oxford University Press, 1959.

———. *The Sufi Orders in Islam.* London: Oxford University Press, 1971.

Tucker, Peter L. *Origin and Philosophy of the Sierra Leone People's Party.* Freetown, Sierra Leone: Mount Everest Publishing House (MEPH), 2001.

———. *The Sierra Leone Constitution (1991) For Laypersons.* London: Copyzone, 2003.

Turay, E. A. D., and A. Abraham. *The Sierra Leone Army: A Century of History.* London: Macmillan, 1987.

Waldie, Kevin. "'Cattle and Concrete': Changing Property Rights and Property Interests among the Fula Cattle Herders around Kabala, North East Sierra Leone." In *Property, Poverty, and People: Changing Rights in Property and Problems of Pastoral Development*, edited by P. T. W. Baxter and R. Hogg, 2129–39. Manchester: University of Manchester, Department of Social Anthropology and International Development Centre, 1989.

Weekes, Richard V., ed. *Muslim Peoples: A World Ethnographic Survey.* 2nd ed. Vol. 1. Westport, CT: Greenwood Press, 1984.

White, E. Frances. *Sierra Leone's Settler Women Traders.* Ann Arbor: University of Michigan Press, 1987.

White, H. P. "The Railways of Sierra Leone." *Railway Magazine* 106 (1960): 231–37.

Williams, G. J., and D. F. Hayward. "The Changing Land-Transportation Pattern of Sierra Leone." *Scottish Geographical Magazine* 89 (1973): 107–18.

———. "Recent Development of the Sierra Leone Airways System." *Geography* 58 (1973): 58–61.

Willis, J. R., ed. *Studies in West African Islamic History*. Vol. 1. London: Frank Cass, 1979.

Wurie, A. "The Bundukas of Sierra Leone." *Sierra Leone Studies* 1 (1953): 14–25.

Wurie, Ahmadu, and Elizabeth Hirst. *Rassin*. London: University of London Press, 1968.

Wylie, Kenneth C. *The Political Kingdoms of the Temne: Temne Government in Sierra Leone, 1825–1910*. New York: Africana Publishing, 1977.

Wyse, Akintola J. G. *H. C. Bankole-Bright and Politics in Colonial Sierra Leone, 1919–1958*. Cambridge: Cambridge University Press, 1990.

———. *The Krio of Sierra Leone*. London: C. Hurst, 1989.

———. "The 1919 Strike and Anti-Syrian Riots: A Krio Plot?" *Journal of the Historical Society of Sierra Leone* 3 (1979): 1–14.

Yusuf, Ahmed Beita. "Capital Formation and Management among the Muslim Hausa Traders of Kano, Nigeria." *Africa* 65 (1976): 167–82.

Zacharia, K. C., and Julian Conde. "Crossing Borders in West Africa." *West Africa*, April 27, 1981.

Zack-Williams, A. "Merchant Capital and Underdevelopment in Sierra Leone." *Review of African Political Economy* 25 (1982): 74–82.

———. "Sierra Leone: Crisis and Despair." *Review of African Political Economy* 49 (1990): 22–33.

———. "Sierra Leone: The Political Economy of Civil War, 1991–98." *Third World Quarterly* 20 (1999): 143–62.

———. *Tributors, Supporters, and Merchant Capital: Mining and Underdevelopment in Sierra Leone*. Brookfield, VT: Ashgate, 1995.

Zack-Williams, A., and Stephen Riley. "Sierra Leone: The Coup and Its Consequences." *Review of African Political Economy* 56 (1993): 91–98.

Index